Build the Best Data Center Facility for Your Business

Douglas Alger

Cisco Press

800 East 96th Street
Indianapolis, Indiana 46240 USA

Build the Best Data Center Facility for Your Business

Douglas Alger

Cisco Press logo is a trademark of Cisco Systems, Inc.

Published by:
Cisco Press
800 East 96th Street
Indianapolis, IN 46240 USA

Printed in the United States of America   4 5 6 7 8 9 0

Fourth Printing May 2008

Library of Congress Cataloging-in-Publication Number: 2003116567

ISBN: 1-58705-182-6

Warning and Disclaimer

This book is designed to provide information about the design and management of Data Centers. Every effort has been made to make this book as complete and as accurate as possible, but no warranty or fitness is implied.

The information is provided on an "as is" basis. The authors, Cisco Press, and Cisco Systems, Inc., shall have neither liability nor responsibility to any person or entity with respect to any loss or damages arising from the information contained in this book or from the use of the discs or programs that may accompany it.

The opinions expressed in this book belong to the author and are not necessarily those of Cisco Systems, Inc.

Trademark Acknowledgments

All terms mentioned in this book that are known to be trademarks or service marks have been appropriately capitalized. Cisco Press or Cisco Systems, Inc., cannot attest to the accuracy of this information. Use of a term in this book should not be regarded as affecting the validity of any trademark or service mark.

Corporate and Government Sales

Cisco Press offers excellent discounts on this book when ordered in quantity for bulk purchases or special sales.

For more information please contact: **U.S. Corporate and Government Sales**   1-800-382-3419
corpsales@pearsontechgroup.com

For sales outside the U.S. please contact: **International Sales**   international@pearsoned.com

Feedback Information

At Cisco Press, our goal is to create in-depth technical books of the highest quality and value. Each book is crafted with care and precision, undergoing rigorous development that involves the unique expertise of members from the professional technical community.

Readers' feedback is a natural continuation of this process. If you have any comments regarding how we could improve the quality of this book, or otherwise alter it to better suit your needs, you can contact us through email at feedback@ciscopress.com. Please make sure to include the book title and ISBN in your message.

We greatly appreciate your assistance.

Publisher	John Wait
Editor-in-Chief	John Kane
Executive Editor/Acquisitions Editor	Mary Beth Ray
Cisco Representative	Anthony Wolfenden
Cisco Press Program Manager	Jeff Brady
Production Manager	Patrick Kanouse
Development Editor	Tracy Hughes
Project Editor	Marc Fowler
Copy Editor	Paul Wilson
Technical Editors	Andy Broer, Mike Lavazza
Editorial Assistants	Raina Han
	Tammi Barnett
Book/Cover Designer	Louisa Adair
Composition	Interactive Composition Corporation
Indexer	WordWise Publishing Services

CISCO SYSTEMS

Corporate Headquarters
Cisco Systems, Inc.
170 West Tasman Drive
San Jose, CA 95134-1706
USA
www.cisco.com
Tel: 408 526-4000
    800 553-NETS (6387)
Fax: 408 526-4100

European Headquarters
Cisco Systems International BV
Haarlerbergpark
Haarlerbergweg 13-19
1101 CH Amsterdam
The Netherlands
www-europe.cisco.com
Tel: 31 0 20 357 1000
Fax: 31 0 20 357 1100

Americas Headquarters
Cisco Systems, Inc.
170 West Tasman Drive
San Jose, CA 95134-1706
USA
www.cisco.com
Tel: 408 526-7660
Fax: 408 527-0883

Asia Pacific Headquarters
Cisco Systems, Inc.
Capital Tower
168 Robinson Road
#22-01 to #29-01
Singapore 068912
www.cisco.com
Tel: +65 6317 7777
Fax: +65 6317 7799

Cisco Systems has more than 200 offices in the following countries and regions. Addresses, phone numbers, and fax numbers are listed on the
Cisco.com Web site at www.cisco.com/go/offices.

Argentina • Australia • Austria • Belgium • Brazil • Bulgaria • Canada • Chile • China PRC • Colombia • Costa Rica • Croatia • Czech Republic
Denmark • Dubai, UAE • Finland • France • Germany • Greece • Hong Kong SAR • Hungary • India • Indonesia • Ireland • Israel • Italy
Japan • Korea • Luxembourg • Malaysia • Mexico • The Netherlands • New Zealand • Norway • Peru • Philippines • Poland • Portugal
Puerto Rico • Romania • Russia • Saudi Arabia • Scotland • Singapore • Slovakia • Slovenia • South Africa • Spain • Sweden
Switzerland • Taiwan • Thailand • Turkey • Ukraine • United Kingdom • United States • Venezuela • Vietnam • Zimbabwe

About the Author

Douglas Alger is a team lead and project manager for the Cisco Data Center Infrastructure Team, where he designs, supports, and manages the company's worldwide Data Centers. He has participated in more than fifty major Data Center design and construction projects and possess more than eight years' experience working in Data Centers of various sizes, functions, and infrastructure. He deals first-hand with the space, electrical, cooling, and other infrastructure challenges facing these critical environments. Prior to coming to Cisco, Doug was a writer and editor in the News & Publications office of Syracuse University and, before that, a full-time stringer for the *Los Angeles Times*. He has a bachelor's degree in journalism from San Jose State University. He lives in San Jose with his wife and their son.

About the Technical Reviewers

Andy Broer is IT manager of the Cisco Data Center Infrastructure team. Andy has worked throughout Silicon Valley in a variety of roles for the better part of the past two decades. He has worked in IT for 10 years. He has also been employed as an on-air radio talent, a digital animation artist, software build engineer, and digital sound engineer/editor. He holds two degrees: a BA in creative arts with a minor in radio television and film and an MA in Chinese geomancy/Feng Shui studies.

Mike Lavazza is manager of operations and engineering for the Cisco Workplace Resources team. He is responsible for the building infrastructure system design, building automation systems, and maintenance engineering at Cisco for more than eight years. Mike and his team are also responsible for critical environment design and operations and energy management programs for the Americas. His team participated in all aspects of electrical, mechanical and building automation system designs and implementation.

Mike has been in the operations and engineering industry for twenty years, working as an operations and engineering manager for 3Com, IBM, Hughes Aircraft Company, and John Deere. He holds a BS in industrial/electrical engineering with an emphasis in building systems and operations.

About the Data Center Infrastructure Team

The Cisco Data Center Infrastructure Team (DCIT) manages more than forty-five server environments distributed among eleven countries and ten time zones, encompassing more than 125,000 square feet (11,613 square meters) of space. The group is responsible for room design for both business function and R&D Data Centers worldwide. DCIT partners with the Cisco Workplace Resources teams to provide a reliable and easy-to-use environment for the company's critical IT systems. As part of the Cisco IT organization, the Data Center Infrastructure Team has supported dozens of acquisitions around the world, providing a wealth of actual Data Center experiences from which to learn and draw best practices from.

Dedications

To my wife, Melynda, for support during this project and love throughout our relationship. To our son, Bryan, for choosing us to be your family. You two are my sunshine.

Acknowledgments

First and foremost, thank you to my teammates—past and present—on Cisco's Data Center Infrastructure Team: James Chillquist, Daniel Cole, Chris Gamez, Glenn Hasbrouck, John Lira, Mitch Lyman, Paul Martin, John McKee, Mete Osten, Christian Pama, Paul Paquette, Chris Posas, Bridget (Carino) Quast, Dave Rogers, Craig Schauman, and Kevin Squarcia. Each in their own way has shaped how we design and manage Cisco's Data Centers and therefore contributed in material ways to the contents of this book. I feel privileged to know and work with such talented and resourceful people.

Thank you to Andrew Broer, my friend and manager. He largely pioneered the distributed infrastructure model presented in Chapters 6 and 7 (and now standard in our company Data Centers). He has also proven many of the room management strategies that are presented. The value of his guiding hand for both Cisco's Data Centers and the Data Center Infrastructure Team is immeasurable.

Thank you to Ken Welch, for the opportunity for me to join Cisco.

I am indebted to Mike Lavazza and Al Valcour, coworkers who generously shared their technical expertise. Mike provided invaluable information on mechanical systems and electrical infrastructure, Al on connectivity and structured cabling. Thank you both.

All drawings in this book were originally created in AutoCAD by Glenn Hasbrouck. May everyone tasked with designing a Data Center have someone with such skill at their disposal.

Thank you to everyone at Cisco Press who shepherded this book from inception to completion. To a person, everyone I have worked with—Chris Cleveland, Raina Han, Tracy Hughes, Dayna Isley, Mary Beth Ray, Jim Schachterle, and Marc Fowler—has been helpful and encouraging.

Finally, thank you to my ever-present writing supervisor, Good Boy. This tuxedo cat spent countless hours curled up next to my laptop computer while I wrote, providing welcome company and occasionally walking across the keyboard to remind me to take a break.

This Book Is Safari Enabled

The Safari® Enabled icon on the cover of your favorite technology book means the book is available through Safari Bookshelf. When you buy this book, you get free access to the online edition for 45 days.

Safari Bookshelf is an electronic reference library that lets you easily search thousands of technical books, find code samples, download chapters, and access technical information whenever and wherever you need it.

To gain 45-day Safari Enabled access to this book:

- Go to http://www.ciscopress.com/safarienabled
- Complete the brief registration form
- Enter the coupon code NLOP-74GN-QZYZ-YUN1-044L

If you have difficulty registering on Safari Bookshelf or accessing the online edition, please e-mail customer-service@safaribooksonline.com.

Contents at a Glance

Table of Contents

Chapter 4   Laying Out the Data Center   83

Command Syntax Conventions

The conventions used to present command syntax in this book are the same conventions used in the IOS Command Reference. The Command Reference describes these conventions as follows:

- **Boldface** indicates commands and keywords that are entered literally as shown. In actual configuration examples and output (not general command syntax), boldface indicates commands that are manually input by the user (such as a **show** command).

- *Italics* indicate arguments for which you supply actual values.

- Vertical bars (|) separate alternative, mutually exclusive elements.

- Square brackets [ ] indicate optional elements.

- Braces { } indicate a required choice.

- Braces within brackets [{ }] indicate a required choice within an optional element.

Foreword

Doug Alger's book provides an in depth look at the Data Center [md]the heart of IT's information flow. From the days of mainframe computing to today's environments that support our ability to conduct business in the 21st century, the Data Center is core to the success of any IT organization. The Cisco Data Center provides IT with the ability to protect and recover critical information and support business applications in a robust, resilient infrastructure capable of delivering performance, reliability, and scalability. The Data Center has a profound impact on any company's ability to meet today's growing and changing requirements. Building on his valuable experiences, Doug shares insights on strategies, lessons learned and pitfalls to avoid in the Data Center.

R. Lance Perry
Vice President,
IT Customer Strategy & Success
Cisco Systems, Inc.

Introduction

Data Centers are critical environments for companies, and the need to correctly design and manage their physical infrastructure is paramount.

The goal of this book is you becoming familiar with all aspects of a Data Center's physical components so you can best design, manage, support, or work in such a facility. The book is a primer on Data Center infrastructure (power, data cabling, cooling, fire suppression, and so on), a strategy guide for creating a server environment that meets the specific needs of your company, and a diary of Data Center-related experiences—both successes *and* failures—you can learn from.

Be aware that this book is *not* about network architecture, Internet/extranet/intranet functions, applications, or other topics unrelated to the physical elements of a Data Center facility.

Motivation for Writing This Book

In talking with executives, Information Technology (IT) professionals, and facilities personnel from a multitude of companies over the years, it is clear that many businesses want to learn about (and implement) best practices for their Data Centers. While there is certainly Data Center expertise available in the marketplace—data cabling standards are endorsed by a technical association, several worthy Data Center industry organizations exist, and countless consultants can be hired to provide design assistance—there has never been a comprehensive handbook about how effectively to design, manage, support, and work in such a facility. This book is meant to fill that gap.

Understanding how to create a productive Data Center and manage it for maximum effect is especially valuable today, since several factors are driving companies to undertake major Data Center projects:

- The proliferation of inexpensive high-density servers that require more power, data connections, and cooling in Data Centers than in the past. Older rooms lack the infrastructure to support these machines and often require retrofitting or expansion.

- An increased awareness of terrorism, natural disasters, and vulnerability of commercial power is prompting more companies to consider building backup Data Centers.

- Businesses looking to save operational costs by shedding real estate, leading to the consolidation of servers into new and larger Data Centers.

- Companies that have experienced explosive growth are discovering their server environments are inadequate in capacity or infrastructure and require upgrades or wholesale replacement.

Sources for This Book

This book draws upon the collective experience of Cisco's Data Center Infrastructure Team. The team—my team—has worked on hundreds of Data Center-related projects. Among them have been all-new construction, comprehensive infrastructure upgrades, expansions of existing facilities, site consolidations, and large-scale (1000+) server relocations.

During these projects, we dealt with the same physical challenges you undoubtedly face in your Data Center: greater equipment densities, increasing heat production, growing weight loads, and more demanding cable management needs. We worked alongside hundreds of IT and facilities personnel on these projects, listening carefully to what clients need from their server environment(s) and what support staff find the most difficult challenges to overcome.

Data Center Infrastructure Team members have toured scores of server environments belonging to other businesses as well, cataloging the strengths and vulnerabilities of those rooms. We've had the opportunity to evaluate still more Data Center designs, and occasionally step in to upgrade them, thanks to Cisco's multiple acquisitions of other companies—ninety-seven as of this writing.

Who Should Read This Book?

This book is for anyone who comes into contact with a Data Center. If you design, support, manage, maintain, or otherwise work in a server environment—or you want to learn how to—this book can help.

There are strategies and lessons here for IT or Data Center managers who design or supervise server environments, facilities managers who keep Data Center mechanical infrastructure running, as well as architectural, engineering, and facilities consultants who design these specialized rooms. The material in this book can also assist IT and network engineers who support individual servers, since the more you know about a Data Center's physical infrastructure and design the more effectively you can use it.

How This Book Is Organized

This book is divided into two sections. The first portion, encompassing Chapters 1 through 9, covers the design of a Data Center and consists of the following topics:

- **Chapter 1, "Approaching the Data Center Project"**—This chapter discusses the critical function that the Data Center serves for your business and explains the need for communication and cooperation among key personnel for its successful design and construction. The chapter presents the five principles of good Data Center design and explains traditional server environment infrastructure, including options for redundancy. Finally, the chapter highlights the people and documents that are normally involved when designing a Data Center, and offers tips for a winning project.

- **Chapter 2, "Choosing an Optimal Site"**—This chapter explains how to choose an appropriate location for your Data Center, from the hazards you should avoid to the physical attributes you want. The chapter spells out the risks that can jeopardize a Data Center site, how to safeguard your server environment against them, and what agency to go to learn if a specific parcel of land is susceptible. Finally, the chapter outlines what seemingly minor building elements can make or break a property's suitability to house a Data Center.

- **Chapter 3, "Quantifying Data Center Space"**—This chapter discusses the physical footprint of your Data Center—how to size it, what's a good configuration, where to locate a server environment within a multipurpose building, how to make it adaptable for the future needs of your business, and how to construct the Data Center to protect the valuable equipment inside effectively. The chapter also outlines what additional dedicated areas are necessary to make your Data Center function effectively, including the required infrastructure of each area and where those areas should be located in relation to the Data Center.

- **Chapter 4, "Laying Out the Data Center"**—This chapter explains how to efficiently arrange all elements of a Data Center during the design phase, from large infrastructure objects to buffer zones to server rows. The chapter addresses how various server layouts affect the amount of floor space that rows occupy, what's the best way to lay out a room when dealing with super heavy equipment, and how to accommodate unavoidable obstacles. Finally, the chapter explains where to place essential Data Center infrastructure controls and what layout-related problems to watch for and avoid.

- **Chapter 5, "Overhead or Under-Floor Installation?"**—This chapter outlines the benefits and drawbacks of running power, data connections, and cooling into the Data Center by way of the ceiling versus installing a raised floor system and routing it underneath. The chapter details the components involved and offers sample illustrations for both overhead and under-floor systems as well as provides common problems to watch out for and avoid.

- **Chapter 6, "Creating a Robust Electrical System"**—This chapter presents the key elements for creating a reliable Data Center electrical system to power your company's critical servers and insulate them against surges, utility power failures, and other potential electrical problems. The chapter provides design strategies for both in-room and standby electrical infrastructure and offers best practices for labeling and monitoring the system, which are important for user safety and to avoid accidental downtime. Finally, the chapter outlines end-to-end testing procedures to ensure that when your standby infrastructure is called upon it performs as intended.

- **Chapter 7, "Designing a Scalable Network Infrastructure"**—This chapter discusses the Data Center's structured cabling and outlines the importance of a well-organized physical hierarchy. The chapter explains the differences between common cabling media, suggests which are most appropriate in various scenarios, and outlines best practices for installation and testing.

- **Chapter 8, "Keeping It Cool"**—This chapter explains the features of a Data Center's environmental control and protection systems—cooling and fire suppression. The chapter includes tips to promote good airflow within a server environment and outlines the advantages and disadvantages of various fire suppression technologies.

- **Chapter 9, "Removing the Skeletons from Your Server Closet"**—This chapter offers guidance on how to upgrade an existing Data Center that is lacking in space or infrastructure, has been poorly maintained, or can no longer meet your company's hosting needs because of changes in the types of equipment that are to be installed. While the design principles are the same as discussed in prior chapters, this section specifically addresses the special challenges of retrofitting a less-than-perfect server environment with the least impact to devices that are already on line.

The second portion of the book, Chapters 10 through 15, covers how to effectively manage a Data Center and consists of the following topics:

- **Chapter 10, "Organizing Your Way to An Easier Job"**—This chapter focuses on how to manage incoming servers and networking devices so that they integrate seamlessly within a Data Center, making individual machines easier to support and the server environment as a whole more productive for your company. The chapter outlines strategies for allocating floor space and arranging equipment as well as recommends processes and standards for reviewing equipment for suitability in your Data Center.

- **Chapter 11, "Labeling and Signage"**—This chapter discusses the role of clear and instructive Data Center labeling in promoting best use of the room's infrastructure, simplifying troubleshooting, and avoiding accidental downtime. The chapter explains different numbering schemes for a server environment and provides examples of essential Data Center signage.

- **Chapter 12, "Stocking and Standardizing"**—This chapter explains the value of providing standardized items within a Data Center to make the room safer to work in, more convenient for troubleshooting server problems, and easier to manage. The chapter calls out specific supplies, from server cabinets to stepladders, and details their potential benefit to a server environment.

- **Chapter 13, "Safeguarding the Servers"**—This chapter presents access control options for a Data Center and recommends standards of operations for people working in the room. The chapter also provides best practices for equipment installations and suggested guidelines when touring visitors through a server environment.

- **Chapter 14, "Mapping, Monitoring, and Metrics"**—This chapter specifies what Data Center-related information should be documented and maintained and how such data is helpful for managing rooms, troubleshooting during emergencies, and planning future Data Center expansions. The chapter also suggests inexpensive tools that can be used to monitor a server environment and recognize problems before they affect servers.

- **Chapter 15, "Maintaining a World-Class Environment"**—This chapter discusses the importance of maintaining your Data Center in a pristine state, diligently removing unwanted materials and having the room professionally cleaned on a regular basis. The chapter also offers instructions for contracting with a professional cleaning company and outlines common mishaps that can occur.

Register Your Book for Additional Content

Two documents are available on the Cisco Press website that supplement the materials in this book. Become a ciscopress.com member and register your book to receive this free supplemental content:

- **Data Center Design Guidelines**—This template provides instructions for the installation of electrical, cooling, fire suppression, structured cabling, and other infrastructure within a Data Center. The guidelines follow the design principles of this book and include both written specifications and sample drawings. The template is customizable and serves as an excellent starting point for anyone who needs to design a Data Center.

- **Data Center Cleaning Policy**—This document provides vendor instructions for the professional cleaning of a Data Center.

If you're already a ciscopress.com member, simply log in and register this book to receive this benefit. After you register the book, a link to the supplemental content will be listed on your Manage Registered Books page of the My Account section.

Visit www.ciscopress.com/register to log in or join.

Designing the Data Center Infrastructure

CHAPTER 1

Approaching the Data Center Project

This chapter discusses the critical function that the Data Center serves for your business and explains the need for communication and cooperation among key personnel for its successful design and construction. The chapter presents five principles of good Data Center design and explains traditional server environment infrastructure, including options for redundancy. Finally, the chapter highlights the people and documents that are normally involved when designing a Data Center, and offers tips for a winning project.

Understanding the Value of Your Data Center

Data Centers are specialized environments that safeguard your company's most valuable equipment and intellectual property. Data Centers house the devices that do the following:

- Process your business transactions
- Host your website
- Process and store your intellectual property
- Maintain your financial records
- Route your e-mails

A well-planned and effectively managed Data Center supports these operations and increases your company's productivity by providing reliable network availability and faster processing.

In many ways your Data Center is the brain of your company. Your business' ability to perceive the world (data connectivity), communicate (e-mail), remember information (data storage), and have new ideas (research and development) all rely upon it functioning properly.

This book tells you how to protect that brain, help it function efficiently, and develop its full potential for your business. It guides you through all major decisions involved in the physical design and construction of a Data Center as well as shows how to customize the environment to meet your company's needs. This book also provides instruction on how to organize and manage your Data Center effectively so downtime is minimized, troubleshooting is easier, and the room's infrastructure is fully used. This enables your company to get more from its financial investment and delay future construction, and the associated costs, by years.

Whether you are looking to design, build, retrofit, manage, support, or simply work more effectively in a server environment, there are lessons here for you. There is information to benefit facilities managers, information technology (IT) managers, system administrators, network engineers, and architectural consultants to the IT industry—anyone who works regularly with Data Centers.

As businesses seek to transform their IT departments from support organizations into sources of productivity and revenue, it is more important than ever to design and manage these specialized environments correctly. A well-built Data Center does not just accommodate future growth and innovation; it acts as a catalyst for them. Companies that know their Data Center is robust, flexible, and productive can roll out new products, move forward with their business objectives, and react to changing business needs, all without concern over whether their server environment is capable of supporting new technologies, high-end servers, or greater connectivity requirements.

Deciding Whether to Outsource

Before launching a Data Center project, the decision must be made whether to outsource the facility, that is rent server environment space from an outside company, or build it in-house. Outsourced server environments may go by various names such as Internet Data Center (IDC) or colocation facility, but the scenario is the same. Your servers are housed away from your company site, in a Data Center that is owned and operated by an outside vendor. These are usually massive raised-floor server environments that use wire mesh fencing to physically separate one tenant's equipment from another's. The hosting company provides and maintains all of the room's infrastructure—power, connectivity, cooling, cabinet space, and protective systems such as fire suppression and temperature monitoring. You might own the networking devices, or they can also be provided by the vendor. Rental costs for an outsourced Data Center are usually dictated by the amount of floor and rack space your servers occupy, how much power they draw, and what level of connectivity and staff support they require.

If you build the Data Center in-house, then the room and all of its infrastructure belong to your company. You dictate the room's design, oversee its construction, and then support and manage the facility once it is online. This puts the responsibility for the server environment squarely on your company's shoulders while also giving you complete control over it, from inception to how it operates on a daily basis.

When is it better to outsource your Data Center needs, and when should your company have its own server environment? In some ways this decision is like choosing between an apartment in a high-security building and the construction of your own home. At an apartment, the landlord is responsible for making sure that the lights and plumbing work correctly. If anything breaks, he or she fixes it. In exchange for this convenience, you pay rent every month. Your belongings are kept in the locked apartment, and someone at the front desk opens the door when you want to enter. You are not allowed to really change the apartment itself—you can't knock down a wall to make more room for your furniture, for example. Unless you sign a long-term lease, you can stop renting on short notice without penalty.

In contrast, building your own home—or Data Center—means a big investment of money up front, but then it is yours to keep and control as you like. You can do anything with the space that you want—remodel it, buy a better roof, shore up the foundation, whatever you like. You can come and go whenever you please, and you're the only one with keys to the front door. It's also up to you to keep everything in working condition.

The key differences between outsourced and in-house Data Centers, then, are ownership, responsibility, access, and up-front costs. Whom do you want to be the keeper of your company's most critical equipment and data? Whom do you want to be responsible for making sure the room is properly built, managed, and maintained? When something breaks, whom do you want to be responsible for fixing the problem?

NOTE   I'm not a proponent of outsourcing Data Centers in most situations. Because a server environment contains my company's most valuable items and handles our business critical functions, I want our own employees to be its caretakers. No one can know my company's server environment needs like our own people who are dedicated to supporting it, and no matter how good an outside vendor is, it does not have a personal stake in making sure that my Data Center runs correctly the way that my coworkers and I do.

The two situations for which I do consider an outsourced Data Center appropriate are when you have a short-term need for a server environment, perhaps until a permanent Data Center is constructed, or when you want a standby facility ready to take over for a primary Data Center in the event of a catastrophic event. If you don't have enough servers to warrant building a second Data Center, outsourcing to have a standby space makes sense.

Even if you opt to outsource your server environment, do not stop reading this book. Knowing how to effectively design and manage a Data Center helps you evaluate an outsourced server environment, identify what types of infrastructure you want the facility to have to support your servers, and foresee what challenges even your rented space might face. It can also prepare you for the day when you may want to build your own Data Center.

Defining Requirements and Roles

Assuming you have decided that building your own Data Center is the right business decision, then the first step in a successful Data Center project is defining the room's purpose. Why is your company building this Data Center? What needs must it meet? What specific functions does it need to perform, and perform well, to be considered a success? What level of availability does your business require? These are obvious questions, but in the rush to get your complex, potentially multimillion-dollar environment designed, built, and brought online in a cost-effective and timely manner, it is easy to move forward based on outdated or incorrect assumptions. The time to verify beliefs is at the beginning of the project when changes can be made on paper at minimal cost rather that at the construction site where most alterations involve significant expense.

All server environments are not created equal, or at least shouldn't be. Servers come in various shapes, sizes, and weights and have unique electrical, connectivity, and cooling requirements. Your company's unique needs determine which and how many servers are purchased and installed in your Data Center. Whatever that combination of machines, your Data Center infrastructure must be able to accommodate the variety of demands that these different servers place upon it. Defining these needs as you design the Data Center ensures that the room is a success.

It is also important at the start of the project to delineate which departments and people are responsible for what tasks. Who designs the Data Center's electrical infrastructure, for example?

- An IT person who manages the room and knows about the incoming server equipment?
- A facilities person experienced with electrical systems?
- An outside architect knowledgeable about regional building codes?

Most likely all three are needed to offer their particular expertise and perspective.

Assign these roles at the start of the project and then make sure that the people responsible for them share information and work together. Poor communication is the most common cause of mistakes, delays, and cost overruns in a Data Center project. As the project gets underway and vendors are brought in to the process, establish clear points of contact for them as well. Stay in frequent contact with these designated representatives and make sure that all discussions about project changes or problems are routed through them.

NOTE   In 1999 I worked on the design and setup of a 680 square-foot (63.2 square-meter) server environment in Uxbridge, England, near London. Although the project featured contributors based in multiple countries and time zones, local participants often held in-person meetings to discuss project issues. Decisions made in these meetings were not consistently communicated to others in the project, which caused confusion and duplication of effort.

At one point, three different Data Center networking plans were submitted to the cabling vendor because there was no clear definition of whose responsibility it was to do so. One plan came from the U.S.-based network engineer assigned to the project, and reflected his team's current design philosophies. A second plan came from the U.S.-based Data Center infrastructure engineer assigned to the project—me—and illustrated the company's cabling standards for worldwide Data Centers. A third one came from a network engineer working at the Uxbridge site and incorporated a network design used commonly in their lab environments. The cabling vendor, either from genuine misunderstanding or seeing an opportunity to increase his fees, installed *all three designs*. This not only tripled the project's labor and materials costs, but because many of the connections terminated directly into the server cabinets, it also wasted installation space that was at a premium in the small room.

Client Needs

Among the best sources of information you have when designing a Data Center are your clients. Talk to the people who work in the room, and find out the following:

- What servers they want it to support
- How much connectivity those devices need
- What their power requirements are
- Whether clients see trends among the equipment they are ordering most commonly

Focus not only on servers being ordered today, but also on what is expected to be ordered in the future. If equipment is growing in size, the Data Center's server rows have to widen to accommodate machines with larger footprints. If equipment is shrinking, the room might occupy less total area but require additional power and cooling to support more devices in the smaller space. If new server technology is emerging, the Data Center's cabling infrastructure might need to change to accommodate it.

When having these conversations, be sure to understand what Data Center users truly need and what they merely want. When clients propose a technology or design element for the Data Center, drill down and find out what issues they're trying to address with their request or suggestion. A Data Center is a multilayered environment that all business functions connect to. At most companies, employees are specialized in their area of expertise, but aren't as knowledgeable about others. This means that their proposed solution might fix their problem but inadvertently create other problems in a different area. A client's requirement may also be based upon incorrect assumptions about the Data Center infrastructure. Part of the Data Center designer's job is finding and implementing solutions that address as many different client needs as possible.

Assume, for instance, that a Data Center user asks you to increase the copper ports provided to a row of server cabinet locations. The user plans to upgrade from current servers to ones that are smaller and more powerful. The new devices have the same copper requirements as the larger machines they replace, but the user plans to install more of them into each cabinet and therefore wants the surplus copper. Rather than automatically installing the additional structured cabling, focus on the underlying issue: How can the user obtain additional copper connections?

Adding cabling is certainly one way to accomplish the acquisition of more copper connections. Doing so increases cabling density to each cabinet location, though, and that solution might not scale if the servers are eventually deployed throughout the entire Data Center. If the cabling is indeed only needed at one server row, then it is a relatively inexpensive solution, and you don't have to worry about scalability. Running additional infrastructure as a one-off solution does make the environment more complicated to manage in the long run, however, because it is no longer uniform. If you are dealing with an existing and online server environment, having a cabling vendor route and terminate cable around live equipment also introduces the risk of an unexpected outage.

A second option is installation of a network switch at multiple server cabinet locations, using them to provide more connectivity. This solution is particularly attractive if you are dealing with a Data Center facing change. This could be a room that often hosts test equipment or new technology, meaning that the client might need only the additional copper ports for a finite amount of time. It could also be for a Data Center that might be online for only a couple of years, either because it is located within a leased building or because it is going to be replaced by a new server environment. Networking equipment can be removed and redeployed when a server row begins to house different equipment or the old room is eliminated, whereas structured cabling can usually only be abandoned.

Yet a third option is maintainance of the existing copper cabling and simply spreading out the smaller servers. Distribute them across the same area that the larger original servers occupy. This avoids the cost of adding cabling or networking devices, but has its own drawbacks. You are deliberately wasting cabinet space in the Data Center, and, assuming you are facing additional equipment arriving over time, this is only a temporary measure. Eventually you must choose between spending considerable money to expand the Data Center and following one of the first two options after all and then dealing with downtime as you ultimately compress the distributed servers.

There is more than one right answer to this example. Each option has its own advantages and disadvantages, and what works best depends upon your circumstances and server environment. The important thing is going past the surface of what a client requests and exploring how to best address the needs behind it.

Cross-Functional Support

Responsibility for a company's Data Center is typically shared among multiple departments and personnel. For example, a corporate Security manager typically governs physical access into the Data Center, an IT manager coordinates where servers are physically deployed, frequently separate network and system administrators install and support individual routers and servers, and facilities engineers maintain the Data Center's physical electro-mechanical systems. These roles might be consolidated to some degree at a smaller company, but the principle is the same. Each organization and person is an important part of the cross-functional support of your company's Data Center. Make a point to understand the various goals of these departments and their representatives to head off potential "us versus them" disagreements.

For instance, the Security representative might push for a restrictive Data Center access policy because it is easier to protect the environment when the fewest people are allowed in, while the IT representative might insist that more people need ongoing Data Center access so they can best support their machines, especially in an emergency. Each person has a valid point and is trying to fulfill their own group's charter.

Seek a compromise, perhaps a short list of IT personnel with around-the-clock Data Center access privileges. Or maybe a tiered policy that generally prohibits access but becomes less restrictive during designated times or when certain emergency conditions occur. Or maybe something else entirely. The point is to work toward a solution that acknowledges the goals and concerns of both groups. Avoid turf wars. Do not let the resolution come from a confrontation over which group has greater authority to decide Data Center issues. Power struggles create bad feelings that make it uncomfortable for those involved to work together. At worst, such conflicts might cause participants to withhold information in an attempt to leverage their authority on the project.

Foster communication and cooperation among key players whenever possible. Reinforce the message that everyone on the project has the same ultimate goal — helping the company succeed by creating an effective Data Center. This can be facilitated through incentives that reward people for working together. If you have the budget or staffing for it, award monetary bonuses or days off for examples of teamwork. If you do not, at least commend cooperative people to their managers and others on the project. Do this with outside vendors as well as company employees. Also consider rewards for the successful early completion of milestones.

Publicly praise the lab manager who volunteers to lend you networking cabinets, enabling servers to come online immediately rather than having to wait until your cabinet shipment arrives, for instance. Congratulate the electrical and cabling vendors who devise a plan to work side by side in the Data Center, reducing the time it would take to install their components independently. Commend the electrician who provides comprehensive circuit information in a timely manner to the architectural firm, so that accurate and thorough as-built electrical drawings can be produced. Rewarding this behavior causes it to proliferate.

Architecting a Productive Data Center

A server environment designed with your company's long-term needs in mind increases productivity and avoids downtime. When your Data Center continues functioning during a utility power outage thanks to a well-designed standby power system and servers avoid connectivity interruptions due to properly managed cable runs, your employees keep working and your business remains productive. To create such a resilient and beneficial server environment, you must follow five essential design strategies.

Make It Robust

Above all, your Data Center has to be reliable. Its overarching reason for existence is safeguarding your company's most critical equipment and applications. Regardless of what catastrophes happen outside — inclement weather, utility failures, natural disasters, or something else unforeseen—you want your Data Center up and running so your business continues to operate.

To ensure this, your Data Center infrastructure must have depth: standby power supplies to take over when commercial electricity fails, and redundant network stations to handle the communication needs if a networking device malfunctions, for example. Primary systems are not the only ones susceptible to failure, so your Data Center's backup devices might need backups of their own.

Additionally, the infrastructure must be configured so there is no Achilles Heel, no single component or feature that makes it vulnerable. It does little good to have multiple standby power systems if they are all wired through a single circuit, or to have redundant data connections if their cable runs all enter the building at one location. In both examples, a malfunction at a single point can bring the entire Data Center offline.

Make It Modular

Your Data Center must not only have a depth of infrastructure, it must also have breadth. You want sufficient power, data, and cooling throughout the room so that incoming servers can be deployed according to a logical master plan, not at the mercy of wherever there happens to be enough electrical outlets or data ports to support them.

To achieve this uniform infrastructure, design the room in interchangeable segments. Stock server cabinet locations with identical infrastructure and then arrange those locations in identical rows. Modularity keeps your Data Center infrastructure simple and scalable. It also provides redundancy, on a smaller scale, as the standby systems mentioned previously. If a component fails in one section of the Data Center, users can simply plug in to the same infrastructure in another area and immediately be operational again.

Make It Flexible

It is safe to assume that routers, switches, servers, and data storage devices will advance and change in the coming years. They will feature more of *something* than they do now, and it will be your Data Center's job to support it. Maybe they will get bigger and heavier, requiring more power and floor space. Maybe they will get smaller, requiring more data connections and cooling as they are packed tighter into the Data Center. They might even incorporate different technology than today's machines, requiring alternate infrastructure. The better your server environment responds to change, the more valuable and cost-effective it is for your business. New equipment can be deployed quicker and easier, with minimal cost or disruption to the business.

Data Centers are not static, so their infrastructure should not be either. Design for flexibility. Build infrastructure systems using components that are easily changed or moved. This means installation of patch panels that can house an array of connector types and pre-wiring electrical conduits so they can accommodate various electrical plugs by simply swapping their receptacle. It also means avoiding items that inhibit infrastructure mobility. Deploy fixed cable trays sparingly, and stay away from proprietary solutions that handcuff you to a single brand or product.

Inflexible infrastructure invariably leads to more expense down the road. Assume, for example, that you need to install a large data storage unit that requires different data connections and more electrical outlets than your Data Center already provides. If the room's existing patch panels can house the new cable connectors and its electrical conduits simply need their receptacles swapped to another type, it is straightforward and inexpensive to modify a server cabinet location to accept the unit. It requires significantly more effort and money if the Data Center contains proprietary patch panels, incompatible electrical conduits, and cable trays; each will need to be removed or maneuvered around to accommodate the new unit.

Part of a Data Center's flexibility also comes from whether it has enough of a particular type of infrastructure to handle an increased need in the future. You therefore make your server environment more adaptable by providing buffer capacity—more data ports, electrical circuits, or cooling capacity than it otherwise seems to require, for example. Boosting these quantities makes a Data Center more expensive during initial construction, but also better prepared for future server requirements.

Standardize

Make the Data Center a consistent environment. This provides stability for the servers and networking equipment it houses, and increases its usability. The room's modularity provides a good foundation for this, because once a user understands how infrastructure is configured at one cabinet location, he or she will understand it for the entire room. Build on this by implementing uniform labeling practices, consistent supplies, and standard procedures for the room. If your company has multiple server environments, design them with a similar look and feel. Even if one Data Center requires infrastructure absolutely different from another, use identical signage, color-coding, and supplies to make them consistent. Standardization makes troubleshooting easier and ensures quality control.

When building a new facility, it might be tempting to try something different, to experiment with an alternate design philosophy or implement new technology. If there are new solutions that truly provide quantifiable benefits, then by all means use them. Do not tinker with the design just to tinker, though. There are many situations in which it is appropriate to experiment with new ideas and infrastructure—your Data Center project is not one of them. (If you are really interested in trying out a new technology, consider deploying it in a lab environment first. Labs are built for testing, so experimenting with different materials or designs is more in line with their purpose.)

Once you find a design model or infrastructure component that provides the functions and features you are looking for, make it your standard. Avoid variety for variety's sake. While it is good to know that several products can solve a particular problem for your

Data Center, it is a bad idea to deploy several of them in the same room, at least not unless they are providing another benefit as well. The more different components in the Data Center, the more complex the environment. The more complex the environment, the greater the chance that someone will misunderstand the infrastructure and make a mistake, most likely in an emergency. It is also much easier to support a Data Center when fewer materials have to be stocked—a single universal power strip rather than a different model in every country, for example.

NOTE   Establish standards for your Data Centers, but also be ready for those standards to evolve over time. The server cabinet that so perfectly meets your needs today may not work so well in five years if server dimensions or power requirements change, for example. Standardize for clarity and consistency, but make sure that even your Data Center standards exercise some flexibility.

Promote Good Habits

Finally, the Data Center should be engineered to encourage desirable behavior. This is a subtle element, rarely noticed even by those who work regularly in the environment. Incorporating the right conveniences into the Data Center and eliminating the wrong ones definitely make the space easier to manage, though.

Data Center users are busy people. They are looking for the fastest solution to their problems, especially when they are rushing to bring a system online and are up against a deadline. Given a choice, most of them follow the path of least resistance. You want to make sure that path goes where you want it to go.

Construct a nearby Build Room where system administrators can unbox servers to keep the Data Center free of boxes and pallets, for example. Make primary Data Center aisles larger than those between server rows, creating an obvious path for users to follow when rolling refrigerator-sized servers through the room for deployment. Install wall-mounted telephones with long receiver cords throughout the Data Center if you are concerned about interference from cellular phones and want to reduce their usage. Provide pre-tested patch cords to promote standardized cabling practices. Design the Data Center so users can easily exercise good habits and they will.

Data Center Ergonomics

An important but often overlooked quality of a server environment is how easily and efficiently people can work there. The harder it is for a Data Center user to complete a task in a server environment, obviously the less productive that room is for your company.

Data Center ergonomics derive from hundreds of minor decisions made when designing the room. Is it easy to reach power and data under a raised floor or do objects above overlap key floor tiles and make access difficult? How easy is it to make connections among servers, networking devices, and other equipment? Are infrastructure controls clearly labeled and within easy reach or obscure and difficult to find? Is the Data Center organized in a manner that can be quickly recognized and understood by a newcomer, or is the room exceedingly complex or, worse, not arranged logically at all?

Seemingly minor details make the difference between a merely serviceable Data Center and one that boosts productivity. Suggestions are provided throughout this book about how to make a server environment easy to use and therefore more productive. These ergonomic recommendations follow a few general principles:

- **Make things accessible**—This means putting items close by that Data Center users need to perform their job. It also means designing work areas, say within an electrical panel or where data cabling terminates, to be free of clutter.

- **Choose simple over complex**—The more straightforward a Data Center's details are, the less chance there is for someone to make a mistake and perhaps cause an outage. Following this principle can influence how you arrange server equipment and major infrastructure in the room.

- **Remove mystery**—If there is a chance someone might not understand an element of a Data Center, add some form of written instructions—signage, labeling, or even maps.

- **Consider human nature**—People typically follow the path of least resistance. As suggested in the preceding section about making the Data Center intuitive, take this into account when designing the room. If you want someone to use a particular type and length patch cord, for example, you should provide them in the Data Center.

Previewing Data Center Components

The word infrastructure has been used several times in this book so far, most often in reference to the electrical and data cabling provided to Data Center cabinet locations. In truth, it is a broader term that traditionally applies to seven basic Data Center facility systems: physical space, raised flooring, in-room electrical, standby power, data cabling, cooling, and fire suppression. (The term can also apply to the collection of networking devices in a Data Center, but since the focus of this book is purely on a server environment's physical design, that definition doesn't apply here.)

Here is a brief introduction to these systems, all of which will be discussed in greater detail in their own chapters.

Physical Space

Physical space refers to the footprint that Data Center-related items occupy. This generally applies to the overall area of the Data Center and its associated spaces, such as electrical rooms or storage areas. On a smaller scale this might refer to key dimensions within the Data Center, such as the external measurements of a server cabinet or aisle clearances.

Raised Flooring

Raised flooring is an elevated grid system that is frequently installed in large Data Centers. Cooled air, electrical whips, and data cabling are routed through the space under the raised floor, promoting better air flow and enabling easier management of power and cable runs. Water pipes, fire suppressant cylinders, moisture detectors, and smoke detectors may be located here as well.

Raised flooring can vary in height from a few inches to several feet, or a few centimeters to several meters. In extreme cases they are as tall as the story of a building, enabling workers to walk upright under the plenum. Regardless of their height, the floors are typically composed of standard 2 foot (60 centimeter) square floor tiles. The tiles can vary in weight, strength, and finish depending upon their use. Tiles featuring either small perforations or large cut-out sections are placed in key locations to enable pass-through of air and cabling between the areas above and below the floor.

In-Room Electrical

In-room electrical refers to all power-related facilities within the Data Center. This normally includes electrical panels, conduits, and several types of receptacles. Power to this system usually comes from an outside commercial power source, namely your local utility company, and is likely conditioned at the company site. Voltage varies from one country to another.

Standby Power

Standby power includes all backup power systems responsible for support of the Data Center's electrical load in the event that normal utility power fails for any reason. This system traditionally includes large batteries, known as an uninterruptible power source or uninterruptible power supply, and one or more generators.

Cabling

The cabling system is all structured cabling within the Data Center. Copper and fiber cabling are the typical media and are terminated via several types of connectors. Common components include fiber housings, patch panels, multimedia boxes, and data faceplates. Cabinets, raceways, and other items used to route structured cabling are also considered part of the cabling system. Users plug servers in to the Data Center's structured cabling system with pre-terminated patch cords.

Cooling

The cooling system refers to the chillers and air handlers used to regulate ambient temperature and control humidity within the Data Center. This system might incorporate the air conditioning system used to cool regular office space within the same building, known as house air, or might be independent of it. Individual server cabinets can also possess their own cooling measures, such as fans or water-cooling.

Fire Suppression

Fire suppression includes all devices associated with detecting or extinguishing a fire in the Data Center. The most obvious components are water-based sprinklers, gaseous fire suppression systems, and hand-held fire extinguishers. Others can include devices that detect smoke or measure air quality.

Other Infrastructure Components

There are also some infrastructure items that do not strictly fall under the prior categories but are commonly found in server environments. These include leak detection devices, seismic mitigation, and physical security controls such as card readers and security cameras.

Establishing Data Center Design Criteria

Armed with the knowledge of what your clients need and want, the essentials of good Data Center design, and the general infrastructure that a Data Center includes, you are ready to define the final factors driving the design of your server environment. You need to decide upon its scope.

How many layers of infrastructure should your Data Center possess? Will it be the only server environment for your company or one of several? Will the room house production servers and be a business-critical site or contain a minimum of equipment for disaster recovery purposes and serve as a failover location? How long is its initial construction expected to meet your company's needs? And, the bottom line question for many projects: What is it all going to cost? Addressing these issues provides the framework for your Data Center's design.

Availability

As stated earlier, the most important aspect of a well-designed Data Center is its ability to protect a company's critical equipment and applications. The degree to which Data Center devices function continuously is known as the room's availability or its uptime.

NOTE   The term *availability* is commonly applied in several different ways. When network engineers talk about availability, they are referring to the routers and switches that form their company's networks. When system administrators speak of availability, it is in regards to the uptime of a particular server or application. When facilities personnel talk about availability, they are referring to the electrical infrastructure that powers all devices in the Data Center and the mechanical systems that keep them cool. The focus of this book is the Data Center's physical infrastructure, and therefore the third use of the term. It is also relevant to note that, because the Data Center's networking devices, applications, and mechanical equipment are all dependent upon the room's electrical infrastructure—routers, servers, and air handlers obviously cannot function without power—a company's network and server availabilities can never be higher than its Data Center availability.

Availability is represented as a percentage of time. How many days, hours, and minutes is the Data Center's electrical infrastructure operational and supplying power over a given time period? Just as a baseball player's batting average drops any time he or she fails to hit and safely reach base, so does a Data Center's availability number suffer whenever the electrical infrastructure fails to provide power to the room. Unlike in baseball, a .400 average does not make you an all-star.

Most companies want extremely high availability for their Data Center, because downtime affects their ability to be productive and perform business functions. How high, though, can vary significantly and is represented by the concept of *nines*. The more nines of availability, the closer to 100% uptime a system has achieved. Say, for example, that your company brings the Data Center's electrical system offline for one hour of maintenance every month. Assuming there are no additional outages of any kind, that means that the Data Center is running for all but 12 of the 8760 hours in the year. That's 99.863% of the time, or two nines of availability.

For some, that's a perfectly acceptable amount of downtime. Other companies that rely the most upon Data Center availability—financial institutions, government agencies, hospitals, companies with a sizable Internet presence or that do business across multiple time zones, for example—set five nines of availability as their standard. That's 99.999% uptime, or little more than five minutes of downtime in a year.

Table 1-1 outlines the amount of downtime involved at the highest availability levels.

Table 1-1   *Data Center Availability*

Level of Availability	Percent	Downtime per Year
Six Nines	99.9999	32 seconds
Five Nines	99.999	5 minutes, 15 seconds
Four Nines	99.99	52 minutes, 36 seconds
Three Nines	99.9	8 hours, 46 minutes
Two Nines	99	3 days, 15 hours, 40 minutes

When discussing availability, remember that any downtime, even if scheduled beforehand so that it affects fewer clients, is a reduction in the room's uptime. On the other hand, if a utility power outage occurs and the Data Center runs on electricity from backup batteries, that does not reduce the room's availability because there is no interruption to devices in the Data Center.

Infrastructure Tiers

The higher the availability you want your Data Center to achieve, the more layers of infrastructure it must have. Logically, if one standby generator keeps the Data Center running when utility power fails, then two provide even more protection. The second generator is there to take over in case a problem occurs with the first during a power outage.

The amount of infrastructure required to support all servers or networking devices in the Data Center, assuming that the space is filled to maximum capacity and all devices are functioning, is referred to as *N capacity*. N stands for need. The term can apply to all types of Data Center infrastructure, but is most commonly used when discussing standby power, cooling, and the room's network.

Exactly how many infrastructure components are required to achieve N capacity for your Data Center depends upon several factors, including the room's size, how many electrical circuits it contains, and the maximum number of servers and networking devices the environment can house. For a small server environment, N capacity might consist of one air handler to adequately cool the room, one small generator to hold its electrical load in the event commercial power fails, and three networking devices to route all network traffic. For a large Data Center, providing that same functionality might require 15 air handlers, two generators with much larger capacity, and 20 networking devices. Remember, the Data Center's capacity refers to the level of functionality it provides, not the number of its infrastructure components.

N is the lowest tier a Data Center's infrastructure is typically designed and built to. It is possible to equip a Data Center with infrastructure that can adequately support the room only when it is partially full of servers, but that is not good design. Imagine an expectant couple buying a two-seater automobile. The car might meet their transportation needs in the short term, but a future upgrade is inevitable.

N+1 is the next tier. N+1 infrastructure can support the Data Center at full server capacity and includes an additional component, like an automobile with a spare tire. If the large Data Center mentioned previously requires 15 air handlers, two generators, and 20 networking devices to function at maximum capacity, it can be designed at N+1 by adding a 16th air handler, a third generator, and at least a 21st networking device—maybe more depending on the design and need. A Data Center built to this tier can continue functioning normally while a component is offline, either because of regular maintenance or a malfunction. Higher tiers of N+2, N+3, and beyond can be likewise achieved by increasing the number of redundant components.

An even higher tier is N * 2. Alternately called a 2N or system-plus-system design, it involves fully doubling the required number of infrastructure components. Still using our earlier example, designing that large Data Center N * 2 means installing 30 air handlers, four generators, and 40 networking devices.

Because components come in many different configurations and capacities, a Data Center can achieve an infrastructure tier in several different ways. For example, say your Data Center requires 1500 kilowatts of generator support. This room can be designed to N by installing one 1500-kilowatt generator. It can also achieve N by sharing the load between two 750-kilowatt generators or among three 500-kilowatt generators. The configuration options become more important as you achieve a higher tier. Adding a single generator will make the Data Center N+1, which means two 1500-kilowatt generators, three 750-kilowatt generators, or four 500-kilowatt generators. If you choose to install the two largest generators, you are actually providing the room with N * 2 infrastructure.

Even higher tiers exist or can be created: 3N, 4N, and so on. There is theoretically no limit to how many redundant systems you can install. As you consider how deep you want your infrastructure to be, however, be aware that just because you *can* build a Data Center with quadruple-redundant power systems and state-of-the-art connectivity doesn't mean you *should*. You want infrastructure tiered to best meet your company's needs, now and in the foreseeable future.

It is quite possible to have too much redundant infrastructure. Although each extra layer adds protection, they also add complexity. The more complex the system, the greater the chance of a mistake occurring through human error, whether during installation of the system or during an emergency when the standby system is needed. There's also a point of diminishing returns. While it is *possible* that during a power outage your primary, secondary, and tertiary generators might all develop problems and your quaternary generator is the one that keeps the room running, the odds are much higher of someone misunderstanding the complicated system and causing an outage by accident. There is also the issue of cost—quadrupling the number of generators that support your Data Center also quadruples what you spend when building the room in the first place.

NOTE   I have maintained Data Center incident logs for years and consistently find that more than half of the unplanned downtimes are caused by human error. It is an observation corroborated by several Data Center industry groups and in conversations with dozens of other Data Center managers. From a janitor tripping a full server cabinet's power strip by plugging a vacuum cleaner into it, to a security guard flipping a circuit breaker to silence an irritating server alarm, to a maintenance worker crashing an entire Data Center after mistaking an Emergency Power Off button for an automatic door-opener, people are a Data Center's worst enemy. It is impractical to keep everyone out of your server environment all of the time, though, and in fact all of the people in the listed incidents had permission to do the work they were doing, if not in the questionable way they went about it. The lesson to take away from these incidents is to make your Data Center infrastructure as simple and straightforward as you can. Balance the benefit of greater redundancy against the hazards of a more complicated system.

One Room or Several?

Although this book generally refers to your server environment as *the* Data Center, it is just as likely that your company has multiple rooms to host servers and networking equipment. They might all be fully functioning server environments, or some might be standby facilities intended to come online only in the event a primary Data Center is affected by a catastrophic event. Depending upon the size of your company, they might be distributed among several buildings on a single campus or among several countries around the world. If you have the ability to choose whether your Data Centers are centralized within one location or decentralized among many, it is important to understand the advantages and disadvantages of each configuration. Actually, even if you cannot choose because the arrangement is already in place, it is helpful to be aware of the strengths and weaknesses of the arrangement of your hosting space as a whole.

One large Data Center is simpler to manage than several smaller ones. Consistent standards can be applied more easily to a single, uniform environment, and all of its support personnel can be located at the site. One large Data Center is also generally less expensive per square foot or square meter than several smaller environments because construction materials cost less per unit when bought in greater quantities. In addition, the greater block of floor space is more forgiving for designing around obstructions such as structural columns. Any upgrades to the Data Center environment, such as increasing the room's cooling capacity or installing additional security measures, are also maximized because the improvements benefit all of the company's servers.

On the other hand, having only one server environment puts all of your eggs in one basket. A natural disaster, major infrastructure failure, or act of sabotage can cripple your business functions. Multiple smaller Data Centers, whether several miles or kilometers apart or even in different buildings on the same company site, are less likely to fall victim to a single catastrophic event. Servers with the same functions can be placed in more than one room, creating an additional form of redundancy.

Alternatively, smaller Data Centers don't achieve the economy of scale that larger rooms do. If building codes require a wide walkway through your Data Center, for example, you sacrifice more usable space providing aisles in several rooms rather than just one. It is also a greater challenge to standardize the construction of server environments located in multiple countries or states. Supplies are not universally available or even allowed in all regions, and building practices can vary from one city to another, let alone from one country to another. For example, Heptafluoropropane, known commercially as FM-200 or HFC-227, is commonly used in the United States as a Data Center fire suppression agent, but is prohibited in some European countries.

The overriding factor for whether your company's Data Center space should be centralized or distributed depends upon where employees are located and what level of Data Center connectivity they require to perform their jobs. Connection speeds are limited by geographic distances, and some computing functions tolerate only a limited amount of latency. This can be improved to a degree by installing more media to provide greater bandwidth, but requires additional networking hardware and higher performance connection lines from service providers.

Ideally, a company is large enough that a few large or moderate Data Centers in total can be located at various company sites where employees require server access to perform their jobs. Functions can be consolidated at these few locations, providing the redundancy of multiple rooms while still achieving the economy of scale that larger installations provide.

Life Span

Another factor that helps define the scope of your Data Center is how long it is expected to support your company's needs without having to be expanded or retrofitted, or otherwise undergo major changes. A server environment that is expected to handle a company's hosting and computing requirements for one year should be designed differently than a Data Center to support those functions for 10 years.

When does it make sense to build a Data Center for a shorter time period? This would be when there is uncertainty surrounding the room or site, such as if the Data Center is constructed in a leased building that your company is not guaranteed to renew in the future. Perhaps your company is large and has acquired another business, and your mission is to create a server environment that will serve its needs only until all of its employees, equipment, and functions are transferred to a new site. Perhaps your company is a startup, and your goal is to design a temporary Data Center, enabling your young business to delay the design and construction of a permanent one until growth warrants a larger room and more funds are available.

As with the decisions about how many Data Centers to build and what level of infrastructure should be employed, your Data Center's projected life span depends upon the needs of your company, and the ideal is likely between the extremes. Equipping a server environment that is going to exist for only several months with abundant infrastructure is not advisable because your business would see only a short-term benefit. On the other hand, designing a Data Center to last at least a decade without alteration understandably requires the commitment of significantly more floor space and infrastructure to accommodate future growth and technology.

The most effective strategy, then, is to design a Data Center with a projected life span of a few years, with the intention of expanding it when it appears close to being filled with servers. Specific instructions on how to size your Data Center are provided in Chapter 3, "Quantifying Data Center Space."

Budget Decisions

It is understandable to want a utopian Data Center, an impenetrable bunker with ample floor space, abundant power, and scorching fast connectivity, capable of withstanding any catastrophe and meeting all of your company's hosting needs for decades to come. The deep infrastructure needed to create that theoretical ideal costs very real money, however, so it is important to understand what expenses you are incurring or avoiding based on the design choices you make. It is no good to spend millions of dollars on a server environment to protect your company's assets if that cost drives your business into bankruptcy. You want to spend money on the amount of infrastructure that is appropriate for your business needs—no more and no less.

The most obvious costs for a Data Center are labor and materials associated with its initial construction, which, even for a room smaller than 1000 square feet or 100 square meters, normally runs into hundreds of thousands of dollars. Consulting fees accrued during the design portion of the project add tens of thousands of dollars to the price. For brand-new sites, there is also the cost of real estate, which varies greatly depending upon the property's location and the physical characteristics of the building. After initial construction, ongoing operational expenses associated with the Data Center normally include utility power costs for providing the room with power and cooling. There is also the running tally for servers and networking devices that are installed into the room over time.

So, how much is acceptable to spend on the construction of your Data Center? That depends. To determine the answer, you need to know the value of what your Data Center is protecting. This is not the purchase price of the servers and networking equipment, although that in itself can far outstrip the cost of the Data Center. It is how much money your company loses when devices in your Data Center go offline. Depending on what task an individual server performs, an outage could shut down your company's website and thereby halt all online ordering, or it could lose data that was the result of thousands of hours of work by employees. Downtime might also shut down your company's e-mail and print capabilities. Your business might even face financial penalties if it is unable to provide contracted services during a Data Center outage.

There are several ways to measure downtime costs. One is to define the cost of a generic employee at your business and then multiply this by the length of the outage and by how many employees are unable to work during downtime. An employee's total cost includes every expense they cause the company to incur, directly or indirectly. Salary, medical plans, retirement benefits, telephone bills, even the fraction of operational costs for lights, air conditioning, and cubicle or office retail space. The personnel expenses, the three listed first, can be calculated by your human resources department, while the operational costs can be figured by your facilities or real estate organization.

Say, for example, a generic employee costs your company a total of $150,000 a year. (Remember, this is all costs combined, not just salary.) That is about $60 an hour, assuming the employee works a traditional 40-hour work week, and 52-week calendar year. If your Data Center goes offline for two hours and stops the work of 100 employees at that site, that is $12,000 for that single outage. It is fair to argue that the length of the downtime should be calculated beyond two hours, because once the Data Center is online it takes more time before all of the affected servers are back on and their applications are running again. (It takes only a second for machines to lose power and go offline, but bringing them all back up again can take hours.) The more servers are involved, the longer it takes for them to be brought back up and the more staff time it takes to do so. For the purpose of this example, let us say that all of the servers are up and running after another two hours after the Data Center itself comes back online. That doubles the cost of the outage to $24,000 in soft dollars.

There is also the time that Facilities personnel spend on the outage and its aftermath, rather than doing their other job functions. Facilities employees might not require the Data Center servers to be operational to do their jobs, but their time spent identifying, fixing, and reporting on Data Center infrastructure malfunctions associated with the outage is certainly a relevant cost. If just 20 hours of staff time is occupied with the outage, that is another $1200, bringing the cost of this one event to more than $25,000.

If your company's business transactions are handled via a website whose servers are housed in the Data Center, then the downtime is also affecting your incoming revenue. Your finance department can tally how much online revenue is traditionally processed through your website during a typical month or quarter. Divide that by the number of hours that the website is online in that time period, and you have its hourly income rate. Multiply that by the number of hours it takes for the Data Center and the web-related servers to come back online, and you have a second data point regarding the outage's cost. For instance, assume that your company typically brings in $1 million a year in online business. If the website accepts orders around the clock, then divide $1 million by 8760, the number of hours in a year. That works out to $114 an hour, which means that the four hours of downtime also disrupted about $500 in sales.

The most difficult value of all to quantify comes from when a server crashes and data is destroyed. When this happens not only are the man-hours that went in to creating that data gone, but there is also a chance that difficult-to-replace intellectual property has been destroyed. Some of this can be protected and later restored by regular data backups, but at many companies such backups are performed only weekly. Such loss can also prolong how long it takes a business to bring a product to market, which in turn leads to missed opportunities for sales or gaining an advantage over a competitor or both.

All three of these costs—lost employee productivity, disrupted sales transaction revenue, and missing intellectual property—are soft dollars. They are challenging to evaluate because they do not appear as concrete expenses on your company's financial records. They do affect your business, though, and it is important to weigh them against the price tag of various Data Center infrastructures.

Installing a generator to provide standby power to your server environment might cost $200,000, and providing a second one for redundancy doubles the expense to $400,000—significant increases to the overall cost of the project. The price for a single generator is easy to justify if power outages occur even a few times a year and cost the $25,000-plus in lost productivity in the previous example. Your company might not want to spend the additional funds for a second generator, however, unless it is for a much larger Data Center hosting additional servers that, in turn, support many more employees and customers.

Managing a Data Center Project

As you have undoubtedly concluded, designing and constructing a Data Center is an immense task involving myriad decisions and details. It is also brimming with opportunities to make a mistake that can cost your company millions of dollars. It is no surprise, then, if it feels overwhelming, especially for anyone who has never managed a Data Center project before.

Fortunately, such an undertaking does not rest solely on the shoulders of one person. There are experts who can and should be tapped for your Data Center project, tips that can help you avoid problems, and one very useful tool to help you guide the project to success.

The Design Package

Once decisions are made about the design of your Data Center, the information must be assembled, documented, and ultimately given to the contractors tasked with performing the work. This is done by first creating a design package. This document can be as minimal as a sketch jotted on a napkin or as involved as a multimedia package of written guidelines, blueprint schematics, and videotaped installation practices. The important thing is that it include clear instructions about how the Data Center is to be constructed and what infrastructure it must include. Pay careful attention to detail and accuracy. The design package is your most powerful tool for ensuring that your server environment is built to your specifications. Mistakes or ambiguity in this document lead to installation errors and can cost your company hundreds of thousands of dollars to correct.

NOTE   In 2000 I was involved in the construction of a 964 square foot (90 square meter) Data Center in Dallas, Texas. The parent company was building the new environment for an acquired company that specialized in software systems for IP-based wireless infrastructure. During construction, the cabling contractor misunderstood the amount of fiber cabling to be installed. He ran 12 *strands* of fiber to each server cabinet location instead of the 12 *ports* that were specified. Fiber ports consist of two strands each, so the room's 40 server cabinet locations ended up with only half of the connectivity they needed. Installing the missing fiber could have cost the client company an extra $150,000, twice what was first quoted for the work. Because the quantities were clearly spelled out in the design package, the contractor kept to his original bid for the project.

At minimum, design guidelines for a Data Center must have basic instructions for installation of the room's infrastructure, calling out how much and what types of pre-structured cabling media and electrical receptacles are required. More thorough packages include testing procedures, relevant building codes, part numbers for preferred materials, and even illustrative drawings. Whatever form your design package takes, it must be detailed enough that workers unfamiliar with your Data Center design philosophy can follow its instructions.

A comprehensive Data Center design package template, including all of the philosophies outlined in this book, is available at the Cisco Press website at http://www.ciscopress.com/1587051826.

Working with Experts

As with any construction project, designing and building a Data Center involves many people from several different fields. Some ensure that the construction is done in accordance to the law. Others add value by providing knowledge and guidance in areas that are critical to the successful design and operation of a Data Center. Here is an overview of common Data Center project participants, their functions, and what expertise they provide:

- **The facilities manager**—This person's specialty includes all mechanical devices within the Data Center infrastructure, from air handlers and power distribution units to fire sprinklers and standby generators. The manager can provide information about your company's infrastructure-related standards. These might include preferred vendors or suppliers, standardized wiring schemes, existing service contracts, or other design philosophies your company follows when building Data Centers, labs, or similar specialized environments. Once the Data Center is online, the facilities department will provide ongoing maintenance of the mechanical systems.

- **The IT manager**—This person is responsible for the servers installed in the Data Center. This manager has insight into the power and data connectivity requirements of these devices. Once servers are online, the IT department supports, monitors, and upgrades them as needed.

- **The network engineer**—This person designs, supports, and manages the Data Center's network. Just as the IT department supports servers, so is the Networking group responsible for all networking devices. Some companies have multiple networks—perhaps one internal network, a second external network, and a third dedicated entirely to backup functions. In that instance, each may be represented by a different engineer.

- **The Data Center manager**—This person designs, supports, and manages the Data Center's physical architecture and oversees the layout and installation of incoming servers. He or she governs physical access into the room and enforces its standards of operation. This manager also serves as a bridge among the facilities, IT, and networking organizations, ensuring that the Data Center infrastructure meets the needs of its users. Some companies do not have a distinct Data Center manager role, instead splitting responsibility for the architecture among the three roles listed previously.

- **The real estate manager or building planner**—This person governs how company building space is used. In a Data Center project, this manager/planner coordinates the floor space requirements of the server environment and its associated rooms with the floor space needs of other rooms and departments.

- **The project manager**—This person manages the Data Center construction project as a whole, including its budget, timelines, and supervision of outside contractors. His or her project might cover an entire building or company site, making the Data Center only one portion of what he or she must supervise. Some companies outsource this role, but most often this person is a facilities manager.

- **The architectural firm**—This outside company ensures that your Data Center design complies with local building codes. They are also a conduit to specialized subcontracting work, such as a structural engineer to confirm the weight bearing ability of a Data Center floor or a seismic engineer to approve its proposed earthquake safeguards. After receiving a design package and other instructions from the client company, the architectural firm creates formal construction documents that local municipal officials review and that the project's various contractors follow when building the Data Center.

- **The general contractor**—This person oversees and acts as a single point of contact for all other contractors on the project. Project changes are normally directed in writing to the contractor rather than through individual contractors.

- **The electrical contractor**—This contractor installs, labels, and tests all of the Data Center's electrical and standby equipment.

- **The mechanical contractor**—This contractor installs and tests all of the Data Center's cooling equipment. Ducting is typically the contractor's responsibility as well.

- **The cabling contractor**—Not surprisingly, the cabling contractor installs and tests all of the Data Center's structured cabling. Its staff also installs any racks or cabinets that cabling terminates into, and labels the room's cable runs.

Tips for a Successful Project

Although each Data Center project has its own quirks, all of them generally have to overcome similar challenges in order to succeed. Budgets must be followed, materials must be installed, and timelines must be adhered to. People must be managed, work must be inspected, and unanticipated issues must be dealt with as they arise. Fortunately, because the challenges are the same, often their solutions can be as well. Several fundamental practices have proven useful in keeping a Data Center project on track and avoiding possible pitfalls.

- **Define expectations and communicate them early and often**—It is hard to have a successful project if everyone involved does not understand what's expected of them. Establish clear deadlines and provide thorough instruction to all contractors. The design package is your most powerful tool for doing this. Also have a formal kickoff meeting early in the project. Involve all of the principal members of the project to make sure that the design package is thoroughly read and that any potential problems are identified and discussed up front.

- **Expect long lead times on infrastructure items**—Certain components used in the construction of a Data Center can take months to arrive from their manufacturers, so it is important that the person responsible for obtaining materials, either the project manager or a particular contractor, order them early. Call this out directly to the contractors, who often prefer to wait as long as possible to order infrastructure components. This is understandable because they themselves often do not get paid until near the end of the project, and delaying purchases helps their cash flow. It can cause problems for your project, though, so it should be discouraged. Additional delays occur when working in countries that have stringent customs procedures. If you know ahead of time what specific infrastructure items are difficult to obtain, it might be worth purchasing and storing spares. This probably is not practical for high-priced or large items, like a generator, but can be effective for smaller components such as patch panels or fiber housings.

Note   It is amazing what infrastructure can be difficult to obtain. Generators, raised-floor tiles, server cabinets, and fiber cabling are the most common culprits, but they are not alone. During construction of the Data Center in Dallas, mentioned previously, the cabling contractor located and purchased all of the project's thousands of individual parts and materials, except for a mere handful of violet jacks. They were required for the copper cabling that terminated into the room, and the contractor spent weeks unsuccessfully trying to order them. The violet jacks miraculously appeared on the day the Data Center came online. I never asked the contractor where they came from, and he never volunteered the information. I suspect a lab somewhere on the site was missing a few connections for several weeks, however.

- **Establish deadline-based incentives for time-sensitive projects**—If your Data Center project absolutely must be completed quickly, include incentives in your vendor contracts that reward for the timely completion of key tasks and penalize for delays. Tasks can almost always be expedited if the right incentives exist. If you take this approach, do not allow safety to suffer in the rush to meet deadlines. It is better to have a project take longer than to put workers at risk or skip procedures that exist to ensure Data Center infrastructure works correctly.

Note	In January 1994 the Northridge Earthquake struck southern California, heavily damaging and causing the closure of four major freeways—the Santa Monica Freeway (I-10), the Simi Valley Freeway (SR-118), the Golden State Freeway (I-5), and the Antelope Valley Freeway (SR-14). At the time, I lived in the city of Santa Clarita just a few miles from where the Newhall Pass portion of I-5 had collapsed. I worked in the San Fernando Valley to the south, and this break in the freeway made it exceedingly difficult to get anywhere by car.
	Initial estimates said it would take two to three years to repair the damage. The California Department of Transportation established contracts that paid $200,000 per day to contractors for finishing ahead of schedule and penalized them $200,000 for every day the project was delayed. Freeways reopened in just over two months, and all of the damaged highways were repaired before the end of the year.

- **Document everything**—Although the design package is intended to cover all details of the project, questions inevitably arise during the course of construction. Can a different product be substituted for the one specified in the design package? Is it acceptable to route cables along a different path? Is the wording on a particular sign acceptable? No matter how minor the clarifications or changes, document them thoroughly. The Data Center is large and complex and might be only one part of a larger project. With all of the tasks everyone is trying to accomplish it is easy to forget or misunderstand a verbal agreement made weeks earlier about a minor issue. Also, although most people in the construction industry are honest and professional, some attempt to profit by taking shortcuts or creating more work for themselves and passing on additional fees to the client company. Clear and thorough documentation is the best weapon against both honest confusion and questionable practices. E-mail is particularly effective because messages are dated and simple to archive, and can include the entire thread of a conversation.

- **Visit the construction site frequently**—No matter how many phone calls are made, e-mails are written, meetings are held, and documentation is kept in association with the project, there is no substitute for walking the site to make sure your Data Center is being built according to the intended design. If budget or scheduling limitations prohibit regular visits, arrange to have someone on the site take pictures at least once a week and send them to the project's key representatives. Digital cameras are ideal for this. There is no cost or time spent to process the images, and they can be distributed quickly.

Summary

Your Data Center houses and protects the servers that perform your company's vital business functions, from processing sales transactions and storing financial records to routing e-mail and developing future products. It is a specialized environment that must be customized to meet the unique needs of the devices it houses and people who use it.

Assign roles and responsibilities early in the Data Center design process, and foster communication among key players to ensure that the project proceeds smoothly. When designed, built, and managed correctly, a Data Center helps foster growth and innovation for your company.

Five key design strategies should be followed to create a productive Data Center. First, make the Data Center robust by including redundant infrastructure and avoiding single points of failure in the design. This provides essential protection for your servers and networking equipment. Second, make the room modular for simplicity and consistency. Third, choose infrastructure components that are interchangeable and movable. Doing so makes the environment flexible and able to accommodate future change. Fourth, standardize your Data Center's labeling, supplies, and operational procedures. This simplifies troubleshooting, again promotes consistency, and ensures quality control. Last, design the room with intuitive details that make it easy for users to adhere to operational procedures.

Traditional Data Center infrastructure includes its physical space as well as raised flooring, in-room electrical, standby power, structured cabling, and fire suppression. The greater availability you want the Data Center to achieve, the more redundancy that must be built into these infrastructure systems. Countless layers of redundancy can conceivably be installed, but the added mechanical protection must be balanced against both the cost of additional infrastructure and the desire for a simple design. Overly complicated infrastructure increases the risk of downtime due to human error. The Data Center's projected lifespan, whether it will serve as your company's only server environment or one of many, and the available budget for the project also influence how much infrastructure is incorporated into its design.

In Data Center projects, a design package is created outlining the infrastructure for the Data Center and how it is to be installed. The overall project is run by a project manager, and key players are involved from the company's facilities, IT, networking and Data Center organizations. An outside architectural firm is hired to incorporate the design package into official construction documents, and specialized contractors are employed to install cabling, electrical, and other Data Center infrastructures.

A handful of practices can make the Data Center project proceed more smoothly. Clearly communicate deadlines and instructions to the contractors. Instruct contractors to order Data Center materials early, and prepare contingencies for inevitable delays. Document all project communications, especially changes, in writing to reduce misunderstanding or confusion after the fact. View the project site often to catch errors or problems as early as possible.

CHAPTER 2

Choosing an Optimal Site

This chapter explains how to choose an appropriate location for your Data Center, from the hazards you should avoid to the physical attributes you want. The chapter spells out the risks that can jeopardize a Data Center site, how to safeguard your server environment against them, and what agency to go to in order to learn if a specific parcel of land is susceptible. Finally, the chapter outlines what seemingly minor building elements can make or break a property's suitability to house a Data Center.

Assessing Viable Locations for Your Data Center

When the time comes for your business to build a server environment, it is essential that the people responsible for the Data Center's design have an opportunity to provide input into where it is constructed. Traditionally, upper management decides what property to purchase, based upon a variety of a company's wants, needs, and business drivers. Other purchase considerations might include a parcel's price tag, its proximity to a talented labor pool, advantageous tax rates, or the desire to have a corporate presence in a particular geographic area. Whatever the drivers are, a property's suitability to house a Data Center must be among them. Purchasing or leasing a site without considering this greatly hampers the Data Center's capability to protect company servers and networking devices. Not making this a consideration also invariably leads to additional expense, either to retrofit the land's undesirable characteristics or to add more infrastructure to compensate for them.

An ideal Data Center location is one that offers many of the same qualities that a Data Center itself provides a company:

- Protection from hazards
- Easy accessibility
- Features that accommodate future growth and change

These qualities are fairly obvious, like saying that it is easier for an ice chest to keep drinks chilled when it is also cold outside. Less apparent are what specific characteristics improve or hamper a property's usability as a Data Center location and why.

Building Codes and the Data Center Site

The first step when evaluating an undeveloped property's suitability as a Data Center site is a determination of how the property is zoned. Zoning controls whether a server environment is allowed to be built there at all. Zoning is done in a majority of countries and reflects how the local government expects a parcel of land to be used. Some classifications prohibit a Data Center.

Zoning information is maintained at the planning or public works department of the municipality whose jurisdiction the parcel is in. Many of these agencies even maintain their own websites and publish up-to-date zoning maps on them. Because land is frequently zoned in consistent blocks, a rudimentary way to estimate how a property is classified is to look at its neighbors. If the land is surrounded by private homes, it is probably residential. If the land is bordered by businesses or manufacturing, it is likely commercial or industrial. If the land is framed by open fields as far as the eye can see, it might be any of the previous zoning classifications or even agricultural land.

If a property you are interested in isn't zoned to allow a server environment, that doesn't mean you have to give up on the site. You can ask local government officials to rezone the parcel for a different type of use, although this might add time for them to review and approve your construction plans. As long as your construction project doesn't have a significant and negative impact on the surrounding area, it is likely to be approved.

Even if you are dealing with a developed site that contains existing structures, it is just as important to be familiar with the zoning, building codes, building control standards, and other government regulations (local, state, and national) that apply to the property. Ordinances vary significantly among cities, and even more so from country to country. They can regulate anything from how many hours a Data Center's standby generator is permitted to run per year to what time of day delivery trucks can travel through the neighborhood. Some countries even control the ratio of manpower and materials that can be imported, requiring that a project use a clear majority of in-country resources. Knowing the restrictions that apply to a given site enables you to either prepare for them or altogether avoid the location if you believe the rules aren't conducive to your business.

NOTE   In early 2001, I helped plan an 8300 square-foot (771 square-meter) Data Center at an office site in Pleasanton, California. The property contained four buildings and was located in an area featuring small business parks and nearby residential neighborhoods. A major point of discussion with city planning officials focused on the proposed loading dock, which was to be in the same building as the Data Center and whose primary function was to receive incoming server equipment. The neighborhood had limitations on commercial truck travel, so Pleasanton representatives wanted detailed explanations of how much and what type of truck traffic the dock would incur. Fortunately, equipment deliveries were to occur infrequently, which allayed their concerns and enabled the project to move forward.

Site Risk Factors

Every parcel of land comes with unique hazards. Knowing the hazards associated with any property upon which you consider placing a Data Center is very useful and should be a serious consideration. Maybe the site is in a region known for earthquakes. Maybe it is in a flood plain. Perhaps it is close to an electrical tower that generates electromagnetic interference. Regardless of whether the dangers are naturally occurring or man-made, it helps to understand how they can affect a server environment, how to alter your Data Center's design to prepare for them, and who can provide information about whether a hazard applies to a particular property. In many cases, the local planning or public works department is an excellent resource. Your company can also hire a risk management firm to gather applicable hazard information about a site.

As you read the descriptions that follow about various hazards and the suggestions for how to mitigate their influence, keep in mind that the absolute best way to avoid a threat to your Data Center is by keeping it out of harm's way altogether. If a property has multiple risk factors, your company needs to decide if the merits of the site outweigh the cost of additional infrastructure to compensate for those hazards and the possibility that a colossal disaster can still overwhelm those preparations.

Natural Disasters

When considering risk factors connected to a property, most people think of natural disasters—catastrophes that devastate a broad geographic area. That's understandable. These events affect countless lives, do tremendous property damage, and garner significant media coverage. The following sections describe several that can threaten a potential Data Center location.

Seismic Activity

Earthquakes are caused when tectonic plates within the earth shift, releasing tremendous amounts of stored energy and transmitting powerful shock waves through the ground. The closer to the surface a shift occurs, the stronger the quake that is felt. Earthquakes are measured in two ways:

- Magnitude refers to its size, which remains the same no matter where you are or how strong the shaking is.
- Intensity refers to the shaking, and varies by location.

The most powerful earthquakes can topple buildings, buckle freeways, and cause secondary disasters, including fires, landslides, and flash floods—all extremely hazardous conditions that you want your Data Center to be well away from, or at least as insulated as possible against. Even a moderate quake that causes minimal property damage can tip over Data Center server cabinets, sever underground data cabling, or induce utility power outages.

Major earthquakes occur regularly around the world. Table 2-1 lists those of 7.5 magnitude or greater that have occurred just since the start of the 21st century, according to the United States Geological Survey.

Table 2-1   *Recent Major Earthquakes*

Date	Magnitude	Region
March 28, 2005	8.7	Northern Sumatra, Indonesia
December 26, 2004	9.0	West coast of northern Sumatra, Indonesia
December 23, 2004	8.1	North of Macquarie Island, Antarctica
November 11, 2004	7.5	Kepulauan Alor, Indonesia
November 17, 2003	7.8	Rat Islands, Aleutian Islands, Alaska
September 25, 2003	8.3	Hokkaido, Japan
August 4, 2003	7.5	Scotia Sea
July 15, 2003	7.6	Carlsberg Ridge
January 22, 2003	7.6	Offshore Colima, Mexico
November 3, 2002	7.9	Central Alaska
October 10, 2002	7.6	Irian Jaya, Indonesia
September 8, 2002	7.6	North coast of New Guinea
August 19, 2002	7.7	South of Fiji Islands
August 19, 2002	7.7	Fiji Region
March 5, 2002	7.5	Mindanao, Philippines
November 14, 2001	7.8	Qinghai-Xinjiang border, China
October 19, 2001	7.5	Banda Sea
July 7, 2001	7.6	Near the coast of Peru
June 23, 2001	8.4	Near the coast of Peru
January 26, 2001	7.7	Bhuj, India
January 13, 2001	7.6	El Salvador
January 1, 2001	7.5	Mindanao, Philippines

Up-to-date listings of earthquakes around the world, major and minor, are available at http://neic.usgs.gov/.

If your Data Center site is in an area known for seismic activity, the entire building should be designed to lessen earthquake impacts. Limit the planned heights of buildings, consolidate weight onto the lowest floors, and use high-quality building materials that can withstand shaking and won't easily catch fire. Anchor the building's structure to the foundation and use earthquake-resistant technologies such as steel frames and shear walls. Finally, limit the number of glass exterior walls and, no matter what architectural style is applied to the building, make sure that all balconies, chimneys, and exterior ornamentation are securely braced.

Similar earthquake mitigation should be applied within the Data Center itself, and more than one technique can be employed. One approach is structural reinforcement of all server and networking cabinets and their secure attachment to something immobile, by either bolting them directly to the Data Center subfloor or securing them with cables to anchor points set in to either the floor or ceiling. Alternatively, seismic isolation platforms can be installed below the cabinets. Bolting or tying the cabinets is intended to restrict their movement in a quake, whereas isolation platforms are to shift with an earthquake's motion, enabling the cabinets to surf over the movement and more likely stay upright.

Another good idea is the securing of all Data Center servers and networking devices by either tethering them with straps or directly mounting them to the cabinets. Miscellaneous Data Center supplies such as storage cabinets or tools should be tied down as well to reduce the number of objects that can become airborne in a quake. This both reduces the likelihood of injury to anyone in your Data Center during an earthquake and cuts down on how much debris has to be cleaned up once the shaking stops.

NOTE   I've lived in California for more than 20 years and personally experienced several quakes, most notably the 6.9 magnitude Loma Prieta Earthquake in 1989 and 6.7 magnitude Northridge Earthquake in 1994. I can vouch firsthand that preparing for a quake ahead of time greatly reduces the damage and messes that are caused. As a newspaper reporter in 1994, I toured several structures that were moderately damaged during the Northridge Earthquake. The most common damage in private homes came from unsecured brick chimneys that pulled away from the house and collapsed. In office buildings, the quake's impact varied widely. In the same workspace, unrestrained bookcases and desktop computers were thrown more than 10 feet or 3 meters and smashed, while those tethered with safety straps moved only a few inches or centimeters.

When choosing among earthquake mitigation options, be conscious of how they affect your Data Center's design. Bolting cabinets reduces the room's flexibility, for example, while installing seismic isolation platforms means server rows need additional buffer space around them so that the platforms can shift from side to side during a quake.

How do you find out if a site you are interested in is prone to earthquakes? Maps showing seismic activity are available at the planning or public works department local to the property. These agencies also have relevant information about the parcel's overall geologic makeup. Land consisting of bedrock, for example, is more stable and therefore more desirable in a seismically active area than land consisting of soft soil. Additional information about seismic activity, from what to do in an earthquake to where major quakes have occurred in the past, is also available through the United States Geological Survey, which you can find online at http://www.usgs.gov/.

Ice Storms

When weather conditions are right, freezing rain can blanket a region with ice, making roads impassable and triggering widespread utility power outages for hundreds of square miles or kilometers. These ice storms occur when relative humidity is near 100 percent and alternating layers of cold and warm air form. Unlike some natural disasters that occur suddenly and dissipate, severe ice storms can last for days. Because they cover a huge area and make it difficult for repair crews to get around, it can take several weeks for normal utility service to be restored to an area.

If your Data Center site is in a region susceptible to ice storms, operate under the assumption that the room might need to run on standby power for extended periods of time and that contracted services for refueling your standby generator, assuming you have one, might be unreliable. Consider this when deciding what tier of infrastructure to build your Data Center to. Additional battery backups or standby generators with greater fuel capacity might be in order.

Be aware that the wintry cold that contributes to an ice storm can itself threaten your building's infrastructure. When temperatures approach 32° Fahrenheit (0° Celsius), ice blockages can form within water pipes. High pressure then occurs between the blockage and an end faucet or valve, which can cause the pipe to burst. Because the liquid inside is frozen, a break in a pipe might go unnoticed until it thaws. Thoroughly insulate your building's piping and perform regular maintenance to reduce the likelihood of a burst pipe.

NOTE   More than once, I've encountered a Data Center overheating despite—and actually because of—frosty outdoor temperatures. One of these instances occurred during an early winter morning in 2002 in a small server environment that I helped support in Wuppertal, Germany. Chilly outdoor temperatures caused water that was normally produced by the air conditioning system to ice up overnight, which made the system shut down. Once the Data Center's sole air handler was offline, the temperatures in the room skyrocketed. Fortunately, the server environment was monitored by sensors programmed to set off an alarm if ambient temperatures reached 90° Fahrenheit (32.2° Celsius). Local support staff responded to the alarm by propping open the Data Center's door, setting up large pedestal fans, and blowing in cold air that was conveniently available from outside. Their actions moderated the room's temperature until a technician arrived, cleared ice from the air conditioning system, and restarted the air handler.

Local meteorologists as well as those in the planning or public works department can tell you if a property is susceptible to ice storms or freezing temperatures.

Hurricanes

Hurricanes, alternatively known in parts of the world as tropical cyclones or typhoons, are severe tropical storms capable of generating winds up to 160 miles per hour (257.5 kilometers per hour). (A tropical storm is not officially considered a hurricane until its winds reach at least 74 miles per hour [119.1 kilometers per hour].) Hurricanes form over all of the world's tropical oceans except for the South Atlantic and Southeastern Pacific. Although they do not start on land, powerful hurricanes have been known to come inland for hundreds of miles or kilometers before dissipating, causing widespread utility power outages and sometimes spawning tornadoes. Hurricane season begins in mid-May in the eastern and central Pacific basin and in June in the Atlantic basin, including the Gulf of Mexico and Caribbean Sea, and ends in November.

If your Data Center site might be in the path of a hurricane in the future, design the room without exterior windows. Transparent views into your server environment are not a good idea at any time, because they create an unnecessary security risk, and should especially be avoided should the building be struck by a hurricane. A hurricane's high winds can propel large debris through a glass window, even one that has been taped or boarded over.

Locate the server environment at the center of the building, if possible, and surround it with cement interior walls. If the Data Center must be near an external wall, surround it with a service corridor. All of your site's major infrastructure components should likewise be sheltered to withstand high winds.

Additionally, because hurricanes often cause power failures that last for days, design your Data Center with adequate standby power to continue functioning for that long. (Chapter 6, "Creating a Robust Electrical System," includes details about providing a Data Center with backup power.)

Besides high winds, hurricanes carry tremendous amounts of water. If a hurricane passes anywhere in the vicinity of your Data Center site, there is an increased chance of moisture entering the buildings there. For instance, external air vents on a building are typically oriented downward and covered with a protective lip. Although this is sufficient to keep out moisture from even a heavy rainstorm, a storm driven by hurricane winds projects water in all directions—including up into a downward-facing vent. Install additional barriers in the Data Center building to make it more water resistant. Consider having a subroof, for example, that can continue to protect the Data Center if a storm damages the main roof.

Hurricanes are unlikely to be a risk factor for a property if it is well inland. However, local meteorologists can tell you for certain if a property has a history of hurricane activity.

Tornadoes

A tornado is an intense rotating column of air. Created by thunderstorms and fed by warm, humid air, they extend from the base of a storm cloud to the ground. They contain winds up to 300 miles per hour (482.8 kilometers per hour), and can inflict great swaths of damage 50 miles (80.5 kilometers) long and more than a mile (1.6 kilometers) wide. Tornadoes can cause significant property damage, trigger utility power outages, and generate large hail. The most powerful tornadoes are capable of throwing cars and other large debris great distances, leveling homes, and even stripping bark off of trees.

If your Data Center site is in an area where tornadoes occur, it should be designed with the same safeguards as for a hurricane—avoid external windows on the Data Center and provide enough standby power systems to do without commercial power for extended periods of time.

Tornadoes can form any time of year. They occur predominantly in the United States, but are also known to appear in Australia and Europe. A portion of the central United States, roughly bordered east and west between the Appalachians and Rocky Mountains and north and south from Nebraska and Iowa to central Texas, is nicknamed Tornado Alley because of the high frequency of tornadoes. Local meteorologists can tell you if a property is susceptible to tornadoes.

Flooding

Flooding most often occurs because of torrential rains. The rains either cause rivers and oceans to rise dramatically and threaten nearby structures or else trigger flash flooding in places with non-absorbent terrain, such as pavement, hard-packed dirt, or already saturated soil. Although less frequent, flooding can also occur from a break in a dam or other water control system. Severe flooding can uproot trees and move parked cars, breach walls, and make roadways impassable. Flooding can also trigger utility outages and cause landslides.

If your Data Center site is in an area prone to flooding, make sure that the building's walls are watertight, reinforce the structure to resist water pressure, and build on elevated ground. If the property has no elevated ground, then consider building the Data Center above the ground floor. This keeps your company's most important equipment out of harm's way if water does reach the structure.

Placing the Data Center above the ground floor, however, affects other elements of the building's design. First, a building's weight-bearing capability is less on its upper levels than the ground floor. To compensate for this, either structurally reinforce the Data Center area or else accept significant limitations upon the acceptable weight of incoming server equipment. Current trends in server design are for more compact form factors that make for heavier weight loads, so in most instances reinforcement is the better option.

Second, if the Data Center is not on the ground floor, the building must have a freight elevator to accommodate incoming equipment and supplies. The elevator must be tall, wide, and deep enough to accept server cabinets, tape libraries, or pallets of materials. The elevator must also have the ability to support the equipment's weight as well as that of the pallet jack and people transporting them.

To find out if a property is located in a flood plain, contact the local planning or public works department. In the United States, flood plain information is also maintained at local offices of the Federal Emergency Management Agency (http://www.fema.gov/). The agency's Technical Services Division performs hydrologic and hydraulic analyses to identify flooding hazards in communities throughout the United States.

Landslides

A landslide occurs when a hill or other major ground slope collapses, bringing rock, dirt, mud, or other debris sliding down to lower ground. These flows can cause significant property damage, either in a single fast-moving event or gradually over time. Slides, also known as earthflows or mudflows, are propelled by gravity and occur when inclined earth is no longer stable enough to resist its downward pull. Earthquakes, heavy rainfall, soil erosion, and volcanic eruptions commonly trigger landslides.

If your Data Center site is in an area prone to slides, the environment should be designed with safeguards similar to those for flooding—make exterior walls watertight and strong to withstand sliding muck and debris and build on elevated ground. Other advisable practices are the construction of a retention wall or channel to direct flows around the Data Center building and the planting of groundcover on nearby slopes.

Parcels at the base of a steep slope, drainage channel, or developed hillside are more susceptible to landslides. Slopes that contain no vegetation, such as those burned by fire, are also more vulnerable to them. Trees, fences, power lines, walls, or other structures that are tilted on a site might be an indication of a gradual slide. Local geologists as well as those in the planning or public works department can tell you whether a particular property is vulnerable to landsliding.

Fire

Fires are the most common of natural disasters. They cause significant property damage, spread quickly, and can be started by anything from faulty wiring to lightning strikes to intentional arson. Even a coffee maker in a break room is a potential source of a fire. Large fires can span tens of thousands of acres and threaten numerous buildings. Even the act of extinguishing a fire once it has entered a structure can lead to millions of dollars in losses from water damage. Additionally, a fire that fails to reach your Data Center can still cause problems. Minor amounts of smoke from a blaze can clog the sensitive mechanisms within servers and networking devices, causing them to malfunction later.

The best ways to deal with fire in the design of your Data Center are prevention and early detection. Install fire-resistant walls and doors, smoke detection devices, and fire suppression systems, both in the Data Center and throughout the building. (Fire suppression system options for a Data Center are outlined in Chapter 8, "Keeping It Cool.") It is also desirable for the building to have adjustable dampers on its ventilation and air conditioning system. This enables you to prevent outside air from entering the server environment during a nearby brush or building fire.

Once your server environment is online, remove potential fuel for a fire by equipping the room with fireproof trash cans and prohibiting combustible materials in the Data Center such as cardboard. Be sure to keep brush and other flammable items cleared away from the building, too.

NOTE   There are mixed opinions among building agencies and firefighting organizations about the value of landscaping with "fire-resistant" vegetation. Some people believe that this practice is beneficial, while others point out that high-intensity fires burn any plants, regardless of type.

Although many causes of fires are unpredictable, the local fire department can tell you if a property has experienced wildfires in the past and where controlled burns are conducted in a region to eliminate unwanted brush.

Pollution

Just as smoke particles from a fire can interfere with the proper functioning of servers and networking devices, so too can other airborne contaminants such as dust, pesticides, and industrial byproducts. Over time, these pollutants can cause server components to short-circuit or overheat.

If your Data Center is built in a region where contaminants are present, protect your equipment by limiting the amount of outside air that is cycled into the room. The percentage of external air that must be circulated into a Data Center is normally controlled by regional building codes or building control standards. The ratios of internal and external air are based upon the size of the server environment and its expected occupancy. A Data Center that has personnel working in it throughout the day is typically required to incorporate more outside air than a Data Center the staff of which are in the room less frequently. Some municipalities even allow zero external air if no employees work throughout the day in the server environment.

A second method of protecting your Data Center is incorporation of high efficiency air filtration into the environment's air conditioning system. Be sure to schedule frequent and regular filter changes for all Data Center air handlers.

NOTE   Keeping away pollutants is also important if your Data Center is equipped with sensitive smoke detection devices. In October 2003, a brush fire came within several hundred yards of a Data Center that I manage in San Jose, California. Although the fire was never a threat to reach the Data Center, it registered on the room's smoke detection system. The system had to be quickly disabled to prevent it from releasing the Data Center's fire suppression agent.

Some municipalities have an agency responsible for managing regional air quality that can provide information about known sources of pollution in an area. Pay special attention to this risk factor in areas known for strong winds, since they are more likely to kick up dust or carry contaminants a significant distance.

Electromagnetic Interference

Electromagnetic interference, or radio frequency interference, is when an electromagnetic field interrupts or degrades the normal operation of an electronic device. Such interference is generated on a small scale by everyday items ranging from cellular phones to fluorescent lights. Large sources of interference, such as telecommunication signal facilities, airports, or electrical railways, can interfere with Data Center servers and networking devices if they are in close proximity.

Electromagnetic interference is particularly challenging because it's not always easy to tell that your Data Center devices are being subjected to it. Even when that is known, you may not be able to immediately ascertain what the source of interference is. System administrators, network engineers, and others who work directly with the equipment are most likely to see symptoms first, even if they don't realize their cause. If you learn of a server experiencing unexplained data errors and standard troubleshooting doesn't resolve the problem, check around for possible sources of electromagnetic interference.

If your property is near an identified source of interference, locate the Data Center as far away as possible to limit the effects. All manner of shielding products—coatings, compounds, and metals; meshes, strips, and even metalized fabric—are available to block electromagnetic interference, but most of them are intended for use on individual devices rather than over a large Data Center. Again, distance from the source of interference is the best protection. That's because electromagnetic interference works according to the inverse square law of physics, which states that a quantity of something is inversely proportional to the square of the distance from a source point. The law applies to gravity, electric fields, light, sound, and radiation.

So, if a Data Center is located twice as far from a source of electromagnetic interference, it receives only 1/4 of the radiation. Likewise, if a Data Center is 10 times as far away, it receives only 1/100. To see an example of this effect, shine a flashlight (torch) against a wall. Back away from the wall, increasing the wall's distance from the light source (the mouth of the flashlight), and the circle of light against the wall becomes larger and fainter. Move closer, reducing the distance between wall and the light source, and that circle of light becomes smaller and more intense.

Figure 2-1 illustrates the inverse square law.

Figure 2-1   *Inverse Square Law*

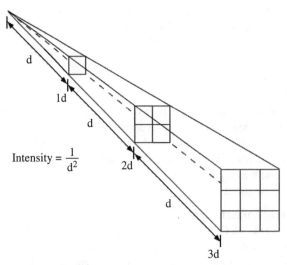

The intensity (I) of electromagnetic radiation is inversely proportional to the square of the distance (d) from the source.

The local planning or public works department can provide the location of airports, railways, and other facilities known to produce electromagnetic interference.

NOTE   The first Data Center I ever worked in taught me how electromagnetic interference, together with a ramshackle environment, can harm a server. That Data Center began as a networking closet, was outfitted with the infrastructure necessary to host servers, and then expanded as needed to accommodate more devices. Because the room grew piecemeal, and wasn't designed to be a Data Center in the first place, its footprint was irregular—squarish, but with multiple indentations from adjacent rooms. The odd shape created uneven server rows and caused its power distribution units, which provided power to those rows, to be installed wherever they could be shoehorned in, sometimes in less than ideal locations. Also, when the Data Center came online, there were no standards for what server cabinets or power strips could be used. As a result, power capacity varied widely from one server location to another. As time passed and various cabinets were used, it became increasingly difficult to know if installing a new server into a half-empty cabinet would trip a circuit breaker or not. To eliminate guesswork, an electrician was called in periodically to measure the power draw on the circuits that fed questionable cabinets.

The first hint of trouble appeared when a system administrator complained about a mysteriously malfunctioning server. It would operate correctly for weeks, then generate error messages. Replacing drives halted the problem, but only temporarily. When I examined the server, I discovered that it had been installed—incorrectly—at the end of a truncated server row, beyond (what was supposed to be) its final server cabinet location. This put it on a short diagonal, about three feet or one meter, to a power distribution unit.

Because the unit fed several of the cabinets with unknown electrical capacity, its circuits were often tested. Measuring the power draw on circuits required removing the power distribution unit's protective shielding, which meant we had been sporadically bathing the nearby server in electromagnetic interference. Small wonder that the device had malfunctioned, or that relocating the server cabinet immediately resolved the issue.

Vibration

Servers and networking devices, like other complex and sensitive electronic equipment, are vulnerable to vibrations as well. As when dealing with electromagnetic interference, there are several commercial products available to inhibit vibrations from reaching Data Center servers—from springs to gel-filled mats to rubber mounts—but the most effective solution is simply avoid locating your Data Center near large vibration sources. Airports, railroads, major thoroughfares, industrial tools, and road construction are common sources of vibrations.

The local planning or public works department can provide information about what major road construction is scheduled to occur near a property, as well as which of these other facilities are in close proximity.

Political Climates

Among the most challenging risk factors to diagnose and prepare a potential Data Center site for are the man-made kind. Political instability in a region can delay the delivery of Data Center equipment and materials, make utility services unreliable, and—worst of all—threaten the safety of employees. Depending upon how contentious conditions are, workers of certain nationalities might even be prohibited from traveling into the region.

When dealing in an area with conflict, adjust your Data Center project timelines to accommodate delays. Design the server environment itself with standby power systems to support the room if utility services fail. Reinforce building walls to withstand explosions. Install safety bollards around entrances and any external infrastructure, such as generators, to protect against someone ramming a vulnerable area with a car or truck. Consider placing security fencing around the entire site. To find out whether or not a property is in a politically unstable area, check with the local embassy and news outlets. The United States Department of State, Bureau of Consular Affairs (http://travel.state.gov/) issues travel warnings for known trouble spots, as do the consular offices of most countries.

NOTE   I received an abject lesson in 2001 about the realities of working on a Data Center project in a politically unstable area. My team had created a design for a server environment under construction in South Natanya, Israel. Several weeks into the project, word went out that the son of one of the contractors on the project had just been killed. A nail bomb had exploded on a public bus that the young man was in the vicinity of.

Flight Paths

If there's an airport in the region of a potential Data Center site, be aware of the flight paths that incoming and outgoing planes regularly follow. Although crashes or debris falling from aircraft are rare, the effect can be devastating if something does strike your Data Center.

How should you prepare for this unlikely event? Even if your property lies in the path of a busy airport, it is probably not cost effective to make your Data Center an impenetrable bunker. A more practical solution is to distribute your servers. Build two smaller server environments and place them in separate locations, even if just two different buildings on the same property. As unlikely as it is for your Data Center to be struck by an out-of-control plane, it is that much less likely for two rooms to suffer the same fate.

The local planning or public works department can inform you if a property is in the flight path of any local airports.

Evaluating Physical Attributes of the Data Center Site

Once you are aware of the risk factors facing a potential Data Center site, it is time to assess the physical features of the property by answering the following questions:

- Where is the site?
- Is it easy to reach?
- Does it have existing structures?
- If so, how suited are they to housing a server environment?
- Specifically, how well does the site support the key design strategies for constructing a productive Data Center?

Remember, you want your Data Center to be robust, modular, flexible, standardized, and to intuitively promote good practices by users.

Relative Location

There's an old saying in real estate that the three most important features about a property are location, location, location. The saying is equally true when evaluating a potential Data Center site, albeit for a different reason. Whereas a home buyer might care about location because of a residence's vicinity to a posh neighborhood, a Data Center designer cares because of how easy it is to reach the property and where it is in relation to the company's other server environments.

Accessibility

When examining a property, make note of how easy it is to enter and leave by answering questions such as the following:

- Is the site visible from a major roadway?

- Are their multiple routes to reach the property or just one?
- Could a hazardous materials spill or major traffic accident at a single intersection block access to the site?

Treat the property's accessibility the same as other Data Center infrastructure details—look for redundancy and stay away from single points of failure.

An ideal Data Center site can be reached easily and has several means of ingress and egress. A property with limited access affects the everyday delivery of equipment, because large trucks might be unable to reach the site. Limited access also influences the response time for emergency service vehicles to reach the site in a crisis.

Finally, determine if the property is located near large population centers. This influences how close your employees live and therefore how long it might take someone to reach the Data Center after hours if an emergency occurs.

Disaster Recovery Options

There are countless publications that thoroughly explain how and why to create a business continuation strategy for your company. While that topic isn't the focus of this book, it is a good idea to think about how a potential Data Center site fits in to your company's disaster recovery plan.

If your plan calls for transferring business functions from one Data Center to another, for example, note the distance between the property you are evaluating and your company's other server environments and answer the following questions:

- Are the locations close enough that network latency won't be a problem?
- Can employees travel from one site to another in a reasonable amount of time, even if major roadways are blocked or airline flights aren't operating normally?
- Are the locations far enough apart that they are both unlikely to be affected by a single disaster?

Likewise, if your company backs up information from the servers in your Data Center and stores the data tapes off-site, where are those facilities in relation to your potential Data Center property? The greater the distance between your Data Center and off-site storage facility, the longer it will take to retrieve and restore the data after a disaster.

Pre-Existing Infrastructure

Many sites evaluated for housing a Data Center are at least partially developed, whether they have little more than an empty building shell or a fully equipped office building with a pre-existing server environment. Whatever the building was previously used for, diagnose if the infrastructure that's already in place can accommodate your needs or at least be retrofitted to do so. Important infrastructure considerations are power systems, cooling systems, and structured cabling, as described in the sections that follow.

Power Analysis

Assess the property's power systems, including its electrical infrastructure and standby systems by answering the following questions:

- How much power is readily available?
- Are there enough electrical circuits to support your Data Center?
- If not, is there enough physical capacity at the site to add more?
- Do power feeds come in to the building at more than one location?
- What alterations must be made to accommodate battery backup systems and standby generators?
- If the site already has standby systems, are they of sufficient capacity to support your Data Center?
- If the site doesn't have them, does it at least have the physical space and structural support for them to be installed?

Make note of how much redundancy is present in the electrical infrastructure and what single points of failure exist.

Cooling Capabilities

Data Centers require significantly more cooling infrastructure than the equivalent amount of office space. Therefore, measuring the cooling capacity of a potential Data Center site is important. To assess the cooling capacity of the site, determine the following:

- Can the building's existing cooling infrastructure provide adequate cooling for a Data Center?
- Is there adequate space and structural support on the site to support air chillers, condenser units, or cooling towers?
- How much modification must be done to the building's existing air ducting to reroute cooling?

Structured Cabling

Determine how much and what type of structured cabling already exists in and to the building. Determine if enough connections exist to support your Data Center and if cabling comes in to the building at more than one location.

Certain cabling media have distance limitations, so it is a good idea to measure how far cable runs must travel, both for the Data Center and throughout the building. Also make note of how much redundancy is present in the cabling infrastructure and what single points of failure exist.

Amenities and Obstacles

Aside from whatever power, cooling, and cabling infrastructure a building already possesses, there are several less obvious features that make a structure more or less amenable for housing a Data Center, including the following:

- Clearances
- Weight issues
- Loading dock placement
- Freight elevator specifications
- Miscellaneous problem areas
- Distribution of key systems

Some of these elements can make a site completely unsuitable to housing a Data Center, while others are merely matters of convenience. The sections that follow examine these elements in greater detail.

Clearances

One of the most basic features to examine about an existing structure is its physical dimensions. Some of the questions you need to answer about the site's dimensions are as follows:

- Is there enough contiguous floor space to house your Data Center?
- How tall are the doorways?
- How wide are the halls?
- What's the distance from floor to ceiling?

These dimensions all need to be sufficient to enable Data Center equipment to pass through easily.

The area for the Data Center itself normally requires a minimum of about 13 feet (4 meters) from floor to ceiling, and much more is preferable. The clearance is to accommodate the raised floor, the height of most server cabinets, the minimum buffer space between the cabinet and the room's drop ceiling that is typically required by local fire codes, and space above the drop ceiling where ducting is routed. Additional space above the drop ceiling allows for easier and more effective cooling of the server environment—more area means that a greater volume of cold air can be pumped in to the Data Center—and so is desirable.

An unobstructed pathway must also exist among the Data Center, its corresponding storage room, and the exterior of the building, for transporting equipment. All entrances, corridors, doorways, and other openings along this path must be at least 8 feet (2.4 meters) high and at least 4 feet (1.2 meters) wide. These measurements are chosen to enable your tallest server cabinets and widest pallets of supplies to be transported within the building and into the server environment easily. If you have Data Center-related items that are larger in size, look for larger building clearances accordingly. That brand-new disk library you purchase to perform data backups can't do you much good if it does not fit through the Data Center doors.

Weight Issues

Once you've determined whether server cabinets and pallets of materials can be transported without difficulty through the building, you need to make sure that none of them damage or crash through the floor. Consider the structural capacity of the building and how much weight the floor is designed to support, especially in the Data Center area. Pay particular attention to this if you intend to place the server environment on an upper level—their weight-bearing capability is normally less than on the ground floor.

Loading Dock

Servers, cabinets, networking devices, or backup storage units can sometimes be damaged during transport to your Data Center. When this does happen, it is often attributed to the equipment being shaken while rolled across uneven ground or dragged over the lip of an entrance and having the item thump forcefully to the ground under its own weight. Although you can't control what happens during shipment, you can safeguard how equipment is treated once it arrives at your site.

Having a loading dock in close proximity to your Data Center reduces the chance of equipment damage, so it is very helpful if a property you are evaluating has one. Equipment can be rolled a short distance across level ground, either directly into the server environment or an associated storage room, rather than having to be offloaded from an elevated truck bed and shuttled a longer distance.

Freight Elevators

As stated earlier in the chapter, a freight elevator is mandatory if your Data Center is located anywhere but on the ground floor. As with the doorways and corridors, the freight elevator must be at least 8 feet (2.4 meters) high and at least 4 feet (1.2 meters) wide so as to accommodate everything from tall server cabinets to wide pallets of equipment. The freight elevator must also have enough weight-bearing capability to carry a fully loaded server cabinet. Today's heavier systems can exceed 1500 pounds per server cabinet location, and it is reasonable to assume that that number will increase.

If your company site doesn't have a suitable freight elevator, you might be forced to take drastic measures to bring large equipment in and out. Figure 2-2 shows workers raising a backup tape library six stories above the ground with ropes and pulleys, for its installation into a Data Center in Bangalore, India.

Figure 2-2   *Moving Equipment Without a Freight Elevator*

Image provided by courtesy of Cyril Gnanaprakasham

The lack of a freight elevator in this building means that large equipment bound for the Data Center must be raised by hand.

Happily, the tape library was undamaged during transit. Ignoring for a moment the hazard that transporting a piece of equipment poses for the device itself, it is certainly potentially dangerous to those who participate. Look closely at Figure 2-2 and you can see that one of the workers is straddling the external stairwell railing as he helps pull on the rope to lift the equipment crate. When the time comes for the device to be removed from the Data Center, it will have to be lowered from the sixth floor in this same manner.

NOTE   A passenger elevator is no substitute for a freight elevator, either. In August of 1998, I helped fitup a 12987 square-foot (1206 square-meter) Data Center in San Jose, California, that was located on the second floor of a building that had no freight elevator. The fitup stage includes all prep work that happens after major construction finishes and before the room comes online. Signage is installed, tools and supplies are stocked, and server cabinets are wheeled in.

The building's two passenger elevator cars were about 7 feet (2.1 meters) tall, shorter than the server cabinets used in the Data Center. With the help of a coworker, I had to tilt and steer each 155-pound cabinet into an elevator, support it at an angle during the ride to the second floor, and then wheel it in to the Data Center. Because the cabinet had to lean at a steep angle while in the elevator, only one person and one cabinet fit at a time. We spent an entire afternoon shuttling more than 100 cabinets up to the Data Center this way. While this was inconvenient to do with empty server cabinets, it would have been impossible to do with ones that were even partially loaded with servers. The building was retrofitted with a freight elevator several weeks later, at great cost and with the assistance of a helicopter to rip out the old lift.

Problem Areas

A key reason to have someone with Data Center design and operation experience help evaluate a building is to identify inobvious trouble spots. Determining whether a structure has adequate infrastructure or tangible facilities such as a loading dock or freight elevator is a straightforward exercise; however, some buildings might have problem areas—from a Data Center perspective—that are not as easily noticed.

Carefully examine all aspects of the building, large and small, to ensure that nothing can interfere with the operation of a server environment. Consider issues such as the following:

- **Where are immovable building elements such as structural columns and stairwells?**—These might restrict how much floor space is usable for a Data Center.

- **Does the building have a kitchen or cafeteria?**—This is a potential fire hazard, and if a site has multiple structures, kitchens or cafeterias should be located in a different building from the Data Center.

- **Where are the building's water pipes?**—Plumbing can leak and therefore shouldn't be routed above the server environment.

Distribution of Key Systems

As you examine the site's existing infrastructure, look closely at how the systems are configured. You ideally want important systems, such as power feeds and data cabling, to be spread out, each entering the building at more than one location. Such physical separation helps protect infrastructure systems—two cable runs following different paths are less likely to both be damaged by a single event than if they each follow the same path, for example. Standby power systems such as generators or backup batteries make the site more robust, and are even more beneficial if they are dispersed on a property rather than clustered together.

Confirming Service Availability to the Data Center Site

Arguably more important than what infrastructure already exists at a potential Data Center site are what utility services can be provided to it. It is fairly simple to have a contractor come out and install data cabling if a property lacks it, for example, but you still can't communicate with the outside world if there's no service provider offering connectivity. Make sure that the property has—or can be provided with—adequate power and data connections for the Data Center, along with the standard water, telephone, gas, and other utilities that any office environment requires.

Aside from power outages that can be caused by natural disasters, some parts of the world simply have less reliable electrical infrastructure than others. Brownouts or momentary dips in power might be common in these regions, which increases the need for your Data Center to have dependable standby power. Just as a car engine undergoes the most stress when it is first started, so too does a standby power system experience the most strain when a server environment's electrical load is first placed upon it. Frequently cranking a car's engine—or transferring a Data Center's electrical load—causes much more wear and tear than if the same equipment ran continuously for an extended time.

NOTE   If you are reviewing a potential Data Center site that's in a large city with well-developed infrastructure, it is easy to assume that commercial power is abundant and reliable. *Don't.* During the first three months of 2001, 6 of the 10 California-based Data Centers that I manage were forced to run on standby power multiple times due to rolling blackouts. The outages, each lasting 90 to 120 minutes, were mandated by the California Independent System Operator to manage electricity shortages in the state. Rolling blackouts reduce electrical demand and are intended to prevent a drop in system frequency that can damage transformers or switching gear and therefore cause much longer, unplanned outages. At the peak of the blackouts, I had Data Centers in the cities of Petaluma, San Jose, and Santa Cruz—93 miles (150 kilometers) apart as the crow flies—lose utility power within 24-hours.

The repeated power transfers took their toll. During one outage, a logic board in an uninterruptible power source failed, preventing the standby power system from holding the Data Center's power load. Several dozen servers abruptly shut down as a result.

The corresponding local service providers can tell you what power and data lines exist on and around a property. When talking to the electric company, ask if it is possible to have the Data Center fed by more than one substation or power grid, thereby providing your facility with another layer of redundancy. When talking to the Internet service provider, determine what types and quantities of cabling are in the ground, both on the property and in the surrounding area.

Prioritizing Needs for the Data Center Site

As you review potential Data Center sites, you'll find that there are no perfect properties, that is, parcels with zero risk factors, all of the physical features you want, and the specific types and amounts of infrastructure you are looking for. Many properties are completely inappropriate for housing a Data Center, while even the most suitable are a mixed bag. Perhaps a site is in a seismically stable area and well away from sources of pollution, electromagnetic interference, and vibration, but is vulnerable to hurricanes or tornadoes. Maybe a property has an existing building that's easily accessible and possesses adequate electrical capacity and incoming data connectivity, but has no loading dock. Whatever the details, all parcels have their unique features and conditions, advantages and drawbacks.

Prioritize what characteristics are most important based upon the specific needs of your company. If you know your business uses large, floor-standing servers, for example, then a building with ample clearances and a loading dock is essential. If your business strictly employs high-density, low-profile servers, then those characteristics are less valuable than a building with abundant cooling capacity and available electrical circuits. Both scenarios, however, require a structure with high weight tolerances.

During the process of selecting a site, you have to answer the Data Center design version of "which came first, the chicken or the egg?" In this case, the question involves a property's risk factors versus your Data Center's infrastructure. Do you opt to add extra layers of infrastructure because the Data Center must be built in a more hazardous area, or do you agree to build in a more hazardous area because the room is equipped with additional infrastructure? You might be less concerned with locating your server environment in a region with less reliable commercial power if you already plan to build a Data Center with 3N standby power, for example.

Summary

When a company buys new land, it is important to consider the property's suitability to house a server environment. Failing to do so often means having to spend more on Data Center infrastructure, either to add what's missing or to overcome shortcomings on the site. The most desirable type of location is one that supports the Data Center's mission to safeguard server equipment and accommodate growth and change.

Learn the zoning, building codes, building control standards, and other regulations that apply to a property. These can affect both your Data Center design and normal business operations. You should likewise understand the risk factors facing a potential Data Center site. These can include natural disasters such as earthquakes, ice storms, hurricanes, tornadoes, flooding, and landslides, as well as fire, pollution, electromagnetic interference, vibration, political climates, or airport flight paths. If you decide to build in a region susceptible to these hazards, you need to adjust how the Data Center is designed, such as upping the capacity of its standby power systems or increasing the structural strength of the building, depending upon the particular threat that's posed.

An ideal Data Center location is strategically placed among your company's other Data Centers and any designated off-site storage facilities—close enough so employees can quickly reach them after a disaster, but far enough away that they are unlikely to all be affected by a single catastrophic event.

When evaluating a property, assess the physical features of all existing buildings. Determine what power, cooling, and data cabling already exist and how easily their capacity can be increased to support a Data Center. Also make sure that the structure has adequate clearance and weight-bearing ability to accept incoming server equipment. A loading dock, freight elevator, and distributed infrastructure all make a site more conducive for housing a Data Center, while immovable building elements and potential hazards such as water piping and a kitchen are unfavorable. Finally, confirm with local service providers that adequate power and connectivity can be provided to support the Data Center.

Because each property has its own advantages and disadvantages, you must decide what characteristics are most important for your business and choose accordingly.

CHAPTER 3

Quantifying Data Center Space

This chapter discusses the physical footprint of your Data Center—how to size it, what a good configuration is, where to locate a server environment within a multipurpose building, how to make it adaptable for the future needs of your business, and how to construct the Data Center to effectively protect the valuable equipment inside. The chapter also outlines what additional dedicated areas are necessary to make your Data Center function effectively, including the required infrastructure of each area and where those areas should be located in relation to the Data Center.

Sizing the Data Center

Nothing has a greater influence on a Data Center's cost, lifespan, and flexibility than its size—even the Data Center's capability to impress clients. Determining the size of your particular Data Center is a challenging and essential task that must be done correctly if the room is to be productive and cost-effective for your business. Determining size is challenging because several variables contribute to how large or small your server environment must be, including:

- How many people the Data Center supports
- The number and types of servers and other equipment the Data Center hosts
- The size that non-server areas should be depending upon how the room's infrastructure is deployed

Determining Data Center size is essential because a Data Center that is too small won't adequately meet your company's server needs, consequently inhibiting productivity and requiring more to be spent on upgrading or expansion and thereby putting the space and services within at risk. A room that is too big wastes money, both on initial construction and ongoing operational expenses.

Financial and Other Considerations When Sizing the Data Center

A smaller Data Center is obviously less expensive in the short term to build, operate, and maintain than a larger one. Data and electrical cables are routed shorter distances, less fire suppression materials are needed to provide coverage over a reduced area, and—as anyone who has ever moved from a cozy home to a spacious one has discovered with their utility bill—it costs less every month to power and regulate temperature in a small space than a large one. From a risk management perspective, there is also a benefit from constructing a smaller Data Center and then, when the Data Center fills up and more hosting space is needed, building a second Data Center at another location. For these reasons, it is no surprise that many companies decide to dedicate the least building space possible to host their servers, only devoting greater area when absolutely necessary. While a small server environment is completely appropriate in many cases, it can prove limiting—and ultimately more expensive in the long run—in others.

As discussed in Chapter 1, "Approaching the Data Center Project," the best practice is to design a Data Center with a lifespan of a few years and intend to expand that server environment when it becomes close to full with equipment. If it is certain your company must have a significant amount of Data Center space eventually, consider building a larger room up front. The larger a server environment, the greater the economy of scale that is achieved. Just as having a house painter complete two bedrooms doesn't cost twice as much as working on one, having a cabling vendor run 10,000 yards or meters of data cabling doesn't cost twice as much as running 5,000. There are basic expenses that are always incurred on a construction job, large or small. Many materials are also less expensive per unit when purchased in greater quantities, which can save hundreds of thousands of dollars over time. Quantity price breaks can apply to not only infrastructure components used in the construction of the Data Center, but also to consumables and other supplies that are used on a day-to-day basis in a functioning server environment, including:

- Server cabinets
- Patch cords
- Custom signage
- Multimedia boxes and patch panels into which structured cabling terminates
- Even rolls of hazard tape for marking electrical infrastructure are frequently eligible for discount when bought in bulk

---

NOTE   I've seen dramatic price breaks while buying Data Center supplies. The biggest single discount I was ever directly involved with—thanks to having a large-enough Data Center to take advantage of—occurred in 2002 on a bulk purchase of server cabinets. In the autumn of that year, one of the Data Centers I manage was expanded from about 9000 to 19,000 square feet (836.1 to 1,765.2 square meters), increasing its capacity from 347 server cabinet locations to 773. Fewer than 300 of the original locations had been occupied when the Data Center was expanded, leaving nearly 500 available for future use.

Rather than continuing to buy about a dozen cabinets each month for the next year, which kept enough on hand to stay ahead of incoming servers and deferred each purchase until absolutely necessary, I spoke with the cabinet vendor about buying in bulk to quickly stock much of the suddenly spacious Data Center with server cabinets. (Cabinets are the

Data Center industry equivalent of toothpaste or toilet paper—there's never a question of whether they will be used, just a matter of how quickly.) The manufacturer could save money by producing in larger quantities, and so offered to slash the price by $300 per unit and provide free shipping if I committed to buying 100 cabinets at a time. I did, and making just one bulk purchase in this manner saved approximately $32,500. (I ultimately made a second purchase of 100 cabinets a few months later, during a new fiscal quarter. This addressed my company's cabinet needs for a long time to come and, all together, saved $65,000 that would have been spent on cabinets over the next year and a half.)

If the business had chosen to build a small server environment to stay incrementally ahead of incoming equipment and had not had a sizable Data Center, the purchase would have been impractical. There would have been no suitable location to store the cabinets and no way to justify their purchase.

A bigger Data Center also addresses a company's server hosting needs for a greater period of time, because it obviously takes longer to fill the available floor space. You don't want to spend months constructing a new Data Center, only to have it fill up within a year and require you to start the process all over again. Running two back-to-back Data Center projects instead of one is an inefficient use of staff time and, assuming you are expanding the same server environment, unnecessarily exposes servers to the chaos and downtime risks that any major construction effort brings.

With the costs of labor and material normally rising over time, a business is likely to spend less money overall to build a large Data Center all at once, rather than building a small room to start and then expanding it to the larger size within a couple of years. When laying out a Data Center, a larger footprint also provides greater flexibility. Structural columns, dogleg spaces, and mandatory clearances are all easier to accommodate when the Data Center floor space is larger. It is like trying to put a suitcase into a car trunk that already contains a spare tire. The bigger the trunk, the easier it is to work around that tire.

Finally, don't forget that the size of a Data Center has a psychological effect upon those who are toured through or work within the Data Center. While psychological impact should not be the overriding factor for determining the size of this facility, be aware of it. A large Data Center teeming with rows of servers and networking devices presents an image of technology, substance, and productivity—more so than a small server environment. If your business provides tours of its facilities to clients, prospective employees, or members of the public, a sizable Data Center can be a showpiece that helps reinforce your company's professional image and credibility.

So, as you size your Data Center, keep in mind the advantages and disadvantages provided by both smaller and larger footprints. Ideally, you want to create a server environment that is large enough to accommodate your company's server needs for a reasonable length of time and achieve an economy of scale, but not so large that money is wasted on higher operational expenses and portions of the Data Center that are unoccupied.

NOTE "How big will the Data Center be?" is the first question I get at the start of every project that includes a server environment. It is never about what servers or networking devices are going into the room, or whether any specialized infrastructure is needed. The initial question is not even about how much the Data Center will cost or how many weeks it will take to build. I guess it is assumed all of those details will work themselves out—and I suppose they always do—just as long as I can answer how big the room will be.

Employee-Based Sizing Method

A good initial approach to sizing a Data Center is to determine the number of employees the Data Center is intended to support and allocate a certain amount of floor space per person. The premise is that the more employees your company has, the more critical equipment that is required for them to perform their work; the more critical equipment your company possesses, the larger the Data Center must be to host the equipment.

This method is most appropriate for Data Centers that house engineering or development servers. Such machines are directly supported and worked upon by company employees— the more employees working to develop future products, the more servers that are typically necessary. Production or business Data Centers that host predominantly information technology (IT) functions are less influenced by employee populations—your company needs servers to perform certain core business functions whether 50 people are employed or 5000.

When using the employee-based method, count only those employees whose roles are associated with Data Center servers and networking devices. Your administrative staff is undoubtedly composed of indispensable people who keep your business functioning like a well-oiled machine, but if their work does not involve your company's servers, don't count them when sizing the room that houses that equipment. Either a human resources representative or the IT manager working on the Data Center project can provide a tally of people whose work depends upon your company's server environment.

Understanding that the proportion of Data Center floor space to number of employees the Data Center supports is *not* linear is the key to sizing a Data Center on a per capita basis— the ratio changes. A large Data Center cannot only support more employees than a small one, it can support more employees per square foot (square meter). The Data Center can support more employees per square foot (square meter) because a minimum amount of floor space in any Data Center has to be devoted to non-server functions, regardless of whether the room is large or small. This non-server space includes areas for infrastructure equipment, such as air handlers and power distribution units, as well as areas to transport equipment through, such as entrance ramps (assuming that the Data Center has a raised floor) and walkways. Once non-server areas are established in the Data Center's design, they do not grow proportionally as the rest of the room does.

For instance, assume that a Data Center has five server rows. Wide aisles surround the rows, and an entrance ramp is located inside the room. The space is sufficiently cooled by two air handlers, but because the room is designed to N+1 capacity, it has a total of three air handlers. Compare that with another Data Center, designed to the same level of infrastructure, but containing 15 server rows instead of five. Because the larger Data Center has triple the number of server rows, does it need to be three times the size of the smaller Data Center? No. The larger server environment does need a proportional increase in space for its server rows and aisles, but not for other non-server areas. For one, only six air handlers are needed to provide adequate cooling and a seventh to achieve N+1 capacity—not nine. Also, the entrance ramp doesn't occupy any more floor space, even if there are more server rows. The cumulative space saved from not having to proportionally increase these non-server areas is considerable.

Figures 3-1 and 3-2 show two Data Centers of similar design but different sizes. The larger server environment hosts a greater number of servers per square foot (square meter) because less of its overall floor space has to be devoted to non-server elements.

Figure 3-1   *Hosting Ratio of a Smaller Data Center*

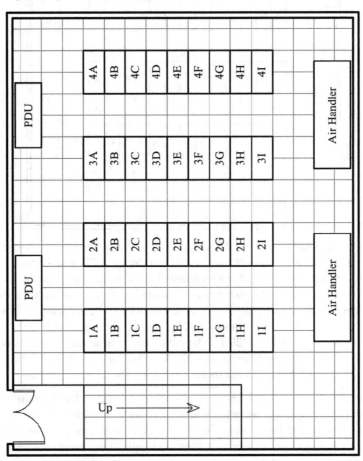

Figure 3-2 *Hosting Ratio of a Larger Data Center*

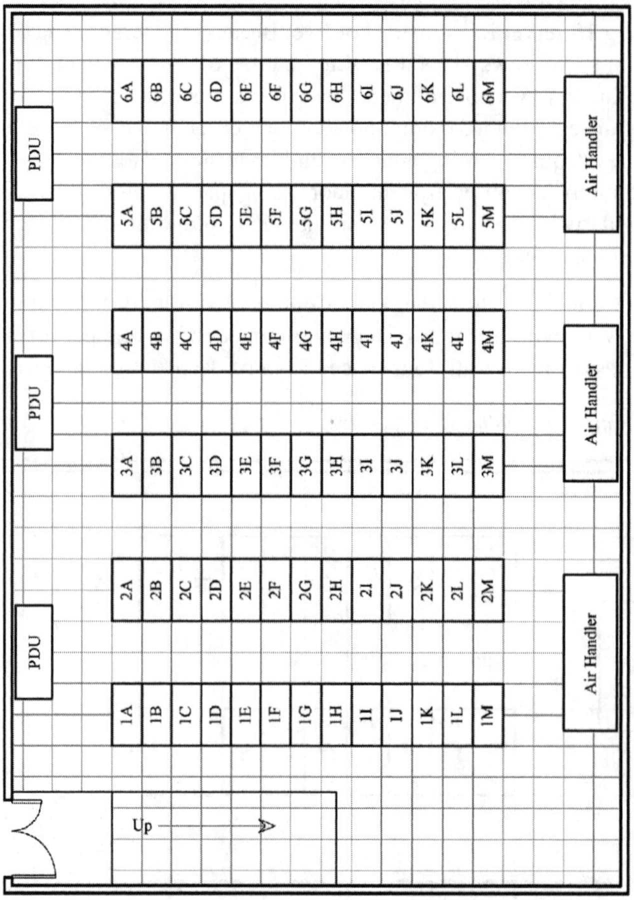

The smaller Data Center is 1301 square feet (120.9 square meters) in size and contains 36 cabinet locations, whereas the larger Data Center is 2270 square feet (210.9 square meters) and contains 78 cabinet locations. That is more than twice the cabinet locations while only increasing the size of the server environment by about three-quarters. To put it another way, a company devotes 36.1 feet of floor space per server cabinet in the smaller room—1301 ÷ 36 = 36.1—and only 29.1 feet of floor space per server cabinet in the larger room—2270 ÷ 78 = 29.1. (The metric equivalents are 3.4 meters of floor space per server cabinet in the smaller room—120.9 ÷ 36 = 3.4—and only 2.7 meters of floor space per server cabinet in the larger room—210.9 ÷ 78 = 2.7.)

If you are asked to provide an approximate size for a Data Center before having a chance to put pen to paper—or more likely mouse to AutoCAD drawing—begin with an estimate of about 10 square feet (1 square meter) for every Data Center-related employee. The formula is easy-to-remember as it allocates roughly one server cabinet of equipment per person and accounts for a similar amount of non-server space, such as walkways or places for infrastructure components. Use this formula when dealing with about 100 employees or less. Adjust the formula steadily downward when dealing with larger numbers of employees, because bigger Data Centers can accommodate a greater proportion of servers.

NOTE   Sizing a Data Center strictly by the number of employees obviously isn't an exact science. After working on dozens of Data Center design projects, though, I've found that 10 square feet (1 square meter) per employee is a reliable starting point for sizing smaller server environments. The rare times that the formula has been off, it has designated slightly too much area for the Data Center, providing me the luxury of giving back floor space during the design phase. This has always been welcomed by other project representatives, who are usually needing additional room for something.

Table 3-1 lists some ballpark sizes for a Data Center, based upon the number of relevant employees working at the site. Note the economy of scale that is achieved—the larger the Data Center, the higher the ratio of employees the Data Center can support.

Table 3-1   *Data Center Sizing by Employee*

Employees	Approximate Data Center Size
Fewer than 100	10 square feet per employee
	1 square meter per employee
200–250	5 square feet per employee
	.5 square meter per employee
400–500	4 square feet per employee
	.4 square meter per employee
1500–6000	2 square feet per employee
	.2 square meter per employee
15,000	1 square foot per employee
	.1 square meter per employee

Do not consider the preceding table a blanket formula for sizing your Data Center. The information in the table is only a starting point, intended to demonstrate the principle of sizing by employee, and must be modified for your company's unique requirements. The square feet (square meter) measurements are rounded for simplicity rather than exact conversions.

Equipment-Based Sizing Method

Although the number of people your Data Center supports should influence the size of the room, don't let it be your only guide. Refine your calculations based on the number and type of servers the room must host.

The more you know about what servers are coming in to the Data Center, both when it first opens and over time, the more accurately you can size the room. The IT manager and network engineer involved with the Data Center project are excellent resources for what servers and networking devices are to be ordered and must be hosted in the server environment in the future. The IT manager and network engineer can also tell you about the physical dimensions of these items, which can come in a variety of shapes, sizes, and weights.

Some servers, for example, are bigger than a refrigerator while others are no larger than a pizza box. Most servers, fortunately, are configured to fit within one of a few standard cabinet profiles prevalent in the server industry. Some devices are intentionally designed to fit only in proprietary cabinets, however—forcing you to buy the manufacturer's cabinets along with its servers—and these unique cabinets can be oversized or irregularly shaped. Still other servers require that they be installed on rails and then pulled out entirely from the cabinet—imagine fully extending a drawer on a filing cabinet—to perform maintenance or to upgrade their internal components. Don't forget that the size and type of servers used in your Data Center affect not only the depth of the server rows, but also the space needed between those rows.

The current trend in server design is to make them more compact—smaller in height but also deeper than older models, which can increase the depth needed for your Data Center's server rows. The lower profile of these servers enables more to be installed in a cabinet— if your server environment can accommodate the greater port density, heat generation, and weight that comes with having so many servers in a small area. If your Data Center is designed to support these more infrastructure-intensive machines, then your company can take advantage of their space-saving potential and likely house them in a smaller room. If not, you might need to spread out the servers so that they take up about as much space as their larger predecessors.

When considering incoming equipment for purposes of sizing a Data Center, pay special attention to any devices that aren't specifically designed to go in to a server environment. These miscellaneous items frequently require greater floor space due to their irregular footprints, inability to fit into standard server cabinets, or access panels that require a large clearance area to open and perform maintenance.

NOTE   The most extreme case I've ever experienced of fitting a square-peg device into a round-hole server environment involved a T-shaped tape library. The tape library was more than 10 feet (3 meters) wide and about 4 feet (1.2 meters) deep. The device clearly was not designed for deployment in a modern server environment. In addition to the device's irregular footprint, the tape library possessed access panels on three of its four sides. Each panel required an additional 2 feet (61 centimeters) of clearance so employees could fully open the panels to insert or remove backup tapes, as needed. The library also had multiple servers associated with it that occupied four server cabinets of their own and had to be placed immediately adjacent to the tape library. Altogether, this cluster of equipment required about 160 square feet (15 square meters) of floor space.

The Data Center where the device was to be installed, meanwhile, had shallow server rows intended to accommodate server cabinets no more than about 3 feet (91 centimeters) deep. Even after placing the tape library so that one of its access panels could swing into an empty aisle, the tape library and its associated cabinets occupied a whopping 14 server cabinet locations in the Data Center. The placement of the tape library is illustrated in Figure 3-3.

Figures 3-3 shows how a piece of equipment fits awkwardly into a Data Center when neither the device nor the server environment is designed with the other in mind. Note that even the proprietary cabinets associated with the tape library are oversized, overlapping beyond than the Data Center's standard cabinet locations and making it harder to access under-floor infrastructure.

Figure 3-3   *Large Tape Library Meets Narrow Server Rows*

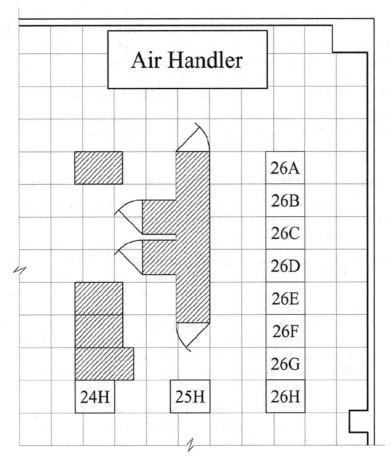

Use data about incoming equipment to estimate how many server cabinet locations are to be occupied when the Data Center first opens, and how rapidly more servers are to arrive. You can learn a lot about future hardware by talking with your IT manager. Ask what major projects are budgeted for in the coming fiscal year, including their timelines and what specific servers are expected to be ordered. The more you know, the better you can size the Data Center, not to mention ensure that cabinet locations have the appropriate electrical and data infrastructure in place.

For example, suppose that your initial equipment—servers, networking devices, and backup gear—fills 20 cabinets and that your IT manager expects to buy servers to fill three more cabinets every month for the next six months. If this is considered typical growth, extrapolate that to estimate 56 cabinets occupied by the end of the year, 112 in two years, and 168 in three. You want your Data Center to accommodate incoming equipment for a few years before needing to expand, so in this example the server environment should definitely have enough floor space for 112 cabinet locations and likely closer to 168.

Note that, when extending the equipment growth rate from the first year, you include the devices that were initially installed in the Data Center. The assumption is that demand for that equipment is going to grow at the same rate as for servers that are installed later. Even if the equipment that's arriving in the first few months is for a special project rather than typical growth, it is probably valid to include the equipment from the special project in your estimate because future special projects are likely to crop up as well.

When in doubt for sizing, round up. It is better to have a handful of extra spaces for servers in your Data Center than to prematurely run out of capacity.

Other Influencing Factors When Sizing Your Data Center

Once you have an idea of how many people your Data Center is to support and of the number and size of incoming servers and networking devices, there are still other elements to consider when sizing the room:

- **Do you want to locate major infrastructure components within the Data Center or elsewhere?**—Traditionally, air handlers and power distribution units are located in the server environment, but it is possible to place them somewhere else. If you choose to put air handlers and power distribution units in a space adjacent to the Data Center rather than inside, for example, less space is needed in the server environment itself but more must be set aside immediately next to the room to house those infrastructure components. In addition, fire suppression containers are most often located in a dedicated closet area, off of the Data Center, but can also be placed within the server environment.

- **How much space do you want around server rows?**—Building codes often require a minimum of 36 or 42 inches (91.4 or 106.7 centimeters) for walkways. If you plan to give tours of the Data Center on a regular basis, consider making the main thoroughfares wider. The additional space makes it easier to accommodate large tour groups and reduces the chances of a visitor accidentally snagging a dangling patch cord or power cable. If your Data Center is in a seismically active area and you choose to install seismic isolation platforms, you must provide additional clearance to enable the platforms to sway in an earthquake.

- **Do structural reinforcements need to be accommodated?**—If the Data Center is in a region at risk for hurricanes, earthquakes, or terrorist attacks, the room may require thicker walls and structural columns. A secondary roof may also be appropriate. Reinforcements add to the size of these Data Center elements, which can in turn alter the overall size of the room.

- **Assuming that your Data Center has a raised floor, is the entrance ramp going to be located inside the Data Center or in a corridor leading up to it?**— Alternatively, the room can be sunken so that the surface of the floor is level with the entrance, and no ramp is required at all. This approach requires significantly more depth for the floor, but saves the need to dedicate floor space for a ramp.

Each of these decisions can occupy or free up considerable floor space, affecting the size of your server environment.

Determining Shape and Placement of Your Data Center

With the approximate size of the Data Center in mind, it is time to figure out its footprint and where to locate the Data Center within the host building.

Square or rectangular shapes are the most conducive for a server environment. Square or rectangular shapes provide consistent boundaries in which to place large Data Center elements—air handlers, power distribution units, and server rows—that are square or rectangular themselves. Avoid shapes containing curved or angled walls, small alcoves, or dogleg spaces. The irregular shapes create pockets of unusable space. Imagine parking an automobile, which is essentially a rectangle, into a one-car garage. If the garage stall is rectangular or square it is a fairly simple task to align the front and sides of the car in relation to the garage's three walls. If the garage is a circle or has a small alcove in each of its walls, though, the car still fits inside but there are always pockets of space between the car and the walls.

Shape and placement are obviously issues only if your Data Center is one of multiple spaces on a building floor. If the Data Center occupies the entire story, its shape is automatically that of the building itself, and placement isn't a problem.

Desirable and Undesirable Spaces to Place Your Data Center

The guidelines for positioning a Data Center within a building are similar to those for choosing a Data Center site in the first place. You want to place the server environment so that it is easy to reach for servers and incoming server equipment and conveniently located near other spaces that support the Data Center. You also want the Data Center to be away from potential hazards that can threaten servers, and clear of building fixtures that might inhibit the room's flexibility.

Specifically, avoid areas adjacent to bathrooms or cafeteria kitchens. Not only are they potential sources of water leaks or fire, as mentioned in Chapter 2, "Choosing an Optimal Site," but bathrooms or kitchens can be problematic to remove if the Data Center needs to be expanded in the future. You want your Data Center located so that it has a pre-determined area to expand in the future—a growth path of some sort for when the room eventually fills to capacity with servers.

Growth Paths for Your Data Center's Space

Plan for later expansion of your Data Center during the initial design of the room. Planning for expansion ensures that the expanded server environment space is just as well-designed, compatible with the building, and productive for your company as the initial floor space. Choose space for your Data Center's growth path that is easy to remodel and is not critical to the function of your business. Employee cubicles, storage rooms, and conference rooms are all excellent for a Data Center growth path because they are relatively easy to relocate and replace. Electrical rooms, lab spaces, and manufacturing facilities are problematic, on the other hand, because relocating them is difficult and disruptive of your company's daily operations. Worst of all are stairwells, structural columns, or other building components that simply cannot be removed. Structural building components landlock your Data Center, making future expansion extremely difficult.

Figure 3-4 shows a building floorplan with three options for locating a Data Center. Note that the building itself has some advantages for housing a Data Center:

- It possesses a loading dock.
- Ample room on the first floor exists for a server environment and its associated spaces.
- Visitors can be routed through a main lobby before accessing the Data Center, providing an additional measure of security.

Based on the preceding discussion of how to place a server environment, which of the three locations in Figure 3-4 is most desirable?

Area A has some initial appeal for placing the Data Center—it is rectangular and in close proximity to the building's loading dock. Unfortunately, there is an irregular space in the southwest corner, including a curved wall. Area A has no desirable growth path, either. The building's main lobby and a stairwell limit expansion to the south, while the walls to the north and west are at the end of the building. It is possible to grow eastward into Area B, but only by blocking the main corridor that runs north-south through the building and narrowing into the space between the stairwell to the north and the loading dock to the south. Place a server environment in Area A only if a more suitable space isn't available.

Figure 3-4   *Data Center Placement*

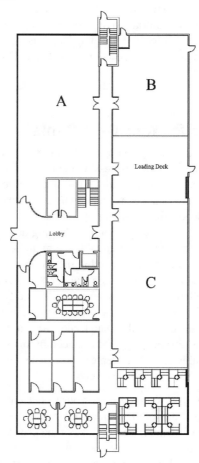

Area B is the worst location of the three for a Data Center. Although the shape of Area B is good and it, too, is near the loading dock, the space is smaller than areas A or C and has an external door. More troubling, Area B lacks a good growth path. The space can't expand past the building's exterior walls to the north or east, and is blocked to the south because of the loading dock. Area B can conceivably expand westward, but that has the same drawbacks as trying to expand Area A—blocking the building corridor and having to wrap around the north stairwell. Locate a server environment in Area B only if no future growth is expected and no better space is available.

Area C is the most desirable location for a Data Center. Area C is a large rectangle with no irregular shapes, and is close to the loading dock. Area C also has no external doors or windows, and there is a workable growth path to the south through existing office cubicles.

NOTE   Figure 3-4 isn't just a hypothetical example. The drawing is from the design plans for a Data Center in central Colorado that I designed and that came online in March 2001. The Data Center is indeed located in Area C, and the room's growth path is to the south. Cubicles occupy Area A, and a lab is in Area B. The Data Center is 2030 square feet (188.6 square meters).

Consolidation Options for Your Data Center

Nearly as important as including a provision to expand your Data Center is having a reduction plan. Hopefully your business will only ever have to deal with the need for more and more server space as your company grows and additional equipment arrives over time, but some circumstances can lead to the downsizing of your server environment. Your company may decide to shift its base of operations to another city or country, for example, scaling back at its original location but not shutting down the site altogether. With less manpower and fewer projects, there could be a reduction in the number of servers and therefore less Data Center space needed in the old location. Alternatively, if your server environment is located in a leased building, upper management could opt to trim operational costs by renting less building space and require that all types of space be "given back" to the landlord, including a portion of the server environment. It is also possible that some of the drivers that existed when the Data Center was first designed may change over time. Large, floor-standing servers might be replaced by ones that are significantly smaller, occupying considerably less Data Center floor space. Or, projects that were to require a large number of servers could be canceled.

Whatever the reason, you want to design your Data Center so that it can scale down just as easily as up. Making the room modular and standardized, as discussed in Chapter 1 goes a long way toward easily modifying the size of the Data Center. Because the Data Center's infrastructure is identical from one server row to another, the room doesn't lose its depth of functionality if several rows are removed to reduce floor space. The consolidated room may be unable to support as many servers as when the Data Center was larger, but the infrastructure provided to each server cabinet location that remains is still the same.

Potential Data Center consolidation can be facilitated in other ways. Where possible, cluster the various types of Data Center infrastructure together, preferably near the floor space the specific component supports. For instance, if a Data Center has a pair of circuit panels that supply power to five server rows, and an air handler that provides cooling to the same area, locate those infrastructure components in close proximity to one another. Repeat this form of modularity throughout the room. If the server environment ever has to be reduced in size, each block of server rows can be isolated along with the corresponding infrastructure within them, and preserved or given up as needed.

Plan your Data Center's reduced footprint. Know exactly how to subdivide the Data Center in the future, if needed. Then strategically arrange and install infrastructure elements that provide coverage for the entire space. Piping for fire sprinklers, for example, must run throughout the Data Center. Once you've defined where the new walls would be if the Data Center was consolidated, you can make sure the sprinkler piping runs parallel to that area rather than perpendicular across it. Running the sprinklers parallel to the server area provides the necessary coverage of the existing server environment, and if the room ever needs to be consolidated, construction is simpler because less piping must be removed or rerouted.

If feasible, also leave extra floor space available around any server rows that would become adjacent to new walls in the consolidated Data Center. Extra floor space allows a proper aisle to be created, and lessens the chance of those server rows being disrupted by construction.

A Data Center Consolidation

During March 2004, I assisted in consolidating a Data Center as part of the overall reduction of a site in Austin, Texas. The facility had opened more than five years earlier and expanded over time to encompass about 207,000 square feet (19,231 square meters) of space in three office buildings. I took part in the original design and setup of the Data Center in late 1998. The site was to be a major hub for the company, with 700 engineers needing a Data Center to perform their work. Based on the number of employees, projected equipment, and predictions of future growth, I helped design a 3719 square-foot (346 square-meter) Data Center that had 14 server and networking rows and 182 cabinet locations. By 2004, though, upper management had relocated much of the site's functions to Richardson, Texas, about 200 miles (322 kilometers) away. (A new site was built, complete with its own server environment.) Roughly half of the engineers remained in Austin, and only one-third of the Data Center was occupied with servers. Some of the Austin leases were up for renewal, so there was an opportunity to save considerable money by consolidating from three office buildings down to two.

To facilitate the consolidation, the Data Center was divided, with one half continuing as a server environment and the other remodeled as a lab. Dividing the area left enough space for the Data Center to accommodate future growth, while enabling other lab space in the building to be returned. Because the Data Center had been designed with consistent infrastructure, it was a fairly straightforward matter to install a wall across the space and modify the fire suppression system and certain electrical controls so that the lab and consolidated Data Center became distinct environments.

Only two things kept the consolidation from being completely transparent to clients who used the Data Center servers. First, a power distribution unit was located where the dividing wall was being constructed and had to be relocated, something I could have avoided if I had thought of consolidation during the original design. Second, servers had been installed across the entire Data Center during the last five years. A few dozen of the servers had to be brought offline as those machines were relocated into the smaller Data Center space. Again, had I planned ahead that the Data Center might need to shrink, all servers could have been kept in one half of the room in the first place and downtime avoided altogether.

When finished, the Data Center was cut practically in half, down to 1913 square feet (178 square meters). It had seven rows and 91 cabinet locations. The overall consolidation reduced the space leased by the company down to about 138,500 square feet (12,867 square meters) and saved more than $1.2 million a year in rent and operational expenses.

Structure and Finishes of the Data Center

The shell that surrounds your Data Center must insulate the room from undesirable external conditions. Think of it as a protective cocoon around your company's servers and networking devices. To help make this cocoon as strong as possible, avoid windows or transparent walls in your Data Center. Windows or transparent walls make the room more vulnerable to a break-in, enable unauthorized personnel to potentially view sensitive data, and—if they are located within an external building wall—increase the chance of incurring damage during a major storm or high winds.

If your Data Center must have windows facing the outside, seal over them from the inside of the room to diminish the security risk the windows create. Whatever blinds or shades are placed in other windows around the building should be installed in the Data Center window bays as well. Although the coverings are never to be opened for the Data Center windows, you want the exterior of the building to present a uniform image. Don't advertise the presence of your Data Center through the absence of window coverings.

For Data Center windows that face the interior of the building, make sure that the inside of the server environment can only be viewed after someone has first passed through some sort of access control measures, such as a door with a badge reader system or electronic combination lock. Locating a window inside a secured area enables you to have a transparent viewing area into the Data Center for guided tours, while protecting sensitive information from unauthorized or unescorted visitors.

Also advisable is avoidance of external doors on your Data Center, that is no doors leading directly to the outside. As with windows, external doors into a server environment make the room more susceptible to physical intrusion. External doors also permit dirt and other unwanted contaminants to be tracked in from the outside. If the Data Center must have an outside door, perhaps as required by local fire codes or due to restrictions against modifying the building, make the door exclusively for egress. Keep the external side locked at all times and install an exit bar, or panic bar, on the inside. If the external door is purely an emergency exit, equip the door with an audible alarm.

Another characteristic for keeping the Data Center cocoon strong is for all of the room's walls to be full height. No one should be able to gain access by entering the space above the false ceiling in a hallway and scaling a partial-height Data Center wall or by lifting a floor tile from the ramp to the Data Center door and crawling underneath the raised floor. All Data Center walls and doors should furthermore be fire resistant and able to keep fire suppression gas within the room. The gas is much less effective at extinguishing a fire if it leaks out of the server environment.

Finally, all interior finishes within the Data Center should be static- and dust-free surfaces, because either can be disruptive to servers and networking devices.

Associated Data Center Support Rooms

When allocating building space for your Data Center, set aside an additional area for several support rooms. Some of these rooms are simply convenience spaces that make tasks easier for Data Center users, while others are integral to the proper operation of a server environment. Most of the infrastructure that runs in to your Data Center must first terminate into another area—power in to an electrical room or structured cabling into a networking room, for example. Just as a chain is only as strong as its weakest link, so is your Data Center only as productive and secure as its associated rooms.

These dedicated areas include the following:

- Electrical room
- Networking room
- Loading dock
- Build room
- Storage room
- Operations command center
- Backup room
- Media storage area
- Vendor service areas

Figures 3-5 represents a Data Center and its associated support rooms as they might be arranged within a building. The room marked with the grid is the Data Center, while the areas with hatch marks are occupied by miscellaneous building features such as elevators, stairwells, bathrooms, janitorial closets, or conference rooms. Numbered spaces are explained in the paragraphs that follow.

Electrical Room

The main electrical equipment that supports your Data Center is located in a dedicated electrical room, separate from the server environment to avoid electromagnetic interference. Switching gear for the Data Center's primary and standby electrical systems are located in the electrical room. The Data Center's backup batteries, known as an uninterruptible power source, are traditionally placed in this room as well. Area 7 in Figure 3-5 is the electrical room.

Figure 3-5   *A Data Center and its Support Rooms*

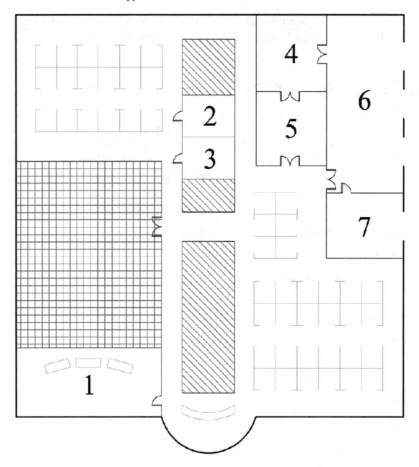

Networking Room

The networking room is the centralized area where all structured data cabling for the site—not just one building—terminates. Other names for this area include data room, communications (comms) room, or campus distributor. All things networking, including those in the Data Center and others (such as a separate network for desktop computers), route through here. Aside from its obligatory structured cabling, this room is traditionally equipped with the same level of standby power, cooling, and physical security measures as the Data Center.

Many companies support their Data Center and networking room from the same standby power system. Because devices in the Data Center cannot communicate with the outside world if the networking room goes offline, the theory is that there is little point in having distributed standby power. Depending upon what additional networks are routed through your network room and how much functionality your Data Center servers still have when they are isolated from an external network, there may or may not be an advantage to having distinct standby power systems for each room.

The networking room does not have to be located immediately near the Data Center to support it, although doing so can save money during initial construction because cable runs are shorter. Area 3 in Figure 3-5 is the networking room.

Loading Dock

As explained in Chapter 2 having a loading dock in the building where your Data Center is located is very useful. Incoming servers, networking devices, server cabinets, and other large supplies can be easily received and transported to either a storage area or build room, as required. The dock should be able to accommodate trucks of varying lengths and configurations and possess a leveler, enabling incoming items to be rolled directly from the truck bed into the receiving area.

It is convenient if the loading dock is located close to whatever rooms are designated to receive incoming items for the Data Center, although this is not mandatory. Do not incorporate a dock into the Data Center space itself, or have your server environment open directly into the dock. This receiving area is likely to contain a lot of dust and dirt because of all of the incoming cardboard boxes, wooden pallets, and other shipping materials. You don't want contaminants from this area tracked or blown in to the Data Center. Loading dock rollup doors, through which equipment is brought in, also have a way of being left open for significant periods of time. If a loading dock is part of the Data Center, that creates a huge opportunity for unauthorized personnel to gain access into the room.

Area 6 in Figure 3-5 is the loading dock.

Build Room

The build room, alternatively called a fitup room, staging area, or burn-in room, is a dedicated area for system administrators and network engineers to unpack, set up, and pre-configure equipment that is ultimately bound for the Data Center.

At minimum, this space is merely an empty room where machines sit temporarily until ready for installation. Having users open their servers and networking devices in this area keeps boxes, pallets, dirt, paperwork, and other miscellaneous trash out of the Data Center.

More sophisticated build rooms are equipped with their own power, data cabling, cooling, and fire suppression infrastructure. Some build rooms are essentially mini Data Centers, right down to having their own raised floor and standby power.

NOTE   Personally, I believe that it is a good idea to equip your build room with a certain degree of conditioned power and data cabling infrastructure—say the equivalent of one or two server rows in your Data Center. This infrastructure enables system administrators and network engineers to initially configure their equipment, and encourages them to use the build room rather than bypassing the space and bringing still-boxed servers directly in to the server environment. I don't think you should provide standby power for the build room, though. The room is meant to be only a temporary holding area. If you make the space as robust as a Data Center, users will have no incentive to move devices to their eventual destination.

The build room should be located in close proximity to the Data Center and the loading dock, so incoming equipment can be conveniently transported to and from the room. The amount of floor space required for the build room depends upon how many devices it is expected to house and for how long. The room should be at least large enough to accept several large servers arriving on a pallet jack. Area 5 in Figure 3-5 is the build room.

If possible, try to match the build room's ambient temperature to that of the Data Center. This helps acclimate incoming equipment to the server environment, especially if the two rooms are near one another. If you have ever brought a fish home from the pet store, you are familiar with this process. After transporting the fish home in a bag of water, it is recommended that you put the entire bag into your aquarium for a while rather than dump the fish in immediately. This protects the fish from being shocked by any temperature difference between the water in the bag and that in the aquarium. Due to the high dollar value of the equipment that resides in the build room—a single server can cost tens of thousands of dollars—provide the build room with the same physical security measures as the Data Center. (Specific recommendations about what physical safeguards to place on your server environment are provided in Chapter 13, "Safeguarding the Servers.")

Storage Room

While the build room can accept incoming items on a short-term basis, designate another space to store Data Center–related materials for longer periods of time. There are many items that can and do accumulate in and around a server environment. It is best to store the spare items in a separate area rather than allow them to take up valuable Data Center floor space. The stored materials can include:

- Decommissioned servers, waiting to be turned in for credit to the manufacturer when newer systems are purchased during an upgrade cycle.

- Custom shipping crates for servers still under evaluation.

- Excess consumables, such as cabinet shelves or filters for the Data Center air handlers.

The size of the storage room is driven by the size of the Data Center—a large server environment is going to accept more incoming equipment, go through more consumable items, and decommission more servers than a small server environment and therefore needs more storage space. A good rule of thumb is to size the storage room at about 15 percent that of the Data Center. As with other sizing guidelines in this chapter, fine-tune the footprint of your build room based on the actual physical factors of your company site.

Equip the Data Center storage room with the same physical security measures as the Data Center and build room. Although your company undoubtedly has other storage needs, stay away from using a common storage area and co-mingling Data Center–related materials with other items. Even if you have an excellent inventory control system, materials in a common storage area are more likely to be borrowed or scavenged and therefore unavailable when needed for the Data Center.

Area 4 in Figure 3-5 is the storage room. Note that the loading, dock, storage room, and build room are situated so that incoming equipment can be conveniently received (Area 6), moved in to storage for a time if needed (Area 4), moved in to the build room to be unboxed (Area 5), and then transported to the Data Center.

NOTE	Although, occasionally, expensive servers disappear from a shared storage room, the Data Center-related items that most frequently go missing are convenience items: pallet jacks and wheeled carts for transporting supplies, stepladders for reaching the top of storage racks or server cabinets, or storage bins for holding patch cords and small supplies, for example. People usually take items to deal with whatever problem they are wrestling with at the moment, and don't bother to return them.
	Having these items disappear at a crucial time is not only frustrating but can also prevent work from being done. I've lost count of how many times over the years I have needed to retrieve something heavy from a common storage area, only to discover that the pallet jack, moving dolly, or wheeled cart that is supposed to be in the storage room is missing. The longer it takes to track down the item, the longer it takes to finish the task.

Operations Command Center

The operations command center, alternatively known as a call center or control room, is a workspace where employees remotely monitor Data Center servers. If a problem arises with a device, command center staff contacts the appropriate employee or vendor resources to address the issue, and helps coordinate remediation efforts until the problem is resolved. Some companies have a separate network operations center to monitor and address networking devices, while others consolidate them into a single space.

Command center facilities are typically equipped with large, wall-mounted display screens, multiple telephones, and computer console furniture with recessed display screens at each seating location. This configuration enables employees to conveniently monitor multiple servers at one time.

Because command center tasks all involve monitoring devices that are in another location, this room does not have to be near the Data Center. In fact, it is preferable if this facility is located a significant distance away for disaster recovery purposes. Some companies choose to outsource their call center functions. When outsourcing, no facility needs to be constructed at all.

Area 1 in Figure 3-5 is the operations command center. Although the room doesn't have to be adjacent to your server environment, its relative location to the Data Center and lobby in this arrangement provides an interesting opportunity. If you equip the command center with physical access controls and provide a good line of sight from that room in to the Data Center, you can use the command center as a viewing area for tours. This enables you to show your server environment without bringing people in to the space.

Backup Room

A backup room is a workspace for support personnel who perform and monitor backups for the servers in the Data Center. Providing a backup room enables the appropriate employees and vendors to perform backup functions without having to be stationed full time in the server environment. As with any operational practice that reduces how many people are in the Data Center and for how long, having backup personnel do their work outside of the Data Center reduces the risk of accidental downtime. Providing a backup room may also help justify a lower occupancy rating for your Data Center. As mentioned in Chapter 2 lower occupancy can reduce how much external air is required to be cycled in to the Data Center, therefore decreasing the Data Center's exposure to outside contaminants.

A backup room is normally equipped with the same level of power and connectivity as standard desktop locations. Although a backup room has its benefits, consider it a convenience rather than a mandatory space associated with a Data Center. If limited space is available in a building for Data Center-related functions, this is one of the first rooms to sacrifce.

The backup room can be located anywhere, but because workers have to enter the server environment to perform certain tasks, it is most convenient if located a short walk from the Data Center. Area 2 in Figure 3-5 is the backup room.

Media Storage Area

A media storage area is for the storage of magnetic, optical, or whatever other media is employed to regularly back up content from the servers in your Data Center. Much like the build room, establishing a separate area for these backup materials keeps dirt, debris, and unnecessary equipment weight out of the Data Center.

Most disaster recovery strategies recommend storing backup media several miles (kilometers) away from your server environment, so that a single catastrophic event doesn't destroy both your original data and backup copies. Not all businesses choose to do that, however, due to the associated costs. If your company maintains its backup media on site, the materials are likely stored in fireproof safes, which can weigh thousands of pounds. A media storage area can accommodate these safes. Your Data Center must already support increasingly heavy servers, and there is no reason to add unnecessarily to the room's weight-load. Even if your company does store its backup media off site and has no heavy safes, it is still useful to have a media storage area. Backup tapes have to be collected and sorted before they are transported off site, and the media storage room enables the work to be performed outside of the Data Center. Incoming tapes can also be stored in the media storage room and then unboxed when needed.

It is not necessary for a media storage room to be placed in the immediately vicinity of your Data Center. If you expect the media storage room to house media safes, locate it on the first floor to better accommodate their excessive weight. Area 2 in Figure 3-5 also serves as the media storage room.

NOTE   Technology advances in recent years have increased fiber transmission capacity. This increased capacity has in turn enabled many companies to build multiple Data Centers and back up their data from one location to the other, using smaller disk-based backup systems rather than tapes. If you have more than one server environment and opt for such an arrangement, your need for a dedicated backup room and media storage area is much less. Inter-site connectivity is discussed in Chapter 7, "Designing a Scalable Network Infrastructure."

Vendor Service Areas

If vendors do a significant amount of work in your Data Center, you might want to dedicate areas for them to work out of or store materials in. This can be appropriate if vendor representatives, rather than your company's own system administrators, install and perform maintenance upon many of your Data Center servers. A provided vendor service area gives these non-employees a place to work other than in your most sensitive environment, the Data Center. If you have people from competing vendor companies working at your site, consider creating more than one of these areas. While it is unlikely that one vendor might try to sabotage a competitor, establishing separate work areas can remove the opportunity altogether.

No vendor storage area is shown in Figure 3-5.

Summary

You must accurately size your Data Center so that it effectively meets your company's server hosting needs for the coming years. A server environment that's too small causes you to rapidly run out of hosting capacity and to invest more time and money creating additional server space. A server environment that's too large wastes money, both on initial construction and ongoing operational expenses. Both are inefficient.

Sizing your Data Center is a complex task, influenced by how many people it supports, how many and what kind of servers it hosts, and how you want to deploy the room's infrastructure components. Many businesses devote the smallest area possible to house their servers, because the limited space is less expensive to build and maintain. Using a small area may be appropriate, but be aware that a larger Data Center can foster bulk discounts on labor and materials—saving your company money in the long run.

Begin sizing the Data Center based upon how many employees rely upon the room to perform their jobs. A simple formula of 10 square feet (1 square meter) per employee is a good starting point for up to 100 or so people. Adjust the formula downward as the amount of people and size of the Data Center increase, to reflect the economy of scale that a larger room enjoys.

Further refine the Data Center's size based upon what kind of and how many servers and networking devices are projected to be installed, allocating additional floor space for non-standard equipment. You want the Data Center to have enough server cabinet locations to accommodate incoming equipment for the next few years.

Square or rectangular spaces are the most conducive for a Data Center, while those with angled walls or irregular shapes waste floor space and should be avoided. Plan ahead when designing the Data Center by making sure that it has a dedicated path for expansion and can be easily consolidated without disruption to the Data Center's pre-existing infrastructure.

Make the structure around the Data Center strong and secure. Avoid having windows or external doors on the Data Center, which make the room more susceptible to physical intrusion, and make sure that all walls and doors are full-height construction from floor to ceiling.

When allocating building space for the Data Center, also set aside space for several dedicated areas that directly or indirectly support the Data Center. Some of these spaces are critical for the proper functioning of the server environment, while others make the room more productive by keeping non-essential personnel and equipment outside of the Data Center.

Support areas include the electrical room, which houses both the main electrical equipment for the Data Center and standby battery system, and the networking room where all of your site's structured cabling and networks route through, including those associated with the

Data Center. Other support areas include a loading dock to receive equipment, a build room to unpack and pre-configure servers and networking devices, and a storage room to safeguard valuable items and keep non-operational equipment out of the Data Center floor. Still more associated rooms are separate work areas for staff who remotely monitor Data Center equipment or perform regular data backups, an area to securely store backup tapes, and dedicated work areas for vendors.

CHAPTER 4

Laying Out the Data Center

This chapter explains how to efficiently arrange all elements of a Data Center during the design phase, from large infrastructure objects to buffer zones to server rows. The chapter addresses how various server layouts affect the amount of floor space that rows occupy, what the best way is to lay out a room when dealing with super heavy equipment, and how to accommodate unavoidable obstacles. Finally, the chapter explains where to place essential Data Center infrastructure controls and what layout-related problems to watch for and avoid.

Drawing Tools Available to Create Your Data Center Layout

Part of creating a productive Data Center is a logical layout of all its constituent parts. From air handlers to electrical panels, sprinkler pipes to server rows, floor tiles to telephones, you must specify not only what components go in your server environment but also where exactly the components are to be located. One of the most effective ways to communicate the layout is the creation of a detailed map of the Data Center.

While it is possible to create an informative design package without drawings, illustrations are often easier to understand than written instructions. Drawings are especially helpful if the contractors working on your Data Center have not built a server environment for your company before, making them unfamiliar with your design concepts, or when key people involved in the project are not all native speakers of the same language. When done correctly, drawings provide a clarity and comprehensive amount of detail that written text can't.

NOTE   I've participated in Data Center projects in multiple countries and more than once had to work through confusion when a turn of phrase was misunderstood or the term for an infrastructure component differed from one part of the world to another. Other mix-ups happen even without a language barrier, due to imprecise wording.

One such misunderstanding occurred over the wiring of monitoring lights used to indicate when the Data Center receives power from its standby generator rather than its normal utility source. The design documents for the project stated that the monitoring lights should activate "as soon as the generator goes off." The intention of the phrase was for the lights to turn on when the standby generator activated, but the contractors wiring the system interpreted "go off" literally and thought the lights were supposed to be on continuously, only turning off when the generator was actively supplying power to the Data Center. Fortunately, because monitoring lights are prominent in the Data Center, the misinterpretation was immediately noticed and fixed.

In later design packages, I replaced the vague wording with an illustration of the wiring scheme for the monitoring lights as well a table that listed whether the lights were to be off or on, depending upon the status of utility power and the standby generator.

The simplest way to sketch a Data Center layout is with pen, straight edge, and graph paper. Using pen and paper is also the most primitive. Making design revisions can be tedious, sometimes requiring you to redraw the entire illustration. Fortunately, several commercial software programs are available that can be used to draw your Data Center layout. AutoCAD®, by Autodesk, is one application often used to create building blueprints, making AutoCAD a good choice if you want your Data Center maps to be compatible with other construction drawings. Visio®, by Microsoft, is another common application. AutoCAD and Visio are powerful tools that are in use around the world and that enable you to create sophisticated renderings of a server environment. Be aware that each program can take time to master. If you plan to use one for your Data Center design, try to become familiar with the program before the project begins.

In the end, work with whatever media you're comfortable with and be sure that the maps you create are clear, detailed, and accurate enough for others to follow—especially the architectural firm that is to incorporate the maps into the Data Center's final construction documents.

The Floor Grid

To begin laying out the Data Center, start with a map of the building area the Data Center is to occupy and draw a grid over that space. The grid, consisting of squares 2 feet (61 centimeters) on each side, helps align objects in the room and simplifies where to place everything. If you intend to install a raised floor in the Data Center, also use this grid to represent floor tiles, because the grid squares are the same size. (Information about whether to install a raised floor system in your Data Center and what attributes such a floor should have are spelled out in Chapter 5, "Overhead or Under-Floor Installation?") If you draw the Data Center on graph paper, use the squares on the paper for the floor grid.

Be sure that the map of the Data Center area that you begin planning from is accurate and that details shown are in correct proportion to one another. You want to make full use of the floor space within the server environment, and if measurements or placement of key items are off by just a few inches (centimeters), problems can arise. If possible, walk the Data Center area with the map in hand, checking to make sure no details have been omitted. It is also helpful to obtain pictures of the space, because they might show details more clearly than a two-dimensional map.

NOTE   In November 1997, I was involved with a Data Center project where a single incorrect detail on the map caused the loss of several server cabinet locations. The server environment, constructed in San Jose, California, was about 3000 square feet (278.7 square meters). It was designed to have 11 rows consisting of 132 cabinet locations. With floor space at a premium, the Data Center was laid out so that each row ended 36 inches (91.4 centimeters) from the edge of the southern wall that ran perpendicular to them—the minimum clearance allowed by local building and fire codes.

After contractors installed the raised floor and placed most of the major infrastructure in the Data Center, it was discovered that the southern wall was actually thicker than was shown on the map used to plan the layout of the room. The difference was barely more than the width of someone's hand, a few inches (a handful of centimeters) at most, but it meant that the rows ended too close to the southern wall. The narrower clearance not only violated local codes, but also made it more difficult to transport equipment through on a pallet jack.

The northern wall of the Data Center had just enough additional floor space, originally set aside to provide a larger path to transport equipment through, to shift everything in the Data Center to the north and recreate the necessary clearance along the south wall. Moving the server rows would have required detaching much of the previously installed infrastructure and then removing and reinstalling the raised floor system, however, and the labor costs were considered prohibitive. The decision was instead made to eliminate a cabinet location at the end of each of the Data Center's 11 rows, sacrificing nearly one-tenth of its server hosting capacity.

Because relocating a raised floor is expensive and time-consuming even in a Data Center that's offline—and extremely disruptive to one containing functioning equipment—it is crucial to correctly place your room's floor grid. In most cases you want the grid's lines to synchronize with the Data Center walls. Aligning the grid lines with the walls makes it simpler to install the raised floor and usually requires fewer floor tiles to be customized for the room, which means reduced time and labor costs. The exception to placing the grid even with the walls is if aligning the grid differently enables better access to under-floor infrastructure or makes obstructions in the room occupy fewer tile locations. Figures 4-1 and 4-2 illustrate how placement of the grid influences under-floor accessibility and usability of floor space.

In each of the following figures, the air handler and structural column extend down to the Data Center subfloor. Floor tiles are removed or cut in half to accommodate the objects. The disk library, meanwhile, rests atop the Data Center raised floor and overlaps any tiles that it obscures in the figures.

Figure 4-1   *A Poorly Aligned Data Center Grid: A Disk Library, Air Handler, and Structural Column Overlap Multiple Floor Tiles*

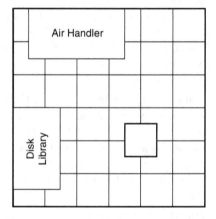

Figure 4-2   *A Well Aligned Data Center Grid: Repositioning the Grid Enables the Same Objects to Overlap Fewer Tiles*

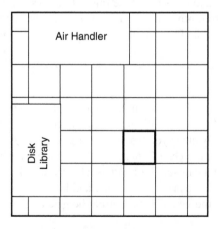

In Figure 4-1, it is difficult to access the under-floor area around any of the Data Center objects. The half-sized tiles in front of the air handler are awkward to remove and replace.

Any data ports and electrical outlets below the disk library are hard to reach because the unit overlaps most of the tiles that are immediately adjacent, preventing them from being lifted. Figure 4-1 also requires that all 10 floor tiles surrounding the air handler and structural column be specially cut to fit around the objects, whereas Figure 4-2 only three floor tiles to be modified. In a large server environment, a poorly grid can require hundreds of tiles to be custom fitted around the objects. be modified by hand, adding to the project's labor costs.

Having half of a floor tile between you and the area directly below a server or of equipment may not sound like much, but in practice it is a significant difference. Center device comes to the edge of a floor tile, enabling you to lift an immediately a tile for access, you can plug in to or unplug from the under-floor infrastructure by sin crouching down and reaching any necessary data ports or electrical receptacles. If that same Data Center device overlaps a floor tile halfway and the closest spot you can gain access below is half a tile away, that means you need to lie down on your belly and stretch to reach under the device. It is also harder to see where patch cords and power cables are supposed to connect when the floor tile you are lifting isn't immediately adjacent to the device. It is dark under the raised floor, and light shining in to the open tile space is what normally illuminates the area. Bring a flashlight (torch) if the tile opening is not immediately adjacent to the device.

As mentioned in Chapter 1, "Approaching the Data Center Project," you want to design your server environment to promote good habits. If the devices in your Data Center overlap floor tiles, users may not intuitively know how to correctly access the infrastructure below. At best, this might lead people to use the room's infrastructure inefficiently, plugging servers in to electrical outlets intended for other equipment or running long patch cords between servers instead of using pre-existing structured cabling. At worst, it can lead to dangerous and costly mistakes.

NOTE   In November 2003, I received an urgent call saying that a server cabinet had tipped over in one of the Data Centers I manage. I ran in to the room to discover a fully-loaded cabinet on its side and two others askew from their regular locations. All three had prominent scrape marks on their sides and obviously damaged cables.

A company employee and two vendor representatives had been installing a cabinet full of new servers. Not understanding our standard design and that structured cabling was available at all server cabinet locations, they had tried to connect directly to a networking device in an adjacent server row by running long patch cords. Rows in this particular Data Center are aligned so that the back of each server cabinet is even with the floor tiles underneath it, while the front of the cabinet overlaps halfway onto a second tile. Users are supposed to access the under-floor cabling by lifting the tile immediately behind any cabinet. The employee instead tried to run patch cords to the adjacent row from the front side. To do so, he pushed the full server cabinet off of the tile it overlaps. (The cabinets have lockable castors, enabling a person to unlock the wheels and roll them to a different Data

Center cabinet location if needed.) Not finding what he wanted, he then went to the other side of the row and rolled the cabinet back to its normal position *without first replacing the missing floor tile on the other side of it.* The 800-pound (362.9-kilogram) cabinet tipped like a domino and crashed into a full cabinet in the next row, driving it into yet a third. Miraculously, no one was hurt. Fortunately, all of the equipment that was damaged was either already offline or was performing research and development functions—no business-related applications or machines went offline from the incident.

While the employee had been taught the correct use of the Data Center infrastructure and can be rightly blamed for breaking several rules of the room, he would not have tried to move the server cabinet if it hadn't partially overlapped a floor tile. Wherever cabinets in the row lined up flush with a floor tile, he understood to lift an adjacent tile, but the overlap confused him.

Figure 4-3 illustrates this incident.

Figure 4-3   *A Server Cabinet Falls After a Floor Tile It Normally Overlaps Is Removed*

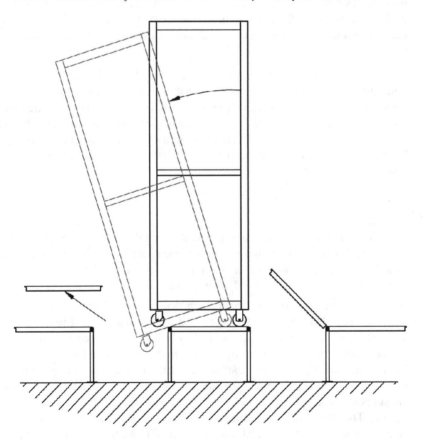

Defining Spaces for Physical Elements of Your Data Center

Laying out all of the physical elements of a Data Center is like working on a complicated, three-dimensional jigsaw puzzle. Mechanical equipment, mandatory clearances, walkways, server rows, and miscellaneous obstacles are all pieces that must be interconnected properly for the server environment to function efficiently. Force one piece into the wrong place and others won't fit well, if at all. Data Center layouts are trickier than the hardest puzzle, though. There is no number on the side of the wall saying how many pieces your server environment has or what it must look like when finished. You are just left to fit as many servers, networking devices, and infrastructure elements into the room as you can.

Also unlike the puzzle, there are several ways to arrange Data Center items:

- Do you place air handlers in the middle of the room or against a wall?
- What about power distribution units?
- How wide do you make the areas surrounding each server row?
- Which direction should the rows face?
- Do you orient all of them the same way, or alternate their direction?

You might think having multiple options makes the task of designing the room easier. In one sense, having several options does make the task easier, because more than one solution is possible. However, some layouts maximize floor space and coordinate Data Center infrastructure better than others, and it takes an experienced eye to know the difference between a mediocre solution and a great one.

To best lay out your Data Center, define the amount of floor space that each item must occupy in the room and arrange each strategically. Whenever possible, overlap clearance areas so that they do double-duty in the room. For example, if a power distribution unit requires a buffer area to protect surrounding equipment from electromagnetic interference and an air handler needs a clearance area to swing open an access panel on the side, place these two items in mutual proximity. The buffer for one can serve as the clearance area for the other. This conserves space in the Data Center and enables it to be used for other purposes.

For smaller items that can conceivably be tucked anywhere within the server environment, consider how frequently and where in the room the items are most often needed. Storage cylinders for the Data Center's fire suppression system, for example, need to be accessed only occasionally for maintenance, so it makes sense to put the cylinders in a remote corner rather than the middle of the room. In contrast, having access to a telephone while working on a server is helpful, so phones should be placed within easy reach of the room's server rows.

Mechanical Equipment

The largest individual objects in a Data Center are typically its major infrastructure components:

- Power distribution units that provide electrical power
- Air handlers that regulate cooling
- Fire suppressant containers

Because this mechanical equipment is essential for a server environment and can take up large chunks of floor space, place it on your Data Center map first.

Power Distribution Units

Electrical equipment of varying shapes and sizes is employed to provide power to your Data Center. Typically, power feeds in to your building from a utility source, where the power is conditioned and then routed into your Data Center. Server cabinet locations are provided power by way of individual electrical conduits, which run back to banks of circuit breakers. The breakers are within floor-standing power distribution units, known as PDUs, or distributed circuit panel boards that are essentially industrial versions of the type of circuit breaker panels found in your home. More information about this electrical equipment, including the advantages and disadvantages of PDUs and how to calculate the number of circuits your Data Center needs, is covered in Chapter 6, "Creating a Robust Electrical System."

For purposes of laying out the Data Center, assume that PDUs will be used and set aside space for them. You can reclaim that floor space if you ultimately don't use PDUs. Power distribution units vary in size by model, based upon how many circuit breakers they contain. A typical size used in server environments is about 7 feet wide and 3 feet deep (2.1 meters wide and 91.4 centimeters deep). Circuit panel boards also vary in size, and can be either wall-mounted or free-standing units on the Data Center floor. If you opt for free-standing circuit panel boards, choose a model that is less than 24 inches (61 centimeters) wide. This lets you place the free-standing unit within a single floor tile location. The height of the panel board varies, again depending upon how many circuits it holds, but the depth is typically no more than about 8 inches (20.3 centimeters).

When placing PDUs, you must balance two factors. First, the closer a unit is located to the server cabinet locations it feeds, obviously the shorter its electrical conduits need to be. As with most Data Center infrastructure, shorter conduits are easier to route neatly and less expensive than longer ones. Second, PDUs generate electromagnetic interference and, even with shielding, shouldn't be placed within close proximity to servers or networking devices. While it is possible to place PDUs in the middle of the Data Center floor, locating them along a Data Center wall has the advantage of reducing how much floor space must be provided as a buffer around the unit. With the back edge of the PDU up against a wall, a buffer area need only be provided on three sides rather than four.

Circuit panel boards serve the same function as fully loaded PDUs but hold fewer circuits. With less electrical capacity running through them, they are also much less a source of electromagnetic interference. This enables you to place the panel boards much closer to servers and use shorter electrical conduits. If your Data Center is short on floor space, consider using wall-mounted panel boards because they are located off the floor altogether.

Air Handlers

Air handlers, the large cooling units that regulate temperatures in the Data Center, are typically installed along the walls at regular intervals to provide even cooling throughout the server environment. Although they can provide cooling anywhere in the room, it is best to place the air handlers perpendicular to your server rows. The structured data cabling and electrical conduits that are installed under the rows may inhibit airflow if the handlers are placed parallel to them.

Figure 4-4 shows potential locations for air handlers within a Data Center.

Air handler A is in the middle of the Data Center floor. Placing the unit here occupies floor space that might otherwise hold server cabinets.

Air handler B is against a Data Center wall. Although the placement is an improvement over the placement of Air handler A, the unit is parallel to the room's server rows and will therefore be less efficient at cooling.

Air handler C shows the preferred placement—against a wall, perpendicular to server rows.

Air handlers' physical dimensions vary from model to model, depending upon capacity. Some of the largest units traditionally used in a Data Center are 10 feet wide and just under 4 feet deep (about 3 meters wide and just under 1.2 meters deep).

An alternative design involves building a secure corridor on either side of the Data Center, placing the air handlers in them and providing pass-through areas under the raised floor and overhead for airflow. This enables maintenance workers to have access to the equipment without needing to enter the server environment. Such a configuration is uncommon, though, probably due to the extra building space that is needed for the corridors. The air handlers have the same footprint no matter where they are placed, but the corridor requires additional space for someone to walk around, which is already included in the Data Center through its aisles.

Figure 4-4 *Air Handler Placement Options*

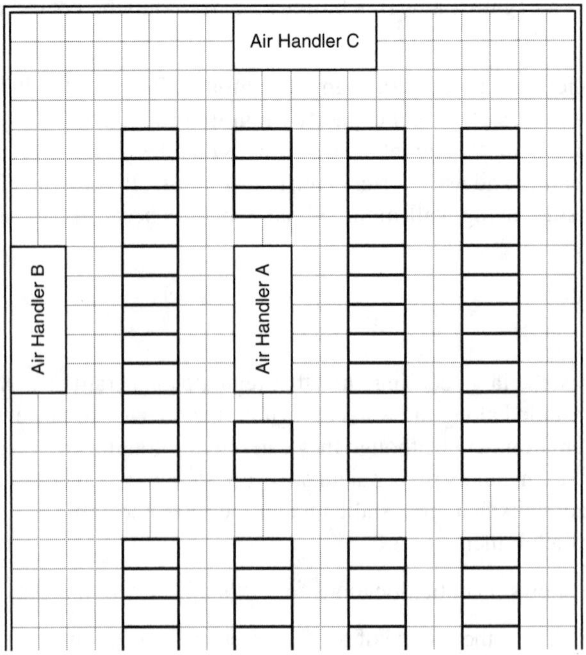

Chapter 8, "Keeping It Cool," provides more information about air handlers, including how to determine how many are needed to cool your Data Center.

Fire Suppression Tanks

If you have chosen to use it, also set aside space for the cylinders containing fire suppressant that is to be dispersed into the Data Center in the event of a fire. Their size, and therefore the area needed to house the cylinders, varies based upon how much and what type of suppressant they contain. The larger the Data Center space the fire suppression system must cover, the larger the cylinders are likely to be.

Ideally you want to place these tanks in a lockable closet outside of but immediately adjacent to the server environment. This keeps the cylinders protected and enables them to be serviced without maintenance workers having to enter the Data Center. If such space outside the room isn't available, create it inside. Although it is possible to install them in an empty corner of the Data Center, a lockable closet is again preferred. This prevents the storage tanks from being intentionally tampered with or accidentally disturbed.

A Data Center can contain fire suppression cylinders under the raised floor, but this is less desirable. The cylinders are more exposed to damage and can restrict airflow. More information about designing a Data Center fire suppression system is provided in Chapter 8.

Buffer Zones

When laying out Data Center objects, don't forget to provide necessary clearance areas. Power distribution units, air handlers, and storage closets all require enough space for doors and access panels to swing open. Building codes in many areas prohibit Data Center doors from opening outward into a main corridor, so clearances must be provided inside the room.

Because PDUs can be a source of electromagnetic interference, provide a clearance area of at least 4 feet (1.2 meters) around them. The units are shielded to block such emissions, but the shielding may need to be removed during maintenance or when taking power readings.

Air handlers normally require a buffer of 36 to 42 inches (91.4 to 106.7 centimeters) between them and the Data Center servers they cool. This cushion of space optimizes how cold air reaches cabinet locations in the room, preventing air from passing too quickly by cabinet locations or short-cycling by the air handler. Air handlers also require a buffer area of 8 to 10 feet (2.4 to 3 meters) to enable the periodic replacement of their main shaft.

Aisles

Perhaps surprisingly, the preponderance of floor space in most Data Centers isn't occupied by computing equipment, cabinets, or infrastructure components. It is made up of empty space that surrounds these items. Although devoid of costly equipment, aisles are a key part of your Data Center. Don't overlook the aisles when laying out the room and don't skimp on them when allocating floor space. Walkways that appear adequately sized on a map can often seem much smaller once you are in the constructed room. When designed properly, aisles enable people and equipment to move or be moved easily through your server environment and promote good air circulation. When planned poorly, these thoroughfares become the first trouble spots as a Data Center fills with servers.

So, how large do you make your Data Center aisles? Building codes in many regions require minimum walkways of 36 or 42 inches (91.4 or 106.7 centimeters). This is adequate for one person (internal doorways in private homes are smaller) but fairly narrow for maneuvering a pallet jack or oversized equipment through, especially because many aisles are between server rows where devices can protrude from their cabinets or cables can dangle and present a snagging hazard. If possible, set aside 4 feet (1.2 meters) for aisles between server rows and 5 feet (1.5 meters) or more for any major thoroughfares where you expect frequent equipment and people traffic.

If you're used to packing as much equipment in to a Data Center footprint as possible, large aisles might seem like a waste of space. Don't underestimate their value. A server environment with insufficient aisle space is more likely to have difficulty regulating temperature and hosting large equipment. And while it is relatively simple to add power or cabling to an operational Data Center that was not made robust enough in its original design, it is practically impossible to carve out additional space between server rows without incurring downtime. Even if your Data Center has to be a few hundred square feet (few dozen square meters) larger to accommodate larger aisles between rows, that does not add much to the overall cost of the room. It is the labor and materials cost associated with the infrastructure that are expensive, whether that infrastructure is placed in a smaller or larger room.

NOTE   Yes, you can get by with narrower aisles in your Data Center. I have worked in nearly a dozen tiny server environments that have tight corners and narrow spaces—some with barely 30 inches (76.2 centimeters) between cabinets and walls. There is no reason to design a server environment that way if you do not have to, though. Such rooms are difficult to maneuver through, cramped to work in, and usually have temperature problems.

Figure 4-5 illustrates the initial stage of a Data Center layout, in which a floor grid is drawn and major mechanical equipment, clearances, and aisles are placed strategically along the walls. Aisles and buffer zones are hatched, and areas that serve dual purposes are cross-hatched.

Note that, as shown in Figure 4-5, overlapping clearance spaces and aisles onto one another conserves Data Center floor space. Placing the PDUs near walls additionally reduces how much area must be reserved for their buffer space.

Figure 4-5 *Mechanical Equipment, Buffer Areas and Aisles*

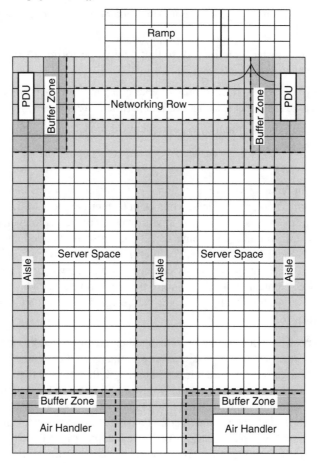

Equipment Rows

The final space to lay out is, ironically, the one most people probably think of first when discussing a Data Center—the equipment rows. These rows are where your company's servers and networking devices are installed and to which all of the room's other infrastructure systems ultimately connect. Electrical and data cabling run to these rows, air handlers blow cooled air at them, and the fire suppression provides coverage for them. The equipment that goes there is what the room is ultimately all about, so plan the space carefully.

Form Versus Function

A key influence on the layout of your Data Center is how you opt to physically arrange your servers, such as:

- Do you cluster them by task so that devices performing similar functions are together?

- Do you group them according to your company's internal organization so that machines associated with a given department are together?

- Do you organize them by type so identical models are together, creating so-called server farms?

All are valid approaches.

If you group your servers by function—either of the first two methods—or even if you do not particularly organize your Data Center devices at all, you generally end up with a heterogeneous mix of gear in your rows. This tends to even out the need for infrastructure over an area—some servers in a row might need a lot of connectivity, with others requiring very little. You therefore want to lay out your rows consistently across the Data Center, so that any cabinet location in any server row can accommodate incoming equipment. This may require the rows to be somewhat deeper to handle a variety of server footprints but makes the design of your Data Center uniform and straightforward.

If you choose to bunch similar servers together, be aware that this creates uneven demand for both infrastructure and physical space in the room. For example, if Row 1 consists entirely of large servers, it requires greater depth than Row 2 that contains only small servers. Row 2 may in turn need many more cabling ports, because it is hosting so many more devices in the same amount of floor space. This goes against the design principle of making your Data Center infrastructure consistent, so any server can be installed in any room location. If you plan to strictly organize incoming servers by type, you can customize sections of the Data Center—laying out rows to differing depths and even scaling infrastructure. This can maximize the use of floor space, structured cabling, and electrical circuits, but makes the room inflexible in the long run. You may eventually find yourself having to completely retrofit any specialized server rows as technology changes and new machines arrive with different demands.

NOTE   While it is possible to group identical servers together in your Data Center, I generally advise against organizing an entire room in this manner. It forces you to micromanage each server row, which is time consuming and doesn't work if you have a lot of Data Center floor space to support—whether in one large room or spread across several.

There is some value in creating specialized server rows in your Data Center but these should be done on a *very* limited basis, such as having a single oversized row to accommodate large servers or one with surplus data connections to handle high-demand equipment.

Of course, if your Data Center is dominated by just a few server models then grouping them together becomes your de facto standard. Server farms, where one model of server fills a section of a Data Center, have been around for many years. The newest configuration of these farms is termed composite hosts, where banks of servers are clustered, and their computing resources are allocated to various tasks as needed. The devices can pool their processing to serve the function of one large server or be distributed to act as separate machines.

Setting Row Dimensions

Knowing that your Data Center rows might have to accommodate equipment of various sizes and shapes, how large should you make them? The answer depends. In most cases, the majority of servers and networking devices in your Data Center are going to be installed into server cabinets that are one of a few dimensions common to the server industry—generally about 24 inches wide and anywhere from 30 to 48 inches deep (about 61 centimeters wide and 76 to 122 centimeters deep). Use these cabinet measurements as the basic building blocks for your rows, and then be sure that those devices can fit easily within your Data Center. To accommodate the deepest servers, set your row depth at 48 inches (122 centimeters).

For the width of your rows, decide how many cabinets you want each row to house and set aside the appropriate amount of space. Many Data Center infrastructure components—fiber housings, copper patch panels, multimedia faceplates—are grouped into multiples of 12. Clustering 12 or 24 server cabinets per row therefore leads to a matching number of infrastructure components. This avoids half-filled patch panels or fiber housings wasting valuable cabinet space that could otherwise hold additional servers.

Depending upon whether you want your Data Center's structured cabling to connect directly to each server cabinet location or to be distributed through a substation, you may need to include one or more cabinets in the server row to act as a networking substation.

Networking devices for a given server row are installed in a substation, and from here Data Center users can plug patch cords into a patching field to connect to individual server cabinet locations. Chapter 7, "Designing a Scalable Network Infrastructure," provides a full explanation of how these networking substations function and their value for a server environment. If you choose not to incorporate them into your design, you can reduce the width of the row accordingly.

NOTE	Building codes in many areas prohibit dead-end corridors that are more than a certain depth (the exact distance varies by region). The restriction is to prevent someone from being trapped in that space in the event of a fire. It is often applied to Data Center server rows, because most server cabinets are tall enough to be an effective interior wall in the room. If you choose to design long server rows into your Data Center, include periodic gaps to avoid creating a dead-end corridor.

When choosing the width and depth of your server rows, translate them into how many floor tiles they occupy—a server row 4 by 26 feet (122 centimeters by 7.9 meters), for example, would be 2 tiles deep by 13 wide. This makes it easier to lay out the Data Center, align cabinets along the floor, and discuss space allocation with anyone around the world without having to convert between measuring systems to understand one another.

Networking Rows

Not all of the cabinet locations within your Data Center are for servers. Some house networking equipment that enable your servers to communicate with one another. While it is feasible to distribute networking devices through your Data Center, it is more common to cluster the major devices together in their own row and then have servers throughout the room connect to them. As with the networking substations mentioned previously, Chapter 7 discusses the networking row in more detail.

At this point, just be aware that you need to include a networking row in the Data Center layout. Its depth and surrounding aisles are the same as for server rows. Because the networking row houses less equipment, it doesn't need to be as wide. If you have the available floor space, however, it is not a bad idea to match its width to that of the server rows. You can use any spare cabinet locations in the networking row to house those rare devices that do not fit in to the rest of your Data Center's organizational scheme, such as IP telephony switches.

Figure 4-6 illustrates the second stage of a Data Center layout, in which server and networking rows are positioned in the room. The H-like symbols at the end of each row are circuit panel boxes placed back to back.

Server cabinet locations are placed in parallel rows in Figure 4-6. The networking row is perpendicular to them in this design, but could alternatively be placed parallel to the server rows.

Figure 4-6   *Data Center Networking and Servers Rows*

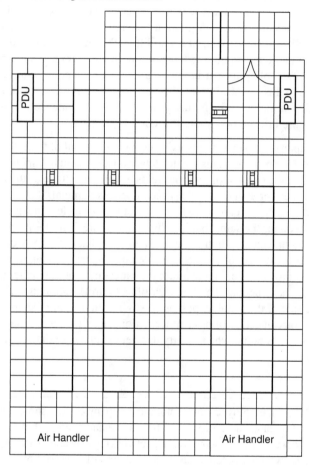

Orienting Rows

The final layout detail for your server rows is how to orient them. You want all devices within a row to face the same direction for simplicity and consistent organization. Orientation of the devices affects where users in the Data Center work on equipment as well as airflow patterns in the room.

One popular strategy is alternation of the direction of server rows, so that the backs of servers in one row face the backs of servers in an adjacent row. This locates all of the patch cords connecting to those devices in the same aisle while keeping the aisles on either side free of them. Because many servers and networking devices vent their exhaust out of their backside, this configuration can create distinct hot and cold areas in your Data Center. While this may sound like a problem, the practice of creating hot and cold aisles is a popular tactic for regulating temperature in a server environment. If you design your Data Center's cooling infrastructure to address such a configuration up front, there are advantages to this layout. In fact, this server row arrangement is the only one endorsed by the Telecommunications Industry Association for Data Center design. Chapter 8 provides more information about this cooling strategy.

A second approach to orienting server rows is to have all of them face a single direction, like books in a bookcase. This creates fewer concentrated hot spots than the alternating approach, but the exhaust of one row vents toward the intake of the row behind it, which makes the need for abundant aisle space in between crucial. It also cuts in half how many patch cords and power cables are located in any given aisle—the overall amount of cabling obviously remains the same, but it is distributed more. This additional physical separation, although minor, can help in the event of a mishap that potentially damages cabling in an aisle. The biggest asset of this design, though, is a purely intangible one. Having all Data Center server rows and equipment face the same direction is simpler and therefore easier to navigate for many people. Think of a gasoline (petrol) station in which the fuel nozzles are all on one side of the gasoline pumps versus a station where the nozzles are in different locations. You can get gasoline at either station, but at the second station there may be some guesswork or hesitation when you try to orient your car so that its gas cap is closest to the pump nozzle.

NOTE   In April 2003, an employee from a storage company caused some minor damage in a Data Center that I manage in San Jose, California. He had been pushing a wheeled cart, stacked high with backup tapes, past the room's networking row and drifted slightly off course. The cart snagged two fiber patch cords, stripping both of them out of the machine they were plugged into. The vendor heard a noise when the incident happened, but didn't see the actual damage, so he continued down the aisle. The device continued to function, although at a degraded ability until the cables were replaced. Fortunately, the vendor didn't catch any other cords.

While the orientation of server rows cannot entirely prevent such accidents, it can reduce their likelihood. Arrange server rows so that hanging patch cords or power cables (typically at the back of server cabinets) don't face high-traffic areas.

However you orient your server rows, be consistent throughout the Data Center. While there is no functional requirement that your equipment rows all be arranged the same, a uniform layout makes the room easier for users to understand and work in.

Weight Issues

In recent years, Data Centers have had to accommodate increasingly high structural loads. Data Center devices big and small have gotten heavier, putting greater strain on the rooms and buildings that house them. When designing your server environment, it is prudent to prepare for equipment that can weigh 1500 pounds (680.3 kg), 2000 pounds (907.2 kg), or even more, in a single cabinet location. (Even if your room doesn't have to support such massive equipment today, it may need to in the future.)

Lay out the room to have extra floor space, floor tile locations that are empty rather than housing equipment, around any server rows that run parallel to structural columns. These rows have the greatest weight-bearing ability and are prime locations to place your heaviest equipment. The additional unoccupied space enables them to support items with overly large footprints, which is helpful because big equipment is usually heavy as well. Even if the extra area is unoccupied, it serves a purpose—it lowers the overall weight on the Data Center floor, therefore enabling other nearby cabinet locations to support more.

NOTE   If there's any doubt about whether your Data Center floor can support a piece of incoming equipment, hire a structural engineer to evaluate the area. If a piece of equipment falls through a raised floor, it can damage not only Data Center infrastructure, the floor, and the device itself, but it can also pose a serious safety risk to anyone nearby—or below if the room is above the ground floor.

Seismic Mitigation

If your Data Center is in a region where earthquakes occur and you choose to install isolation platforms to mitigate their effect, increase the amount of space allocated for any server rows that they are installed in. This is to accommodate both the footprint of the platforms themselves, which are usually made to match the size of the server row they are installed in, and the additional range of motion they require to function properly during a quake. This movement is typically about 10 inches (25.4 centimeters) in every direction.

Dealing with Obstacles

Unfortunately, infrastructure components are not the only things you have to be concerned with when designing your Data Center. Like it or not, your server environment also unavoidably contains a variety of obstacles. Most are characteristics of the building you are in—oddly shaped floor spaces and support beams, for example. You want your Data Center to be as productive as possible, so your goal when laying out the room is to use obstacles to your benefit when you can and minimize their presence when you cannot.

Irregular Spaces

As much as you strive for a uniform shape for your Data Center, you may find that the room has some uneven walls or dead-end spaces. These can be created by adjacent rooms or immovable building infrastructure, for example. If your server environment does have irregular spaces, they are probably unsuitable for hosting servers. They may serve another function, however, and should not be forgotten when designing the Data Center.

If uneven walls create a recessed area, consider what can be placed there. Perhaps the recessed area is the right size to park a pallet jack that can be used to help someone move heavy servers. Maybe it can be occupied with replacement filters for the room's air handlers (stored in a fireproof container so as to not be fuel for a fire), spare server components to fix a malfunctioning machine, or pre-tested patch cords for server installations.

The point is, if you have an odd space, try to make it useful. Maximize every square foot (meter) of Data Center floor space. The entire infrastructure installed there, combined with the monthly cost to keep it cool, makes the room some of the most expensive real estate within your company's building. You don't want to waste any of it.

Structural Columns

Sometimes the space within a Data Center includes structural columns. The larger your server environment, the more columns it is likely to have. While columns provide necessary structural support for the building and even enable Data Center server rows closest to them to support greater weight loads, they are also an obstruction to positioning server cabinet locations. The columns obviously cannot be removed or relocated, so the goal is to mitigate their presence as much as possible.

If any columns are close to an edge of the Data Center, consider moving the wall so that those columns are embedded inside. It is easier to orient Data Center elements in relation to a consistent wall than to have to work around dead space created by the column, so it may be worth surrendering a small amount of floor space to eliminate the dead space. This option is only practical if the Data Center is still in design on paper and no walls have been constructed. Again, consider this only if a *small amount* of floor space must be sacrificed.

For columns located in the middle of the Data Center floor, design the external area of each column to be as small as possible—without sacrificing any of their structural strength, of course. Frame the outside of the column tightly around the internal beam. Then orient the Data Center floor grid so that each column overlaps as few tile locations as possible. Columns are usually identical in size and spaced at regular intervals through a building, so if one is aligned to fit within a single tile location, they all should fit.

Note that, in Figure 4-2, shown previously in this chapter, the structural column fits within the 24 by 24 inches (61 by 61 centimeters) of a single floor tile. This conserves available floor space and, by not overlapping additional panels, makes it easier to access the area under the floor.

Piping

Two Data Center infrastructure systems—cooling and fire suppression—include associated piping that must reside in your room. As you lay out your server environment, route this piping to be as unobtrusive as possible. Tuck the chilled water pipes that flow to and from the room's air handlers close to the units themselves, making sure that the access panel on the handlers opens on the side opposite the pipes. Place water feeds for the sprinkler system outside of the Data Center or, if inside, in a rarely trafficked corner of the room or perhaps in a dead space against a structural column.

Placing the pipes in such areas is intended to safeguard them from accidental damage as well as keep them from occupying significant Data Center floor space. It is also a good idea to insulate the pipes or, even better, construct a solid frame around them with an access panel to reach their controls. Don't forget to account for the larger footprint of the framing when you lay out the pipes in the room.

Avoid having any piping in your Data Center that is not directly associated with the room. Every pipe is a potential risk to leak moisture, so you want as few as possible in the environment.

System Controls

Place the controls for key Data Center infrastructure immediately inside the main entrance(s) to the room. These include controls to cut off electrical power in an emergency, controls to manually deploy or abort the fire suppression system, and even switches for the room's overhead lights. Cluster the controls and install them at a convenient height to make them easy to locate and use. Installing controls 44 inches (112 centimeters) above the surface of the floor is common and enables most people to reach them from either a standing or seated position.

Chapters 6, 8, and 11 provide more information about what specific types of controls to install—push-buttons, pop-up buttons, levers, switches, and so on—and how to label them.

Telephones

Distribute telephones liberally throughout the Data Center, particularly near the infrastructure controls. Wall-mount them in strategic locations so that someone standing in front of practically any server, networking device, or infrastructure component can make a phone call. This enables Data Center users to contact the appropriate support group or vendor for assistance without having to walk away from the item that needs to be fixed. To further facilitate this, install long cords—say, 25 feet (7.6 meters)—between the handset and receiver of each telephone and make sure that the phones are configured to call external numbers. As with the infrastructure controls, wall-mount the telephones at a convenient height.

NOTE   Your company might use a Voice over Internet Protocol (VoIP) telephone system at your
Data Center site to take advantage of the lower costs and additional features it provides. If
you install a VoIP phone system in your Data Center, I recommend also installing a single
analog phone line in the room for redundancy. In the event an outage occurs and affects
the network that your VoIP equipment is connected to, you can still place calls via this
phone line. If nothing else, this line can be helpful while troubleshooting the networking
outage itself. Cellular phones can obviously function during an outage as well, but there is
no guarantee of someone in the Data Center having one with them at the time. The cluster
of system controls near the Data Center's primary entrance can have more influence on your
servers than any other single infrastructure component—pushing one button can power off
the entire room—so locate the redundant phone close to these system controls.

Figure 4-7 shows placement of the Data Center's infrastructure controls and telephones.
Triangles represent telephones, the letter P stands for emergency power off (EPO) controls,
and the letter F represents fire suppression controls.

Figure 4-7   *Placement of Infrastructure System Controls*

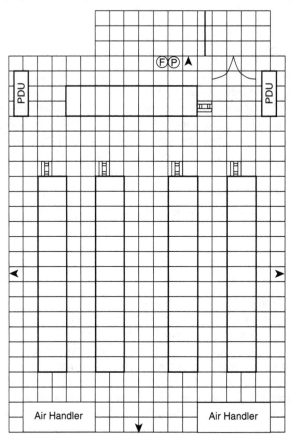

Common Problems

Even with seemingly clear instructions and a detailed map of the room, mistakes can and do happen when laying out a Data Center. Some are caused by the room's designer, who fails to specify the placement of an item or doesn't anticipate how some objects in a server room can conflict with one another. Others occur when a contractor misinterprets or simply fails to follow the Data Center design package. The sections that follow describe some common layout-related mistakes to avoid.

The Floor Grid Is Positioned Incorrectly

Misaligning, by just a few inches (centimeters), the Data Center's raised floor from what is shown on the map is a subtle problem with large consequences. Not usually noticed until the entire raised floor and other major infrastructure are installed, this error causes all objects in the room to drift from their originally intended locations. Buffer areas in the room are likely affected, possibly causing server cabinet locations to be sacrificed to recreate mandatory clearances.

Infrastructure Items Are Installed Backwards

Clearly mark on your Data Center design map in which direction you want objects in the room to face. Pay special attention to items that at first glance appear the same from more than one side. For example, certain air handlers can be ordered with service panels on either their right or left side, enabling you to customize the device according to where you plan to locate it in the Data Center. The different models are mirror images of one another and can appear very similar to anyone who doesn't specifically check for the panel location. If you intentionally order an air handler with an access panel on a given side, say with a right-sided access panel so that the unit can be placed with its left side close to a Data Center wall, make sure the installers put the correct handler in that location.

NOTE   In various Data Center projects over the years, I have had stationary cabinets for networking equipment bolted to the floor upside down, facing the wrong direction, and even with temporary wheels still attached, all because contractors couldn't tell the difference between front to back or top to bottom of the cabinet, and I neglected to spell it out clearly and repeatedly in the design package.

In one instance in early 2000, a cabling contractor placed a row of 13 networking cabinets backwards and terminated 1500 fiber and copper connections into them before the mistake was discovered. To be fair, the mistake was not solely his fault. He had asked a company employee who was based at the Raleigh, North Carolina, site about the positioning, and that person suggested an orientation for the row rather than pointing the contractor to me. Truly remediating the problem would have required rotating the entire row—as a unit—180 degrees and relocating all structured cabling that terminated there. Cabling would have to have been swapped so that cable runs would go to their original destinations. This would have meant rerouting cables from the first cabinet to the thirteenth, the second to the twelfth, the third to the tenth, and so on—and then repeating the process on the opposite end. Unfortunately, none of the cable runs included much slack, certainly not enough to be relocated by several cabinet locations. The only way to terminate cables into their correct positions would have been to run completely new structured cabling—a sizable undertaking for a Data Center nearly 8000 square feet (743.2 square meters) in size.

Rather than arguing over the mistake and potentially delaying the project, we reached a compromise. The cabinets in the row were individually turned around and, although the cables were reterminated to face the opposite (correct) direction, they stayed in the same cabinet. This created a functional networking row, albeit one that is a mirror image of those in all other Data Centers I manage.

Floor Space Between Rows Is Too Narrow

This layout oversight occurs in the design phase and may not become apparent for a year or more after the Data Center is constructed. It is tempting to try to maximize floor space by allocating the smallest space possible between servers rows. If you do, the room's layout is likely to seem fine until equipment is ordered that is oddly shaped or larger than expected. Then you are forced to install the oversized gear in existing rows, wasting infrastructure (and the money it cost to have it installed) as non-standard machines hog two or more cabinet locations in your Data Center. Never forget that the room must accommodate not only servers you know are coming in the next few months, but also those you don't know about that are to arrive over the next few years. No one has a crystal ball, but you can safely predict that the smaller the space between the rows in your Data Center, the less ability the room has to accommodate future equipment.

Infrastructure Items Are Uncoordinated or Misplaced

With dozens of contractors from several different trades working simultaneously to build your Data Center, it takes careful attention to synchronize the work so that the end result is an integrated whole and not merely a hodgepodge of infrastructure. For instance, your Data Center map may show fire system controls, electrical system controls, light switches, and a telephone clustered near the room's main entrance. Unless your design package is *extremely* detailed, their exact placement on the appropriate Data Center wall is likely to be decided by nothing more premeditated than which individual contractor—the one working on the fire suppression, power, lights, or telephone—finishes his or her wiring job first. While this may work out fine, sometimes the results are chaotic. An access panel for one control system may open atop the controls for another, or light switches may be placed so close to unprotected push buttons that someone reaching for one could accidentally activate the other.

The lesson here is that anything your design package doesn't spell out clearly and repeatedly is subject to misinterpretation.

NOTE	In December 2000, I helped convert a 392 square-foot (36.4 square-meter) conference room in West Columbia, South Carolina, into a small server environment. My tight design shoehorned two rows of 10 cabinets into the room and required careful placement of infrastructure for everything to fit. When the cabling contractor went to install raceways to route data cabling overhead, he discovered that the electrician had already installed ceiling lights where they were to go—directly above the cabinet locations. He therefore installed the raceways about 18 inches (45.7 centimeters) to the side. This meant that patch cords could not exit each server cabinet directly upward to connect with data ports overhead, as I had designed. They instead would connect at an angle, sagging and presenting a risk of being accidentally pulled out. With servers sitting in the hall awaiting installation, there was no time to properly fix the error. The only option was to rotate each server cabinet so that their backsides were as close to underneath the off-kilter data ports as possible. Essentially, all servers in the room had to be installed backwards until the room was eventually decommissioned in mid-2004.

In another project in October 2000, an electrical contractor placed the light switches for a new Milpitas, California, Data Center at the top of the entrance ramp, 25 feet (7.6 meters deep) into the room. All but a few of the Data Center's lights are shut off at night to conserve energy. This means that whoever first enters the server environment for the day has to walk several steps to reach the light switches. The last Data Center user leaving for the night faces the reverse situation, having to take their final steps to the exit in dim lighting.

The wiring is routed through a very sturdy fire-resistant wall, so it was decided not to go through the effort to relocate the switches. While not affecting the operation of the Data Center, it is a minor inconvenience that irks me every time I enter the room because it was completely avoidable. I just hadn't bothered to specify the location of the light switches in past design packages because previous contractors had always placed them immediately inside the Data Center door.

Summary

It is important to create clear, detailed instructions for the physical layout of your Data Center to ensure that the room is built accurately. A detailed map can be a powerful tool for this purpose, whether you use pen and paper or drawing software.

Begin the layout process by drawing a grid over a map of the room. It is a guide for placing objects and represents the Data Center's raised floor tiles. Place Data Center objects—mechanical equipment, server rows, structural columns, and so on—so that they align evenly with this grid. This enables easy access to under-floor infrastructure around these items.

Some layouts coordinate Data Center infrastructure better than others. When possible, use floor space for multiple purposes—as a walkway for people, buffer zone for electrical equipment, and space to open an access panel, for example — to maximize space. Place commonly used infrastructure items close to where they are most often needed and those that are rarely used or vulnerable in less-traveled corners.

Lay out pieces of mechanical equipment in the Data Center first, because they are fundamental to the operation of the room and are usually the largest single objects. Circuit breakers are housed in large power distribution units (PDUs) and circuit panel boards — place PDUs against the Data Center walls and circuit panel boards close to where servers are to be located. Place air handlers along the wall as well, perpendicular to server rows. Locate fire suppression cylinders in a lockable closet adjacent to the Data Center. Provide clearance areas around PDUs to guard against electromagnetic interference and around air handlers to optimize their ability to cool servers.

Be generous with aisle space. Wide aisles enable easy movement of people and equipment and help keep the Data Center cool. Narrow aisles are choke points, making a server environment difficult to work in and incapable of hosting large equipment.

How you group the servers in your Data Center — either by form or function — affects the design of your server rows. Arranging them by department or task leads to a mix of equipment, lessening demand for infrastructure in any single server row. Clustering identical servers spawns uneven demand across the Data Center, requiring customized infrastructure and micromanaging of server cabinet locations. If your Data Center hosts servers that require more than the room's standard infrastructure, create a small number of specialized rows to address their needs.

Size your server rows to be two floor tiles deep and as many tiles wide as you want server cabinets in a row. Consider increments of 12, because Data Center infrastructure components often come in groups of 12. If your server rows are to include a network substation to house networking devices, allow for their width as well.

There are two common patterns for orienting server rows:

- Having every other row alternate directions
- Having them all face the same way

Alternating directions locates server cabling together and creates hot and cold areas in the room, which can be incorporated into an overall cooling plan. Facing rows in the same direction is straightforward for users and more evenly distributes cabling and temperature.

Data Center weight loads have been gradually increasing over time, and there's no sign of this trend stopping. Design your room to accommodate 1500 pounds (680.28 kg), 2000 pounds (907.18 kg), or more per cabinet location. Also design extra floor space around any server rows that run parallel to structural columns, because these areas can support greater weight loads.

Most Data Center spaces include obstacles of some sort that must be designed around. Look for creative ways to incorporate irregular floor spaces into your layout, such as storing non-flammable supplies in those areas. Frame tightly around structural columns to reduce how much floor space they occupy. Place piping for the air conditioning and sprinklers system in lightly traveled areas, either against an air handler or in a remote corner, to safeguard them and reduce their influence on the room's floor space.

Cluster electrical shutoff controls, fire suppression system controls, and light switches inside major Data Center entrances. Make them easy to find and at a convenient height to use in an emergency. Scatter telephones throughout the room so it is possible to place a call while standing in front of any Data Center server or infrastructure equipment.

Anything your design package doesn't spell out clearly and repeatedly is subject to misinterpretation. Common layout-related problems that can occur include misalignment of the Data Center's floor grid, installation of infrastructure components backwards or upside down, inadequately designed space between server rows, and a failure to integrate infrastructure components that are competing for wall space in the room.

CHAPTER 5

Overhead or Under-Floor Installation?

This chapter outlines the benefits and drawbacks of running power, data connections, and cooling into the Data Center by way of the ceiling versus installing a raised floor system and routing it underneath. The chapter details the components involved and offers sample illustrations for both overhead and under-floor systems as well as provides common problems to watch for and avoid.

Overhead Installation

In an overhead installation, structured cabling and electrical conduits are typically routed above the Data Center's false or suspended ceiling and then terminated directly above the room's server rows. Cooling is channeled above the false ceiling as well, then directed to the server environment below by way of adjustable vents.

The primary advantage of locating infrastructure overhead is that it enables you to forego a raised floor system for your server environment. Overhead installation is therefore less expensive, occupies less floor space, and fits more conveniently in shorter building spaces. Cable trays, ladder racks, and raceways are less expensive than a complete raised floor system, contributing to the cost savings. Less floor space is needed for an overhead installation because there is no entrance ramp, which—depending upon the height of the floor and how steeply the ramp is angled—can have a footprint of more than 200 square feet (18.6 square meters). This also provides some cost savings. Because likely there already has to be a pocket of space above the Data Center's suspended ceiling to accommodate wiring for the overhead lights and piping for sprinklers, any electrical and data cabling needed for the Data Center can be included in the overhead area as well. Elimination of a raised floor also does away with space required for the subfloor.

Be aware that installing infrastructure overhead and forgoing a raised floor does present a greater challenge for circulating air within the Data Center. Raised floor server environments are typically cooled by drawing warm air away through overhead ducted returns while blowing cold air under the floor. This process leverages the natural behavior of hot air to rise. It is significantly more difficult to cool a server environment by pushing cold air downward. Other effects of routing infrastructure overhead are mixed. Patching power cords and data cabling atop cabinet locations rather than below reduces the chances of someone snagging or damaging the cords as he or she walk by, with or without a pallet jack of equipment in tow. Data Center users must climb a stepladder to plug in to the room's infrastructure, however, which is potentially unstable and arguably more likely to trigger an accidental disconnect.

There is also a possibility of a power cable or patch cord coming unplugged due to gravity and the weight of the cord. If you choose to use an overhead system, mitigate this risk by using twist-lock power receptacles on your electrical outlets and corresponding plugs on your server cabinet power strips. Twist-lock electrical components require you to insert and then rotate an incoming power plug clockwise to lock it into position within the receptacle. Once in place the plug can't be pulled directly outward. It must first be rotated counter-clockwise. Likewise, make sure that the patch cords used in your server environment have unbroken tabs and, preferably, some form of support ladder to lessen the strain on their connectors. The patch cords should click firmly into place when inserted in an infrastructure port or server. This makes accidental disconnects less likely to occur.

Under-Floor Installation

In an under-floor installation, a system of horizontal and vertical bars is mounted on the Data Center's true floor, creating an elevated grid in which flat panels are placed. This creates a raised floor surface, under which structured cabling, electrical conduits, and cooled air may be routed. Sprinkler piping and leak detection infrastructure might be located here as well.

Structured cabling and electrical infrastructure typically terminates in the subfloor below each server cabinet location in multimedia data boxes and power receptacles that are either free-standing or incorporated into raceways under the Data Center server rows. Alternatively, infrastructure can be routed through pre-made openings in the raised floor and terminate into patch panels and power receptacles that are installed within the Data Center cabinets. Cooling is directed into the server environment above by the placement of solid and perforated floor tiles.

Most Data Centers are built with a raised floor system. Despite the additional cost, a raised floor provides several benefits for a server environment:

- The raised floor creates a dedicated space to channel cooled air through. By strategically placing perforated or grated floor tiles, you focus and direct this cooling wherever it is needed in a server environment. There is no equivalent mechanism for controlling airflow in an overhead system. While it is possible to install multiple air vents overhead and adjust how far they are open or shut, they can't direct air in the same pinpoint manner that floor tiles can.

- Routing infrastructure under a raised floor keeps hundreds or thousands of associated patch cords and power cables out of sight, which makes them less susceptible to damage or being unplugged accidentally. The absence of cabling or raceways in the

Data Center's common area also gives the room a more professional and less cluttered appearance.

- Although infrastructure is out of sight, it remains easily accessible under the floor, much more so than when located above Data Center server cabinets.

NOTE   The needs of your particular Data Center are going to determine whether it is worth the price and physical space necessary for installation of a raised floor system. When I design a server environment, I let its size drive whether to run infrastructure overhead or under floor.

- **If the Data Center is small**—In round numbers, generally less than 1000 square feet (100 square meters)—or is being constructed in a building that has limited space from floor to ceiling, I design it with overhead infrastructure. The ramp needed for a raised floor and the height it occupies simply take up too much space in such a small room.

- **If the Data Center is larger**—I design it with a raised floor and place its various infrastructure down below. I find the raised floor system essential for controlling airflow and neatly routing infrastructure. I've also learned that it is much simpler to lift a floor tile and plug in to or disconnect from infrastructure components than to climb a stepladder and stretch above a server cabinet to make connections.

Separation of Power and Data

No matter where you choose to route structured data cabling and electrical conduits in your Data Center, provide physical separation between the two. Electrical wiring can generate enough electromagnetic interference (EMI) to distort the information transmitted along nearby data cabling. Mixing power and data in a common bundle or within a single raceway can also be problematic if either infrastructure needs servicing. A vendor working on one faces the risk of disturbing or damaging the other.

Exactly how much separation to have between data cabling and electrical conduits, or between data cabling and any power source for that matter, is a gray area. No firm industry standards exist, although many cabling vendors or Data Center design consultants can recommend minimum distances.

Three factors contribute to how powerfully electromagnetic interference affects data cabling and therefore the amount of physical separation needed—the strength of the interference, whether the data cabling is unshielded or shielded, and whether cabling is encased in a raceway (typically metal or plastic).

Tables 5-1 and 5-2 show suggested minimum separation distances between data cabling and power sources. The distances, which are rounded off rather than straight conversions between measuring systems, are recommended by The Siemon Company.

Table 5-1   *Recommended Minimum Separation for Unshielded Twisted Pair (UTP) Cabling*

Power Level	Spaces	Pathways
Less than 3 kva	2 in. (50 mm.)	2 in. (50 mm.)
3–6 kva	10 ft. (3 m.)	5 ft. (1.5 m.)
6 kva or more	20 ft. (6 m.)	10 ft. (3 m.)

Table 5-2   *Recommended Minimum Separation for Shielded Twisted Pair (STP) Cabling*

Power Level	Spaces	Pathways
Less than 3 kva	0 in. (0 mm.)	0 in. (0 mm.)
3–6 kva	2 ft. (.6 m.)	2 ft. (.6 m.)
6 kva or more	3 ft. (1 m.)	3 ft. (1 m.)

While the characteristics of structured cabling are discussed in detail in Chapter 7, "Designing a Scalable Network Infrastructure," it is important to understand the difference between UTP and STP cabling.

Unshielded twisted pair cabling contains multiple pairs of twisted copper conductors, which are gathered in a single sheath (typically four pairs for data communication). Each wire is surrounded by plastic insulation. Shielded twisted pair cabling is similarly constructed, but also contains a metallic foil or braid around each pair of wires. As the STP cable's name suggests—and as the preceding tables bear out—this metal shields the cable from electromagnetic interference.

Despite the greater interference protection of STP cabling, most Data Centers use UTP cabling because it is less expensive and easier to install—two significant issues because server environments usually involve large quantities of structured cabling. If you are particularly concerned about the nearness of your data cabling and electrical conduits, you may wonder whether to run one form of infrastructure overhead and the other below a raised floor—all data connections above each server cabinet location while all electrical conduits within the subfloor, or vice versa. It is certainly possible to do so, but such arrangements essentially provide the disadvantages of each system—the clutter and difficulty of reaching overhead infrastructure along with the cost and additional height requirements of a raised floor—without any particular advantage. Moreover, it is unnecessary. Merely running electrical conduits and structured data cabling several inches (centimeters) apart provides sufficient separation to prevent signal interference.

For an overhead installation, you can run the two types of infrastructure in separate channels and then terminate them in parallel raceways over server cabinets to permit easy access to both. Keep data cabling not just away from the electrical conduits but also from the Data Center's overhead lights, which are sources of interference as well.

NOTE	Fluorescent lights in particular are known to generate electromagnetic interference. Because copper cabling is vulnerable to such interference, keep it at least 5 inches (12.7 centimeters) away from fluorescent light fixtures. More information about structured cabling and interference is provided in Chapter 7.

For an under-floor installation, you don't even need the channels, although many companies opt to use some sort of tray system to route infrastructure—just place the electrical conduits and structured cabling so they don't follow identical paths. You can locate data cabling directly below server cabinet locations and place electrical conduits one floor tile space behind, for instance. Orient whatever multimedia boxes and power receptacles they terminate within so that they face toward one another. As with the overhead scenario, data and power are separate from one another but still within reach.

Plenum and Non-Plenum Spaces

In most regions, building codes permit only specially rated cables to be used in the plenum—those pockets of space used for air distribution in your server environment. These are normally the cavities above the false ceiling or below the raised floor. The codes are intended to reduce the chances or effects of a fire, because once a blaze reaches these spaces, there is little to stop its smoke and flames from spreading rapidly. Because plenum space is more vulnerable to fire, stricter standards are applied to its cabling.

While these regulations don't directly affect your decision of whether to run infrastructure above the ceiling or below the floor, be aware of what types of cables you must use when routing them through different Data Center spaces. Three types of cabling are typically used in server environments:

- **Non-plenum/riser-rated**—These cables are used in general purpose cabling installations. They are very flexible and the least expensive of the three types. In a server environment, non-plenum cables are usually enabled for use in the main area of the room—below the ceiling or above the raised floor. Non-plenum cables are often made of polyvinyl chloride, or PVC, and if they catch fire produce toxic smoke.

- **Plenum**—As indicated by their name, these cables are intended for use in air distribution spaces. Plenum cables emit less toxic smoke when burned than non-plenum cables. They are preferred for use in the United States, but prohibited in many European countries.

- **Low smoke/zero halogen**—These are preferred for use in Europe, but restricted for use in the United States. They produce little toxic smoke in a fire.

These classifications apply to both structured cabling and to patch cords. Plenum and low smoke/zero halogen cables fall into the same general category of cabling, but because each has different properties, one type of cable cannot be directly substituted for one another. Their usage or prohibition in different parts of the world are based upon how local countries measure toxicity. Specify in your design package the appropriate cabling type to be used in your Data Center's air distribution spaces—plenum or low smoke/zero halogen—based upon regional building codes.

In specific situations, you may be able to reduce costs by strategically using non-plenum cables, which are less expensive, in chosen locations. If you route structured cabling in a cable tray or ladder system above the server rows but below the ceiling plenum, for example, it is probably permissible to use non-plenum cabling. You can also use non-plenum patch cords for connections that don't go above the Data Center ceiling or below its raised floor, such as direct connections from a server to peripheral equipment within the same cabinet.

Such scenarios should be attempted sparingly, however. They require you to micromanage how patch cords are used to ensure that non-plenum cables are not routed where they are not enabled and that more expensive plenum or low smoke/zero halogen cables are not wasted in Data Center locations where they don't need to be. In a large server environment, the cost savings probably are not worth the logistical challenges. It might be worth attempting in a small Data Center, perhaps one with one or two server rows, or in one that is intended to be temporary.

NOTE   When you install plenum-rated or low smoke/zero halogen structured cabling in your Data Center plenum, make sure that other supporting components used in your cabling infrastructure, such as cable ties or patch cords, are similarly rated. They, too, can be a source of toxic fumes if burned.

The regional fire marshal is usually the ultimate authority over what type of cabling can be used in an installation. In some instances, they may require the use of plenum cabling in a space typically considered a non-plenum environment. This most often occurs in schools, but be aware that it might happen to your Data Center project as well.

Ceiling Components

There are several elements involved in an overhead infrastructure system. Structured cabling and electrical conduits are typically installed above a Data Center ceiling, supported and routed by cable trays or ladder racks. Cable tray is a shallow basket made of crossed metal bars. Ladder rack is a narrow ladder frame that is also made of metal and installed horizontally. Both items are secured by brackets to the Data Center's true ceiling and configured along whatever paths you want your infrastructure to follow. Electrical conduits and data cabling are then placed atop them. Cable trays and ladder racks have gaps between their metal bars, enabling air to flow through wherever cords and cables aren't gathered together to restrict it.

The data ports and power receptacles that the infrastructure terminates into are normally housed in metal raceways that are secured to the ceiling and suspended overhead. The raceways help organize the infrastructure, enabling it to be clustered above each server cabinet location. An alternate approach is secured vertical posts through the ceiling above each cabinet location and individual power outlets and data faceplates mounted directly to those. This practice is more commonly done in lab environments.

Be aware that fire codes in many regions require an 18- or 19.7-inch (45.7- or 50-centimeter) gap between automatic sprinkler heads, most often installed in the suspended ceiling, and any solid or opaque objects. In a Data Center, the fire codes generally apply to raceways or ladder racks filled with cables, server cabinets, infrastructure equipment, or boxes. Make sure that your cable management components are installed to provide sufficient clearance. Don't place them too low, however, as you want to be able to reposition server cabinets in the room without worrying about jostling any overhead raceways.

NOTE	Many of the Data Centers I manage possess four-post server cabinets that are open at the top, bottom, and sides, rather than solid. (This style of cabinet is shown in all of the figures in this chapter.) Inspectors in some cities have enabled these cabinets to intrude slightly into the clearance area, ruling that they only present an opaque surface at the highest point at which a server can be installed in them, which is a few inches (several centimeters) below their open top. While I don't recommend trying to hedge any codes, if you are designing a server environment in a building with limited ceiling heights, you may want to request clarification from local inspectors about how close open-top cabinets may come to the ceiling. Using them in your Data Center might enable you to gain a little more space.

You might be tempted to terminate data ports and power receptacles directly into the ceiling tiles, mounting them flush above the server cabinet locations and skipping the use of raceways. While faceplates installed in this manner typically must be secured to the overhead ceiling deck, to keep weight off the tiles, this configuration still causes patch cords to constantly pull on the termination points for the structured cabling. With no strain relief, the weight of the cords can damage this cabling over time. Mounting infrastructure against the ceiling also shifts the location of the data ports and power receptacles higher above the server cabinets. This makes it harder to reach and plug in to the infrastructure and requires longer patch cords and electrical cords.

Figures 5-1 and 5-2 show a sample termination of power and data cabling into back-to-back raceways, above a Data Center's server cabinet locations.

Figure 5-1   *Overhead Termination Example—Front View*

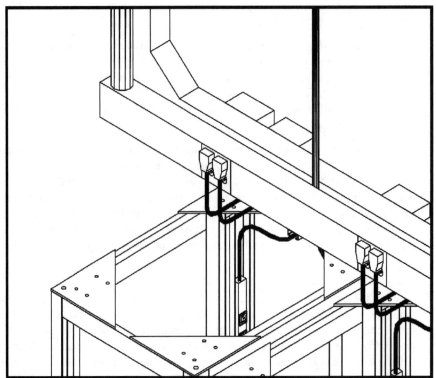

Note that the front of the server cabinets faces the same direction as the electrical outlets overhead, while the back of the cabinets faces the same way as the data ports. Orienting the raceways so that the data ports appear above the back of the server cabinet locations enables patch cords to directly connect to them from the back of any servers installed within a cabinet. Unfortunately, the electrical cords for the cabinet's power strips can't connect to the overhead power outlets without first being threaded through to the front side of the cabinet. This is admittedly awkward. It is an inescapable fact of having overhead infrastructure that Data Center users have to plug in most patch cords and even some power cables well above their heads—usually at least 8 feet (2.4 meters) off the ground. That means repeatedly climbing a stepladder. It is fairly straightforward to make connections when cabling runs directly up the back side of the cabinet to the raceway on the same side, but much more challenging when you have to reach around to the raceway that faces front.

Because power and data must be separated, this awkward routing is nearly unavoidable. Reversing the position of the raceways would enable the server cabinet power strips to plug in easily but then require the patch cords to be on the opposite side of the raceway with the data ports. Because there are usually more patch cords that exit a server cabinet location than electrical cords, thanks to the presence of cabinet power strips, this is an even less convenient setup.

Figure 5-2   *Overhead Termination Example—Back View*

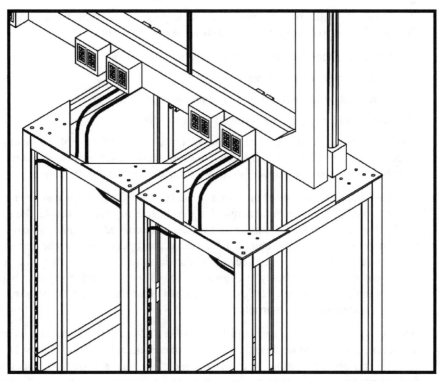

One solution would be to redesign the server cabinets or change the orientation of how devices are installed into them, so that the power and data cabling exit on opposite ends of the cabinet—front and back—just as they appear on the overhead raceways. This is a not a standard configuration, however, and would need to be examined closely to make sure that installed servers could still easily plug in to the cabinet power strips.

Raised Floor Components

If you choose to use a raised floor system in your Data Center, there are several elements that you must specify as part of its design. These include:

- Floor height
- Mechanisms for bringing in equipment
- Weight-bearing capacity
- Types and numbers of floor tiles
- Instructions for terminating infrastructure
- Other subfloor details

Floor Height

Data Center raised floors vary significantly in height from one facility to another. The ideal elevation for your particular floor depends upon several factors:

- Size and shape of the server environment
- How much equipment it contains
- How much cold air you want to channel in to the space
- How much infrastructure is routed under the floor

Except for that last detail, all of the factors are tied directly to the use of the under-floor area for cooling. Once the floor is tall enough to clear whatever infrastructure you route along the subfloor, the rest of the space is really only necessary for air circulation.

So, what's the ideal floor height for your particular Data Center? You can pay a cooling engineer to calculate an optimal height, but the general principle is simple: the greater the height of your raised floor, the more air that can be circulated through that space. A taller raised floor means that more chilled air can collect and pass through. The greater the volume of chilled air, the more effect it has when it is then channeled above the floor. Also, air obviously flows more freely through a 24-inch (61 centimeter) cavity than one half the size, especially if there are electrical conduits, structured cabling, or other items running through the area that act as barriers.

While every server environment is different, 18- and 24-inch (45.7 and 61 centimeter) raised floors are very common and may be considered default heights for most Data Center designs. This distance enables an ample volume of air to pass through the plenum, even with a large amount of infrastructure routed through the space, but isn't so deep that someone lifting a floor tile cannot easily reach the subfloor. This is helpful for contractors installing infrastructure under the raised floor and for Data Center users who later use that infrastructure.

NOTE   In late 1998, I refurbished a server environment in Dallas, Texas. The pre-existing room was about 850 square feet (79 square meters). It had a raised floor, but only in the most generous use of the term. The floor was just 4 inches (10.2 centimeters) high, barely tall enough to route infrastructure under the floor. Power cables from server cabinet power strips had to be carefully threaded so as to not bend too sharply when plugged into under-floor receptacles. These outlets often tipped on to their sides after a floor tile was removed, and it was impossible to replace the panel without first rotating the receptacle upright again and carefully tucking power cables out of harm's way. The plenum was considered too small to channel cooling through, so the server environment's air handlers were configured to circulate air above the ceiling. Fortunately, this room was a temporary space. Within 18 months, all of its servers and networking devices were relocated to a more properly designed Data Center.

I used the under-floor space because it was there, but in my opinion such a small raised floor is useless. Putting any infrastructure under such a short floor inhibits airflow, and connecting to under-floor data ports or power receptacles is awkward and tedious and has the potential to damage patch cords or power cables. Even without placing any infrastructure in that space, I'm skeptical that the under-floor air volume can effectively cool even a moderately sized Data Center. If you are not going to have a raised floor that is at least 12 inches (30.5 centimeters) high, I say don't bother having one at all. A small raised floor might make your server environment look neater, but it is not worth the price tag and other drawbacks that come with it.

If you have the building space to spare and you want vendors to work on under-floor infrastructure without actually entering your Data Center space, you may consider a *very* tall raised floor—high enough for workers to stand upright and install, remove, or test structured cabling or electrical conduits. For this design, cable trays or some other management systems are needed to elevate the infrastructure so that it is within easy reach from the top of the raised floor as well as from the work area. Lighting is also necessary for this space, so that workers are not forced to rely on flashlights or other portable light sources. As with the innovative idea of installing air handlers in a secure corridor adjacent to the Data Center, mentioned in Chapter 4, "Laying Out the Data Center," this is a commendable design idea that is only rarely implemented due to the additional space and money it requires.

Even if you don't make your raised floor tall enough to walk in to, be aware that as the height of your raised floor increases additional air handlers may be needed to cool and circulate the increased volume of air.

In conjunction with calculations about the height of the raised floor, you must choose whether the top surface of your Data Center floor is to be elevated or at the same level as other (non-raised) floors in the building. The simplest and therefore most common option is having the raised-floor height elevated. This enables the bottom level of the floor—the concrete—to be one consistent level throughout the building. It requires the use of a lift or ramp to bring equipment onto the Data Center, however.

The second option, making the *top* of the raised floor flush with other floor surfaces, requires the Data Center subfloor to be set into the ground. In this configuration, what is normally called the height of the raised floor becomes its depth. The more space needed for the subfloor, the deeper the cavity below the surface this space must be. Constructing a sunken Data Center floor in this manner is more expensive, but does provide certain advantages.

A major benefit from this arrangement is that no ramps or lifts are needed to transport equipment into the Data Center. The floor surface never changes elevation between the Data Center and adjoining rooms or corridors, so items can be rolled in or out of the room without assistance. Eliminating these mechanisms from a Data Center conserves floor space and adds convenience for users. Materials and equipment can be brought in to the room from multiple access points—any door that is wide enough—rather than only by way of specially equipped entrances. Depending upon how the areas are designed and where they are located in relation to the Data Center, a level floor may enable you to forgo otherwise-needed construction of raised floors in adjacent support areas such as a Build Room or storage area—recouping at least some project costs due to the sunken floor.

If you choose to have a viewing area into your server environment, perhaps for a control center or to facilitate tours, the uniform floor surface height also enables you to avoid making the choice between having to look up into the elevated server environment or building up the height of the viewing area.

Because this decision can affect the building's foundation or require greater heights between stories, depending on what level the Data Center is located on, it should be made as early in the design process as possible.

Ramps and Lifts

Assuming that your Data Center's raised floor surface is elevated, there are two mechanisms for bringing equipment into the room and level with the floor—ramps and lifts.

Ramps are the most popular choice. They enable either people or materials to be brought into the Data Center and have no moving parts to malfunction. Their length is determined by two factors—the height of the raised floor and the slope used to reach that height. In the Unites States, Data Center ramps feature a 1 in 12 incline—a 1 inch increase in height for every 12 inches in length. Such a slope is considered acceptable under the Americans with Disabilities Act of 1990, which is designed to make all workplace areas accessible to those with disabilities. Using such an incline, a room with a 15-inch high raised floor needs a ramp that is 15 feet long, while one with a 24-inch raised floor needs a ramp 24 feet long. (Although the formula doesn't translate as gracefully in the metric system, that is 4.6 meters long for a 38.1-centimeter high floor, or 7.3 meters for a 61-centimeter high floor.)

Although this requirement doesn't apply in other countries, still consider a 1:12 incline. A shallower incline requires more space for the ramp, which doesn't help your design. A steeper incline means a shorter ramp, but makes it significantly more difficult to steer heavy equipment in or out of the Data Center. Full server cabinets can be quite heavy, and if you have ever had to push an object up an incline—say a stalled car or a piece of heavy furniture—you know that it is much harder to move it up a steep rise than a shallow one.

Data Center ramps are ideally going to be 6 feet (1.8 meters) wide and have landings at both ends that are 6 feet (1.8 meters) square. These dimensions enable sufficient room for maneuvering large equipment in or out of the Data Center. When designing your Data Center ramp, keep in mind the advantages of having floor space serve multiple functions. It is completely acceptable to have the bottom landing for the server environment located in the building's hallway, for example, as long as there is sufficient clearance.

Building codes in many regions require some form of handrail on both sides of the ramp, to prevent a person or piece of equipment from accidentally slipping off a ramp edge. For the same reasons, it is advisable to install slip-resistant tread on the ramp. Depending upon the size of your Data Center and the wording of regional building codes, you may be required to have more than one ramp.

The alternative to having a ramp for your Data Center is a lift, an adjustable platform that enables you to raise an item up to the height of the raised floor or down to the level of the regular floor in the adjoining room or corridor. A lift occupies less floor space than a ramp, but is more expensive. As such, it is best reserved for sites where floor space is at a premium.

Weight Bearing Ability

Arguably the most important element of any Data Center floor, whether it includes a raised floor system or not, is its weight-bearing ability. The more weight your Data Center floor can support, the more equipment, large and small, that can potentially be installed in the room. Ideally, your Data Center floor should be able to support 1500, 2000, or more pounds (680.4, 907.2, or more kilograms) per server cabinet location. Those were considered exorbitant weight loads a few years ago, but current design trends for servers and other Data Center devices are producing heavier and heavier equipment. The most prudent approach is to assume those trends are to continue and to design your server environment accordingly.

Ultimately, the overall weight-bearing ability for a Data Center floor is limited by the structural makeup of the building—the thickness and integrity of the building's concrete slab if the room is on the bottom floor and the same characteristics of its steel skeleton if the server environment is above the ground.

Specify in your design package how much weight you want your raised floor system to bear. You want the system to have essentially the same strength as the subfloor. Lesser weight-bearing ability doesn't take full advantage of the building's strength, while greater ability increases construction costs without providing any benefit.

Overall weight isn't the only characteristic that must be specified for your Data Center floor. There are several types of load that are applied to the floor, and they fall into two overall categories:

- **Static loads, which involve constant weight:**
  - **Concentrated or point load**—Weight applied on a small area, such as where the pegs or casters of a fully loaded server cabinet touch the floor. For example, if a cabinet is filled with equipment and weighs 2000 pounds, the load is distributed evenly among its four casters, 500 pounds each. To support this cabinet, floor tiles must be rated for a point load of at least 500 pounds.
  - **Uniform or static load**—Weight distributed over a larger area. Common occurrences in a Data Center are heavy boxes or large equipment that sits flush on the ground and possesses no support pegs or wheels. This load

can also be an accumulation of point loads. If two of the casters from the previous example rested upon the same floor tile, that tile would have a static load of 1000 pounds upon it. To successfully support such weight, the panel must be rated for a static load of at least that amount.

- **Dynamic loads, which involve the movement of weight over an area:**
  - **Rolling load**—Weight rolled over an area from passing equipment. This load is defined not only by the weight of the object but also by the size and hardness of the wheels that make contact with the tile and how many passes are made. Practically anything transported across a Data Center floor— server cabinets on casters, supplies moved by way of a pallet jack, backup media transported by mobile cart, even a person sliding across the floor in an office chair with wheels—is a rolling load.

  - **Affect load**—The force put on a raised floor by a dropped object. This is defined by the weight of the item and distance it falls. Although items aren't regularly dropped or tipped over in a Data Center, the floor must be able to withstand such force in the event that an accident does occur.

  - **Ultimate load**—The minimum weight that exceeds a floor tile's ability to support a load. This is essentially the breaking point of a floor panel, past which an object crashes through to the subfloor. This may be represented as an independent weight or as a multiple of a panel's concentrated load.

Although concentrated and uniform loads place ongoing pressure on the raised floor, the dynamic loads have the most potential to cause damage in the Data Center. Rolling items over the same floor tiles can cause wear and tear over time, while dropping an item on the floor may cause small cracks in the floor system as well as damage panel surfaces.

When specifying the weight load requirements of your Data Center, apply them to whatever ramps or lifts the room is equipped with as well. It does little good for your server cabinet locations to be able to support thousands of pounds each if the equipment can't make it past the entrance because of a weaker lift or ramp.

NOTE   Consider setting the structural capacity of the Data Center so that all cabinet locations can support at least 20 percent more than the heaviest item you ever expect to house. So, if the heaviest fully loaded server cabinet will be 1500 pounds (680.4 kilograms), specify 1800 pounds (816.5 kilograms) per tile location. This provides a buffer to accommodate unanticipated equipment weights and density in the future.

If you are constructing a server environment in an existing building, obtain a map that indicates the weight-bearing abilities of the structure. Such information can typically be acquired through the architectural firm and can help you lay out the Data Center space most efficiently.

Types of Floor Tiles

Three types of floor tiles are involved in a raised floor system:

- Blanks
- Perforated
- Notched

These floor tiles come in one standard size—2 feet (61 centimeters) square—and are typically made of steel, with wood or concrete at the core, or cast aluminum. Tiles can be ordered in various colors, or even made transparent, although beige and light gray are the most common.

Blank or solid tiles are the most abundant in any Data Center. They have no openings and are capable of supporting the most weight, and therefore are traditionally placed in all aisle locations, directly under Data Center equipment, and on the room's ramp.

Perforated or vented tiles have dozens of tiny holes in them, enabling air to flow through. These panels are most often placed immediately in front of server rows, although they may be located anywhere in the room depending upon how you want to direct airflow. Where specifically to place them in your Data Center is explained in Chapter 8, "Keeping It Cool." Perforated tiles can be configured with a sequence of adjustable metal plates on the bottom. Adjusting a single control mechanism on the tile, usually with a hexagonal wrench, shifts the position of the plates. In this way you can restrict as much or little airflow through a perforated tile as you want.

NOTE	So, if perforated tiles enable you to better control airflow in the Data Center and it is possible to completely close them, why not put them in the ramp and aisles, too, and not bother with any blank tiles? It is because perforated tiles are weaker than blanks due to all of the holes in them. Installing perforated tiles throughout the room would reduce the weight-bearing ability of your raised floor.

Notched or cut tiles are similar to blanks except that they have one or more openings for patch cords and power cables to be threaded through. You can have the openings made to practically any size or shape and placed anywhere on the tile. You want the openings to be large enough to accommodate an average-sized bundle of power and data cables routed through your Data Center, but not so large that air from the floor can escape. The more air that escapes out of your Data Center's cut tiles, the less that comes out of your perforated tiles, which are where you want the cooling.

There are multiple products available to help prevent air from leaking out of oversized tile cut-outs. Some consist of foam padding or wiry bristles that enable cables to be threaded through a tile opening but prevent air from passing through. They work reasonably well but, over time, might become weighted down or frayed and no longer function as effectively.

Others are caps of wood, metal, or plastic that rest in tile cut-outs. These can be adjustable in size, enabling cables to pass through while occupying the remainder of the opening. These continue to function for years, but are vulnerable to human nature. Data Center users often remove and set tile caps aside, requiring additional time from the room's support staff to track down and replace them. The caps, no matter what they are made of, may also give people a false impression about how much weight they can hold. Data Center users transporting cabinets or equipment across the raised floor are usually conscientious enough to steer around notched tiles with open cut-outs, but may not think twice about rolling heavy equipment over one with a cap. The result is a broken or damaged cap and possibly a toppled server cabinet.

It is important to maintain air pressure in a server environment so that air can circulate properly through the room and thereby regulate ambient temperatures humidity. Data Center air pressure is affected by how floor tiles are deployed—the more openings in the floor from perforated and notched panels, the harder it is to maintain pressure. Your proposed deployment of floor tiles in the Data Center should therefore be reviewed by the project vendor responsible for the room's cooling. They may recommend a limit for the total number of perforated tiles in your Data Center.

NOTE   Because a raised floor system is, literally, the foundation of your server environment, it is important to protect it. Here are several recommended practices for maintaining your raised floor system:

- When lifting floor tiles, limit how many are removed from their normal position at any given time. Also remove panels in a line rather than a block. Removing several tiles or even a small number in a block exposes support pedestals to damage or displacement.

- Avoid placing heavy items on notched tiles because they are weaker than blank tiles. If you must position equipment on a cut tile, keep concentrated loads, such as the support pegs of a device, as far from the cutout as possible.

- After removing floor tiles, set them back down carefully upon the raised floor. The panels can be heavy and awkward to handle. With rough edges on the bottom and sharp corners, one tile can easily damage another if dropped or set down roughly.

- When transporting heavy equipment across the Data Center raised floor, take measures to protect the tile surfaces. Place protective covering along the path of travel and avoid rolling items over cut or perforated tiles.

- If a floor tile becomes damaged for any reason, replace it immediately. Don't allow minor cracks or gouges to worsen.

If you're concerned about wear and tear on your floor panels, you may want to periodically rotate tiles between high-traffic and rarely traveled areas of the Data Center.

Floor Tiles and Static

The raised floor panels installed in your Data Center should have static-control qualities. Because static can disrupt or damage sensitive electronic equipment, you want to limit how much static your servers are exposed to. Static control tiles help reduce the voltage that is generated from people walking across the surface of the floor.

Floor tiles are commonly either static dissipative, which means that they inhibit the creation of static, or conductive. Raised-floor vendors typically recommend dissipative tiles for areas where various users will walk across the floor, and conductive tiles for rooms where personnel will wear static-control footwear. Choose accordingly based upon what type of foot traffic will occur in your Data Center.

The Electrostatic Discharge Association is a good resource for more information about electrostatic discharge (ESD), including various ESD-related industry standards. The association's website is at http://www.esda.org.

Termination Details

There are several methods and components for routing and terminating Data Center infrastructure under a raised floor. Electrical outlets, for example, can be individually terminated as follows:

- At the end of a flexible conduit
- In a cluster on the same conduit
- Along a floor-mounted guide rail
- In a stationary raceway, on a vertical power pole
- Up in a server cabinet.

Equivalent options are available for structured cabling, too. Each approach has its advantages and disadvantages.

Running individual electrical conduits and cable bundles to each server cabinet location is the most flexible configuration, enabling quick and easy redistribution of Data Center infrastructure. This is a tremendous advantage when incoming servers arrive with new or additional requirements for power or connectivity. Infrastructure can be repositioned or altered with minimal disruption to the environment as a whole.

Cable bundles and electrical conduits can be routed along the Data Center subfloor, carefully secured to the raised floor system's vertical pedestals by soft cable ties or fasteners such as Velcro. If you design your Data Center in this manner, include specific instruction in your design package about what paths electrical conduits and data cables are to follow under the raised floor. This configuration involves a significant number of power receptacles and multimedia boxes under the floor, and careful routing enables them to be managed more easily and efficiently.

NOTE   I recommend against terminating Data Center infrastructure into under-floor raceways
              or directly into cabinets, although both are common practices. While raceways help
              organize infrastructure under the floor, they also restrict airflow, inhibit flexibility,
              and add expense to the price of your server environment. It is much easier to relocate
              freestanding structured cabling bundles and electrical conduits than those terminated
              in raceways or cabinets.

If you decide to use cable trays or raceways under the raised floor, place them strategically
so that Data Center users can easily access infrastructure. If you intend for people to plug
patch cords into under-floor data ports directly under server cabinet locations, make sure
that whatever combination of cable trays, wire management, and multimedia panels you
use keeps the structured cable bundles out of the way while situating the data ports within
easy reach.

Don't restrict access by overlapping or criss-crossing the infrastructure management
devices. For example, don't terminate power into a raceway and then run a cable tray
directly on top of it, forcing someone to put his or her hand through the lattice of the tray—
and between bundles of structured cabling—to reach the electrical outlets. The two distinct
raceways should instead be staggered so that one is not directly over the other.

Prepare for additional power and data cables in the future. Choose management systems
that have space for growth and that are expandable. If your Data Center cable trays are
completely filled by structured cabling the day the room comes online, they are too small.
If space under the floor permits, choose deeper or wider trays that enable more cable
bundles to be added. It is much better to have large cable trays and raceways that are
half-full than small ones that are bulging with infrastructure.

Also, choose infrastructure management components that have a low profile and that can
be easily dismantled and reassembled elsewhere. This limits their effect on under-floor
airflow and provides an opportunity to reconfigure your Data Center infrastructure.

The last option is terminated power and cabling above the Data Center floor directly into a
server cabinet. The primary advantage of this practice is that once infrastructure is in place,
there is no need to lift floor tiles to access connections. Servers and networking devices
can be installed with no risk of damaging a patch cord or power cable when moving floor
panels. This is a very inflexible design, however, because it is very difficult to relocate either
infrastructure or individual server cabinets without incurring downtime. This approach
should therefore be implemented only in Data Centers that have minimal turnover of
equipment.

Figure 5-3 shows power, data, and cooling routed under a raised floor. Electrical conduits
and structured data cabling follow parallel but distinct paths under the floor.

Figure 5-3   *Under-Floor Termination Example*

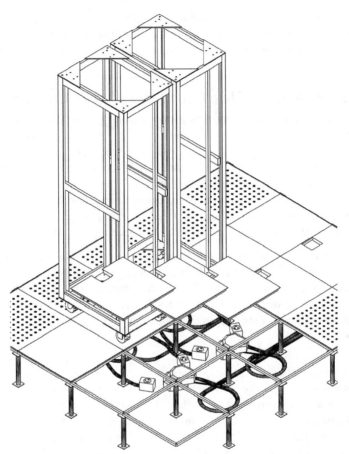

The Subfloor

If you use a raised floor system, make sure that that the subfloor is sealed. This prevents the Data Center air handlers from stirring up minute concrete dust that can in turn damage servers or networking equipment.

Also consider designing troughs into your subfloor. These can provide a degree of protection for your infrastructure in the event that water intrudes into the Data Center. Run the troughs parallel to the server rows, out of the way of under-floor infrastructure. The deeper they can be, the better, because you want them to catch and carry away moisture before it can reach any of the cabling under the floor.

Common Problems

Routing the hundreds or even thousands of cable runs and electrical conduits in your Data Center can be very complicated, so errors of one type or another are likely to occur. The sections that follow discuss some of the more common errors to look out for.

Tile Cut-outs Are Poorly Sized or in the Wrong Location

While a contractor may misread the instructions in your design package, these errors most often occur during the Data Center planning stage. It is easy to miscalculate sizes for tile cut-outs, by either not providing a big-enough opening at cabinet locations where several cable bundles pass through or else making the notches so large that air escapes wherever only a handful of patch cords is routed. One solution to this problem is use of two cut-out sizes for your notched tiles and strategic placement of them. Perhaps use an 8-inch (20.3-centimeter) square opening for panels near cabinets packed with cables and a 4-inch (10.2-centimeter) square cut-out for tiles near sparsely cabled cabinets.

Still more potential for error exists when cutting notched tiles and orienting their cutouts in relation to servers in the Data Center. If cabinets in your Data Center don't have the same width as your floor tiles—2 feet (61 centimeters)—pay careful attention to how they align with your room's notched floor tiles. Different widths can cause tile cutouts and the equipment cables that are to pass through them to drift apart.

NOTE   Many of the Data Centers I manage use server cabinets that are 22.5 inches (57.2 centimeters) wide. While only slightly narrower than the panels on the raised floor, the cabinets are typically situated flush with one another. Over the span of an entire server row, each cabinet drifts a bit more from the center of the floor tile it sits upon. At the end of a server row with 13 cabinets, that is a gap of 19.5 inches (49.5 centimeters). I can—and have—still run cables through cutouts that are offset by this much, but it is awkward, and I have to use longer patch cords and electrical cables. The same problem occurs when cabinets in a row are wider than the floor tile. The drift between servers and tile cutouts just occurs in the opposite direction.

There are three ways to address drifting cabinets:

1. Don't let cabinets become misaligned from floor tiles. Space out cabinets, narrow or wide, so that that they are always centered on your Data Center floor tiles. For wider cabinets, this may mean skipping over tile locations and potentially wasting floor space.

2. Adjust the placement of the notched tile cutouts as you progress down the row, so that they are always centered near the equipment intended to use them. This requires additional customization and may not meet your needs when new equipment arrives for the space.

3. Make sure that your server rows are interspersed with wide and narrow cabinets. This dovetails with the approach of organizing servers by function and getting a heterogeneous mix of equipment, as mentioned in Chapter 4.

Figure 5-4 illustrates how cabinets narrower than Data Center floor tiles can be separated from the notched tiles that their cabling is intended to pass through. Row A shows cabinets becoming misaligned with cut-out tiles, while rows B, C, and D show the possible measures to realign them.

Figure 5-4   *Preventing the "Drift" of Floor Tile Cutouts*

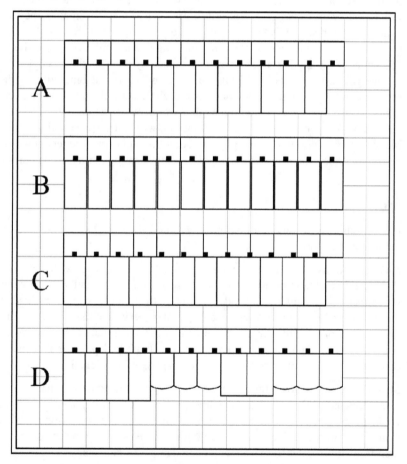

Cabling Installed in Plenum Spaces Aren't Properly Rated

Clearly specify the type of structured cabling you want installed in your Data Center and double-check that you receive the correct materials. Some manufacturers use similar part numbers for their plenum and non-plenum cables, identical except for a single digit.

Mistakes can occur, and you want to quickly catch any errors so there is adequate time to receive replacement supplies. Review the items as soon as possible. Even if you have experience with non-plenum, plenum, and low smoke/zero halogen cables, you may not immediately recognize an incorrect item without close scrutiny.

The Raised Floor System Isn't Strong Enough to Accommodate Equipment

It is easy to plan your Data Center for today's servers, but hard to make accurate predictions for future equipment. Remember: If future devices become larger, they are likely to add weight onto your Data Center floor; if future devices become smaller, they are *also* likely to add weight, because Data Center users are going to install more of them in each server cabinet. For example, a floor-standing machine that occupies one floor tile and weighs 750 pounds (340.2 kilograms) might be replaced by a device that occupies two floor tiles and weighs 1800 pounds (816.5 kilograms), or by a server cabinet filled with 20 narrow servers weighing 75 pounds (34 kilograms) each. That third configuration may seem lighter at first glance, but when you do the math it works out to the heaviest load of all—1500 pounds (680.4 kilograms) in one tile location, with extra space still left in the cabinet! Make your building as strong as physical conditions and your budget allowable, and then design the Data Center floor to match the weight-bearing ability of the building.

Summary

Power, data cabling, and cooling may be routed above a Data Center's false ceiling or below a raised floor.

An overhead installation is less expensive and takes up less space that an under-floor one. Patch cables and power cords all connect above your Data Center server cabinets when infrastructure is installed overhead. This makes them unlikely to be snagged in passing but requires Data Center users to climb a stepladder every time they want to connect to or disconnect from the infrastructure, which is inconvenient and carries its own snagging risks. If you install power and data overhead, use twist-lock plugs and receptacles and patch cords with sturdy connector tabs to reduce the risk of accidental unplugs.

Most Data Centers have a raised floor system despite their cost and space needs. Chilled air can be channeled through the under-floor and directed with greater precision to server cabinet locations by way of perforated and solid tiles better than from overhead vents. Routing infrastructure under a raised floor also makes it easy to access but out of sight, therefore protecting it from accidental damage or disconnects.

Electrical wiring generates electromagnetic interference, so keep it physically separate from any structured data cabling. Do this by routing them along separate paths in the Data Center and, if using an overhead installation, terminating them in distinct raceways.

You must use specially rated cabling and associated materials in the spaces that distribute air through your Data Center, typically located above the ceiling or below the raised floor. These are plenum-rated cabling in the United States or low smoke/zero halogen in most European countries. Non-plenum cabling is acceptable for use in other areas of the server environment.

When routing infrastructure overhead, structured cabling and electrical conduits are typically installed above the Data Center suspended ceiling, routed by cable trays or ladder racks and terminated in raceways below the ceiling. Provide space between automatic sprinkler heads mounted in the false ceiling and any solid objects such as raceways, cable trays, server cabinets, or other Data Center equipment; building codes in many regions call for a minimum clearance of 18 inches (45.7 centimeters). To keep power and data adequately separated, route them in back-to-back raceways, with power over the front of server cabinet locations and data over the back.

When routing infrastructure under floor, begin by establishing the height of the raised floor system. The higher the elevation, the greater the volume of cooled air that can pass through the plenum, and the less obstruction that is presented by infrastructure installed along the subfloor. Floor heights of 18 or 24 inches (45.7 or 61 centimeters) are typical.

Unless you create a Data Center with a sunken subfloor, which requires a compatible building design and additional expense, you must bring equipment onto the raised floor by way of a ramp or lift. Ramps are the most common, and are sized based upon the height of the floor. The taller the floor, the longer the ramp must be. Lifts are a second, more expensive alternative in which equipment is placed on a platform and then elevated to match the height of the Data Center floor.

A critical element of a Data Center raised floor is its weight-bearing ability. The more it can support, the more servers and networking equipment that can potentially be installed in the room. Strive for a raised floor that can support 1500, 2000, or more pounds per floor tile—or whatever the maximum strength of the building is, whichever is greater. Servers are becoming heavier each year, and you want your Data Center to be able to support future equipment.

Three types of floor panels are used in the raised floor system: solid tiles, which are the strongest; perforated tiles, which control airflow; and notched tiles that enable cabling to connect from server cabinets to under-floor infrastructure. Caps or other air-blocking devices may be placed in panel cutouts to prevent air from being misdirected.

Under-floor infrastructure can be terminated in several ways. The most flexible design is to run individual electrical conduits and cable bundles to each server cabinet location. Cable trays and raceways may also be used. If you do install raceways, seek components that are easily reconfigured or expandable. A final option is to terminate directly into Data Center cabinets. This is the least flexible design, but removes the slight risk of patch cords or power cables being damaged when someone lifts or replaces floor tiles.

Properly seal the subfloor to avoid concrete dust in the room.

Common infrastructure-related problems include improper placement or sizing of tile cutouts, installation of non-plenum cabling in plenum spaces, or failing to design a strong-enough raised floor.

CHAPTER 6

Creating a Robust Electrical System

This chapter presents the key elements for creating a reliable Data Center electrical system to power your company's critical servers and insulate them against surges, utility power failures, and other potential electrical problems. The chapter provides design strategies for both in-room and standby electrical infrastructure and offers best practices for labeling and monitoring the system, which are important for user safety and to avoid accidental downtime. Finally, the chapter outlines end-to-end testing procedures to ensure that when your standby infrastructure is called upon it performs as intended.

Recommended Electrical System Features

Above all else, your Data Center electrical system must be dependable—capable of keeping your servers and networking devices running no matter what external conditions might be. It's easy to assume that this dependability comes entirely from the capacity of your Data Center's electrical infrastructure—the greater its source of power, both primary and backup, the more reliable the server environment.

This is true only to a point. The largest power source in the world does a Data Center little good if its electrical system isn't carefully thought out. As you design your Data Center's electrical infrastructure, include the following system features to avert unnecessary downtime.

Isolated Power

Unless the building in which your Data Center is located is dedicated entirely to server space, the building has a mixture of power requirements. Air conditioners, elevators, office equipment, desktop computers, break room refrigerators—everything down to the electric pencil sharpener on someone's desk requires power. Provide separate power sources and infrastructure for Data Center items than for others that are less essential. You don't want the air handlers in your server environment shutting down on a hot day because the air conditioning system for the rest of the building drew in more electricity than a shared power source was able to provide.

Avoiding Single Points of Failure

This point was made at the beginning of this book, but bears repeating—do not allow your server environment, specifically its electrical system, to be vulnerable to failure from any single event or malfunction. To reduce the chances of power interruptions to your servers, do the following:

- Equip your Data Center with a standby power system
- Provide redundancy for all critical functions
- Physically separate key infrastructure systems

Also, don't let Data Center equipment share circuit breakers. It's bad enough to have a server cabinet filled with devices shut down due to a tripped breaker, but you don't want any more to be affected. Also, the power requirements of devices on a shared breaker might increase over time, going beyond what the circuit can handle. This can lead to an unexpected outage for those servers and require additional electrical work in the future.

Maintenance Bypass Options

Design your electrical system so that major components don't have to be brought offline for regular maintenance or, if they do, that electrical loads can first be transferred to other equipment without an interruption of power. You don't want to have to take Data Center servers and networking devices offline for non-emergency work.

Figures 6-1 and 6-2 diagram electrical systems that include a maintenance bypass feature. Figure 6-1 shows a single uninterruptible power source (UPS) configuration (N), and Figure 6-2 shows a system in which two UPS modules support the Data Center and a third provides redundancy (N+1).

Figure 6-1   *A Maintenance Bypass on a Single UPS System*

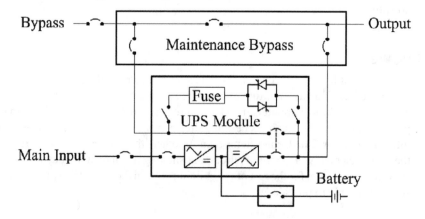

Figure 6-2   *A Maintenance Bypass on a Redundant UPS System*

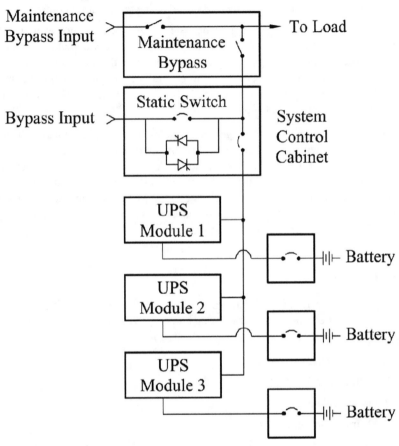

Remote Infrastructure Management

Assuming that your Data Center is part of a company site of at least moderate size, consider using a computer-based building management system to remotely supervise and control your various building infrastructure components, including those associated with your Data Center. Such a system can monitor your server environment's air handlers, power distribution units, and standby electrical devices as well as control the room's lighting and air handlers. (It can also perform similar functions for the environmental controls, elevators, and alarm systems in your office space.)

Proper implementation of a building management system can provide the following:

- Early warning of infrastructure problems
- Reduction of the amount of staff time spent monitoring Data Center systems

- Savings on utility costs by timing when certain building infrastructure components go on and off, such as overhead lights and office temperature controls

Computer-based building management systems are expensive, however, which means they aren't typically cost-effective at small sites. Costs will vary depending upon the type of buildings a management system is coordinating—strictly Data Center or mixed office space—as well as their size, but you can generally expect to pay somewhere in the neighborhood of $2 per square foot ($21.50 per square meter). That covers the cost of software, installation, and support.

Several brands of building management systems are available. Honeywell, Johnson Controls, and Siemens are the market leaders. Others include Alerton, Automated Logic Corporation (ALC), Echelon, Tour Andover Controls, and Trane. When choosing among them, look for systems that have high interoperability, that is, can interface with equipment from a great number of different manufacturers. Most building systems these days have comparable features, so look for those that are easy to program, have a clear graphic interface, and can produce useful data metrics.

In-Room Power

Designing the in-room portion of your Data Center's electrical infrastructure includes deciding what components to use to deliver power to your servers and networking devices. Electrical infrastructure elements include the following:

- Power distribution units
- Circuit breaker panels
- Electrical conduits
- Wiring configurations

You must also choose how to route, terminate, and label the components.

Pre-wire cabinet locations in your Data Center with power receptacles. Managing a room with pre-installed infrastructure is much easier than running new electrical conduits every time a new server arrives. While this practice adds to the initial cost of the Data Center, it is less disruptive and potentially less expensive in the long run, too.

NOTE   I work with both server environments that are pre-wired with electrical conduits and structured cabling and those that aren't. Without question, any cost savings that are enjoyed by not installing infrastructure up front is paid back 10 times over in staff time that is spent wiring cabinet locations one at a time to accommodate incoming servers. Without exception, pre-wire your Data Center whenever possible.

Determining Power Requirements

Your Data Center electrical system must be extensive enough to support the room when it is completely filled with servers. To begin determining your Data Center's power needs, extrapolate from how many cabinet locations are in the room and their maximum possible power draw. The basic formula is simple: (volts * amps)/1000 = kilovolt amps (kva).

Here are four examples:

- Suppose that your Data Center has 50 cabinet locations and that the server cabinets you use each have two power strips rated at 120 volts and 20 amps, a typical configuration in the United States. If you plug both strips from a cabinet into a single circuit, the Data Center's standby infrastructure must be rated to handle a minimum of 120 kva. That is ((120 volts * 20 amps)/1000) * 50.

- Adding some redundancy into the example, assume that each cabinet location is provided with two electrical circuits so that each power strip plugs in to its own dedicated circuit. That is ((120 volts * 20 amps)/1000) * 100, which equals 240 kva.

- Say that your Data Center, still with 50 cabinet locations to house equipment, instead hosts only floor-standing servers. In the United States, many of these require 208 volt, 30 amp power. That is ((208 volts * 30 amps * 2)/1000) * 50, which equals 624 kva.

- In many European countries, 220 volt, 32 amp power is typical. If the Data Center is built with the same redundancy as in the second example, with two circuits provided at each of the 50 cabinet locations, the room's maximum power load is 1408 kva. That is ((220 volts * 32 amps *2)/1000) * 100.

Obviously, the greater knowledge you have of the servers, networking devices, and other equipment coming in to your Data Center, the more accurately you can calculate the room's future electrical needs. Servers and networking devices aren't the only items in the Data Center that need to be powered, however. Account for the draw of your room's air handlers, overhead lights, badge access readers, and miscellaneous convenience outlets, as well.

When designing the Data Center's electrical system, provide an abundant number of circuits. Few electrical devices, including server and networking equipment, draw the maximum power that a circuit can provide. Therefore most server environments run out of available circuits well before they approach the room's maximum electrical capacity.

Power Distribution

Chapter 5, "Overhead or Under-Floor Installation?," explores the initial question of whether to run Data Center infrastructure above the ceiling or below a raised floor. The matter of what specific paths the electrical wiring should follow is still an issue, though. One approach is to run flexible electrical conduits, known as *whips*, from large power distribution units (PDUs) directly to each cabinet location. This works moderately well in a smaller server environment with a limited number of electrical conduits. The conduits travel a relatively short distance and can be managed so they stay neat and organized. This approach doesn't work very well for large Data Centers, however, especially when cabinet locations require multiple power receptacles. Running each electrical conduit directly from the source power panel in more or less a straight line to a destination cabinet requires rivers of conduits to cross over one another. This is problematic when the time comes to relocate whips or perform or electrical work in the Data Center.

Figure 6-3 shows power conduits running directly from power distribution units to a server row.

Figure 6-3   *Direct-Connect Power*

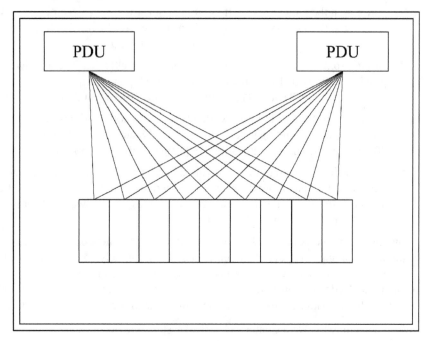

A more manageable design for larger server environments is installation of electrical substations at the end of each row in the form of circuit panels. Run conduits from power distribution units against the Data Center wall to the circuit panels and then a subset of connections to the server cabinet locations.

This configuration uses shorter electrical conduits, which makes it easier to manage, less expensive to install, and more resistant to a physical accident in the Data Center. If a heavy object is dropped through a raised floor—say a floor tile slips out of someone's hand—the damage it can cause is greatly reduced in a room with segmented power, because fewer conduits overlap one another in a given area.

Figure 6-4 shows power conduits running from power distribution units to circuit panels and then from panels to cabinet locations.

Figure 6-4   *Distributed Power*

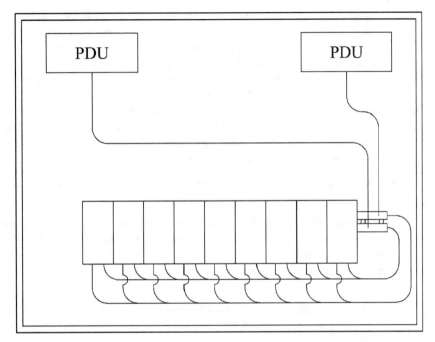

Power Redundancy

For greater reliability, run the electrical conduits to your server cabinet locations from separate sources, as shown in Figures 6-3 and 6-4. Most server cabinets come with two power strips, so plug each strip into a different receptacle. If one power distribution unit malfunctions — a rare occurrence — your servers remain online thanks to the second power supply. Be sure to only load each PDU to 50 percent of their capacity. That way each unit has can carry the load if a second PDU does falter.

Obviously, this redundancy only makes a difference if the servers installed in your Data Center feature redundant power supplies. If feasible, make it a requirement that all servers and networking equipment ordered for your Data Center have redundant power capability.

NOTE

You want devices that have two power supplies but not three. A server that has three power supplies and needs two of them to be powered isn't redundant, no matter what some manufacturers might claim.

Avoid devices that use an odd number of power cords. A greater number of electrical conduits and circuits are required in your Data Center, and there's no graceful way to accommodate the leftover power cord in a standard server cabinet.

Wiring, Component, and Termination Options

Different regions of the world have their own electrical standards for voltage, frequency, and wiring, not to mention an array of plugs and sockets containing unique shapes, sizes, and prong configurations. For instance, Europe and most other countries in the world generally use between 220 and 240 volts, whereas Japan and North America use between 100 and 127 volts. Make sure you are familiar with local power requirements when designing your Data Center's electrical infrastructure, as well as the predominant power requirements of incoming equipment. Installing uncommon infrastructure into your server environment, if not outright incompatible with servers, is sure to confuse Data Center users. Fortunately, many servers and networking devices have auto-sensing power supplies, enabling them to function at various voltages.

Despite the voltage differences, there are several good design practices to follow, no matter what regional electrical system you are designing to:

- **Use flexible whips**—Routing electrical infrastructure through flexible conduits can be easier to install and therefore less expensive than rigid conduits. Provide extra length for each whip, enabling it to be shifted from its normal location to an adjacent server row. This slack, combined with the use of flexible conduits, enables Data Center power to be rearranged quickly and inexpensively.

- **Use a heavy gauge of wire**—The thicker the wire, the more electrical current it can carry. The lower the gauge of wire, the thicker it is—10-gauge wire is heavier than 12-gauge wire, for example.

- **Don't terminate more than one receptacle on a conduit**—Doing so essentially binds those receptacles together. One can't be moved or rewired without affecting the other, and both can be damaged by a single event—the same reason you avoid sharing circuit breakers.

- **Avoid dirty power**—Some European countries provide two different types of power into their server environments by default: so-called clean power, which is conditioned and backed up by standby infrastructure, and dirty power, which isn't. You don't want your servers subjected to power fluctuations or exposed to a utility power outage, so specify in your design documents that no dirty power is to be installed in your Data Center.

NOTE   An alternate method of running electrical infrastructure is to use busbars, common conductors that connect multiple circuits. This configuration can be installed quicker than running individual electrical conduits and so is less expensive. Linking Data Center electrical circuits together in this manner makes the circuits—and any servers plugged in to them—more vulnerable to damage or downtime from a single event, though. I prefer to avoid busbar installations except perhaps in a temporary server environment where a short-term vulnerability may be acceptable in light of the cost savings.

Finally, here is one country-specific suggestion for wiring electrical conduits. For Data Center electrical infrastructure in the United States, consider using six 10-gauge wires, consisting of the following:

- Three phase conductors
- One neutral
- One equipment ground
- One isolated ground

This configuration provides all of the necessary wiring to provide either a pair of 120 volt, 20 amp circuits or one 208 volt, 30 amp circuit. The pair of 20 amp circuits can power standard Data Center server cabinets equipped with two power strips—typically rated at 15 or 20 amps—while the 30 amp circuit can power most floor-standing servers.

By far, the most common power requirement of Data Centers servers, networking devices, and other equipment in the United States is either a pair of 120 volt, 20 amp circuits or one 208 volt, 30 amp circuit. This configuration provides a huge benefit for managing a server environment. With this wiring in place, an electrician can simply exchange one type of receptacle for another and change the breaker in the electrical panel that supports it; without it, the electrician must also carefully thread new wiring into the enclosed electrical conduit, along its entire length. The first process is much faster, enabling electrical changes to occur more rapidly and with less expense.

Labeling and Documenting

Electrical systems of any type can be complicated and, if not thoroughly understood, dangerous. This is particularly true of Data Center electrical infrastructure because of the high voltage, copious wiring, and multitude of circuits involved. Making a mistake while interacting with a server environment's electrical infrastructure can cause unplanned downtime or, in extreme circumstances, kill or seriously injury someone.

The best way to avoid such hazards is clear and consistent labeling of all Data Center electrical components. Don't just mark them so that your regular, longtime facilities personnel can understand them. You want signage, labeling, and documentation to be so thorough and unambiguous that someone who is completely new to the infrastructure and has just been woken from a sound sleep and rushed to the Data Center—all likely circumstances in an emergency—can understand them.

Label your Data Center power receptacles with the circuits they possess and the location in the circuit breaker panel where they originate. At that breaker panel, list all of the circuits it contains and which cabinet locations they are located at.

Figure 6-5 shows a 120 volt, 20 amp double duplex power receptacle labeled with specific circuit information. Circuit information is provided on the face of the receptacle and side of the electrical conduit. The receptacle contains circuit 22, left, and circuit 24, both from panel M of power distribution unit 9.

Figure 6-5   *Labeled Power Receptacle*

Color-code electrical components to emphasize parallel infrastructure. Suppose that your Data Center has redundant power at each server cabinet location, thanks to electrical conduits running from two different power distribution units. If you use one color of label on receptacles from one PDU and a second color on the receptacles from the other, it becomes immediately apparent that server cabinet locations have redundant power and what PDU is the source. Color-coding the receptacles or electrical conduits is another way to emphasize parallel infrastructure. Either method of color-coding can be as effective as the other, although labeling is probably less expensive and easier to obtain in multiple colors than the receptacles or conduits.

When your Data Center is constructed, have the electrician create a blueprint of the room, showing where every electrical circuit has been placed. This document, known as an *as-built*, is important because actual construction of the room might be somewhat different from your design package. Circuits might be reallocated, or a last-minute power change might be accommodated, for example.

Most Data Centers host such a variety of equipment over time that minor electrical work— swapping from one type of receptacle to another or adding an additional electrical conduit here or there—occurs regularly. Keep this information current. Outdated labeling or documentation is worse than none at all, because it can lead to incorrect assumptions about how a Data Center device is being powered.

Finally, use hazard tape to mark electrical equipment that Data Center users must stay away from. For example, outline a clearance area around power distribution units so people know to keep servers away from potential electromagnetic interference.

Convenience Outlets

Servers and networking devices aren't the only items that need power in your Data Center. On occasion, non-essential equipment must be plugged in as well, such as:

- Rechargeable batteries for a power drill or electric screwdriver used to install equipment
- Pedestal fans to keep temperatures down until an air handler is brought back online
- A vacuum cleaner used by a professional cleaning crew to remove particulate matter from the server environment

Whatever the items, you want surplus electrical outlets available so they don't have to be plugged in to a cabinet power strip or an electrical conduit that is intended for server equipment. That is an unnecessary risk of overloading a circuit or dislodging a power cord for critical equipment, especially in a Data Center heavily populated with servers and networking devices. The so-called convenience outlets should be provided in multiple locations around the Data Center, on each of the walls and structural columns. Don't connect the convenience outlets to your room's standby power system. It is unnecessary, and, as with the Build Room, you don't want equipment plugged in to these receptacles for more than a short time.

NOTE   In June 2003, a cleaning crew was working in a Data Center I manage in San Jose, California. Although the group was supposed to be experienced at working in a computer room environment, one of the workers plugged a vacuum in to the closest power source he noticed—one of the two power strips on a nearby server cabinet rather than into one of the room's many convenience outlets. The cabinet housed a dozen functioning servers, and the additional draw tripped the power strip's breaker. Most of the servers possess redundant power supplies and were unaffected, but not all. Two devices suffered downtime as a result of the incident.

Emergency Power Off

Fire codes in most regions of the world call for Data Centers to have the means to shut down all electrical power prior to the activation of their fire suppression systems. This capability is typically achieved by way of an emergency power off (EPO) system. Setting up an EPO system involves wiring your electrical infrastructure to purposefully halt incoming utility or standby power whenever conditions exist to trigger your Data Center's fire suppression system. Designing the system to have a brief delay — 30 to 60 seconds, for example — —is a prudent action so that if there is a false alarm you can stop the shutoff of power and discharge of the fire suppression system.

NOTE   It is a common misconception that an EPO system is solely intended as a safety feature for Data Center users, enabling power to be cut if someone has come into contact with live electrical wiring and is being electrocuted. While the system does enable you to do that, that is not its main purpose. The EPO system is intended to prevent fire suppression materials from coming into contact with live electrical current.

Manual EPO controls, enabling you to shutdown the room's power even without a fire condition, must be near the server environment's primary exits, and can take several forms. Consider carefully what type of EPO controls you want in your Data Center. The system creates the dangerous opportunity for someone to bring down all of your company's critical servers and networking devices by pressing one button or toggling a single switch. You want your EPO controls to be easy to use, but not unprotected so someone can activate them by accident or without first thinking through what they're doing. As with other Data Center infrastructure, design your EPO controls to promote good habits.

The following are three types of available EPO systems:

- **Push button** — Among the most common EPO controls. The push button is easy to use — just push — and therefore prone to accidental activation.

- **Pop-up button** — A second frequently-used type of system is a pop-up button that is held in place by a glass disk the size of a large coin. Breaking the glass with a small hammer, which is attached to the controls by a short chain, causes the button to extend and power to shut off immediately. Accidental activation is less likely with this configuration, but it is impossible to restore power until a new piece of glass is installed. If you choose this type of control, tape a few spare pieces of glass near the controls so that time isn't wasted searching for replacement glass during an outage.

- **Control knob** — A third option is use of a control knob, similar to controls on a stove. To activate, the user rotates the knob 90 degrees. Although this configuration is less common than the other two, it is arguably a better design. It is simple to use, unlikely to be mistaken for another control, and not susceptible to accidental activation from someone or something leaning against it.

Whatever controls you install, cover them. A transparent plastic shell, wired to an audio alarm, is ideal. It enables someone to see the controls but not bump them accidentally. The alarm is an effective deterrent to someone casually fiddling with the controls, but won't stop a person who is intent on shutting down power due to a critical situation.

Figure 6-6 shows two common types of EPO controls.

Figure 6-6   *Sample Emergency Power Off Controls*

A Push-Button Control, Covered
by a Transparent Plastic Shell

A Pop-Out Button Control

NOTE   I cannot overemphasize the need to cover, alarm, and provide signage for your Data Center's EPO controls. In March 1999, a few months after I helped fitup a Data Center in Austin, Texas, a contractor working in the room noticed the red push-button mounted on the wall inside each entrance. He didn't notice the small signs over them that said "emergency power off," however. When left the room, he pressed one of the buttons, thinking it would cause the door to automatically open, and instantly brought hundreds of servers and associated devices offline.

Standby Power

The Data Center's standby electrical system consists of backup power sources to keep servers and networking devices running when commercial power fails. As with all types of Data Center infrastructure, you must strike a balance among three factors when designing your standby system:

- Redundancy
- Simplicity
- Cost

The more levels of redundancy you employ (N+1, N+2, and so on), the more complex and expensive the system inevitably becomes.

Load Requirements

How to calculate the basic power requirements for a Data Center was covered earlier this chapter. When designing your standby power system, start with whatever maximum kva load the entire room can produce and then adjust it in two ways:

- Size your standby infrastructure to handle 110 to 120 percent of the Data Center's projected maximum power needs. This provides a safety margin to accommodate unanticipated power draws.

- Build out your standby infrastructure based upon what level of redundancy you want for your server environment. If two standby power devices are necessary for N coverage, you need three for N+1, four for 2N, and so on.

Because your Data Center's standby infrastructure sees action on only a limited basis, it can appear to some as a potential area to trim costs. You might be asked whether it is okay to get by with less standby infrastructure, enough to support only the most critical devices in the room. This scenario is certainly possible, but you don't want to design your Data Center this way. Your server environment should house only devices that require the protection that standby infrastructure provides. Devices that can get by without it shouldn't be in the room at all. If you find that a significant number of servers fit this description, take a second look at how you have sized the Data Center. Shifting low priority devices out of your server environment might enable you to have a smaller Data Center footprint and reduce the quantities of all Data Center infrastructure, which is more appropriate and cost effective than skimping on the standby system.

While you don't want your Data Center's standby infrastructure supporting another space, the one exception to this policy might be the site's network room, especially if the two are in close mutual proximity, such as in adjacent buildings. Both environments must be operational, for servers to perform their normal business functions and for your company's associated employees to be productive. If the rooms are a significant distance apart, having separate standby infrastructure provides some redundancy, but if they are close to one another, their standby infrastructure is going to be located close together anyway. If your standby system is to support both your Data Center and network room, obviously size it to handle the overall power needs of both.

Batteries

The most common source of standby power for a server environment is a bank of batteries. Such a cluster is known collectively as an *uninterruptible power source (UPS)*. Technically, any device that protects your servers from shutting down due to an outage, spike, or other undesirable power condition can be called a UPS, but in the Data Center industry the term typically refers to a battery system.

In its smallest form, a UPS is a single battery that can be mounted in an individual server cabinet. Cabinet power strips are plugged in to the UPS, and the UPS is in turn plugged in to a Data Center power receptacle (one UPS is installed into each cabinet). This type of UPS is acceptable for a very small server environment, such as room with just a few cabinet locations where a minimum of standby power is desired. This type of UPS is also appropriate for a temporary Data Center, because these portable devices are relatively inexpensive and can be taken with you if and when the room is decommissioned.

For most Data Centers, however, large floor-standing UPS models are recommended. They are more robust, have greater capacity, and are located in the electrical room rather than occupying space. Install the UPS in your electrical room and use it to condition the power bound for your Data Center.

How long standby infrastructure can support a Data Center's electrical load is known as its *run time*. When establishing the run time for your server environment, always do so under the assumption that the room is at full capacity, with every circuit holding the maximum possible electrical load. You want to size the UPS so that it can support your Data Center's electrical load for a significant time, certainly long enough to withstand most power outages in the region.

NOTE   If a UPS is going to be your Data Center's sole form of standby power, I recommend a run time of at least two hours. This amount of time provides adequate coverage to ride out most minor utility outages. If an outage is anticipated to last longer than two hours, this time period at least enables system administrators and network engineers to choose what machines they want to shut down themselves. This is typically easier on the equipment than just enabling them to "crash" when their supply of power disappears abruptly.

Keep in mind—if your Data Center is running at less than full capacity, the coverage provided by its UPS system increases proportionally. If the room is only drawing 50 percent of its potential power, for example, a UPS sized to support the fully loaded room for two hours can actually support it for twice as long. That is because you are draining the battery system at only half the anticipated rate. If you are facing an outage expected to outlast the standard capacity of your UPS, you can even shut down less-critical servers to ration your battery power and enable more-critical systems to stay online longer.

Generators

No matter how large the batteries are in your UPS, the power they provide is finite. For a more continuous supply of standby power, use a generator. A generator converts mechanical energy into electrical energy that then supports your Data Center equipment.

Different models of generator run on different types of fuel, such as gasoline, diesel fuel, or natural gas. Because this fuel can be refilled, a generator can run without limit.

NOTE	Theoretically, a generator can run without limit. Generator emissions are typically regulated by local, state, or federal ordinances, which might limit how many hours a generator can run during a quarter or other defined period of time. Two different amounts are usually defined, one for system maintenance and another for actually powering the Data Center. How severely your generator's usage is restricted depends entirely upon where in the world your site is and what type of generator is involved.

As with the UPS, size the generator to support at least 10 percent more than the Data Center's maximum power capacity and provide enough units to provide the desired level of redundancy. As previously stated, this capacity includes both the electrical load of the servers within the Data Center and the cooling devices that support the room.

NOTE	As with other Data Center infrastructure, the size of the room should determine how much standby equipment to use. For a small server environment in an area with generally reliable utility power, look for two hours of runtime from the UPS, and forgo a generator to save cost.
	You definitely want a generator for larger Data Centers and in regions that are prone to frequent utility outages, though. At those sites, I recommend 20 minutes of runtime from the UPS and a generator that can support the Data Center for eight hours before refueling. (Make sure to have service contracts in place with fuel providers that enable refueling of the generator well before eight hours.)

Install your generator in a protected area a short distance from the Data Center building. At a minimum, this protection should include steel barrier posts driven into the concrete to shield the generator from being struck by a vehicle, either accidentally or as an act of sabotage.

A standalone generator enclosure is preferred, because it enables unauthorized personnel to be locked out and might obscure the fact that your building has a generator—and therefore houses an important facility—at all. An enclosure can also protect the generator from the elements and muffle some of the noise and vibration that it produces when in operation. The enclosure must provide adequate ventilation to enable the dissipation of heat, prevent combustion, and include enough clearance around the unit for servicing.

Monitoring Lights

When utility power fails in a region, the first thing that anyone responsible for a Data Center wants to know is whether his or her room is still online, successfully protected by its standby infrastructure, or whether its servers and networking devices have shut down. This can take a nerve-wracking number of minutes to determine as people either travel to the Data Center to perform a visual inspection or get to a system with network connectivity and attempt to log on to devices in the room. This time grows even longer when there are multiple Data Centers in a region to check on or when the server environment is at a small site with minimal support staff available to investigate.

To make this determination faster and easier, install monitoring lights inside and outside each Data Center. Wire them to turn on when the standby infrastructure is actively supporting the room's electrical load. If your server environment has both a UPS and a generator, assign lights with different colored domes for each. The domes can be any color, but to avoid confusion stay away from amber or white, which are frequently used for fire alarms.

Place the monitoring lights on both sides of the Data Center entrance, high up on the wall, and in other strategic locations within the room. You want them to be visible from anywhere in the server environment. Large, rotating beacon-style lights are very effective because their strobe effect is easy to notice even when you are not looking directly at them. Also, locate the lights at the end of your Data Center's major aisles so they are less likely to be obscured by tall server cabinets.

A key benefit of installing monitoring lights outside a Data Center is that someone completely unfamiliar with the room can see them and—with the help of some explanatory signage nearby—realize that the standby infrastructure has engaged. This is especially helpful for a server environment located at a remote location with few Data Center users. Post signage close to the monitoring lights that explains their purpose and provides a telephone number to call to report when the lights are on. This number can be to your operations command center, a facilities manager, or on-call Data Center support staff— whomever you want to initially respond to such an issue.

NOTE   I help manage half a dozen very small server environments—less than 300 square feet (27.9 square meters)—in locations ranging from Ann Arbor, Michigan, to Edinburgh, Scotland, to Seoul, Korea. When I get word that commercial power has failed in one of those regions, I call a receptionist or security guard stationed at the site and politely ask them to confirm that power has failed to the site and to check whether the lights outside the Data Center are on. Employees who don't have badge access to the room or the training to log on to a server can still immediately ascertain the status of the room by checking the exterior monitoring lights.

Chapter 14, "Mapping, Monitoring, and Metrics," provides tips for checking a Data Center's monitoring lights directly, from anywhere in the world.

Figure 6-7 shows the entrance of a Data Center with monitoring lights mounted high on the wall, enabling someone outside the room to determine immediately whether the room is running on standby power. Beacon lights, indicating when the Data Center is running on standby power, are wall-mounted outside the main entrance.

Figure 6-7   *Monitoring Lights for the Standby Power System*

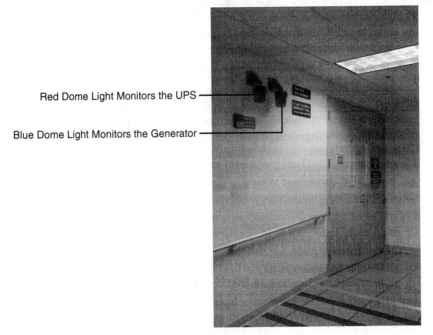

Red Dome Light Monitors the UPS

Blue Dome Light Monitors the Generator

Labeling and Documenting

The electrical room is the hub for all power coming in to the building, including the server environment itself, as well as the location for your UPS. Thoroughly label and document all infrastructure here, as in the Data Center. Make the labeling consistent for both rooms, using the same terms and labeling schemes when possible.

Post a wiring diagram showing how all infrastructure components in the electrical room interconnect. Tracing a circuit is much easier when following a diagram than when searching for and reading labels. Update the diagram when alterations are made to the system.

No common standard exists for orienting electrical switches. The only safeguard against someone incorrectly opening or closing an electrical circuit—causing injury or downtime as a result—is clear labeling. One simple and effective practice is to highlight "on" positions for all circuits and switches in the electrical room. Painting a silhouette behind the control switch or making some other guide mark is an easy way to highlight the correct position.

Figure 6-8 shows the cross-section of an electrical panel. Dots highlight the direction that circuit breakers face when on.

Figure 6-8   *Electrical System Labeling*

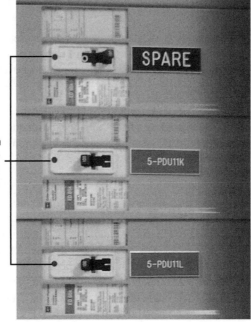

Black Dots Show Which Direction Breakers Must Face When On. The Top Breaker, an Unused Spare, Is Off; the Other Two Are On.

Installation and Grounding

In addition to providing your servers and networking devices with reliable power, it is the job of your Data Center's electrical infrastructure to protect those items (as well as people) from excess electrical charges. Such charges can be generated by anything from faulty circuits to static discharges to lightning strikes. To provide this protection, install a grounding system for your Data Center. Electricity always seeks the fastest route back to its source or the earth, and grounding provides a desirable path for it to follow—instead of going through a person or piece of Data Center equipment.

A Data Center grounding system typically involves installing copper wires below the Data Center raised floor, connecting them to the building's steel, and then linking to a long, copper rod that is driven deep into the ground. How deep depends upon the moisture level of the soil. You want the rod to extend far enough to reach moist soil, which is more conductive than dry soil, and to be located in close proximity to your site's main electrical room. The closer it is to the electrical room, the shorter the building's grounding wires have to be.

NOTE   Many Data Center grounding systems, especially those in dry regions, connect to the building steel in this manner and might also use grounding electrodes encased in concrete. This is known as *Ufer grounding*. Herbert Ufer, a consultant for the U.S. Army, developed the technique during World War II to ground a series of bomb storage vaults in Arizona.

Ufer grounding uses the properties of concrete—quick to absorb water and slow to dry out—to increase conductivity for grounding. Tying in a building's reinforcing steel makes it all part of the grounding system and improves the conductive path to the earth.

With the grounding system in place, make sure that all Data Center items that can potentially be charged by an electrical current, including all power sources and metal cabinets, are linked to it.

Signal Reference Grid

In addition to the safety that a Data Center grounding system provides to people and equipment, it also reduces electrical noise in the room. To further protect your servers and networking devices from interference, install a second grounding system known as a signal reference grid. This grid, also made of copper, specifically reduces high frequency noise. Connect to the signal reference grid from your Data Center's raised floor pedestals and at each power distribution unit and air handler.

Testing and Verification

Once all of your Data Center's electrical components are installed, have the electrical contractor conduct a series of tests on the entire system to make sure that the infrastructure performs the way it is designed to. The tests should include the following:

- **A load bank test**—This involves placing an electrical load on your standby power system to make sure that your UPS or generator components or both can support the level of power they are designed to. The first part of this test checks the maximum capacity of the standby infrastructure, while the second portion confirms the runtime of the UPS.

- **An injection test**—This procedure injects electrical current through circuit breakers and records the level at which they trip. Validating the trip characteristics of your Data Center breakers helps ensure that they perform correctly during a real-life power spike. This test is typically performed upon the breakers at the main distribution points of a Data Center's electrical system, say those that are 225 amps or greater. For additional labor costs, you can widen the scope of this test to involve all Data Center circuits.

- **Circuit and labeling verification**—After all electrical receptacles and circuit breakers in your Data Center have been labeled, verify that breakers are supporting the correct circuits as they are labeled. As with the injection test, this should be done at minimum for the main breakers supporting a server environment and possibly for all circuits.

- **A full power test**—For this test, utility power to the Data Center is cut off to verify that the room's electrical load correctly transfers to the standby infrastructure and then back again. A handful of randomly chosen electrical receptacles in the Data Center are monitored throughout the test to confirm that voltage levels remain steady. Also, monitoring lights are visually inspected during each stage of the test.

- **An EPO system test**—In this test, EPO controls are activated to confirm that all power sources, air handlers, and convenience outlets in the server environment shut down properly.

Conduct all of these tests before any servers or other devices are installed in your Data Center. Some people might balk at testing your Data Center's entire electrical system, because end-to-end testing is time consuming—it might take an entire day to complete—and infrastructure components are usually checked before they are installed. Don't be dissuaded. No matter how well components have been reviewed individually, there is no substitute for testing your entire Data Center electrical infrastructure as a single unit.

NOTE   I have participated in dozens of end-to-end tests of Data Center electrical systems, and a problem was uncovered *every time*. Most often the problem was minor, such as a circuit breaker being in the wrong position or a minor miswiring of some monitoring lights. Occasionally, the problem was more serious, though. In the most dramatic instance, a UPS battery exploded when an electrical load was placed upon in. Whatever the glitch might be, catching it before the room goes online can help to avoid such mistakes that will lead to downtime.

Have someone from the client company who is familiar with the proper operation of the Data Center's electrical system witness the tests. If that is not possible, videotape the tests. Show the key steps in each test.

Table 6-1 shows the steps involved in a load bank test, and what to videotape for the client company. Provide this sort of outline to the electrical contractors who are to perform it on your Data Center infrastructure.

Table 6-1   *Typical Load Bank Test*

Step	What to Do/Video
1. Set up load bank	Video the UPS. Show that it is operational and standing by to support the Data Center.
2. Set load, place on UPS	Set the load bank at 110 percent of the maximum projected Data Center load. Video the UPS. Show its display readout, indicating the amount of load being placed upon it.
3. Transfer load to generator	Video the generator. Show the readout, indicating the load being placed upon it. This should still be at 110 percent.
4. Adjust load, place it back on UPS	Adjust the load bank level to 100 percent of maximum projected Data Center load. Cycle through the UPS displays that indicate system load and how much battery time is available. Continue videoing as battery power drains to zero.
5. Turn load bank off	Continue videoing the UPS. Video readings as the UPS batteries recharge to full.

The two other tests, the full power test and check of the EPO system, can be combined. Table 6-2 shows the steps involved in both.

Table 6-2   *Typical Full Power Test and EPO Check*

Step	What to Do/Video
1. Confirm that Data Center mechanical systems are operating.	Plug three indicator devices into randomly chosen power circuits within the Data Center. Devices should be objects that can be readily identified as receiving power (such as a lamp). Video inside the Data Center. Show each indicator device— powered on—and the label of its corresponding circuits. Show a close-up of each air handler, including instrument panel, to verify that it is running.
2. Verify that necessary circuit breakers are closed (ON).	Video front entrance of the Data Center, focusing on the unlit monitor lights.

Table 6-2   *Typical Full Power Test and EPO Check (Continued)*

Step	What to Do/Video
3. Open (OFF) circuit breaker main, and watch system transfer to backup power.	Continue videoing emergency lights. Once lights activate (one light goes on when UPS supports the Data Center load; the other goes on when generator supports the Data Center load), re-enter the Data Center.
	Video each indicator device. They should still be powered on.
	Show a close-up of each air handler, including its instrument panel, to indicate that it is functioning.
	Video each set of emergency lights in the Data Center, to confirm that it is functioning while backup power is supporting the room.
4. Check emergency power off (EPO) button operation.	Video EPO controls and nearest monitoring lights. Continue videoing as EPO button is pressed and power shuts down.
	Video each indicator device still powered on.
5. Close (ON) circuit breaker main, and watch system transfer to normal power.	Video inside of the Data Center. Show each indicator device, powered on. Show a close-up of each air handler, including its instrument panel, to indicate that it is functioning.

Common Problems

The complexity of the Data Center's electrical system means that installation errors are not uncommon. Here are a few to avoid:

- **Power receptacles or circuit breakers are mislabeled**—A Data Center can have hundreds or thousands of electrical circuits, and it is easy to transpose numbers or misplace labels. You definitely want to uncover labeling errors before your server environment is on line to avoid accidental downtime. To safeguard against this problem, obtain a simple power tester that can signify whether power is active on a circuit. Have two people verify all receptacles in the room—one person plugs the device in to the outlet, while the other flips the corresponding circuit breaker off and then on again. This process can quickly identify mislabeled or otherwise malfunctioning circuits.

- **Monitoring lights for the standby power system are wired incorrectly**—It is not unheard of for electricians to wire the monitoring lights in such a way that there is a 30-second interval before they engage. For a Data Center equipped with both a UPS and generator, when commercial power fails, the electrical load is typically transferred through the UPS and onto the generator within moments. If the standby infrastructure performs as it is designed to, that 30-second delay means that no one is ever going to see the UPS monitoring light activate.

- **Circuit breakers are left off**—Although a simple mistake, failing to turn on all Data Center circuits after electrical infrastructure is installed can lead to confusion and cause people to believe that a more serious electrical problem exists.

NOTE   In April 2001, a Data Center that I helped to design and fitup in Boulder, Colorado, appeared to have a serious problem with its standby infrastructure. The room, 2030 square feet (188.6 square meters), had been on line for just six weeks when local commercial power failed. Although the UPS performed correctly, when power transferred to the generator, its internal batteries couldn't support the load, and servers in the room went down. This was very surprising because the standby infrastructure had passed a complete series of power tests less than two months earlier.

Subsequent investigation discovered that the electrical circuit that the generator's trickle charger was plugged in to had never been turned on. The generator had enough of a charge to function correctly during the power tests, but was drained in the process. Flipping the breaker activated the charger, and the standby device was functional again in short order.

Summary

Incorporate features into the Data Center's electrical system that protect servers from unnecessary downtime. Don't share power sources for Data Center devices and non-essential equipment. Avoid single points of failure by employing a standby power system, physically separating key infrastructure, and not sharing circuit breakers. Also design your electrical system so that maintenance can be performed without incurring downtime. For larger server environments, consider installing a building management system to remotely monitor and coordinate Data Center and other building infrastructure.

Determine your Data Center's power requirements by calculating the maximum possible draw of all cabinet locations as well as other infrastructure such as air handlers, lights, access readers, and convenience outlets. Provide ample circuits, because most server environments run out of available circuits before reaching the maximum capacity of the electrical system.

In small server environments, power can be routed directly from a power distribution unit to cabinet locations, crossing conduits where needed. For larger Data Centers, install a circuit panel at the end of each row, running short connections from PDU to panel and panel to cabinet locations. This configuration is more manageable and less expensive.

Provide power to Data Center cabinet locations from at least two different source PDUs for redundancy and always use servers and networking devices that have dual power supplies.

Electrical systems vary greatly from country to country. Design your server environment's electrical infrastructure to be compatible with common local configurations. Route power through flexible conduits, providing slack for each, and use a heavy (low) gauge of wire. Terminate only one receptacle per conduit, and provide only clean power into the Data Center.

Thoroughly label Data Center electrical infrastructure, both to protect workers and to prevent accidental downtime. Clearly label power receptacles, circuit breaker panels, and PDUs with location information and specific circuit numbers. Use color-coding to illustrate where power is provided from different sources. Have as-builts made of the Data Center electrical system and keep them up to date. Place hazard tape around electrical infrastructure that Data Center users need to stay clear of.

Provide convenience outlets around the perimeter of the Data Center for plugging in non-essential items. Don't connect them to your standby power system.

Your server environment must have an emergency power off system to cut power to the room immediately before its fire extinguishing system discharges. Choose controls for the system that are easy to use but unlikely to be activated accidentally. Cover EPO controls with a transparent shell and alarm it.

Make the capacity of your Data Center standby infrastructure 10 percent greater than the room's maximum possible electrical load. Increase this by how much redundancy you want your server environment to have—double it for 2N, triple it for 3N, and so on. Don't support other rooms with Data Center standby infrastructure, except perhaps a network room that helps maintain Data Center connectivity.

Backup power is typically provided to a Data Center by a cluster of batteries, known as an uninterruptible power source (UPS), and—at larger server environments—a generator. Wire large monitoring lights into the standby infrastructure to enable a quicker determination when the room is running on standby power.

Document and label electrical infrastructure in the electrical room as thoroughly as in the Data Center. Post and maintain electrical diagrams in this room, and use guide marks to highlight normal control positions for equipment.

Install a grounding system for your Data Center and make sure all items that can potentially generate or conduct an electrical charge are connected to it. Also install a signal reference grid to reduce high-frequency electrical noise in the room.

Once all electrical infrastructure is installed, perform end-to-end tests of the entire system. Include a load bank test, to confirm that standby infrastructure can support the Data Center's maximum projected electrical load; a full power test to ensure that the room's electrical load transfers to the standby infrastructure and back again; and a test of the EPO system to make sure that power can be cut to the server environment as intended.

Typical problems with the installation of a Data Center electrical system include mislabeling of circuits, miswiring of monitoring lights, or simply neglecting to turn on circuit breakers.

Designing a Scalable Network Infrastructure

This chapter discusses the Data Center's structured cabling and outlines the importance of a well-organized physical hierarchy. The chapter explains the differences between common cabling media, suggests which are most appropriate in various scenarios, and presents best practices for installation and testing.

Importance of the Physical Network

Arguably, the most intricate part of the server environment's design, from an infrastructure standpoint, is its structured cabling system. While a Data Center's electrical infrastructure is crucial for keeping servers and networking devices running, it is the physical network — cable runs and their terminations — that dictates how (and if) these items communicate with one another and the outside world. Your network's structured cabling must be abundant in order to provide ample connectivity, employ various media to accommodate different machines, and be well organized so that the entire system is easy to learn, and simple to manage. All of this also needs to be done in tight spaces, terminating in multimedia boxes, data faceplates, four-post network cabinets, or two-post relay racks.

A Data Center's usability is greatly affected by the following:

- Cabling media choices
- How many connections are provided
- How cable terminations are organized

These are all key decisions that need to be made during the initial design of a server environment. Space constraints and the presence of running servers make it very difficult to reconfigure cabling infrastructure once a Data Center is online. Design your physical network well and you have a scalable infrastructure that can meet your company's needs for years. Design it poorly and you will likely incur downtime to reconfigure or expand that infrastructure to address shortcomings in the original design.

Following are a few tips to keep in mind as you design your Data Center's physical cabling network:

- **Build the entire structured cabling system during initial construction** — Some companies try to save on the initial cost of their Data Center by installing cabling to only certain server cabinet locations, with the intention of adding more later when additional equipment arrives. This is understandable, but not recommended—for the same reasons as for the installation of the room's electrical infrastructure. Running cabling to all cabinet locations during initial construction makes the room easier to manage and avoids subjecting servers to potential downtime later when additional cabling is run. An up-front installation is also ultimately less expensive than adding cabling piecemeal since labor costs invariably rise over time.

- **Use shorter cable runs whenever possible**—Lay out Data Center cabinets so that devices can be connected with shorter rather than longer runs of cable. Shorter cables are less expensive and provide better performance. Abbreviated cable runs also reduce the potential for outages, since they provide less cabling in the Data Center to be affected by an incident.

- **Choose the right cabling media for the right connection**—What type of structured cabling to install into a Data Center isn't always as obvious as it seems. For instance, some cable solutions are cheaper to install, but require more expensive components (i.e., network cards) to be installed into servers, possibly resulting in a higher overall cost to your company. Choosing the most appropriate cabling also requires anticipating future needs, since you don't want to equip your Data Center with media that will quickly become outdated.

Cabling Hierarchy

There are essentially two ways to lay out your Data Center's physical network. Both approaches begin by creating a row to house the server environment's major networking devices. There are many terms used for this row:

- Room distributor
- Special distribution framework
- Home row
- Main street
- Network hub

It is simply referred to in this book as the *network row*. From the network row, structured cabling needs to be run to server rows.

One approach is structured cable runs routed directly to each server cabinet location. This works moderately well in a smaller server environment, say a room with fewer than 25 server cabinet locations. The cabling travels a relatively short distance and can be managed to stay fairly neat and organized. This approach doesn't work very well for large Data Centers, however. Cable bundles overlap and become tangled, making it very difficult to manage, trace, or remove them in the future.

A second approach is a network substation established at strategic locations in the Data Center—say at the end of each row—and then cable from the network row to the server cabinet locations by way of the substation. This substation, sometimes called a *row distributor* or *zonal cabinet*, serves the same purpose that end-of-row circuit panels do for the electrical infrastructure. Not only do network substations keep structured cabling better organized, but they also provide a level of distribution and redundancy for the Data Center network. By installing a highly available network device into each substation instead of consolidating them within the network row, each row of servers can be supported by a different networking device rather than having them all connect to one or two in the network row. This arrangement also limits the scope of downtime—in the event that a network device fails—to a single server row. Similarly, if an infrastructure problem arises at one cabinet location, you can immediately relocate servers to another row supported by identical infrastructure and networking devices.

Using networking devices at each server row also enables server connections to be aggregated and cable runs back to the network row to be greatly reduced. Fewer cable runs can, in turn, lead to improved airflow below the raised floor.

This approach does come with its own set of challenges, however. For one, data connections must pass through an additional patching field at the network substation. Every additional connection point along a cable run causes a slight degradation in the signal. So, passing through fewer termination points generally means better performance. Network substations in a Data Center also occupy floor space that can otherwise be used as server cabinet locations.

The largest effect of all, though, is that the more network substations you include in a Data Center design, the more networking equipment you must purchase. Because networking devices can be expensive, weigh the benefits of this distributed design against their price tag. If costs become prohibitive, consider using a smaller ratio of substations to server cabinet locations—perhaps one substation to support two server rows instead of one, for example.

Designing for Physical Versus Logical Network Topology

As this book deals with the physical infrastructure of your Data Center, I recommend the distributed model. Using network substations follows good principles of Data Center infrastructure design because the substations make the server environment more robust, modular, flexible, and standardized.

I work in both models of Data Center, some with direct-connect structured cabling and others with distributed structured cabling. As someone who manages physical infrastructure, I find the distributed design much easier to deal with due to its redundancy and organizational benefits. I consider the network substations an effective use of floor space, much like setting aside cabinet space for much-needed wire management, and I have seen no drop in performance because of the substations.

You will find many Data Center network designers who call for a direct-connect approach, however. That is because their designs focus on the *logical topology* of a network and pay little attention to the *physical topology*. That is, their designs streamline the paths that data travels from one point of the network to another but don't address the structured cabling that must be installed to enable the logical functions to occur.

These competing priorities are one of the toughest challenges facing a Data Center designer—more distribution points make the physical network easier to manage and the logical network more complex. Fewer distribution points make the physical network more complicated and the logical network simpler. You must decide upon which network elements are most critical for your Data Center, and design your cabling hierarchy accordingly.

Figure 7-1 shows structured cabling running directly from a network row to multiple server cabinet locations, while Figure 7-2 shows the same number of connections made by way of a network substation at the end of each server row.

Figure 7-1 *Direct-Connect Cabling Hierarchy*

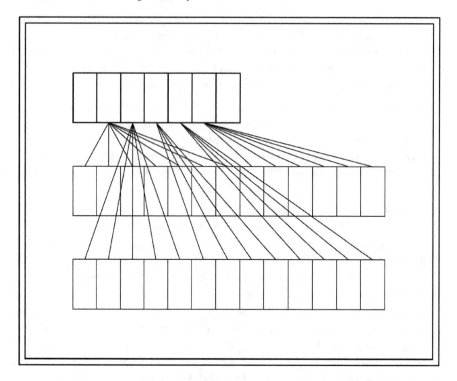

The cabling hierarchies in Figures 7-1 and 7-2 should look familiar. They are similar to the power distribution models outlined in Chapter 6, "Creating a Robust Electrical System," except that they involve data cabling instead of electrical conduits. In addition to the other benefits that a distributed design provides, employing it for both your power and data provides consistency and makes your server environment easier for users to work in. Once a user understands the concept for one system, the user understands it for both.

Figure 7-2   *Distributed Cabling Hierarchy*

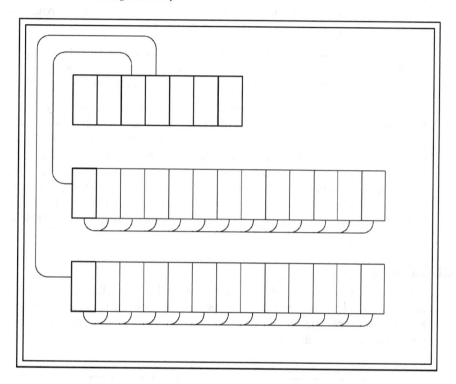

Assuming you use the distributed design for your Data Center, orient the server rows perpendicular to the network row when designing the room. Then place each server row's network substation at the end closest to the network row. This makes the cable run between the network row and the network substations as short as possible, which is less expensive to install. The shorter runs also provide marginally better performance.

Cable Characteristics

Data Center connectivity is provided by two broad types of cabling media—copper and fiber—and they in turn come in different configurations that offer various levels of performance.

NOTE	This chapter focuses primarily on copper- and fiber-structured cabling that is initially installed in a server environment. Patch cords, which are smaller lengths of pre-terminated cable used to connect into these structured cabling systems, are discussed in Chapter 12, "Stocking and Standardizing."

To assess the capabilities of each cable type and configuration and make an informed decision about what to install in your server environment, it is necessary to first understand how cable performance is measured.

The speed at which data can travel across a cable is measured in kilobits per second (Kbps), megabits per second (Mbps), or gigabits per second (Gbps). The capacity of information that a cable can carry, its bandwidth or frequency, is measured in megahertz (MHz).

Bandwidth and speed are sometimes discussed interchangeably, but really shouldn't be. They represent two different qualities of a cable. Imagine that your physical cabling network is a highway. The higher its Mbps rating, the more cars that can drive along the road. The higher its MHz rating, the more lanes the road has. Greater bandwidth won't increase the speed at which information is passed along a cable, but it is necessary in order to accommodate high-end demands such as video broadcasts. Another apt comparison is a water pipe. A larger pipe, enabling a greater volume of water to pass through, equates to greater bandwidth (MHz). More water pressure equates to higher speed (Mbps).

Copper Cabling

Copper cabling has been used for decades in office buildings, Data Centers, and other installations to provide connectivity. Copper is a reliable medium for transmitting information over shorter distances; its performance is only guaranteed up to 109.4 yards (100 meters) between devices.

NOTE   Technically, that distance limitation includes 98.4 yards (90 meters) of structured cabling and a total of 10.9 yards (10 meters) of patch cords on either end.

Copper cabling that is used for data network connectivity contains four pairs of wires, which are twisted along the length of the cable. The twist is crucial to the correct operation of the cable—if the wires unravel, the cable becomes more susceptible to interference.

Copper cables come in two configurations:

- **Solid cables**—Provide better performance and are less susceptible to interference, making them the preferred choice for use in a server environment.

- **Stranded cables**—More flexible and less expensive, and typically only used in patch cord construction.

Copper cabling, patch cords, and connectors are classified based upon their performance characteristics and what applications they are typically used for. These ratings, called categories, are spelled out in the TIA/EIA 568 Commercial Building Telecommunications Wiring Standard. TIA is the Telecommunications Industry Association; EIA is the Electronics Industries Alliance. Both are trade organizations that develop industry technology standards for electronics, telecommunications, and information technology equipment.

NOTE	Consider TIA/EIA 568 and its addendums your bible for recommended Data Center cabling practices. Installation practices, performance standards, and testing procedures are all covered by it. Buy a copy and reference it liberally in your design documents. You can find this document online at http://www.tiaonline.org/.

The lowest rating of copper cable used in modern Data Centers is Category 5. Previous categories were used for telephone systems and, by today's standards, slower network connections. Technically, even Category 5 cable is considered obsolete by TIA/EIA in favor of Category 5E—the E stands for enhanced—but it can still be found in server environments built in recent years.

Table 7-1 outlines the minimum standards for copper cabling, by category. As of this writing, a definition for Category 7 is still under development, so the listed criteria are only projections.

Table 7-1   *Copper Cable Specifications, By Category*

	Cat5	Cat5E	Cat6	Cat7
Ratified	1991	1999	2002	Proposed
Frequency	100 MHz	100 MHz	250 MHz	600 MHz
Attenuation	22 dB	22 dB	19.8 dB	20.8 dB
Characteristic Impedance	100 ohms ±15%	100 ohms ±15%	100 ohms ±15%	100 ohms ±15%
NEXT	32.3 dB	35.3 dB	44.3 dB	62.1 dB
PS-NEXT	-	32.3 dB	42.3 dB	59.1 dB
ELFEXT	-	23.8 dB	27.8 dB	Not yet specified
PS-ELFEXT	-	20.8 dB	24.8 dB	Not yet specified
Return Loss	-	20.1 dB	20.1 dB	14.1 dB
Delay Skew	-	45 ns	45 ns	20 ns

The attenuation and all cross-talk requirements are at a minimum of 100 MHz, while the delay skew is at a maximum of 109.4 yards (100 meters).

So, what do all of these statistics mean? Following are definitions of each characteristic:

- **Attenuation, also called loss**—A reduction in signal strength during transmission. It is measured in decibels (dB) and normally occurs over long distances. The less attenuation, the more efficient a cable is.

- **Characteristic impedance**—The opposition that a cable or component gives to the flow of an alternating electrical current. This impedance can affect the performance of high-speed networks.

- **NEXT, PS-NEXT, ELFEXT, and PS-ELFEXT**—Refer to crosstalk, which is when a signal carried along one set of cable wires interferes with a signal on another nearby set. This is much like if you were talking on the telephone and began to hear a conversation from a nearby phone line. Crosstalk is measured in decibels (dB) and is typically caused by poorly twisted terminations at the connection points. The different types of crosstalk are defined as follows:

  — **NEXT**—When measured at the end closest to the transmitter, it is called near end cross talk (NEXT).

  — **FEXT**—When measured at the end farthest from the transmitter, it is called far end cross talk (FEXT).

  — **Power Sum (PS)**—All possible combinations of interference from adjacent cable pairs added up is the power sum (PS).

  — **ELFEXT**—The subtracted attenuation of a signal due to cable length is equal level far end cross talk (ELFEXT). The amount of crosstalk enabled on a copper cable actually increases with a higher category of cable because its better construction makes it more resistant to interference.

- **Return loss**—Noise that occurs when a signal travels down a cable and encounters a jack or other piece of connecting hardware. The greater the impedance difference between the two items, the more noise—return loss—that results. If the cable and connecting item have the same impedance, there is no return loss.

- **Delay skew**—Refers to the different amounts of time that it takes for a signal to travel down a copper cable's various internal wires. Because a copper cable contains four pairs of twisted wires, those wires can be slightly different in length from one another. The difference between the fastest and slowest pairs is the delay skew. Errors can occur if a cable's delay skew is too great.

When specifying structured cabling and connectors during the construction of a server environment or ordering of patch cords to support an existing room, be aware of what cabling standards have been adopted by industry organizations. Someone is stretching the truth in selling cables, connectors, or patch cords and claiming that they meet standards that haven't been ratified. Really, he or she is selling a cable exceeding existing standards, and assuming that it will meet the upcoming standard.

NOTE   In the years before Category 6 standards were recognized by TIA/EIA, I had several vendors offer to sell me patch cords purported to be Category 6. While the patch cords exceeded Category 5E standards and were fine for my needs, they weren't Category 6, because technically it didn't yet exist.

It is important to note that many cabling products on the market are made to significantly outperform the standards that have been adopted by the cabling industry. Many Category 5E cables are capable of performing well beyond 100 MHz, for example. Manufacturers make better cables and components to attract buyers to their brand of products, and competition drives them to make continual improvements. Therefore, your Data Center's connectivity needs aren't limited to the minimum capabilities associated with a particular rating of cable. If you need better performance and are willing to pay more, you can very likely obtain it.

Category 5, 5E, and 6 cabling materials are all compatible with one another. Mixing components along a connection provides performance that is somewhere in the middle of what the individual items normally offer. For example, terminating a Category 5 cable with a Category 6 jack is going to perform better than if the system consisted entirely of Category 5 components but not as well as if only Category 6 items were used.

Fiber-Optic Cable

Fiber-optic cable is another common medium for providing connectivity. Fiber cable consists of five elements. The center portion of the cable, known as the core, is a hair-thin strand of glass capable of carrying light. This core is surrounded by a thin layer of slightly purer glass, called cladding, that contains and refracts that light. Core and cladding glass are covered in a coating of plastic to protect them from dust or scratches. Strengthening fibers are then added to protect the core during installation. Finally, all of these materials are wrapped in plastic or other protective substance that is the cable's jacket.

Figure 7-3 shows the components of a fiber optic cable.

Figure 7-3   *Anatomy of a Fiber Cable*

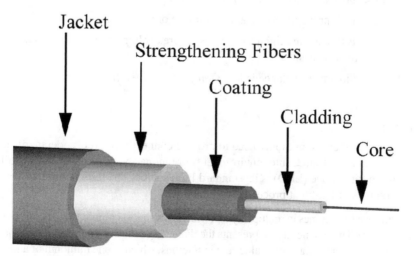

A light source, blinking billions of times per second, is used to transmit data along a fiber cable. Fiber optic components work by turning electronic signals into light signals and vice versa. Light travels down the interior of the glass, refracting off of the cladding and continuing onward until it arrives at the other end of the cable and is seen by receiving equipment.

When light passes from one transparent medium to another, like from air to water or in this case from the glass core to the cladding material, the light bends. A fiber cable's cladding consists of a different material from the core—in technical terms, it has a different refraction index—that bends the light back toward the core. This phenomenon, known as total internal reflection, keeps the light moving along a fiber optic cable for great distances, even if that cable is curved. Without the cladding, light would leak out.

NOTE   To see refraction in action, fill a clear drinking glass with water and drop in a piece of silverware. When viewed from an angle, the utensil appears bent. This is because light waves bend as they pass from the denser water into the less dense air.

Fiber cabling can handle connections over a much greater distance than copper cabling, 50 miles (80.5 kilometers) or more in some configurations. Because light is used to transmit the signal, the upper limits of how far a signal can travel along a fiber cable is related not only to the properties of the cable but also to the capabilities and relative location of transmitters.

Besides distance, fiber cabling has several other advantages over copper:

- Fiber provides faster connection speeds.
- Fiber isn't prone to electrical interference or vibration.
- Fiber is thinner and lighter weight, so more cabling can fit in to the same size bundle or limited spaces.
- Signal loss over distance is less along optical fiber than copper wire.

Multimode Fiber

Multimode fiber is commonly used to provide connectivity over moderate distances, such as those in most Data Center environments or among rooms within a single building. A light-emitting diode (LED) is its standard light source. The term *multimode* refers to the several rays of light that proceed down the fiber.

Multimode fiber comes in multiple types, with the two most common listed as 62.5/125 μm and 50/125 μm. The first number represents the diameter of the cable's core; the second represents the size of the cladding. Both values are in microns, which is one millionth of a meter.

The cable with the smallest diameter core provides the fastest connectivity, because the internal refraction that occurs in a cable moves a signal faster along a narrow core than in a larger one. The reflecting light crosses shorter distances in a narrower core.

Figures 7-4 and 7-5 illustrate how light travels along fiber optic cables with different core diameters.

Figure 7-4   *Internal Refraction Within Multimode Fiber*

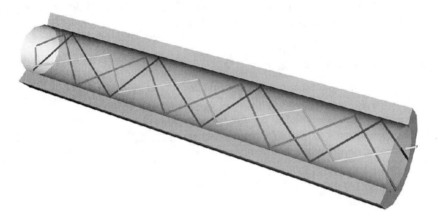

Figure 7-5   *Internal Refraction Within Singlemode Fiber*

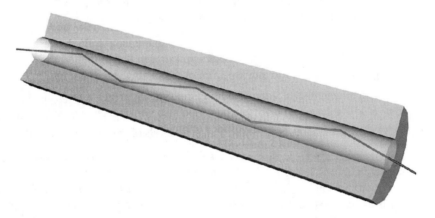

Singlemode Fiber

Singlemode fiber is used for the longest distances, such as among buildings on a large campus or between sites. It has a smaller core than multimode fiber, and a laser is its standard light source. It also has the highest bandwidth. The de facto standard core size for singlemode fiber 8.3/125 μm, although alternative diameters are occasionally used in a few regions of the world. Specify this size in your design documents to avoid confusion.

As newer servers and other devices require faster connection speeds, there is growing interest in installing singlemode fiber deeper into server environments, not just to connect a distant networking room to the Data Center's network row but also to extend that connection to individual server rows. This is still an uncommon practice, however, because network interface cards for singlemode fiber are more expensive than other types. At shorter distances, there can also be a problem of a singlemode fiber's laser light source traveling too rapidly for a receiver to read, requiring installers to intentionally attenuate the signal.

Table 7-2 shows the minimum cable performance capabilities of different types of fiber cable. (Wavelengths are expressed in nanometers.)

Table 7-2   *Fiber Cable Specifications, By Type*

Cable Type	Cable Type Wavelength	Maximum Attenuation	Minimum Bandwidth
62.5 μm MM	850 nm	3.5 dB/km	500 MHz-km
	1300 nm	1.5 dB/km	500 MHz-km
50 μm MM	850 nm	3.5 dB/km	160 MHz-km
	1300 nm	1.5 dB/km	500 MHz-km
8.3 μm SM	1300 nm	1.0 dB/km	n/a
	1550 nm	0.5 dB/km	n/a

NOTE   Don't mix different types of fiber. Unlike mixing different types of copper, which results in an averaged performance, mixing fiber creates substantial signal loss.

Cabling Costs

Because fiber optic cable provides greater performance than copper, you are probably assuming that it is significantly more expensive, too. In truth, the price tags of the two media depend greatly upon the distances involved and levels of performance that are needed.

Copper is generally the less-expensive solution over shorter distances, say the length of your Data Center's server rows, while fiber is less expensive for longer distances such as connections among buildings on a campus. That's because the copper cabling material itself is more expensive than fiber, but the electronic components used in the physical network—namely the network interface cards in each server—are more expensive for fiber than copper. Installations with long cable runs can offset the higher electronics costs, not to mention take full advantage of fiber's greater performance capabilities.

If more than one combination of infrastructure components can provide your Data Center with the features you are looking for, comparison shop to see if you can reduce costs. You don't want to sacrifice functionality or standardization, but you also don't want to buy a $10 item when an equivalent one is available for $5. Don't rely upon vendors to tell you the most cost-effective way of purchasing or configuring your infrastructure components. Many of them won't.

NOTE	My typical Data Center design calls for installing hundreds of copper jacks into the network row and the network substations at the end of each server row. Either of two patch panels from a particular manufacturer can be used to house the jacks—one is a 2U panel with 48 jacks, and the other is a 1U panel with 24 jacks. They are identical in every way except that one is exactly twice the height and capacity of the other; there is no functional or even cosmetic difference between installing four 2U panels or eight 1U panels.

For several consecutive projects, I exclusively used the 1U panels. They enabled me to install an odd number of patch panels where appropriate, and I figured that skipping the 2U panel avoided a superfluous part number and might even have led to a bulk discount on the 1U panels. A later audit of project costs revealed that, although the 1U panels were half the size and capacity of the 2U panels, they were significantly more than half the price. Replacing the 1U panels with 2U panels would have saved thousands of dollars per project!

When this was pointed out to the vendor, he smiled knowingly and said "We just gave you what you ordered."

Storage Area Networks (SANs)

A growing number of server environments now incorporate a storage area network (SAN) into their design. A SAN enables data from different servers to be transmitted over a dedicated network and stored, as needed, on various storage devices. Without a SAN, a server must be cabled directly to its own storage unit. With a SAN, any server in the network can potentially connect to any storage device in the network. This enables greater management of storage resources and, because data isn't residing on the servers themselves, frees up their processing abilities for other tasks.

From the perspective of Data Center infrastructure design, a SAN is largely the same as any other network. If you choose to have one within your Data Center, you must allocate cabinet space for SAN-related devices and provide structured cabling for connectivity. Fifty micron multimode fiber is the current standard medium. One SAN element that is different from the infrastructure perspective, however, is that (at least today) SAN equipment doesn't enable consolidated connections between devices in the way that conventional networking equipment does. This means that a SAN often requires larger amounts of cabling—both structured cabling and patch cords—than other networks.

Because a SAN is the same as any other network from a Data Center infrastructure perspective, consider housing your SAN's disk equipment and patching fields alongside your standard network's devices and cabling. Terminating the structured cabling for both your regular and storage networks provides consistency for Data Center users, making both systems easier to understand. Make sure that the components of both network systems are clearly labeled, so users can readily tell the difference between them.

Determining Connectivity Requirements

Servers and networking devices have a wide range of connectivity needs. A single server cabinet filled with equipment can therefore require dozens of connections or just a few. How, then, do you decide how much structured cabling to provide in your Data Center?

If you organize equipment in your Data Center by type of server, then research what connectivity each server requires and equip accordingly the corresponding rows where you plan to install them. This approach is simple when a server environment first comes online, but can cause headaches in the future. It creates different levels of infrastructure in the Data Center and locks in where equipment must be placed in the room. If you fail to accurately predict how many of a given server your Data Center is going to host or if technology changes, you must periodically retrofit portions of the Data Center to keep up.

If you organize equipment in your Data Center by function or work group, then choose a level of connectivity that can accommodate most servers and combinations of devices that might be grouped together in a server cabinet. Equip all Data Center cabinet locations with this amount of cabling. This might seem a less precise approach because you are designing to a theoretical average rather than specific equipment. It is a superior design, though, because it leads to a uniform amount of infrastructure rather than to peaks and valleys. Because all server rows are identically equipped and the room is organized by function rather than form, servers with high and low connectivity needs can be mixed together so as not to exceed the amount of cabling provided at any single server cabinet location.

NOTE   When specifying fiber quantities in your design documents, choose your terminology—ports, strands, or pairs—and be consistent. Merely calling for "24 fiber" at a location, for example, can be interpreted in two ways.

Depending upon the type of a connector used, a patch cord may occupy one port in a patching field while containing two strands. That same cable can also be referred to as one fiber pair. It is equally correct to describe that connection as one port, two strands, or one pair of fiber, so that request for "24 fiber" could mean 24 strands (12 ports), or 24 ports (48 strands).

I recommend using *strands*. The term is used consistently in the fiber industry, and any misunderstandings that do occur are going to result in an overabundance of connections, which is easier to deal with than not having enough.

As you determine how much connectivity to provide to each server cabinet location, be aware of how much space those cable runs occupy in your Data Center's network substations (or network row, if you choose to make direct connections). Higher cabling density requires more space to house patch panels and fiber housings, which means you might need to set aside additional cabinet locations to house them.

NOTE   My current standard for Data Center connectivity is to provide 24 strands (12 ports) of 50 μm multimode fiber and 24 ports of Category 5E copper to each server cabinet location. That is 432 connections for a row of 12 server cabinets. Placing a network device within each network substation then enables me to reduce the connections to the network row from 432 down to just 36—24 strands (12 ports) of fiber and 24 ports of copper.

These quantities address the connectivity needs of most combinations of servers, although it cannot accommodate a server cabinet filled entirely with 1U servers. I try to avoid such a massive installation anyway, though, because of the intense heat and weight it generates.

Network Redundancy

Where electrical redundancy is provided to your servers by electrical conduits running from more than one power distribution unit, network redundancy is provided by structured cabling running from more than one networking device. Whereas electrical conduits must be hardwired into the PDUs, however, structured cabling is standalone infrastructure that any networking devices can be plugged in to. Each cable is essentially providing its own path, and you just need additional networking devices to make them redundant.

This means that, as long as you provide abundant structured cabling throughout the Data Center, you increase redundancy as much as you want by simply installing more networking devices at the network row and network substations. If you want to provide a minimum level of redundancy over the entire Data Center, install a second set of networking devices in the network row and patch to key components at the network substations. If you want to provide an even greater level of redundancy, double the networking devices at each network substation.

Providing this redundancy may or may not require additional cabling infrastructure. It depends upon how many network connections a given server requires, and how many servers are patched into a Data Center's network devices. Most servers require a minimum of two connections, one for a primary Ethernet connection and another for either a console connection or a secondary Ethernet connection.

Networking Room

While power for your Data Center originates from an electrical room elsewhere in the building, data cabling similarly connects back to a networking room. It is here that structured cabling from the entire building, and in some cases an entire site, terminates.

Typically the networking room contains one or more rows of cabinets to house network devices and patch fields. These rows are often configured similarly to the Data Center's network row. Connections here, however, are to other rooms—the Data Center, labs with networks, distribution rooms with cabling for office computers—rather than to server rows.

Run structured cabling from your Data Center network row into the networking room. Copper, multimode fiber, and singlemode fiber provided between these locations is usually a good idea. The presence of the singlemode fiber enables easy patching into the building-to-building structured cabling system that also terminates in the networking room. This is especially important if your site contains more than one server environment and you want to incorporate them into the same network.

NOTE   As stated previously, my current cabling standard is 24 ports of Category 5E cable and 24 strands (12 ports) of 50 μm multimode fiber to each server cabinet location, and then that same amount—for each entire server row—between each network substation and the network row.

To complete the connection to the networking room, I run 24 ports of Category 5E cable, 24 strands (12 ports) of 50 μm multimode fiber, and 24 strands (12 ports) of 8.3 μm singlemode fiber from the network row.

Common Termination Options

Structured cabling typically terminates into female connectors, known as jacks or ports, within a container such as a fiber housing, patch panel, multimedia box, or data faceplate. (The terms *jack* and *port* can be used universally to describe fiber, copper, or even voice connectors.) While plugs and connectors are rated in the same way that copper and fiber is, the housings themselves are not. From a performance standpoint, it makes little difference what container you terminate a cable into.

Space constraints are usually the biggest challenge when it comes to providing a high amount of connectivity into a Data Center, or when it comes time to expand that system. Look for the housings that:

- Hold the most connections in a given space
- Provide some physical protection for the cabling
- Are easy for Data Center users to access
- Can be readily expanded in the future

Fiber housings and copper patch panels are used for terminating structured cabling directly into cabinets. These are optimal for locations where you want a Data Center user to have immediate access to data connections without needing to lift floor tiles or reach above a cabinet to plug in to a raceway. Avoid using fiber housings and copper patch panels at cabinets that you may reposition later, since these housings are screwed into cabinets and generally expected to be permanent installations. Multimedia data boxes are typically used when terminating structured cabling below a raised floor, while faceplates are used in overhead raceways.

Technically, you can mix what housings are used where—say installing data faceplates under a raised floor or multimedia boxes in a server cabinet, but there is no point in doing so.

NOTE   I have seen structured cabling purposefully terminated into patch panels below a raised floor at empty server cabinet locations. When cabinets arrive with servers, patch panels are then raised above the floor and screwed in to the cabinets. The strategy behind this approach is that, once servers are installed, Data Center users plug in to the patch panels and never have to raise floor tiles and risk damaging patch cords. I believe that such risk is minimal, and that this practice adds an unnecessary step to the installation process. It also reduces the future mobility of a Data Center's server cabinets.

Copper Cabling Terminators

Data Center copper cabling typically terminates into connectors and jacks known as RJ-45s. The plug looks like a wider version of the one that connects to your telephone, complete with a tab at the end that clicks when inserted into its corresponding jack. That telephone plug is actually an RJ-11. Both types are part of the registered jack (RJ) series of telephone and data connectors first established by the Bell telephone companies.

Crosstalk and other performance losses for a copper cable, outlined in the portion of this chapter addressing cable categories, occur predominantly where a cable is terminated. To diminish these losses, use quality RJ-45 connectors and jacks. Using connectors that are of a higher rating than your structured cabling not only reduces signal loss or interference, but it is also a cost-effective method of improving the performance of your entire network. The increased cost per connector is marginal when using Cat 6 jacks rather than Cat 5E, which is much less expensive that running miles (kilometers) of more expensive cabling in a server environment.

NOTE   Although this technique is not endorsed by TIA/EIA standards, it works. Most of the Data Centers I help manage were installed with high-performing Category 5E copper cabling and Category 6 jacks. That particular Cat5E cabling is rated to provide 350 MHz bandwidth and when paired with Category 6 jacks provides Cat6 performance for less than if Cat6 cabling had been installed.

Fiber Cabling Terminators

Three types of jacks and connectors are typically used for the termination of Data Center fiber cabling:

- Subscription Channel (SC) jack
- Mechanical Transfer Registered Jack (MT-RJ)
- Lucent Connector (LC) jack

SCs, the oldest type of connector, were originally developed by Nippon Telegraph and Telephone Corporations. SC plugs contain two small squares that are held side by side in a bracket.

Although still a perfectly capable jack, SCs have been largely replaced by smaller MT-RJ and LC connectors. These two connectors, modeled after the RJ-45 plug used for copper connections, each contain the same number of strands as an SC but at half the size.

Color-Coding Cabling Materials

Consider using different colors of cabling and components to help illustrate how your Data Center is organized. Multimedia boxes, data faceplates, copper jacks, and tie wraps can all be obtained in multiple colors. Perhaps you want to highlight all cable runs that connect the Data Center and networking room. Maybe you want to color-code connections that are part of a highly secure network, enabling them to be obvious for those who know what to look for without having to use labeling that reveals too much. Whatever your goal, color-coding cabling materials is an effective way to emphasize specific connections in your Data Center. Because these components are permanent installations, be sure that whatever you want to mark in this manner is meant to be a longstanding characteristic of your Data Center, too.

NOTE   I find it helpful to color-code copper jacks in the Data Center based upon where they connect—black for those that lead to network cabinet locations, white for those that lead to server cabinet locations, and lavender for those that exit the Data Center. (I would continue this color scheme with fiber ports, too, but they aren't available in multiple colors.) This results in a block of black jacks in the network row, a cluster of white jacks above or below each server cabinet location, and a clear juxtaposition within the network substation of which connections go where.

Figure 7-6 shows a patching field in a network substation. The top jacks (black) connect to the Data Center's network row, and the bottom jacks (white) connect to the server cabinet locations that are supported by the substation.

Figure 7-6   *A Color-Coded Patch Field*

Building-to-Building Connectivity

While this book focuses predominantly upon infrastructure within a Data Center, some mention needs to be made of the external cabling system that must be in place for your servers and networking devices to communicate with the outside world. This is known as *site-to-site* or *building-to-building connectivity.*

Typically, a company owns the external structured cabling on its site and then, once that cabling extends beyond its property lines, leases the conduits with which it connects. (That is assuming that the business owns the property and buildings, of course. If the site itself is leased, then the landlord is the true owner of the onsite cabling.) Conduits off of the property are owned by local service providers, such as a telephone or cable company, or sometimes by the area municipality. If you are uncertain what agencies have conduits in the ground in the region where your site is, ask the cabling contractors who are installing your Data Center's structured cabling.

Due to the distances involved and the desire for fast connection speeds, most connectivity between buildings is accomplished through singlemode fiber. In areas where conventional fiber can't be installed, lasers can be employed to provide point-to-point connectivity over short distances. This was previously accomplished with microwaves, but lasers provide greater bandwidth.

A star-and-ring topology, which provides redundant cabling to each building, is the industry standard configuration for building-to-building connectivity. You always want two different cabling paths into a building, for redundancy. The paths should be at least 50 feet (15.2 meters) apart, and ideally should be on opposite sides of a building. The farther apart they are, the less susceptible both are to damage from a single event.

The number of strands needed for your building-to-building connectivity depends upon how much traffic you expect—24 strands is typical for small company sites; 72 is more appropriate for larger ones.

Figure 7-7 illustrates a standard configuration for structured cabling among the buildings on a site. Each black dot represents a building.

Figure 7-7   *A Sar-and-Ring Topology*

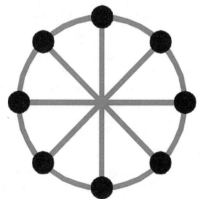

When working with a service provider, be clear about what redundancy you want in your system. Establish service level agreements with the provider that define its response times and repair responsibilities. Also, clarify how representatives from the service provider are to access your site during emergencies. Finally, to reduce repair times, it can be beneficial to maintain spare components on your site, for example, extra power supplies or controller cards.

Recommended Installation Practices

Just as important as how you design the paths of your Data Center's cable runs and what components you choose to use is the manner in which those materials are installed. Include comprehensive instructions in your design documents so that there is no question on the part of the cabling contractor as to what a proper installation is for your project.

General Installation

First, make sure that all cabling installations are done in a professional manner and comply with applicable building codes for the region where the Data Center is constructed. It is advisable to require that the contractors installing the structured cabling into your server environment be trained and experienced at doing so. (Corning Cable Systems' Extended Warranty Program training is an excellent standard for fiber cabling, as is Panduit Corp.'s Integrity Authorized Installer training for copper.) Have the contractor provide training certificates of completion for all technicians who are installing the cable.

Because cable runs coming from the networking room must pass through a Data Center wall, require contractors to redress this opening so that it meets the same fire resistance rating as the rest of the wall.

Bundling Structured Cabling

The structured cabling in your Data Center should be gathered into bundles and organized by destination. Cables running from one point in the Data Center to another should be contained within the same bundle. This enables easy tracing, maintenance, or removal of the cables as needed.

Set a maximum size for the cable bundles. This creates uniform cable runs through your server environment and can help you standardize both the size of cutouts in your notched floor tiles and the wire management on your network cabinets. Twelve copper cables per bundle is a good choice for the following reasons:

- It is a manageable size that occupies minimal space within the plenum.
- It can fit through small floor tile cutouts.
- It is consistent with the by-12 grouping common to Data Center infrastructure components, as mentioned in Chapter 4, "Laying Out the Data Center."

Fiber cabling is much smaller than copper, but you might still want to limit bundles to 12 ports (24 strands) for consistency.

Specify the use of soft hook and loop cable ties to gather the cables into bundles, making sure that they are not cinched too tightly or otherwise stressed. Have all cable bundles combed during installation. This keeps individual cables from twisting within a bundle, making it possible to readily trace any cable along its entire length.

Figure 7-8 shows multiple bundles of structured cabling, gathered with soft tie wraps and combed. Each bundle contains 12 cables and is routed to a different cabinet location within a single server row.

Figure 7-8   *Bundled Structured Cabling*

Copper and fiber cables in Figure 7-8 are bundled with hook and loop tie wraps. What appears to be a lone cable curving away from the copper bundles is a 24-strand bundle of fiber cables.

Minimum Bend Radius

Require that all cables be installed with a generous bend radius so that they aren't kinked, sheared, or otherwise damaged. A sharp bend in a copper cable can disturb how the pairs of wires inside are twisted, reducing the cable's performance and making it more susceptible to interference. A sharp bend in a fiber cable can damage the cladding, enabling light to escape and decreasing the strength of the data signal.

There is no overall standard in the cabling industry for a minimum bend radius. Individual standards are typically specified by the manufacturer of a given cable. The closest things to a common standard are as follows:

- **Copper** — A TIA test that calls for Category 5 cabling to withstand a 1-inch (2.5- centimeter) bend radius under certain conditions

- **Fiber** — A bend radius that is at least 10 times the diameter of the cable, which typically works out to somewhere between 1.2 and 2 inches (3 and 5.1 centimeters).

Be aware that these measurements refer to the radius of curvature that a cable can bend without suffering damage and reduced performance. If you want to specify one universal minimum bend radius in your design documents, rather than look to different manufacturers' guidelines, err on the side of caution and use 2 inches (5.1 centimeters).

NOTE	Structured cabling isn't the only form of data cabling you want to protect from sharp bends. Apply a similar minimum bend radius when using pre-terminated patch cords. More information about how to care properly for the patch cords in your Data Center is provided in Chapter 12.

Reverse Fiber Positioning

When your fiber cabling is installed, it is important that the cable strands be oriented in a consistent manner to maintain polarity in the system. Transceivers on servers, networking equipment, and other devices are standardized so that their transmitter and receiver are always located in the same position relative to a central keyway.

Figure 7-9 shows how the orientation of transmitters and receivers maintains the same position in relation to the keyway.

Figure 7-9   *Transceiver Orientation*

Have the cabling contractor flip the strand positions for each connector between the networking room and Data Center network row, among network rows and each network substation, and between the network substation and each server cabinet location. This practice, known as reverse fiber positioning, enables you to standardize on one straight-through patch cord for all connecting cords on both ends of the system.

Figure 7-10 shows the standard locations of the transmitters and receivers as signals pass between Data Center-related devices.

Figure 7-10   *Transceiver Orientation and Data Transmission*

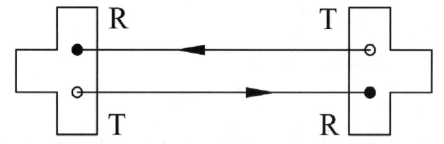

Labeling the Structured Cabling System

The most comprehensive structured cabling system in the world is only as useful as its labeling makes it. If connections are ambiguous in any way, Data Center users are likely to ignore what was so painstakingly installed and simply run patch cords to connect their server where they want it to go. Every place in your Data Center where cabling terminates needs to be clearly labeled with the start and end locations of that cable run (Chapter 11, "Labeling and Signage," offers suggestions for how to number cabinet locations in your Data Center). Extend this labeling scheme down to every fiber housing, patch panel, multimedia box, and data faceplate.

Figure 7-11 shows the array of structured cabling components that should be labeled with destination information in your Data Center.

Figure 7-11 *Labeling of Structured Cabling Termination Points*

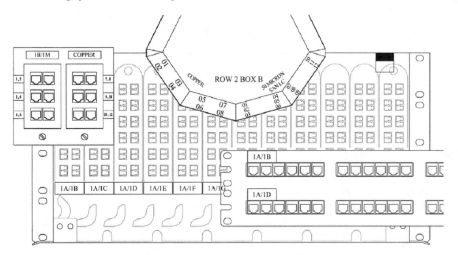

You want your Data Center labeling to be able to pass the novice test. Someone completely unfamiliar with a server environment—not just unfamiliar with yours but having never been in any Data Center before—should be able to easily make or trace a connection from one cabinet location in the room to another. When Data Center connections are simple to follow, equipment installations and troubleshooting become easier, and changes for human error are reduced.

NOTE   I have toured dozens of server environments where every patch cord in the room has some form of labeling tag at both ends. While this is admirably thorough, it takes a lot of staff time to maintain. Even a moderately sized Data Center can use thousands of patch cords, and spending just a few minutes to label each cord can add up to hundreds of hours per year. This extra work is completely unnecessary if your Data Center is well organized and if all of its termination points are clearly labeled.

While most Data Center users are going to examine the labeling only where structured cabling terminates, it is also helpful to provide certain markings on the cable runs themselves. This can avoid later confusion about exactly what kind of cabling was installed in your Data Center and make it easier to troubleshoot any infrastructure problems.

For copper cabling, label all cable jackets with the following:

- Name of the manufacturer
- Gauge of copper wire
- Pair count
- Category rating
- Sequential length markings
- Minimum performance specifications (i.e., EIA/TIA 568B)

For fiber cabling, label all cable jackets with the following:

- Name of the manufacturer
- Fiber size and type (i.e., 50/125 μm MM)
- Sequential length markings

Cabinet Installations

While cable runs to your Data Center's server cabinet locations terminate in multimedia boxes under-floor or data faceplates overhead, cable runs to your Data Center's network row and network substations terminate directly into cabinets by way of fiber housings and copper patch panels. These cabinets are the only ones to house both structured cabling and equipment, specifically networking devices. Both the cabinets and incoming cabling must be installed in a particular manner to function correctly.

NOTE   Copper jacks aren't the only Data Center components that you can color-code. You can color-code the cabinets as well. I use black cabinets for the network row and substations and white cabinets for server rows. This continues the pattern started with the room's copper jacks, and provides an immediate clue to the room's organization to new users and visitors.

Figure 7-12 shows a server row with color-coded cabinets. The two black cabinets at the left end of the row house networking devices; the white cabinets house servers.

Figure 7-12 *Color-Coded Cabinets*

First, secure the network cabinets to your Data Center floor, by running a threaded rod down to the cement and bolting each cabinet at all four corners. With structured cabling terminated in the network cabinets, you aren't going to reposition them in the Data Center as you might the server cabinets whose data connections terminate adjacent to but outside of them. You might as well gain the stability that comes from securing the network cabinets. In some regions, there might even be tax benefits associated with securing the cabinets. Equipment that is secured to a building is considered a capital improvement and therefore deductible whereas unattached infrastructure items are merely expenses.

Second, route structured cabling down the sides of the cabinet. You want to stay within the frame of the cabinet while still leaving as much internal space open for the installation of networking devices as possible.

Here is where limiting the diameter of the Data Center's cable bundles is helpful. Cabling contractors might experience difficulty in routing structured cabling inside your network cabinets. A cable bundle is fairly rigid, but it is not like a wire coat hanger that can be bent and then retain its new shape. Even if it could, a contractor still has to be careful of the path of the cable due to minimum bend radii.

One way to help with this challenge is to install vertical front-and-rear wire management on the sides of each network cabinet. This style of wire manager has two channels—one that extends past the front of the cabinet face and another that sits behind it. Structured cabling can be routed through the "rear" channel, keeping it away from networking devices.

The drawback of this solution is that the wire management requires room between each network cabinet, adding to how much Data Center floor space they occupy. Over the course of an entire network row, that can add up.

A second approach is installation of several horizontal guide rods into each network cabinet with cable bundles secured to them. Typically, #8-32 threaded zinc plate rods, cut to match the depth of the cabinet, along with the same size of hex nuts and washers, work well.

Figure 7-13 shows cable bundles routed along the sides of a network cabinet. The bundles are secured to several horizontal guide rods so as to stay clear of networking devices but remain within the silhouette of the cabinet.

Figure 7-13   *Guide Rods for Structured Cabling*

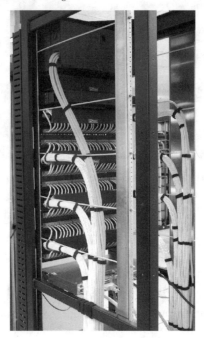

NOTE   Throughout this book, I refer to the use of four-post cabinets to house Data Center equipment. Two-post metal frames, known as relay racks or open bay racks, can also be used in many situations. These racks are lighter and generally less expensive, and have a smaller profile than four-post cabinets.

Such racks often have lesser weight-bearing ability than four-post cabinets, however. I have seen cheaper racks actually warp under the weight of networking devices. Two-post racks also can't stand upright on their own—they must be mounted to the floor. Because of this, two-post racks are suitable for network rows and network substations but not for housing servers.

Testing and Verifying Structured Cabling

Once your structured cabling is in place, have the cabling contractor test all components to make sure that the entire system, both copper and fiber, is providing the level of performance expected of them. Tables 7-1 and 7-2 from earlier in the chapter summarize these values, taken from TIA/EIA 568B.

Although testing requirements differ between copper and fiber cabling, there are certain procedures that you want contractors to follow for both media, including the following:

- **Provide documentation on what testing procedures and equipment are being used**—List specific manufacturers and model numbers, and when the equipment was last calibrated. An approved service provider should have calibrated all test equipment within the past two years.

- **Perform tests on the entire system cabling, not just individual components**—If anything disturbs a termination after it is tested, consider the test invalid and do it again.

- **Provide test results in both hardcopy and computer-readable format**—Cable test results can come in an array of presentation formats, many of which include very small type sizes. Hardcopy is helpful for initially reading the mountain of test results; softcopy is useful for storing the data long term.

Be clear in your design documents that a cabling installation isn't considered acceptable until all terminations meet the appropriate standards, and that any components that do not meet the standards must be removed and replaced at no cost.

Have copper-structured cabling tested to confirm that there are no opens, shorts, or incorrectly crossed pairs, a test known as wire mapping. It should also be tested, per TIA/EIA 568B, to make sure that all components meet the expected parameters for NEXT, PS-NEXT, ELFEXT, PS-ELFEXT, return loss, propagation delay, and delay skew, as outlined previously in Table 7-1.

Current copper testing standards call for what is known as permanent link testing, which eliminates the testing materials—the patch cord and connector used to plug the tester in to the structured cabling that is being measured—from the results. (The prior standard called for a basic link test, which did not eliminate these materials.)

Have fiber optic structured cabling likewise tested to make sure that all components meet the expected parameters for maximum attenuation and minimum bandwidth, as outlined previously in Table 7-2.

Structured Cabling Warranties

While Data Center cabling infrastructure should be tested and verified as part of their installation process, what if you discover bad ports at a much later date? This is not unheard of in very large Data Centers, since data ports at the far end of a room may go unused for months or even years after the room's initial construction.

Malfunctioning ports are typically addressed according to the warranties that accompany the installations. Most structured cabling manufacturers provide a warranty on their materials for at least 20 years and, if an authorized installer performed the work, cover their labor for the same amount of time.

Labor performed by a non-approved installer will be covered according only to that installer's warranty. This is good incentive to use established companies, rather than an unproven vendor who might not still be in business when later problems arise.

In my personal experience, reputable cable installers are quick to stand by their work and remediate a non-working installations for free, even if the original work was done years earlier. Such responsiveness fosters goodwill and makes it more likely for the customer to return with future business.

If you use multiple cable installers at your site, carefully document who does what work. It is unrealistic to expect even the most agreeable vendor to reinstall cabling without charge if there is uncertainty over when they installed it in the first place.

Wire Management

Wire management is an important tool for keeping your Data Center neat and organized and for encouraging Data Center users to correctly patch in to the room's structured cabling infrastructure. These components come in many shapes, sizes, and materials, enabling you to customize a solution for your particular server environment. Some patch panels and fiber housings can also be ordered to include their own wire management. Vertical wire management is typically mounted onto the external frame of Data Center cabinets, while horizontal pieces can be mounted either that way or installed within the cabinet.

Size your Data Center's wire management based upon how many patch cords you expect to route through it—obviously, the more cables a wire manager must accommodate, the thicker it needs to be. A good rule of thumb is wire management that is at least as big as any copper patch panels and half as big as any fiber housings that it is intended to guide cabling to. If you have a copper patch panel that occupies 2U of cabinet space, make sure that there is a total of 2U of wire management adjacent to it. If the jacks that those copper cables plug in to need that much space, it is a safe bet that the cables themselves need at least that much room. Fiber cables are thinner than the ports they plug in to, which is why the ratio is cut in half for them.

Install ample wire management in areas where you want cables routed through and none in those where you don't. A carefully chosen combination of patch fields and wire management can guide how Data Center users' patch cables into the system.

For example, if you don't want patch cords to be routed along the top of your network row, don't install horizontal wire management there. Place those components lower on each cabinet instead. Given a choice between using existing wire management or stringing cables somewhere else, the vast majority of people follow what is already in place.

Install a comprehensive wire management system on the front of your network row, where connections from the Data Center's network substations terminate, to enable users to easily patch to and from anywhere in the room. Use thick, vertical wire managers on either side of each cabinet to accommodate large numbers of patch cords. You also want thinner horizontal components among every couple of patch panels to guide patch cords into the vertical pieces.

Figure 7-14 shows a comprehensive wire management system, which includes both vertical and horizontal components, on a network row.

Figure 7-14 *Horizontal and Vertical Wire Management*

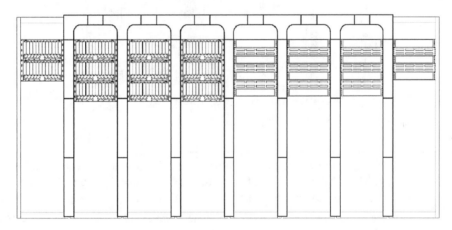

Figure 7-15 shows two examples of how wire management and patch panels can guide Data Center users on how to route patch cords:

- The configuration on the left features wire management that encourages users to patch above and below the patch fields and then into the vertical wire management.

- The configuration on the right relies upon convex, v-shaped patch panels to encourage users to route cabling directly in to vertical wire management.

Be judicious about the installation of wire management into server cabinets, especially pieces that connect cabinets together or unintentionally encourage Data Center users to string patch cords between cabinets. Both conditions inhibit the flexibility of your Data Center and should be allowed only in rare circumstances.

Figure 7-15 *Alternate Wire Management Configurations*

NOTE	Some cabinets come equipped with their own internal wire management. I usually stay away from this style of cabinet because the built-in devices make the cabinet wider or occupy vertical internal space that could otherwise hold additional server equipment, or both.
	If wire management is needed at server cabinet locations, I prefer to install it externally on key cabinets. This conserves equipment space in the Data Center and is more flexible, enabling wire management to be reconfigured or removed as needed. It is also easier to customize than built-in systems, enabling you to install components only where cable density warrants it.

Common Problems

As stated at the start of this chapter, a Data Center's structured cabling is one of its most complex infrastructure systems. As such, it is also the most likely to feature mistakes during initial construction. Here are several installation errors to watch out for in your server environment's cabling:

- **Structured cabling is routed sloppily in the network cabinets**—The neatness of cable runs installed in your Data Center can vary depending upon the contractor. Carelessly routed cable bundles can either block internal cabinet space needed to install equipment or stray outside the cabinet frame and expose them to damage from other cabinets being placed adjacently. Even the most well-intended cabling contractor might not understand when a cable run is in the way of future installations if he or she is unfamiliar with your Data Center design. The best way to avoid this problem is an included drawing or picture of properly routed cables in your design documents.

- **Incorrect structured cabling is ordered and installed**—Chapter 5, "Overhead or Under-Floor Installation?" mentions the possibility of mixing up plenum and non-plenum cabling. That is not the only mixup in materials that can occur.

Note	Although the Data Center design documents I use clearly call for indoor plenum-rated cabling, down to the part number and manufacturer, in separate projects I have had cabling contractors order and begin to install non-plenum cable, heavily jacketed cable designed for outdoor use, and even armored cable. In each case, the contractor took responsibility for the mistake and agreed to fix it, but there was inevitably little time to do so and still have the Data Center come online on schedule. In some instances, the cabling was hurriedly replaced, while in others (in which there was no fire code violation) I simply had to accept the mistake.
	Catching incorrect materials can be especially difficult if the project site is at a remote location that you are unable to visit frequently. Most of the time, the first hint I receive that incorrect cabling has been ordered comes when a contractor complains that they can't route it in to network cabinets in the manner specified. Both the armored and outdoor cabling are thicker than what is normally called for, which prevents it from fitting in the tight spaces.

- **Strand counts are mistaken as port counts or vice-versa**—With no standard for referring to fiber counts by strands or ports (2 strands = 1 port), it is easy for an incorrect amount of fiber to be installed. The best precaution against this mistake is one term chosen and used consistently in your documentation. A drawing in your design package that shows typical fiber terminations at the network and server cabinet locations can also reduce confusion.

- **Labeling of connections is incomplete or unclear**—Make sure that cabling contractors have a good understanding of how your Data Center's patching fields and other components are to be labeled. Labeling can be a tedious and confusing job and so is often skimped on. It doesn't help that some fiber housings come with a pre-printed numbering scheme. It inevitably won't match the one for your Data Center, so it usually just creates confusion. To avoid this problem, provide illustrations of proper labeling within your Data Center design documents.

Note	In early 2000, I had a contractor who thoroughly labeled components in the structured cabling system of a new Data Center in Raleigh, North Carolina. Unfortunately, the planning and facilities consultant involved in the project took the odd step of deciding that the network substation at the end of each server row shouldn't be counted in the numbering scheme.
	That Data Center is 7914 square feet (735.2 square meters) and contains about 730 cabinet locations. Hundreds of multimedia boxes and thousands of patch panels and fiber housings had to be relabeled. Doing so ultimately required three coworkers and me to spend about 300 hours to correct the error.

- **Multimedia boxes aren't fully assembled**—When structured cabling terminates into a multimedia box under a raised floor, make sure that the boxes are assembled completely. Some simply snap together, while others need to have their pieces further secured by screws. Contractors occasionally take a shortcut by snapping the boxes together and skipping the screws. This makes the boxes prone to coming apart and exposing cable strands over time. Spell out the proper assembly of these components in your Data Center design documents.

Summary

A Data Center's physical network is crucial for a company's servers to communicate with one another and the outside world. This network must feature high-performing cabling media and abundant connections and be well organized for ease of use and future expandability.

Provide a full complement of structured cabling to all server cabinet locations when the Data Center is constructed. Incorporate short cable runs into the design for better performance and lower costs. Also, be sure to pick the correct cabling media for your server environment's connectivity, based upon the performance needed and distances involved.

There are two approaches to laying out a Data Center's structured cabling. One is cables directly connected from a network row to server cabinet locations. This can work in small server environments but is difficult to manage and maintain in larger ones. The other is cables run from a network row to a substation at the end of each server row. This is more manageable, shortens the length of cable runs, and adds redundancy to the network.

Copper and fiber-optic cabling are used to provide Data Center connectivity. Copper is used for shorter connections, up to 109.4 yards (100 meters). Copper cabling and components are rated by categories, and Data Center cabling traditionally falls into Category 5, 5E, or 6. These categories define standards for frequency, signal loss, impedance, several forms of crosstalk, return loss, and delay skew. Fiber is used for longer connections, up to several miles. Data Center fiber comes in three types that differ primarily by the diameter of their core: 62.5 μm multimode, 50 μm multimode, and 8.3 μ singlemode. Their specifications included standards for signal loss and bandwidth.

Copper cable costs more than fiber cable, but the associated network cards that must be installed in servers are inexpensive, making this a good medium to use over a shorter distance. Fiber is the opposite—cable material is less, and network interface cards are more. Together with the distance advantages of fiber, this makes it a better solution for longer connections.

Decide how much cabling to run to server cabinet locations based upon how you organize servers and what connectivity they require. If the Data Center is organized by server type, stagger infrastructure levels to meet their needs. If the Data Center is organized by function or work group, provide enough connectivity to meet most combinations of servers. The second approach is preferable because it is more flexible and easier to manage.

Ample structured cabling in the Data Center enables redundancy to be added at any point where additional networking devices are installed.

Data Center structured cabling ultimately terminates back to a networking room. This rooms serves the same role for the building or entire site that the network row does for the Data Center—it is the ultimate destination for all network cabling. Install copper, multimode fiber, and singlemode fiber in the networking room to enable easy patching into any site network.

In a server environment, copper cabling terminates into RJ-45 connectors and jacks while fiber cabling terminates into SC, MT-RJ, or LC connectors and jacks. Consider color-coding these and other cabling components to highlight how your Data Center is organized. While a company usually owns all structured cabling up to its property boundaries, further connectivity is provided by conduits leased from a service provider such as a telephone or cable company. Have redundant cabling paths into your site, and establish clear service-level agreements with your service provider.

Include thorough directions in your design package to ensure that cabling and components are installed correctly. These directions should call for trained personnel to perform the installations, careful bundling and combing of structured cabling, generous bend radii, use of reverse fiber positioning, labeling of all cabling with from/to information, and careful termination of cabling into network cabinets.

Have cabling contractors test cabling materials once they are installed to ensure that they meet expected standards. Require contractors to document their test procedures, test the system as a whole, and provide results in both hardcopy and softcopy.

Install wire management strategically to guide how Data Center users patch into the cabling infrastructure—provide ample wire management where you want cable routed and none where you don't.

Common installation mistakes with structured cabling include sloppy routing in network cabinets, use of incorrect cabling, confusion between fiber ports and strands, inadequate labeling, and failure to fully assemble multimedia boxes.

CHAPTER 8

Keeping It Cool

This chapter explains the features of a Data Center's environmental control and protection systems—cooling and fire suppression. The chapter includes tips to promote good airflow within a server environment and outlines the advantages and disadvantages of various fire suppression technologies.

Cooling Requirements

In addition to supplying power and connectivity, your Data Center must cool the servers, networking devices, and other machines that it houses. The environmental controls within a building that regulate temperatures and air circulation are referred to, collectively, as HVAC—heating, ventilation, and air conditioning. This HVAC infrastructure has three jobs to do in a Data Center:

- Keep temperatures low
- Keep them constant
- Diffuse hot spots created by clusters of equipment

Low temperatures are necessary for the efficient operation of servers. Like most electronic devices, they function more effectively at cooler temperatures—circuit speeds are faster due to lower electrical resistance, components degrade slower, and heat removal is more efficient. In fact, while server environments are typically maintained somewhere between 65 and 75° Fahrenheit (18.3 and 23.9° Celsius), that is usually in deference to the comfort of people working in the room and because it requires tremendous amounts of energy to achieve lower temperatures. If those weren't considerations, Data Centers would probably resemble walk-in refrigerators.

NOTE   There's a rule of thumb among electronics manufacturers that for every 18° Fahrenheit (10° Celsius) increase in ambient temperature, there is a 50 percent reduction in the reliability of a device. Or, to put it the other way, every 18° Fahrenheit (10° Celsius) decrease in temperature doubles a device's reliability.

This ballpark equation comes from the Arrhenius Rate Law. The law, named for Nobel Prize-winning chemist Svante Arrhenius, states that the rate of a chemical reaction increases exponentially according to absolute temperature. It is the reason why foods spoil and metals rust much slower when kept in a cold environment instead of a warm one. For computer hardware, the phenomenon means that capacitors and semiconductors have a shorter lifespan when subjected to higher temperatures.

It is therefore paramount for the health and overall lifespan of servers and networking devices that your Data Center cooling infrastructure maintains the room at low temperature.

Constant temperatures are required in server environments because fluctuations are hard on servers and network devices. It is actually better for such equipment to reside in an always-warm Data Center than in one that varies between warm and cool, provided that that always-warm temperature remains within the manufacturer's operating range. Dramatic fluctuations—more than 10° Fahrenheit (5.5° Celsius)—can cause corrosion and humidity problems, and reduce the lifespan of a machine because its components must work harder in the changing environment.

Finally, diffusing hot spots is necessary to prevent the exhaust from one cluster of servers from adversely affecting other nearby devices. Even when infrastructure provides adequate cooling to your Data Center as a whole, clusters of equipment can create hot spots. Hot spots have become more prevalent in Data Centers in recent years as server manufacturers have moved to smaller chassis, prompting system administrators to install more devices into any given server cabinet. Unfortunately for those tasked with keeping a Data Center cool, future generations of servers are likely to be even hotter. Higher processing speeds are attained largely by increasing electrical consumption, which in turn generates more heat.

NOTE   It is a fallacy of high-density, low-profile servers that a company can install dozens of them into a small area, reducing how much Data Center floor space and supporting infrastructure are needed. In theory, because these servers occupy only 1U and standard server cabinets have 42U of interior space, you should be able to pack them in to a very small area.

In reality, these servers generate so much heat and weight that when you install them close together most server environments can't accommodate them without major structural and cooling upgrades. The only alternative solution is the small equipment spread over a larger area to disperse its effect, which makes it occupy the same space as the larger machines it replaced and is supposed to be superior to.

Chilled Liquid Cooling

Data Center cooling is typically accomplished through a chilled liquid system, which involves three main pieces of equipment—air handlers, chillers, and cooling towers.

Air handlers circulate air within the Data Center, drawing in warm air from the space between the floor and ceiling and discharging cold air into the room's plenum. (This occurs typically below the raised floor if a Data Center has one, and above the false ceiling if it doesn't.) Air is cooled within the handler by passing over coils containing chilled liquid— think of wind blowing across a block of ice—and then expelled into the Data Center. The coils are generally maintained at about 43 or 44° Fahrenheit (6.1 or 6.7° Celsius).

Because warm air rises and is going to gather near the ceiling and most Data Centers include a raised floor, most air handlers have their intake at the top and discharge at the bottom. These handlers are installed either in the Data Center or in an adjacent corridor with connecting ducts that enable air exchange. Assuming that your Data Center has people working inside it on a regular basis, regional building codes likely require a percentage of external air circulated into the room. Most air handlers also possess filtration systems to capture dust and other pollutants, to improve your Data Center's air quality.

Chillers do the work of keeping the air handler coils cold. They contain three components — an evaporator, compressor, and condenser. The evaporator transforms liquid refrigerant into gas and in the process chills the water that circulates to and from the air handlers. The compressor draws in this gas, changing it into high-pressure, high-temperature vapor that can be condensed easily. The condenser transforms this vapor back into liquid, discharging heat, and then returns the liquid refrigerant back to the evaporator.

Figure 8-1 illustrates the flow of air and water through a typical Data Center cooling system.

Figure 8-1   *Data Center Cooling Process*

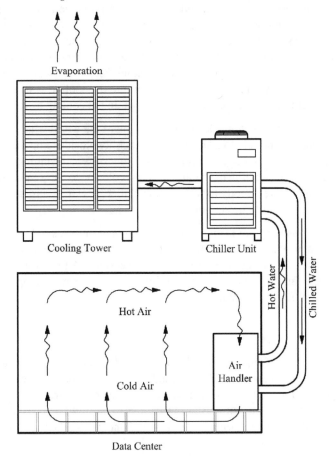

Chillers are typically located outside of the building where the Data Center is. They can be placed at ground level or, if real estate is at a premium, on the roof. A ground-level chiller is somewhat easier to maintain because workers don't need to carry tools up to the roof, but also more vulnerable to tampering.

The processes that occur within the chiller generate a significant amount of heat. It is the job of the cooling tower to dispose of this heat and keep the chiller cool. Hot water is vaporized in the cooling tower to lower its temperature. This process works the same way that your body does. When you exercise or otherwise exert yourself, you sweat and are cooled as that moisture evaporates. Fans within the cooling tower then draw air across a series of filters, which cools the water inside, similar to how the air handler functions. Because water is lost during the evaporation process, so-called makeup water must be added into the system.

Makeup water comes from a municipal water source. Unfortunately, this means that your Data Center cooling system is vulnerable to any failure by this water supply. You can safeguard against this by constructing a water storage container to house your own surplus supply of makeup water. For an added measure of protection, configure your cooling and fire suppression infrastructure so that water within the sprinkler system can be drawn upon to serve as makeup water in an emergency. Sprinkler water should only be utilized as makeup water as a last resort to keep your Data Center from overheating. Not only does diverting this water hamper your ability to extinguish a fire, but because sprinkler water can be stagnant for years at a time, transferring it into the cooling system contaminates the normal water treatment process that occurs within the cooling tower.

If your server environment is located in a region of the world where cold weather is prevalent, you might be able to take advantage of chilly outside temperatures to save energy—and therefore money—needed to run your cooling system. Installing a plate and frame heat exchanger enables water in the cooling tower—cold due to the weather outside—to transfer its cold temperature directly to water in the chiller by way of a metal plate, enabling the chiller's compressor to be shut off.

This saves money by not having to run the compressor, leads to less wear and tear on the device, and provides an ideal opportunity for any required maintenance to be performed on the chiller. This technique is known as free cooling. Admittedly it is not really free, because the fans and pumps in the cooling system must remain operational, but it can provide significant cost savings.

House Air

Most Data Centers require such elaborate and dedicated cooling measures due to the high amount of heat produced by the hundreds or thousands of servers, networking devices, and other equipment they house. However, if you are constructing a very small server environment—say, one with just a few cabinets—it might be possible to cool the room using the same air conditioning infrastructure that cools other spaces within the building. This is known as *house air*.

House air is typically automated for office spaces in the same manner that you set the thermostat in your home. Heating and cooling are used liberally during business hours to provide a comfortable temperature level, and less so after hours and on weekends when employees aren't expected to be in the building. If you opt to cool a small server environment with house air, configure it to provide cooling around the clock, seven days a week—not just during business hours.

Makeup Air

Just as makeup water must be added as part of the chiller process to compensate for water that is lost to evaporation, so too must makeup air be supplied into the Data Center. Makeup air is necessary to prevent the server environment from becoming depressurized. Makeup air is drawn from the outside and should be filtered to prevent contaminants from entering the Data Center.

Cooling Quantities and Temperature Ranges

When designing your Data Center's cooling infrastructure, you must determine two key details:

- How much cooling infrastructure is necessary to cool the server environment adequately?

- What specific temperature you want to maintain the room at?

To determine the first, it helps to understand a few terms that are used to quantify cooling.

- **A ton of cooling**—This term represents the amount of heat involved in melting one ton—2000 pounds—of ice in a 24-hour period. Data Center air handlers generally come in 20- and 30-ton capacities. This means that they provide the same amount of cooling as having an equivalent-sized block of ice in the room.

- **BTUs**—Cooling units are generally rated in British Thermal Units. This term refers to the amount of heat needed to raise the temperature of 1 pound of water by 1° Fahrenheit (.56° Celsius). One ton of cooling equals 12,000 BTUs.

- **Watts per square foot**—The third term is watts per square foot or watts per square meter depending upon what part of the world you are in. This refers to how much energy is used in the Data Center. It is relevant to cooling because energy produces heat. So, when someone says they want 100 watts per square foot of cooling, they are asking for enough cooling to offset that amount of energy usage in that space. One watt equals 3.41 BTUs.

To calculate how much cooling is required for your Data Center space, you need to know how much energy is going to be expended in the Data Center and the size of the room. From there, you can match that amount of energy to its equivalent cooling, in tons.

Table 8-1 illustrates how much cooling is needed in a 10,000 square-foot Data Center, based upon how much energy is used. From left to right, watts are converted into BTUs, multiplied for the size of the Data Center, and then converted into tons of cooling. This cooling tonnage is then distributed among 20- and 30-ton air handlers placed strategically in the Data Center.

Table 8-1   *Projected Cooling Needs Based upon Power Usage (sq ft)*

Watts/sq ft	BTUs/sq ft	DC size (sq ft)	Total BTUs	Tons of cooling	Number of air handlers
50	170.5	10,000	1,705,000	142.1	5–7
75	255.75	10,000	2,557,500	213.1	7–10
100	341	10,000	3,410,000	284.2	10–14
125	426.25	10,000	4,262,500	355.2	12–18
150	511.5	10,000	5,115,000	426.3	14–22
175	596.75	10,000	5,967,500	497.3	17–25
20	682	10,000	6,820,000	568.3	19–29

Table 8-2 provides similar data using watts per square meter, for a 1000 square-meter Data Center. From left to right, watts are converted into BTUs, multiplied for the size of the Data Center, and then converted into tons of cooling.

Table 8-2   *Projected Cooling Needs Based upon Power Usage (sq m)*

Watts/sq m	BTUs/sq m	DC size (sq m)	Total BTUs	Tons of cooling	Number of air handlers
600	2046	1000	2,046,000	170.5	6–9
800	2728	1000	2,728,000	227.3	8–12
1000	3410	1000	3,410,000	284.2	10–15
1250	4262.5	1000	4,262,500	354.4	12–18
1500	5115	1000	5,115,000	426.3	14–22
1750	5967.5	1000	5,967,500	497.3	17–25
2000	6820	1000	6,820,000	568.3	19–29

Chapter 6, "Creating a Robust Electrical System," explains how to determine the maximum power draw of your Data Center.

Obviously, the more energy used in your Data Center, the more cooling that is required. Also, note that more cooling requires a greater number of air handlers, which in turn occupy more floor space within the Data Center. This means that less space might be available for hosting servers and networking equipment.

NOTE   The more air handlers installed in a Data Center space, the greater the height likely required for its raised floor. A deeper plenum enables a greater volume of chilled air to pass through and can better accommodate the increased air pressure that additional air handlers create.

To answer the second question, choose a temperature that falls within an acceptable range for servers and networking devices to function properly within your Data Center. While individual manufacturers specify preferred temperatures for their particular models, generally maintaining a server environment between 65 and 75° Fahrenheit (18.3 and 23.9° Celsius) is fine for hosting all manner of equipment.

Assuming that your Data Center is large enough to have multiple air handlers, use them to good advantage. In areas of the room that are heavily populated with equipment, lower the air handler's settings to below the ambient temperature you want to achieve. In areas that are lightly populated, use slightly higher settings. Even greater temperature control can be obtained through the strategic placement and incremental opening of the Data Center's perforated tiles.

NOTE   In my experience, an ambient temperature of 68 to 72° Fahrenheit (20 to 22.2° Celsius) in a Data Center is a reasonable target. It is well within the operating range for servers and cooler than typical office temperatures, but not so cool as to place unreasonable demands on the air handlers or make the room uncomfortable for people to work in.

Redundancy in Your Cooling Infrastructure

Just as you install additional electrical infrastructure and networking devices so that these Data Center functions are insulated against downtime, so too should you provide redundancy in your cooling infrastructure.

At a minimum, provide at least one more air handler in your server environment than is required to meet its cooling needs. This redundancy enables any one air handler to be shut down for regular maintenance. In the event that an air handler malfunctions, the spare unit can also be activated to maintain sufficient cooling in the server environment. For a large Data Center that includes more than a dozen air handlers, consider installing two spare air handlers.

Because all of the Data Center's air handlers ultimately route back to an external chiller, install a second chiller to keep it from being a single point of failure for the room. Having a spare chiller and at least one spare air handler provides your Data Center with N+1 cooling coverage, in the same manner as having a redundant UPS does for the room's standby electrical infrastructure. It might be impractical to provide much physical separation between the two chillers—if they're located on the roof of the Data Center building, for instance—but do so if circumstances allow.

Follow through on this redundancy by providing an additional cooling tower with each chiller. Although it is possible to feed two chillers from a single cooling tower, this isn't recommended. The cost savings are minimal from doing so, and a lone cooling tower becomes a single point of failure.

Cooling Distribution and Air Pressure

Air pressure must be maintained in your Data Center for cooling to be delivered effectively and efficiently. Unwanted openings in the Data Center plenum inhibit cool air from reaching where it needs to go and force your cooling infrastructure to work harder to compensate. Imagine trying to fill a large bucket with water using a garden hose that has a pinhole leak. The water that escapes out that hole never makes it into the bucket. The more holes in the hose, the more that is diverted.

The level of air pressure in your Data Center is called its static pressure. This measurement, expressed in inches or centimeters of water column or water gauge, refers to the resistance of air as it is pushed in to the room. Data Centers are typically designed to have a static pressure between .2 and .5 in. wc. (.51 and 1.3 cm. wc.). To maintain air pressure in the Data Center, properly seal all walls and doors and carefully manage any openings in the plenum—either the raised floor or space above the false ceiling, depending upon your room's design. Fully open perforated floor tiles at cabinet locations that are packed with equipment and close them near locations that aren't. Also cover tile cutouts to prevent air from escaping. (Chapter 5, "Overhead or Under-Floor Installation?" provides suggestions for how to do this.)

Also be cautious about locating perforated tiles too close to Data Center air handlers. Most handlers require a buffer of 36 to 42 inches (91.4 to 106.7 centimeters) between them and what they are trying to cool. If perforated tiles are placed too close, any of three cooling problems can occur:

- Cold air exiting the handler can travel at such a high velocity that little of it emerges from the perforated tiles within the clearance area, causing servers in the clearance area to not be cooled. Air slows down as it moves away from the handler, enabling it to pass through the perforated tiles that are farther away.

- A pocket of low pressure may be created below the perforated tiles. This condition can draw warm air from above the raised floor down into the under-floor plenum. This unintentially warms the chilled air, reducing the efficiency of the Data Center's cooling system.

- Short cycling can occur. In this case, cold air exits the air handler, comes out through perforated tiles in its buffer area, and returns to the handler—still cool and without getting to any servers. Because the regulating sensors for the air handler are located in the return airflow, the unit is fooled into thinking the Data Center is cooler than it actually is, and turns off prematurely. Short cycling causes air handlers to turn on and off more frequently than normal, causing more wear and tear.

Humidity

Another aspect of your Data Center's HVAC system is its ability to regulate relative humidity in the room. Humidity is the amount of water vapor in the air. Relative humidity is a percentage of how much water is in the air compared to how much that air could hold at whatever temperature it happens to be when you measure it.

Although servers and networking devices can function within a wide range of humidity levels, generally between 20 and 80 percent, it is good to exercise some control over humidity in the Data Center. High humidity can cause condensation and corrosion on servers or infrastructure components, while low humidity can cause static.

Adding or removing moisture from the air can be done by way of properly equipped air handlers or through the use of separate humidification units. Because separate units occupy additional floor space, they can be more expensive than building humidification capabilities into existing air handlers, and require additional water piping. In most cases, it is more advantageous to use air handlers in your Data Center that have humidification capabilities.

Aim for a relative humidity level in the Data Center of somewhere between 45 and 55 percent. This is a favorable setting for servers and infrastructure components and provides a buffer in the event that humidity begins to change in your server environment, giving ample time to correct levels before they become too high or low.

Humidification devices, whether within an air handler or separate, enable you to establish their level of sensitivity—at what point they are to engage and begin adding or removing moisture to adjust the air back to desired humidity conditions. You want this range to be small enough that relative humidity stays at the level you want, but not so narrow that the system must repeatedly turn on and off to make minor corrections. Think of this like the heating and air conditioning systems in your home. If you set your thermostat to keep your home at a specific temperature at all times and allow it to vary by only a couple of degrees, the system has to work much harder than if it can vary by several degrees.

NOTE The Data Centers that I manage are maintained to a relative humidity level of 50 percent, with a sensitivity range of 10 percent. The humidification systems engage when relative humidity reaches above 55 percent or below 45 percent.

Layout, Cabinets, and Cooling

Filling your Data Center with more and more air handlers isn't the only way to address heat. How you arrange items in the server environment—not just the cooling infrastructure but also the server rows and different types of floor tiles—as well as what types of cabinets you deploy can have a significant effect upon how air circulates and where cooling is directed.

Space

The most straightforward solution to reducing heat in a server environment is to simply spread everything out. Allocate more floor space for the Data Center, make aisles wider between server rows, and don't tightly pack equipment into server cabinets. Each of these steps enables the heated air to more easily dissipate. If you have ever sat near a bonfire, you know that simply backing up a bit makes a huge difference to how much heat you feel from it.

As simple as this solution is, it is often difficult to accomplish. Building floor space is usually at a premium, so you might have a difficult time obtaining a larger Data Center footprint. Lightly populating your server environment can also be perceived as wasteful by upper management.

At minimum, evenly distribute equipment among your server rows, mixing low-profile servers with larger ones and hotter devices with cooler ones. This can help reduce the formation of hot spots.

Positioning Air Handlers

When designing the layout of the Data Center, orient air handlers and server rows so that they are perpendicular to one another. Air from the handlers can then pass easily between the electrical conduits and structured data cabling infrastructure associated with each row. When handlers are parallel to server rows, discharged air can be partially blocked by this under-floor infrastructure.

Keep the plenum space immediately in front of the air handlers free of obstructions, so that air circulation is not disrupted. Also avoid placing cable trays or other items under floor that might further restrict airflow.

Hot and Cold Aisles

As stated at the start of this chapter, hot spots are a major challenge that must be addressed by your Data Center cooling infrastructure. One approach to this problem is a Data Center design with heat sources occuring in predictable locations. Cooling can then be more easily directed to deal with them. This is most often done by creating what are called hot and cold aisles.

To do this, arrange the Data Center as follows:

- Face consecutive server rows in alternating directions. The front of each row faces the front of another, and the backs of each row face one another.

- Place perforated floor tiles in front of each server cabinet location, opening their adjustable dampers so that air flows into this aisle.

- Install ducting in the ceiling than begins with a vent above the aisle behind each server row and connects back to the air handler's intake.

Most servers and networking devices discharge exhaust from their rear side. Laying out the Data Center in this manner brings cold air from the air handlers to the front of each server cabinet location—the cold aisle. The air is then drawn in to the server cabinets, cooling the devices inside, and expelled out the back as exhaust, into the hot aisle. Now heated, this air rises and is drawn in by the ducted return overhead and channeled back to the air handler.

Figure 8-2 illustrates the airflow pattern that hot and cold aisles provide in a Data Center.

Figure 8-2   *Airflow Through Hot and Cold Aisles*

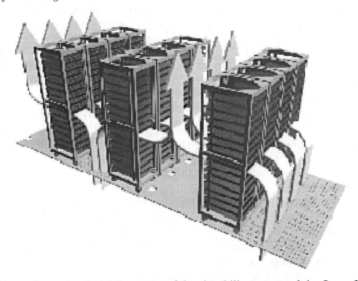

This configuration is only as successful as its ability to control the flow of air. If your server environment contains many servers or networking devices that vent exhaust to the sides or cabinets that direct it up or down, this design is less effective and might not be worth deploying.

NOTE   Even if you don't use hot and cold aisles in your Data Center, you can install ducted returns back to the air handlers to improve how much warm air is drawn back to them, and help dissipate hot spots.

Cabinet Design

To make hot and cold aisles in your Data Center most effective, it helps to use cabinets that have solid walls on both sides. Used in conjunction with devices that discharge heat at their backside, this helps channel exhaust into the hot aisles.

Several other types of cabinets can be used in a server environment to assist with cooling.

Perhaps the most obvious approach to dealing with servers that generate tremendous heat is fans built directly into the cabinets that house them. Cabinet fans can be used to draw cooler room air into a cabinet or to expel warmer cabinet air out, or both. Some cabinets even contain variable flow fans linked to their own temperature sensors—the amount of cooling applied to the servers within the cabinet varies as needed. The chief drawback to this solution is the higher cost for cabinets with fans. Fans can also slightly increase the power draw that each cabinet requires and might be noisy, nothing significant from a single cabinet but usually noticeable when deployed across an entire server row or Data Center. Some cabinet fans also redirect server exhaust straight up from a cabinet, which may or may not coincide with the airflow patterns you want for your server environment. Finally, cabinet fans might have a reduced effect upon servers that are installed in a tight cluster or have a large profile, because those characteristics inhibit airflow within an enclosed cabinet.

Another option is use of open cabinets, that is cabinets without any door, wall, top, or bottom panels. Server exhaust doesn't become trapped in an open cabinet the way it does in one that has doors and panels. This is a potential plus, although the same lack of doors and panels also means that server exhaust can't be channeled as easily into hot and cold aisles. Fortunately, open cabinets are usually lighter and less expensive than other models. Because patch cords and power cables aren't hidden behind cabinet doors, they must be routed neatly by Data Center users so as not to become a snagging hazard.

NOTE	Don't confuse four-post cabinets with two-post racks. Two-post racks can't be used without bolting them to the Data Center floor, which you don't want to do to your server cabinets because it limits the flexibility of the room. Some two-post racks can also be relatively flimsy and might warp when filled with heavy servers. If you do opt for two-post racks, choose a model that can bear the same weight in a cabinet location as your Data Center floor, so that the racks don't limit you in how you deploy servers.

Yet another approach is use of liquid-cooled cabinets. Though their specific operations can vary, these cabinets generally draw server exhaust from the back of the cabinet across a chilled coil or cooling module and then recycle the air back to the front of the servers to cool them. The process, which largely mimics the role of the Data Center's own air handlers, neutralizes the heat that a cluster of servers normally produces. The advantage of this design is that the cabinet is specifically trying to cool the heat source rather than ambient air. As with cabinets containing fans, the main drawback of liquid cooled cabinets is their price. There is also the risk, albeit a minor one, of a leak from a liquid cooled cabinet onto Data Center servers or infrastructure.

Although there are benefits to standardizing what type of server cabinets you use in your Data Center, you might not want or be able to exclusively use fan-cooled, open, or water-cooled cabinets throughout the room. This could be due to costs, noise concerns, or because some servers can only be housed in specific proprietary cabinets. If this is the case, focus the deployment of these cabinets in problematic areas of the server environment where additional cooling assistance can be the most helpful.

Fire Suppression

A Data Center is just as vulnerable to fire as any other conventional office building space. Computer hardware can potentially short circuit, for example, or flames might start in another part of the building and then spread to the server environment. Whatever the cause, protect Data Center users and your company's servers by installing a comprehensive fire suppression system.

Suppression Materials

Materials used to extinguish a fire in a Data Center must be capable of more than simply putting out flames. First, because it is possible that people might be in the server environment when the suppressant is released, they must not be toxic or otherwise harmful. Second, due to the critical nature of what is placed within a Data Center, it is important that the materials don't damage sensitive equipment and cause data to be lost. Third, suppressant must also be environmentally friendly, because building codes in many regions prohibit the use of any materials that are damaging to the ozone layer or potentially contribute to global warming. Finally, it is helpful if the materials are easy to clean up so that your staff can get back to work as soon as possible.

Gaseous suppressant is most commonly used in server environments because it doesn't harm servers or leave a large mess behind after discharging. Here is a list of several commercially available materials that are considered safe for use in areas occupied by people and gentle on servers:

- **Inergen or IG-451**—An inert gas composed of nitrogen (52 percent), argon (40 percent), and carbon dioxide (8 percent). Inergen removes oxygen from the air so that combustion can't occur. Inergen is a preferred suppressant in many European countries and is considered to have no environmental risk due to ozone depletion or global warming.

- **Argonite or IG-55**—An inert gas composed of argon (50 percent) and nitrogen (50 percent). Argonite reduces the oxygen content of the air. It is considered to have no environmental risk due to ozone depletion or global warming.

- **FM-200 and HFC-227**—Made by different manufacturers, but both consisting of heptafluoropropane. Used in server environments around the world, particularly in the United States, but prohibited in some European countries due to its potential contribution to global warming. FM-200 and HFC-227 are not considered toxic, but might break down under intense heat and produce hydroflouric acid, which is toxic.

- **FE13 or HFC-23**—Made of trifluromethane and originally developed as a chemical refrigerant, it absorbs heat from a fire until combustion can no longer occur. As with FM-200/HFC-227, this has global warming potential and, though non-toxic itself, can produce toxic hydroflouric acid as a byproduct.

Countries have different regulations as to what fire suppression materials are permitted, so check with regional building codes to determine which are acceptable for your Data Center site. Fire suppression systems can vary significantly in cost and how much physical space they occupy, depending upon the size of the Data Center and what extinguishing materials are used. When designing your server environment, involve a fire suppression system specialist to provide this information. Whatever suppressant you choose, avoid those with high levels of carbon dioxide. While they are quite capable of extinguishing a fire, they can also asphyxiate people.

Because these fire suppression materials are gaseous, server environment walls and doors must be well sealed for them to function properly. In the event that the system discharges, you want the suppressant to be concentrated within the Data Center and not leak outside.

Sprinklers

Whether or not your Data Center has a gaseous fire suppression system installed, building codes in most regions require coverage from fire sprinklers.

Fire sprinklers are a system of pipes designed to discharge water in specific areas where intense heat, presumably from a fire, is detected. Each sprinkler head contains either a liquid-filled glass bulb or a solder link that bursts at a certain temperature, causing water to be released.

The exact temperature at which the bulb bursts can vary, although it is typically above 155° Fahrenheit (68° Celsius). Data Center servers can generate a tremendous amount of heat, so make sure the temperature break point for your sprinklers is not too low. While a lower break point registers a fire sooner, it is also more likely to be triggered by a heat source other than a fire. This is especially important in a tiny server environment that is supported by a single air handler. One malfunction can cause the room to overheat rapidly.

Sprinklers are configured to dispense water only where the heat source is. If a fire's heat is only below one sprinkler head, only that head discharges. Activation across an entire room occurs only if the fire's heat radiates over a large enough area to warrant it. Most systems additionally include audio and visual alarms to alert people when sprinklers have activated.

There are multiple types of fire sprinkler systems. A so-called wet system keeps pressurized water in the pipes at all times, while a dry system uses compressed air to keep water out of the pipes and behind control valves until a fire condition exists. Because cold weather can potentially freeze the pipes in a wet system, there is also a mixed system that enables you to change between wet and dry configurations during different times of the year. Finally, a pre-action system keeps water out of the piping until electrical or mechanical detection devices determine the presence of a fire.

Install a dry or pre-action system into your server environment. This reduces the risk of water being accidentally spilled into the room. If a sprinkler pipe in the Data Center is somehow damaged, there is no liquid to spill out of a dry or pre-action system.

Manual Controls

Although sprinklers are activated only by intense heat, gaseous fire suppression systems typically include manual controls as well. These controls consist of two push-buttons—one button resets the automatic countdown-to-activation that occurs as fire suppressant is prepared to discharge, and the other button bypasses the countdown and triggers an immediate discharge. The automatic countdown typically lasts 30 seconds.

As mentioned in Chapter 6, Data Centers are usually required by fire code to shut down all electrical power before activating their fire suppression systems. To meet this requirement, all of the controls for your Data Center's fire suppression systems must be linked with the room's Emergency Power Off (EPO) system. This applies to the automated activation of any fire extinguishing system (sprinklers or gas) *and* to manual controls.

This means that the manual controls for your Data Center's gaseous fire suppression system have the same ability to bring the entire room offline as the EPO controls do. As such, you should secure them in a similar manner to deter accidental activation—cover the manual controls with a transparent shell, install an audio alarm, and provide clear labeling.

Sample signage for the manual controls of a gaseous fire suppression system are recommended in Chapter 11, "Labeling and Signage."

NOTE	Be aware that the button that resets a Data Center fire suppression system's countdown-to-discharge doesn't permanently halt it. As soon as pressure on the button is released, the countdown starts again from 30.

Be sure to install a telephone near the manual controls of your fire suppression system, so that any person who is actively pausing the countdown is not trapped in the Data Center and unable to communicate what is happening to other support personnel.

Design Details

Whatever combination of fire suppression infrastructure you install in your Data Center, coordinate the design with the installer to make sure that the system not only provides coverage throughout the entire server environment but also strategically places fire suppression infrastructure components.

For example, if fire suppressant storage tanks can't be located in a dedicated closet and must be placed somewhere within the Data Center floor, at least locate them in a low traffic area. Similarly, make sure that sprinkler heads and dispensing nozzles are not positioned where they might be obstructed by servers and other equipment that are to be installed in the room later.

Be sure to firmly secure the suppressant containers, because their contents are under pressure. If the containers are somehow damaged they could become projectiles.

Air Sampling and Smoke Detection

Data Center fire suppression systems are typically designed to detect heat from a fire and then discharge their extinguishing materials. While this is effective at stopping a blaze, it doesn't provide any opportunity to deal with or respond to a fire before it is well underway. For earlier warning of a potential fire, install a smoke detection system in your Data Center.

The most effective detection systems are those that continuously sample the air. In these devices, air is drawn from the target area—in this case the server environment—by pipes, to a central unit that scans the sample with a xenon lamp. Smoke particles and other common fire emissions cause the light to scatter in a pattern that is recognized by the detection devices. Air sampling can detect smoke during the early stages of combustion, before smoke is visible to the naked eye.

Be aware that these air sampling systems are much more sensitive that conventional smoke detectors—by a factor of 1000 according to some manufacturers. Due to this high sensitivity, adopt the following practices for your server environment to avoid false alarms:

- Prohibit cardboard and other sources of dirt within the Data Center. Although air sampling systems include filters designed to screen out dirt particles, they are not infallible.

- Prohibit smoking or the use of soldering equipment in the Data Center, or in close proximity to it.

- Shut off the air sampling system whenever major construction is performed in the Data Center, or in close proximity. If a lab is being built in a space adjacent to the Data Center, for instance, it is possible for particles to be blown or tracked in to the room.

Turn down the sensitivity of your smoke detection equipment in the event of a fire anywhere near your property. Winds can carry smoke from a hillside fire for miles, possibly triggering your air sampling system.

Fire Alarms

Regional fire and building codes are likely to spell out the proper deployment of fire alarms at your building site, including within your Data Center. In addition to those requirements, make sure that fire-related audio alarms are loud enough to be heard in the Data Center. Air handlers and cabinets containing high-density servers are notably noisy and can drown out quieter alarms. Likewise, orient visual alarms so that they can be seen throughout the room. Tall server cabinets might prevent Data Center users from having a direct line of sight to an alarm, so flashing and strobe alarms are recommended.

Locate the control and display panels for air sampling and smoke detection infrastructure near the Data Center's fire suppression controls. In the event that conditions are detected that make you want to manually activate the fire suppression system, it will be helpful to have them at hand.

It is useful to install explanatory signage near your Data Center's fire alarms and fire suppression system controls so that users know how this infrastructure operates and what they need to do during an emergency. Chapter 11 provides recommendations about this and other emergency instructions.

Handheld Extinguishers

In addition to room-wide fire suppression systems, install portable fire extinguishers throughout the Data Center. Building codes in some regions might enable you to forgo these devices if your server environment possesses the other systems, but it is still a good idea to have them. Smoke and fire detection sensors, no matter how effective, might miss the start of a small fire. Having handheld extinguishers mounted in key locations around the Data Center might enable you to put a fire out before the room's larger suppression systems need to engage and shut off power to all servers in the process.

There are five classes of fire extinguishers—each is intended to quench a different type of fire:

- Class A is for basic fires involving wood or paper.
- Class B is for fires involving inflammable liquids such as gasoline or oil.
- Class C is for electrical fires.
- Class D is for inflammable metals.
- Class K is for cooking oil and grease fires.

Multi-use extinguishers, which can be used on several types of fires, are also available. Suppression materials used by these extinguishers include:

- Water (Class A)
- Chemical foam (Class A and B)
- Carbon dioxide (Class B and C)
- Dry foam (Class B and C)
- Dry powder (Class D)
- Wet chemical (Class K)
- Dry chemical (multipurpose)

Class C fire extinguishers are most appropriate for use in a Data Center. Halogenated or carbon dioxide materials are preferable, because they leave minimal residue when discharged.

Install handheld fire extinguishers in the build room as well, because cardboard boxes, wooden pallets, and other combustible materials are inevitably placed there.

Common Problems

It is pretty easy to tell whether your Data Center's cooling infrastructure has been correctly installed or not—cooling is either being provided throughout the room or it is not. More challenging is the fire suppression system, because any significant installation problems aren't likely to be uncovered until it is time for the system to discharge. Here are couple of common mistakes to watch out for during construction of your server environment:

- **Perforated tiles are indiscriminately left open or closed**—Despite the importance of floor tiles to cooling a Data Center, little thought is usually given to these tiles after a contractor first installs the raised floor system. Their adjustable plates are simply left in the position in which they arrive at the site. This can defeat the design of the Data Center's cooling infrastructure. Check the settings of all perforated tiles to make sure that air is being directed where you want it to go. Be especially vigilant for any tiles that are to have a server cabinet or piece of equipment placed directly upon them. Once something is sitting upon these tiles, it becomes very inconvenient to change their settings.

- **Chilled water pipes are inadequately insulated**—Occasionally contractors fail to insulate the piping that carries chilled water to and from Data Center air handlers. When warm air in a server environment makes contact with bare pipes carrying the cold liquid, condensation can occur and lead to puddles on the floor. Because this water tends to accumulate below the raised floor or in another out-of-the-way area, it might go unnoticed for some time and potentially damage infrastructure. Thoroughly insulate all pipes carrying liquid to and from Data Center air handlers, both to prevent this condensation and help maintain the temperature of incoming chilled liquids.

NOTE An easy way to detect water leaks above your Data Center's false ceiling is to keep an eye on the ceiling tiles. If the bottom of a tile has a brown stain, water has leaked through it. Facilities personnel should investigate the source of the leak and, after repairing it, replace the stained tile with a new one.

Summary

It is the job of your Data Center's cooling infrastructure to keep the room at a cool, consistent temperature and disperse hot spots created by server exhaust. Electronic devices work more efficiently at low temperatures and suffer greater wear and tear due to significant fluctuations. Hot spots created by server clusters are problematic because they can heat up surrounding devices.

A chilled liquid system is most commonly used to provide Data Center cooling. Air handlers circulate air in the server environment—drawing in warm air, passing it over coils of chilled liquid, and then discharging it. An external chiller keeps the coils cold by changing refrigerant to gas, and then returns the vapor back to liquid so that the process can be repeated. A cooling tower uses similar evaporation cooling to then keep the chiller cool, replacing any evaporated water by way of a municipal water supply.

While most Data Centers require dedicated cooling infrastructure, house air might be used to cool the smallest of server environments.

Size your cooling infrastructure based upon how many watts per square foot or square meter of energy is expected to be expended within the Data Center. The more energy, the more cooling that is required. Set the room's target temperature at a level that is acceptable for servers to function at and comfortable for Data Center users.

Provide redundancy within your cooling system by installing at least one spare air handler to provide full cooling coverage during maintenance or a unit failure and a second chiller and cooling tower to avoid having a single point of failure.

Maintain air pressure in the Data Center so that the cooling infrastructure functions properly and efficiently. Seal floors and walls and use perforated tiles to control how cold air is directed in the room. Don't place perforated floor tiles too close to Data Center air handlers. Air might either rush past the opening, failing to cool equipment above the raised floor, or return immediately to the handler and mislead it into thinking the room is cooler than it actually is.

Control the relative humidity within your Data Center to prevent corrosion from too much moisture in the air or static from too little. Do this through properly equipped air handlers or separate humidification units. Allow variation in humidity levels so that infrastructure components aren't constantly working to maintain a pinpoint level.

Lay out your Data Center to achieve maximum cooling. Design wide aisles and spread out servers that generate substantial heat. Place air handlers perpendicular to server rows so that under-floor infrastructure doesn't inhibit airflow. If your servers and networking devices all use front-to-back cooling, alternate how server rows are oriented. Then place perforated floor tiles in front of them and ducted air returns behind them to create hot and cold aisles.

Enclosed cabinets containing fans, open cabinets that enable server exhaust to escape, and liquid-cooled cabinets can all be used to improve spot cooling in the Data Center.

Install a comprehensive fire suppression system in your Data Center to protect against fire. Gaseous suppressants are popular because they don't harm servers or leave a large mess after a system discharge. Common suppression materials include Inergen and Argonite, two inert gases; FM-200 and HFC-227 that are made of heptafluoropropane; and FE13 or HFC-23, which absorbs heat from a fire. Not all materials are allowed in all regions of the world, so you must check with local authorities to determine what is acceptable for installation at your particular Data Center.

Even with a gaseous fire suppression system, most building codes require the installation of a water-based sprinkler system. Dry or pre-action systems are best for a server environment because their water supply is kept outside of the pipes that are routed inside the room. Be sure that piping and sprinkler heads are laid out to provide maximum coverage within the Data Center.

Equip the Data Center with an air sampling system to detect combustion as early as possible. Prohibit cardboard and other sources of dirt, smoking, and soldering inside the Data Center to avoid triggering the smoke detection system. Shut off or lower the sensitivity of the system during nearby construction projects or when an external fire might cause a false alarm.

Install fire alarms in key locations within the server environment so that they are most likely to be seen and heard by Data Center users. Also install handheld fire extinguishers that are suitable for use in a computer room.

When your Data Center's raised floor is installed, check all perforated tiles and adjust them to provide how much or little airflow you want for each server cabinet location. Also make sure that all chilled water pipes are properly insulated so that condensation doesn't form.

CHAPTER 9

Removing Skeletons from Your Server Closet

Not all Data Center projects involve the construction of an all-new server environment. This chapter offers guidance on how to upgrade an existing Data Center that is lacking in space or infrastructure, has been poorly maintained, or can no longer meet your company's hosting needs because of changes in the types of equipment that are to be installed. While the design principles are the same as discussed in prior chapters, this chapter specifically addresses the special challenges of retrofitting a less-than-perfect server environment with the least impact to devices that are already on line. Tips are also provided on how to relocate a Data Center with the least possible disruption and downtime.

Lack of Space

One of the most common reasons for upgrading a Data Center is simply that it has run out of physical space to host new equipment. This could be because the server environment was undersized during its initial design or, hopefully, because a company has prospered and requires more servers and networking devices to handle its expanding business functions.

Space Saving Measures

Before launching a large-scale construction project to expand a Data Center that is running out of hosting space, take steps to make sure that what exists already—both floor space and internal space within each cabinet—is being used as efficiently as possible. Here is a handful of tips that can extend the capacity of a server environment:

- **Rerack servers**—Review how existing Data Center equipment has been installed.

  - Are there gaps between servers? Move devices closer together so that they occupy less cabinet space.

  - Are devices sitting on the raised floor that can be rack-mounted instead? Install them into cabinets to free up floor space.

  - Can large monitors in cabinets be replaced with smaller ones? While a standard computer monitor occupies 10U or more when placed on a cabinet shelf, there are rack-mountable models that open and shut like a laptop computer. They occupy only 1U in a cabinet, and a user slides out an extendable tray to open them to viewing size. It's also possible to link multiple devices to a single monitor, using a switch box to change displays, thereby freeing up even more cabinet space.

Note   Some of the Data Centers I manage are stocked with a KVM switch that is mounted to a movable cart. The switch enables a keyboard, video monitor, and mouse (hence KVM) to control multiple computers at one time. This even further reduces the number of peripherals that need to occupy server cabinet space.

- **Reorient floor-standing devices**—Rack-mountable servers aren't the only items that need to be arranged in order to conserve space. Make sure that floor-standing machines are positioned to occupy as few cabinet locations in the Data Center as possible. For example, if a storage unit has a door on one side that needs to swing open to insert or remove media, place the unit at the end of a server row. This enables the aisle to provide the clearance space for the door rather than sacrificing a usable cabinet location.

- **Upgrade to smaller devices**—Today's servers, networking devices, and storage units are almost universally smaller and faster than yesterday's. Consider upgrading to newer devices as a strategy to recoup floor space. In some instances it can even be cheaper to buy a new model of server than to continue paying service contracts to support older ones. This is especially true when older systems are replaced by a smaller number of new machines. While some approaches to upgrading server performance can be difficult to sell to upper management due to their costs, a solution such as this that saves money, provides better performance, and delays the need to expand a space-constrained Data Center is an obvious winner.

  As you pack equipment tighter in the Data Center, watch out for hot spots. The most dramatic consolidations might require additional electrical and cooling infrastructure. While additional infrastructure doesn't come cheap, it is still much less expensive than paying to expand the entire room.

- **Remove old equipment**—Are decommissioned devices sitting on the Data Center floor or occupying space in server cabinets? System administrators are often diligent about installing new equipment but not as attentive about removing outdated gear. That is understandable, because there is no project or application being held up if a leftover server isn't immediately removed. Allowing old items to accumulate wastes valuable floor and cabinet space and adds unnecessary weight to the Data Center floor, however, so work with Data Center users to have equipment removed in a timely manner. When new servers or networking devices arrive for installation, check with the owner to see if they are replacing devices that can now be removed.

Note	Some system administrators might tell you that they want to keep decommissioned servers because they have a trade-in value toward a future purchase. If so, have those items placed in storage. Data Center real estate is too important to use for this purpose.

- **Reorient major infrastructure to share buffer space**—Depending upon the layout of your existing Data Center, you may be able to reclaim some floor space by relocating air handlers and power distribution units so they begin to share buffer areas. This approach is presented in Chapter 4, "Laying Out the Data Center," for new Data Center designs as well—see Figure 4-5 as an example. Unlike the previous suggestions this alteration is likely to require server downtime.

New Construction

Even after consolidating equipment as much as possible, you might find you are simply outgrowing the existing Data Center and that building additional server environment space is your only option. If the Data Center was designed with expansion in mind and a dedicated growth path already exists, your course of action is easy. Simply design the expansion space the same way that you would a completely new Data Center. Assuming that the existing server environment has successfully met your company's needs to date—how it is laid out, the type and amount of infrastructure components available at each server cabinet location—then duplicate its design in the new space, making what minor adjustments are precipitated by the footprint of the expansion space. (What to do if the design of the old server environment is no longer adequate is covered at the end of this chapter in the section titled Paradigm Shifts.)

It is your decision whether to knock down the wall between the existing Data Center and the expansion space, making one contiguous server environment, or to keep that wall up and create two separate-but-adjacent rooms.

The advantages of two spaces come from their segmentation. If their respective infrastructure systems are kept distinct, it is possible that a problem in one room—say an air handler fails or a fire breaks out—might not spread to the other. This can limit how many servers and networking devices suffer downtime from a single event. Building the new server environment in this manner is also the least disruptive on the existing space, because no construction takes place within the Data Center that is already online. If done correctly, two separate-but-adjacent rooms also enable all of the new server environment's infrastructure to be fully tested without concern about electrical tests causing downtime for equipment that is online in the old space.

The disadvantage of two rooms is that the dividing wall between them occupies significant space. If you knock down the wall of the existing Data Center and expand into the growth area, you don't have to lose usable floor space to a dividing wall and associated aisles. In a large server environment, the additional area can enable one or two additional server rows to fit into the same floor space. Because a lack of physical hosting space is the reason for expanding the Data Center in the first place, you want to consider carefully before giving any floor space away during expansion.

If you opt to make a contiguous Data Center, take precautions to protect servers in the original room during construction. Hang thick layers of material between the old and new spaces to prevent dust, dirt, or other contaminants from entering the old space. Also limit ingress into that area by contractors. Finally, when testing the Data Center's entire electrical system, you must decide whether it is acceptable to incur downtime to servers and networking devices in the original space or whether you want to skip portions of the power tests that shut down all power to the room.

If no dedicated growth path exists for the Data Center expansion, examine your building plans to determine a desirable location. Employee cubicles, storage rooms, and conference rooms are all prime candidates. Chapter 3, "Quantifying Data Center Space," provides more information about choosing a suitable area.

NOTE   I start the process of expanding a Data Center—rounding up key players, creating its design, and initiating construction—when 80 percent of its cabinet locations are filled with equipment. That is close enough to the room's maximum capacity to indicate that more space is warranted while still leaving enough open cabinet locations for equipment to go in to while the expansion space is designed and built.

Because expanding a Data Center is a significant financial investment, you'll likely have to get the project's budget approved even earlier. If server growth is steady, start that process when the room is about half full, because it usually takes time to get a multimillion-dollar project fully approved. Starting at the halfway point is also helpful because you can calculate how long it took the Data Center to get that full and project a similar amount of time as a deadline for when expansion space needs to be completed and on line.

Chaos

Sometimes the driving force behind the retrofit of a Data Center is that the room has become so disorganized and cluttered that it is problematic to install new equipment. Tangled patch cords, unlabeled structured cabling and electrical whips, and poor cooling distribution can all make a server environment vulnerable to downtime every time a new device is installed. Before embarking upon a major construction project to add infrastructure or expand an overworked server environment, see if any of the following can remediate the problems and make the space more usable:

- **Use the right length patch cords for the job**—System administrators sometime plug in servers and networking devices using whatever patch cords happen to be at hand rather than locating the correct lengths of cable that are needed to make connections.

This results in 15 feet of cable being used to go 4 feet (4 meters of cable used to go 1 meter). Excess cable length is left to dangle from the device or patch panel it is plugged into, perhaps coiled with a tie wrap or perhaps not. Over time, this creates a spider web of cable that blocks access to servers, pre-installed cabling ports, and electrical receptacles. This tangled web not only reduces the usability of Data Center infrastructure, but it all presents a snagging hazard that can cause accidental downtime. Replace overly long patch cords and power cables with those that are the correct length. Also, remove cords and cables that aren't plugged in to functioning servers and are simply leftovers from decommissioned equipment. Do this within cabinets and under the raised floor.

Note	Many servers come standard with power cables that are 6 feet (1.8 meters) long. This is useful for reaching a power receptacle under a raised floor or in a ceiling-mounted raceway, but it is much longer than necessary if you are installing the device into a server cabinet with its own power strips. You can tie wrap the excess length, but even that still dangles somewhere within the server cabinet.
	To reduce this problem, I stock power cables that are the same type provided with the servers, but just 2 feet (61 centimeters) long. The shorter cables are much less likely to become tangled or get snagged when someone is installing or removing equipment into a cabinet.

- **Add wire management**—Even when Data Center users run the right length of patch cord, you end up with hanging cables if adequate wire management is not provided. Install new or larger cable management at cabinet locations where cable glut interferes with access to infrastructure or equipment.

Together with replacing correct cable lengths, installing wire management can free up access to existing data ports and electrical receptacles. These steps also make troubleshooting easier, improve airflow around servers, and improve the overall appearance of the Data Center.

Figure 9-1 illustrates how using correct lengths of patch cords and routing them through wire management cleans up patching fields and enables better access to infrastructure.

Note	I spent just 10 minutes replacing patch cords and threading them through the available horizontal wire management. Installing vertical wire management on the front of the cabinet, along both vertical rails, and routing patch cords into it would further improve accessibility to the patching fields, airflow to the networking devices, and the appearance of the substation.

Figure 9-1 *Patch Cord Cleanup*

A Networking Substation in a
Small Server Room with Poorly
Managed Patch Cords

A Networking Substation in a
Small Server Room with Properly
Sized Patch Cords and Partially
Utilized Wire Management

- **Make sure that people are correctly using infrastructure**—You can spend hundreds of thousands of dollars on structured cabling, but it is worthless if Data Center users string patch cords between server cabinets rather than use the infrastructure that is installed. Failing to properly use the infrastructure in a server environment leads to disorganization, makes troubleshooting difficult, and can create situations that are hazardous to both equipment and Data Center users.

  For example, imagine that someone installs a server into a cabinet within the Data Center, and they don't understand that each cabinet location is provided with dedicated circuits from two different power sources. Wanting redundant power for their server's dual power supplies, they plug one power cable in to the power strip of their own server cabinet and then string the other power cable to the strip in an adjacent cabinet. This adds unnecessary electrical draw onto the adjacent power strip, making it more susceptible to tripping a circuit. It also ties the two adjacent server cabinets together. If a time ever comes to relocate either cabinet, and whoever is moving it is unaware that a power cord has been strung between them, an accident might occur that could harm someone or damage a server.

- **Install power strips with known electrical ratings**—Do you know how much equipment you can install into your server cabinets before you overload their power strips? If not, you are either underutilizing server cabinet space or risking downtime every time you plug in new equipment. Swap out any mystery power strips with ones whose amp ratings are known. If possible, have the power strip rated for the same amperage as the circuit it is plugged into. This enables you to maximize existing electrical circuits and server cabinet space.

- **Redeploy floor tiles**—If cooling is a problem and your Data Center has a raised floor, check that floor tiles are deployed to best advantage. Close off unnecessary openings in the floor surface and open perforated tiles closest to highly populated cabinets. Close or relocate floor panels that are especially close to air handlers and might be causing short cycling. Make sure under-floor infrastructure isn't blocking air coming from the room's air handlers. If it is, try to shift the location of structured cabling and electrical conduits to enable better circulation.

Infrastructure Shortcomings

Another reason to retrofit a Data Center is because the room lacks a particular infrastructure. Power, data cabling, cooling, fire suppression, and structural support all have the potential to be lacking as a server environment fills with equipment.

Power

If a Data Center can't provide enough power to servers and networking devices, it is generally because it has no more circuits available, not that its power distribution units are unable to provide enough raw electricity.

Data Centers typically have plenty of power capacity to spare because of two reasons. First, just like many other electronic devices, servers usually draw less power than the labels on their power supplies indicate. To save costs, many manufacturers incorporate pre-existing power supplies into their electronic devices rather than designing and building something new each time. It is easier and cheaper for manufacturers to make a few universal power supplies than to produce custom supplies for each product model. Using universal power supplies doesn't diminish the performance of the device, but it does make it likely that a power supply has the ability to provide more power than the device it is linked to is ever going to draw. (The power supply won't ever be underpowered, because the device then wouldn't function.) That higher capability is what's listed on the power supply. Simply put, your Data Center servers might never draw as much as their power labels claim.

Second, although a Data Center's electrical system should be designed as if every server cabinet is drawing the maximum possible load, few cabinets actually do. Drawing maximum power from a server cabinet power strip poses the risk of tripping its circuit breaker, so most installations leave a margin for safety. This small amount of unused electrical capacity adds up to a lot of amps over the span of a large Data Center. Even if you manage to use 18 of 20 amps on every electrical circuit in a server environment, that is still only 90 percent of the room's maximum capacity. That is like leaving one of every 10 cabinets in the Data Center empty.

NOTE   Do you want to know how much power servers in a particular cabinet are drawing? Some power strips are equipped to provide a live display of how many amps they are providing to devices. While not cheap, these intelligent power strips help monitor electrical usage and might deter Data Center users from installing servers into a cabinet that is susceptible to overloading a circuit.

It is also possible to have an electrician take a power reading of a circuit at its source, the power distribution unit. This provides only a snapshot, however, that is the electrical draw is at the moment the reading is taken. As with any work done at a PDU, it also presents a potential risk for downtime.

Assuming that your Data Center is facing a circuit shortage rather than a lack of power capacity, the easiest solution is installation of circuit panels—known as remote power panels—that connect back to source power distribution units. If floor space allows, place them at the end of each server row. This enables the shortest possible electrical conduits to be run from PDU to electrical panel and then panel to cabinet locations. It is therefore less expensive, reduces under-floor clutter, and is easier to manage. If floor space is unavailable, wall-mount the electrical panels. Again, place these panels strategically between the source PDU and the server rows to enable short electrical conduits.

If your Data Center is the exception, however, and overall electrical capacity is the problem, you must install an additional PDU. Survey the room to determine where there is adequate floor space to fit the unit. As available floor space allows, place the unit and route electrical conduits according the principles covered in Chapter 4 and Chapter 6, "Creating a Robust Electrical System." This includes allowing room for a buffer area to protect servers against electromagnetic interference.

NOTE   If your Data Center doesn't already provide redundant power to each cabinet location, that is electrical circuits run from two different source power distribution units, consider making this upgrade when you perform other electrical improvements. Any major alteration to a Data Center's electrical infrastructure puts the room at risk for downtime, so you might as well make as many upgrades as possible while the server environment is exposed. Doing so can prevent the need for such exposure in the future.

Connectivity

Running out of data ports is perhaps the most common infrastructure shortcoming that occurs in server environments, especially in those whose rows contain infrastructure tailored to support a specific model of server. When it comes time to host different equipment, those cabinet locations must be retrofitted with different infrastructure. Fortunately, lack of connectivity is one of the easier issues to address. It can be remediated in one of two ways.

One option is added structured cabling. As long as the installer is careful to work around existing servers and their connections, the upgrade can usually be completed without any downtime. This cabling needs to terminate somewhere in the Data Center, however, either at a network substation or a main networking row. These added ports might require more space than existing networking cabinets can provide, so be aware that more floor space might need to be allocated for them, which in turn reduces what is available to host servers.

A second option, particularly when the need is for copper connections, is to install either of two networking devices—a console server or console switch—at the cabinet where more ports are needed. These networking devices can send multiple streams of information over one signal, a process known as multiplexing. For example, if you have several servers installed in a cabinet, instead of running a dozen patch cords from those devices to the Data Center's structured cabling under the floor, you run those patch cords to a console server or console switch and—thanks to multiplexing—you then run just one patch cord from that device to the structured cabling. Installing these networking devices can significantly expand the capacity of your Data Center's existing structured cabling.

This second approach is best used when:

- There is limited internal space within the Data Center's network cabinets. Installing these networking devices in key server cabinets can reduce the space needed for additional patching fields.

- Infrastructure within the Data Center plenum is chaotic, and installing more structured cabling may either restrict airflow or pose a downtime risk. Increasing ports by way of these networking devices involves only a fraction of the structured cabling than would otherwise be required.

- The need for additional ports is temporary. Networking devices can be removed and reused more easily than structured cabling.

Cooling

As Data Center cabinets fill up with servers, you might discover that its cooling infrastructure isn't up to the task of keeping the space cool. The overall ambient temperature of the server environment might become too warm, or else hot spots might develop in areas where servers are tightly packed or a large device emits a high amount of exhaust.

Presumably, you have already used the Data Center's floor tiles to good advantage, placing perforated floor tiles so that cooling is directed at known hot spots and sealing unwanted openings to maintain air pressure. There are many techniques for improving cooling in a server environment. Here are five:

- **Relocate air handler temperature sensors**—These devices are generally located at the cooling unit itself, where temperatures are often lower. Placing the sensors deeper within the room gives the air handlers more accurate readings about the Data Center's ambient temperature and can cause them to provide cooling for longer periods.

- **Install ducted returns**—These draw away more of the Data Center's heated air, channeling it into each handler's normal cooling cycle, and can reduce temperatures in sections of the room by a few degrees.

- **Distribute servers**—If tightly packed servers are causing hot spots, spreading such equipment out is a sure way to prevent them. This solution obviously has limited value if your Data Center also has space constraints. However, even if you don't have the option to only partially fill server cabinets in your Data Center, at least try to strategically locate devices so that the highest heat-producers aren't clustered together. It is easier to deal with several warmer areas in a server environment than one that is very hot.

- **Install self-cooling cabinets**—Reinstall the Data Center's most prodigious heat-generating servers into cabinets that are cooled by fans or chilled liquid. This eliminates hot spots at their source and might lower the room's overall ambient temperature.

- **Install additional air handlers**—Finally, if all else fails you might need to put in another air handler to increase how much cold air is being pumped in to the Data Center. Use the same approach that you would when designing the room's cooling infrastructure from scratch—try to place the handler perpendicular to server rows and create a buffer area around it so that short cycling does not occur. For more information, review Chapter 8, "Keeping It Cool."

NOTE   When performing any work on your Data Center's cooling system that might require air handlers to be shut down, have multiple portable fans and spot coolers at the ready. Temperatures can rise quickly when air handlers are turned off. You might need to prop open the Data Center doors and use fans to blow hot air out of the room. For major cooling system work, try to schedule work to occur during colder weather, such as at night or during winter months or both.

Fire Suppression

No matter how full your Data Center becomes with servers and networking devices, the one type of infrastructure that is never going to become overtaxed is the fire suppression system. Because this infrastructure is designed based upon the physical size of the room, its capability isn't affected by how many or few servers have been installed.

It is possible, however, that your company might want to upgrade the fire suppression system that was originally installed in your Data Center. It could be that the room was designed and built with wet pipe sprinklers, and you want to replace them with preaction dry pipe to reduce the risk of water spilling onto servers due to a leak or pipe break. Maybe the Data Center was designed without a gaseous fire suppression system, and at a later date you decide to add it for greater fire protection.

The first option is rarely done. Most companies aren't going to bother tearing out and replacing a wet pipe system if there hasn't been a problem with it. The second option, although still uncommon, is more likely because you can increase fire protection to a Data Center and not alter the sprinkler system that is already in place.

Adding a gaseous fire suppression system to an existing Data Center is essentially the same as installing it into a new room. Installers simply need to take care when working around online servers and existing infrastructure so as to not cause downtime. For more information, review Chapter 8.

Structural Support

Yet another possible shortcoming is your Data Center being unable to support enough weight to accommodate incoming servers. This limitation can be particularly challenging. For one, it is not easy to see. Your Data Center might be only half full to the naked eye and appear quite capable of housing more servers, yet in reality only be able to accommodate a small number of additional machines.

Don't assume that a server environment is subject to weight limitations only if it contains a raised floor. While the floor grid might be a weak point, it is equally possible that the weight-bearing ability of the building itself might be the source of the restriction. This is most likely if the Data Center was built above the ground floor.

NOTE   A few of the Data Centers I manage are located on either the second or third level of a building. In each case, their raised floor system is capable of supporting more weight than the concrete in the floor is able to. When systems weighing more than 900 pounds (408.2 kilograms) are installed, an adjacent cabinet location must be left practically empty to accommodate the excess weight. Needless to say, this occupies floor space in those Data Centers at a much higher-than-normal rate.

Before you reach the maximum weight-bearing ability for your Data Center, take the following steps to lighten the room's load:

- **Shed unnecessary cabinet weight**—If you have a choice among what types of server cabinets are deployed in your Data Center, use those that weigh the least. Remove doors from cabinets that don't need to lock to secure servers. Take off the side panels, too, especially if you aren't using them to channel server exhaust into a hot aisle. Doors and panels might look nice, but they add unnecessary weight. If a server can be placed either upon a shelf or mounted directly onto the cabinet, skip the shelf. No single item is going to remove much weight, but consistently shedding weight from your cabinets can have a measurable effect over an entire server row.

- **Enforce a maximum weight for fully-loaded cabinets**—In addition to removing non-essential cabinet components, restrict how much weight can be placed at the cabinet locations within your Data Center. To effectively enforce this, the people in your company who purchase server equipment must first obtain accurate weight information from the manufacturers. Be aware that this solution is going to help with weight issues but also cause incoming servers to occupy floor space at a faster rate, perhaps leading to a lack of space.

- **Place heaviest items in rows with structural columns**—The greatest weight-bearing ability of a Data Center floor is along the steel beams of the building. Take advantage of this by placing the heaviest equipment in rows containing structural columns.

- **Distribute servers**—Space permitting, redistribute servers over a greater area. This not only disrupts hot spots in the Data Center, as mentioned previously, it also prevents the concentration of weight upon the floor.

If you have taken these steps and weight is still a problem, you must resort to major construction in the Data Center. If the problem is with the raised floor, it is possible to remove and replace its floor grid components with ones that are capable of supporting greater weight. This is a non-trivial task because it essentially means disassembling and rebuilding the entire floor system one piece at a time.As sections of the floor grid are removed and replaced, servers or networking devices in that area must be temporarily repositioned to enable access to the floor components. This usually means downtime for servers, although if enough slack exists in the structured cabling and electrical conduits, it might be possible to carefully shift an entire cabinet of equipment by several floor tiles. Once the floor grid is upgraded at that server cabinet location, the cabinet can then be shifted back. The process is then repeated at the next cabinet location. This is a delicate procedure, but is an option if you are determined to avoid downtime.

If the problem isn't with the raised floor system but with the floor itself, then the solution must occur outside of the Data Center. Structural bracing must be installed to provide additional support to the server environment. This is very likely going to involve installing additional support beams or columns under the Data Center and therefore might be disruptive to whatever rooms are below it.

NOTE   If your Data Center has limitations upon how much weight it can support, consult a structural engineer. He or she can determine how much weight your server environment can support at given cabinet locations and create a plan to increase its structural strength. Pay close attention to the weight-bearing ability of your Data Center. Too much weight can cause the floor to buckle and lead to serious injury or death.

Paradigm Shifts

It is also possible that your Data Center has ample physical room and infrastructure available and yet still begins having problems hosting incoming equipment. This occurs when servers, networking devices, or other machines arrive that the server environment wasn't designed to accommodate.

Maybe server manufacturers alter their designs, making machines that need more physical space or electrical power. Perhaps your company decides to pursue a different business goal, requiring equipment that your Data Center never had to host in years past. It could also be that technology changes, requiring new cabling media to accommodate it. Whatever the cause, this can be the hardest of shortcomings to deal with in a server environment, because you might not be able to overcome it by simply adding a few circuit panels or running more structured cabling. The physical layout of Data Center rows might need to be changed, including the physical relocation of both servers and infrastructure components—all while the server environment remains online.

If you are fortunate—more accurately, if you anticipated the need for future change—you designed your Data Center infrastructure to be easily upgradeable. Flexible electrical conduits and lightly bundled structured cabling, with additional slack provided, can enable you to reconfigure your under-floor infrastructure quickly and concentrate power and data connectivity where it is needed. Infrastructure components that enable you to use different media, such as multimedia boxes that can accommodate multiple connector types and electrical whips pre-wired to terminate in several types of receptacles, also make it easier to change elements of a server environment.

If your Data Center possesses these types of infrastructure components, retrofitting the room might be as simple as having structured cabling and electrical conduits reterminated. More likely, however, you are going to have to make more dramatic and intrusive changes to the server environment. This might include rearranging server rows, removing and rerunning structured cabling, and either adding or relocating power distribution units or air handlers.

Here are several tips to follow when making significant infrastructure changes to your existing Data Center:

- Upgrade the room in phases, say a couple of server rows at a time, rather than trying to overhaul it all at once. Retrofitting a live Data Center is like performing surgery on a conscious patient. Breaking the task down into segments reduces the effect of downtime and makes it less likely for something to go wrong on a large scale. If work can be completed over a long period of time, you might even be able to coordinate infrastructure changes with server lifecycles, that is as servers are decommissioned and replaced with newer models.

- When retrofitting the Data Center dictates physically moving equipment, take advantage of devices that have dual power supplies. Strategically shifting power plugs from an old power receptacle to a new one can enable you migrate a server to a new part of the Data Center, or onto a different power source that won't be shut down, and enable you to avoid downtime.

- If work in the Data Center might produce debris or airborne particles, shut down the fire suppression system to avoid setting it off accidentally.

- If new servers are installed in the Data Center while it is undergoing a retrofit, place them according to how the room is going to be designed ultimately. Arrange them to be part of the new layout, not another piece of equipment that must be relocated later.

An example of a recent paradigm shift for Data Centers is the emergence of 1U servers. At the start of this century, server manufacturers began producing low profile servers that were high performing and relatively inexpensive compared to earlier generations of devices.

IT departments in many companies opted to replace older, larger systems with dozens of 1U servers. They are particularly popular for computing applications that can pool the power of multiple servers. For these applications, a cluster of 1U devices provides both flexibility and redundancy: flexibility, because exactly how many servers are dedicated to a task can be altered as needed and redundancy because even if a server fails there are several others that continue processing. Low-profile servers are also desirable for companies that lease Data Center space. Most hosting facilities charge based upon how much floor space a client occupies, so using smaller servers can reduce those costs.

Despite their merits, 1U servers are difficult to host in many Data Centers. When clustered together, they are heavy, draw large amounts of power, produce a lot of heat, and require a high amount of data connections in a very small space—not what most pre-existing server environments were designed and built to accommodate.

Case Study of a Data Center Retrofit

In 1999, I was faced with retrofitting a Data Center in San Jose, California, that had about 200 cabinet locations and occupied 4522 square feet (420.1 square meters). The room was built in 1994 and contained direct-connect structured cabling and electrical conduits. Although it had dozens of cabinet locations yet to be occupied and some infrastructure remaining to be used, the server environment was in dire need of improvement.

For its first few years of existence, the Data Center hadn't been managed. People used infrastructure haphazardly, finding data ports and power outlets wherever they could under the raised floor and either dragging them to wherever was convenient or using long cords—some more than 50 feet (15.2 meters)—to connect to them. After 5 years of equipment growth, the under-floor plenum contained thousands of criss-crossing patch cords, structured cabling, power cables, and electrical conduits. Any time someone attached or removed patch cords or power cables under the floor, he or she risked disturbing the glut of connections already in place and causing downtime. As a result, Data Center users didn't always remove old connections, which made under-floor conditions even worse.

Also, with no one controlling what was allowed in to the server environment, dozens of questionable cabinets had been installed. Some cabinets were so tall that they partially obstructed the room's ceiling-mounted sprinkler heads, a fire code violation. Others contained power strips whose capacity was unknown. Circuits were tripped occasionally as Data Center users discovered that a power strip was rated to support only 15 amps and not the 20 that they had hoped.

Finally, because accessing electrical outlets and data ports underneath the floor was such a hassle, Data Center users took shortcuts. They strung patch cords from cabinet to cabinet rather than using under-floor infrastructure and plugged devices into the power strips of adjacent cabinets instead of trying to find an electrical receptacle to plug their own cabinet power strips into.

Simply put, the room was a mess. To improve the Data Center's functionality, it was decided to:

- Remove all direct-connect cabling. Install network substations at the end of each server row. Run new copper and fiber cable, in a distributed pattern. Relabel cable runs for greater clarity. This was to create organized cabling patterns and prevent future cabling glut.

- Remove all electrical conduits, most of which contained single circuits. Run new conduits with dual circuits. This was to cut the number of electrical conduits running under the floor by half. (Two circuits coming from one power distribution unit support cabinets in this Data Center. If I were to retrofit the room today, I would also install circuit panels at the end of each row to further reduce conduit lengths. Additionally, I would feed those panels from two different PDUs and multiple standby electrical infrastructure, for redundancy.)

- Reorient server rows to face a single direction. The prior layout had server rows alternate directions, which made it all-too-easy for Data Center users to string cables between cabinets in adjacent rows.

This room was gradually upgraded over a period of two and a half years. Work was done to a few server rows at a time. The process worked like a sliding number puzzle, where you have to put disorganized tiles in a sequence in the fewest moves by sliding pieces into the empty spot. Servers were moved out of a work area, and then infrastructure in those rows was retrofitted. Servers from the next target area were then moved into the rows that had been fixed, freeing up space for more work to be done.

Although most machines in the Data Center had to incur downtime at one time or another, this phased approach enabled the effect to be minimized by scheduling it around the most important tasks that servers were associated with.

As part of the retrofit, the overall number of electrical circuits and structured cabling provided to the room's 200 or so cabinet locations was doubled. This greatly expanded how many servers the Data Center could accommodate, which made the project even more beneficial than simply cleaning up the server environment.

Acquisitions

Finally, your business might acquire or merge with another company, and in the process end up with one or more additional server environments that are functional but inconsistent with your established Data Centers. The challenge here is deciding how much to change in the interest of standardization.

If your company plans to keep the facility, definitely perform any non-intrusive alterations that can make the server environment more consistent with your other Data Centers. (If the site is going to be released in less than six months, with personnel and equipment transferring to another location, it is probably not worth the time and expense to upgrade the room.) Apply your standard labeling scheme to the room's structured cabling and electrical conduits, for example, and install telephones and monitoring lights as you would in a new Data Center. If the server environment is disorganized, use the suggestions listed earlier in this chapter to clean up how patch cords and power cables are routed.

If the acquired Data Center has infrastructure that is less robust or flexible than your existing server environments, weigh the pros and cons of making major upgrades:

- Do you add another power distribution unit to provide redundant electrical circuits to cabinet locations, especially if not all of the servers in the room have dual power supplies?

- Should you add a standby generator or gaseous fire suppression system?

- If the room could use more data connections, should you try to do away with its direct-connect design and begin using network substations? Decide if it is more beneficial to add more structured cabling or deploy new console servers or console switches.

More often than not, you will want to upgrade any acquired Data Center so that it meets the same standards as those you have designed and built, even if this means incurring some downtime. The Data Center must perform the same job as your other server environments, so you want it to have the same quality of design and infrastructure. Also, it is notably more difficult to manage multiple Data Centers that possess different levels of infrastructure. In addition to assigning space based upon ease of physical access, weight considerations, heat distribution, and possibly departmental organization, you must also keep track of whether there are enough power and connectivity to support certain devices.

NOTE   Most of the 45-plus Data Centers that I manage contain the same level of structured cabling, including 24 strands of multimode fiber at each server cabinet location. A few acquired server environments, however, have mixed amounts of fiber throughout the room. As a cost-saving measure, and so as to not disrupt already-functioning servers, no additional cabling has ever been installed.

More than once I have started to dole out space in one of these rooms for the installation of particular equipment, only to belatedly remember it has insufficient fiber to support the incoming equipment. While there are many servers that can be and are housed in those rows, it takes much more of my time and concentration to manage these spaces than rows that have standard infrastructure. Their inconsistent levels of infrastructure slows how quickly new equipment can be deployed.

Large-Scale Server Moves

While many infrastructure upgrades can be performed while a Data Center remains online, truly sweeping changes can require you to displace several rows' worth of servers and networking devices. Your company might even decide that the most expedient way to clean up your server environment is essentially to start over—build an entirely new Data Center and move servers out of the old hosting space altogether. Either scenario involves the daunting task of moving hundreds of servers. Here are several techniques for making such a large-scale equipment relocation proceed smoothly and quickly:

- **Have a plan**—One of the best ways to ensure that a move goes the way you want is to clearly define how you want it to go. Create a schedule that outlines all major steps in the move—shutdown sequences, preparing servers to move, the transportation, restarting systems at their destination. Include target times for completion.

- **Hire professionals**—When you need to move a large number of devices from one Data Center to another—even if the two rooms are at the same company site—contract with professional movers to transport them. Choose a moving company that is experienced at transporting sensitive electronic devices and be sure that movers carefully wrap all server cabinets and the items within them.

- **Prioritize equipment**—Determine the order that various networking devices and servers are to be taken offline and restarted. This order is typically dictated by the importance of the functions of given equipment or how many clients are affected when that server is offline or both. The most vital systems are shut down last and restarted first.

- **Run a special backup**—No matter what your normal schedule is for backing up data from your Data Center equipment, conduct one more backup immediately before the move. Have those tapes or disks readily available in the event data is lost, so that it can be restored quickly.

- **Label items with destination information**—Assign unique colors for each cabinet location in the destination Data Center. Then tag both the server to be moved and the destination floor tile with matching colored paper. If servers are to be reracked into cabinets in a different sequence, sketch what their final placement should look like and tape the image onto the destination cabinet. Both of these practices make it extremely easy for move participants to recognize where cabinets and servers are supposed to go.

- **Pre-cable patch cords**—It can be time-consuming to redo thousands of data connections, from scratch, following a move. If you leave patch cords dangling from servers and secure them carefully during the move process, you can likely just plug them back in at their destination location. For servers that are to be reracked, determine where they will be installed in their destination cabinet and have the correct lengths of patch cords waiting when they arrive. For example, if a server is to be installed 3 feet (91.4 centimeters) high in a cabinet and data connections in the Data Center terminate below the raised floor that is 18 inches (45.7 centimeters) deep, place a sufficient number of 5-feet (1.5-meter) long patch cords at the destination cabinet location ahead of time.

- **Have spares at the ready**—As carefully as equipment is moved, there is always the possibility that a server or peripheral device may fail to come back online. Stocking spare server components and cabinets can reduce how long it takes to overcome an unexpected component failure.

- **Leverage dual power supplies**—If equipment is to be relocated within the same Data Center, you might be able to reduce how many servers must be taken offline. For any devices with dual power supplies, take advantage of their redundancy by transitioning their power feeds—one at a time—from the electrical receptacles at the original cabinet location to the electrical receptacles at the destination cabinet location. In this manner, the server is never without power or offline. If the old and new locations are a significant distance apart, consider running temporary electrical conduits to bridge the distance.

When the time comes for the move, bring all hands on deck. That is, have all of your company system administrators and network engineers who support your Data Center equipment participate in shutting down and later restarting the devices involved in the move. The more employees who take part, the faster that servers can be brought back online.

Don't forget to involve the vendors who normally support your Data Center systems, too. They can provide additional manpower and expertise. The service contracts for some devices might even be voided if they are moved without participation by a representative of the manufacturer.

NOTE   No Data Center manager wants to take servers offline, but if you have to, take full advantage of the downtime. Fix poorly routed cabling, upgrade server components, and reposition servers that were poorly placed to begin with. Perhaps you can disperse server clusters that generate tremendous heat or shift overloaded cabinets into server rows that contain structural columns and can bear the most weight.

Summary

While most Data Center design projects focus on building a new server environment, there might come a time when you need to retrofit an existing room due to one of several infrastructure shortcomings.

One common problem is running out of space to host equipment. To mitigate this, rerack servers close together, share monitors between devices, position floor-standing machines to occupy the least space, upgrade to smaller servers, and quickly remove decommissioned servers from the Data Center floor.

If more space is still needed after taking these steps, you must expand the existing server environment—ideally into a pre-determined growth path. You can either build a distinct second Data Center, which can protect servers and networking devices in both rooms from being affected by a single event, or expand the existing server environment and forgo the additional floor space that a dividing wall and additional aisles require.

Another cause for retrofitting a Data Center is the room having become disorganized with its infrastructure components hopelessly tangled. To mitigate this, swap out overly long cables, remove cords that aren't attached to functioning equipment, add wire management where needed, replace power strips that have unknown electrical ratings, and rearrange floor tiles to improve airflow.

Yet another reason to upgrade a server environment is the room having run short on certain infrastructure. Power shortcomings usually require installing breaker panels to provide more circuits, but if overall capacity is the issue, a new power distribution unit must be installed. A lack of connectivity can be addressed by adding more structured cabling or by installing console switches that enable multiple data signals to be combined over a single data connection. Cooling problems can be improved by modifying existing air handlers to run longer and draw in more heated air, redistributing servers, or installing more cooling equipment.

A Data Center might also need to be upgraded if it does not have enough weight-bearing ability, either in its raised floor system or true floor. To mitigate this, remove cabinet doors, cap the weight of incoming devices, place heavy items near structural columns, and spread out servers. Ultimately, it might be necessary to install additional support beams or columns below the server environment.

Even if a Data Center has adequate infrastructure and space available, it might need to be altered significantly to support new equipment configurations. If the Data Center layout must change, try to limit downtime by performing the work in stages, using dual power supplies to transition power sources, and incorporating incoming devices into the new layout.

Last, you might need to retrofit a server environment that is obtained through the acquisition of another company. Upgrade the room to match your Data Center standards as much as possible. It is much easier to manage multiple server environments if they all contain the same level of infrastructure.

Managing the Data Center

CHAPTER 10

Organizing Your Way to an Easier Job

This chapter focuses on how to manage incoming servers and networking devices so they will integrate seamlessly within a Data Center, making individual machines easier to support and the server environment as a whole more productive for your company. The chapter outlines strategies for allocating floor space and arranging equipment as well as recommends processes and standards for reviewing equipment for suitability in your Data Center.

The Need For Organization

Part I of this book concentrates on strategies for designing a reliable, easy-to-understand Data Center. As important as those principles are, they are only half of what goes in to creating a server environment that is as productive as possible for your business. The second element is effective management of the room. A Data Center that is thoughtfully designed and strategically managed takes less time to supervise because

- The room's layout and infrastructure are easy to understand and work with

- Less accidental downtime occurs due to mechanical failure or human error

- Costs are avoided because fewer alterations to its cabling or electrical infrastructure are needed

- More equipment can be accommodated because floor and cabinet spaces are used to greater effect

No matter how well-designed your Data Center is—how robust, modular, flexible, standardized, and intuitive its layout is—the Data Center can't be productive if it is allowed to fall into disarray. Imagine a library in which books that have been read aren't returned to their proper place on the shelves, arranged by topic or author, but are instead tossed on the floor in a large jumble. In a short time, even the best library with the greatest resources becomes practically useless under those circumstances. The library's books contain the same information in either scenario, but they are much less useful when they aren't organized. Your Data Center is similar. The room must be managed and organized on an ongoing basis for your company to receive maximum benefit from it.

Put another way, if your Data Center is worth spending thousands of hours of staff time and millions of dollars to design and build, it is worth an equivalent level of dedication to support and manage once it is online. Some companies make the mistake of designing a world-class server environment only to then give inadequate attention to managing the space. The people who were gathered to provide input into the room's construction—facilities managers, information technology (IT) managers, network engineers, and project managers—all return to their regular duties once the Data Center becomes operational. Some of them might have responsibilities that continue to bring them into contact with the room, but it is not their primary focus. That is just not the same as having a dedicated person whose sole job is to oversee the server environment.

Wanted: Data Center Manager

Does your company have a Data Center manager, someone who designs, supports, and oversees all of your company's server environments? A Data Center is a focal point for several different disciplines and technologies. It is unlikely that experts in any one of those fields are highly trained in others—networking is a much different skill set than electrical, for example. It is valuable to have an employee whose core responsibility is to coordinate the implementation of these different technologies within a company's server environments.

Also, as mentioned in Chapter 1, "Approaching the Data Center Project," the various departments that support a company's server environments might have different goals. Having someone responsible for the Data Center's wellbeing is beneficial here, too. Imagine if new servers arrive that require more connectivity than is currently provided at each server cabinet location. This need can be addressed by spreading the servers across more cabinet locations, installing additional structured cabling, or installing networking devices to provide more ports. The system administrator installing the servers might want to spread the equipment out—that way they don't need to wait for the time it would take to have cabling or networking devices added. A facilities manager might want to have more networking devices—that solution conserves Data Center floor space and avoids the cost of installing more infrastructure. A networking manager might want either to spread out the servers or have more structured cabling put in—whatever option means they don't have to buy and support more networking devices. Someone responsible for managing your company's server environment space as a whole probably has the best perspective to choose among the three valid approaches.

A Data Center manager additionally provides a bridge between the department that needs the Data Center infrastructure—typically IT—and the one that provides it—facilities. Tales of squabbling between these groups are legendary at some businesses. Much of that is due to the one-dimensional interactions that occur between them. Typically, IT is demanding something from facilities—be it more power and cooling for servers or immediate answers when a major mechanical system malfunctions and applications shut down. These are usually stressful situations with employee productivity, reputations, and large amounts of money at stake, so emotions run high. There is a lot of potential there for an adversarial relationship to develop.

Adding to this challenging dynamic is the fact that the average employee thinks about facilities and company Data Centers about as much as they do the utilities in their home. That is to say not at all as long as things are functioning normally. As long as water flows out of the faucets at the turn of a handle, the lights come on at the flip of a switch, and servers remain on in the Data Center, no one pays much attention. When these items fail, however, everyone sees that there is a problem. So, it is not uncommon that the only time the facilities staff hears from IT personnel is when someone is contacting it about a problem. A Data Center manager who has visibility in both departments can strengthen that relationship by drawing attention to the ongoing successes that generally happen behind the scenes and might otherwise pass unnoticed. Incidents in which standby infrastructure successfully protected servers or facilities personnel took special action to head off potential infrastructure problems, for example.

Finally, a dedicated Data Center manager role is helpful for a company that has server environments in diverse locations. That person can ensure that standards for the room—both design elements and how the Data Center functions—are consistently maintained at all locations. Without someone to provide such a global perspective, local networking, facilities, and other contributors to the Data Center are most likely going to come up with unique—and therefore nonstandard—solutions. In the long run such one-off solutions make the server environments harder to maintain, because anyone supporting a given room must be aware of its abnormal features.

Organizing Equipment: Form vs Function

The first step in managing a Data Center begins the moment the room comes online and incoming equipment arrives. Where servers, networking devices, and other items are deployed can have a significant influence on how the room functions on a daily basis. What systems plug in to which particular infrastructure components, where system administrators and vendors work in the room, and how easy it is for different types of equipment to expand and occupy additional Data Center floor space are just a few of the details that are influenced by this.

There are four common approaches for arranging servers within a Data Center:

- Clustering devices with similar functions
- Organizing them by internal business group or department
- Grouping models made by the same manufacturer
- Not organizing them at all, simply filling server cabinet locations on a first-come, first-served basis

Chapter 4, "Laying Out the Data Center," discusses the effects of these approaches on a Data Center's infrastructure. It is also important, though, to consider which of them makes the room easiest to manage. Although there is no one right way to organize the equipment in a server environment, some require less time and effort to maintain than others.

Clustering by Function

Gathering machines together based upon what they do can result in either a homogenous or heterogeneous mix of equipment, depending upon whether your company standardizes upon one server manufacturer or not. If it does, the approach is essentially the same as option three, grouping by manufacturer, and therefore has the same advantages and disadvantages. If it doesn't, the approach is probably similar to option two, organizing by business group.

Organizing by Business Group

Although arranging Data Center equipment based upon your company's internal business groups might seem arbitrary, in practice it is one of the simplest Data Center organizational plans to manage. For one thing, this approach tends to distribute equipment models throughout the Data Center, which leads to fewer peaks and valleys of infrastructure demand. An occasional server farm might appear under this approach, but they are rare. Second, server rows can be assigned to the manager of each business organization, making them responsible for the upkeep of their own floor space. This isolates changes within the Data Center, and therefore any potential disruption, due to the needs of a specific business group.

For instance, say Group A wants to decommission a dozen older servers and replace them with newer models that require different power receptacles. Most of the work—the wiring change to the electrical whips, the decommissioning of the old servers, and the installation of the new servers—can occur strictly within the rows that are designated for that business group. The chance of downtime in the Data Center as a result of the activity is chiefly limited to Group A's own rows. In contrast, if Group A's servers are spread out across the server environment, any accidental downtime that occurs is just as likely to affect equipment belonging to any group.

(Chapter 13, "Safeguarding the Servers," spells out what types of things can go wrong in a Data Center during routine activities, including the performance of electrical work or installation or decommissioning of servers.)

Be aware that this benefit is reduced if your Data Center has applications or networks that tie equipment together regardless of their physical location in the room. In the prior example, even if Group A's servers are consolidated into their own row, working on them poses a downtime risk to any other servers throughout the entire Data Center that have dependencies upon Group A's equipment.

Grouping by Manufacturer

While placing all of the same machine models together in a Data Center creates uneven pockets of demand upon the room's infrastructure, this approach can be easy to maintain in the short term. Brand A machines all go in to one row, Brand B machines all go in to another, and so on. Data Center users can often easily predict where their incoming systems are going to be installed in the room. This approach also concentrates support personnel within specific areas of the server environment. Doing so can be useful if you want to keep vendor personnel from competing companies away from one another's equipment.

A drawback of having server rows support only one type of machine is that it limits your flexibility when allocating floor space for incoming equipment. Management difficulties can also arise over time when a given type of server either outgrows its assigned floor space or else needs to be decommissioned and upgraded. This can require significant time, effort, and money to retrofit server rows to meet the customized needs of brand-specific equipment.

Not Organizing at All

Initially, this approach doesn't require any effort, certainly not on the part of whoever would otherwise have to allocate floor space. Data Center users just move equipment into whatever server cabinet locations are available. As the room fills up, however, problems can emerge. System administrators who maintain servers must work in all areas of the Data Center, and downtime on the part of a networking device might cut off access to machines that are performing many different functions. Problems aren't isolated to a particular group. Also, because no one truly controls how space or infrastructure is allocated, Data Center users might swipe electrical receptacles and data ports from unclaimed cabinet locations or even try to claim more server space than they require.

Only consider this approach in very small server environments, perhaps a room with three server rows or less, where the limited space makes it impractical to assign complete rows of floor space. Essentially, only skip organizing a server environment that is too small to practically do so.

NOTE   Most of the Data Centers that I manage are organized according to option two, with space allocated to internal groups known as business units. A row is assigned to a business unit manager, and system administrators who report to that manager are responsible for maintaining the equipment within that area. If a problem arises in a given section of the server environment—perhaps a device is sounding an alarm or someone discovers that a handful of servers have been installed incorrectly within a row—I don't have to spend time researching who owns each specific piece of equipment. I merely contact the owner of the row, and they have the correct person on their team address the issue. Devices that perform universal functions affecting multiple business units, such as print servers and backup devices, are in turn consolidated into their own dedicated row. This organizational approach, together with designing Data Centers to have standardized and distributed infrastructure—the networking and electrical substations at the end of each server row—has proven invaluable. It is very scalable, enabling the team of nine I am on to support, assign space for, and manage forty-five to fifty Data Centers around the world—more than half of them remotely.

Planning for Growth

There is a bit of wisdom that is often given in leadership conferences, screenwriting classes, project management courses, and countless other disciplines—begin at the end. Have a clear idea of what goal you want to achieve or situation you want to be in when you start a task. This advice applies equally well to organizing a server environment. You want servers and networking devices to be distributed across the Data Center so that the room is easy to use, equipment is logically arranged, and demands upon the infrastructure are even and manageable. To accomplish this, assign space in your Data Center—from the beginning—with an eye toward how you want the fully-occupied room to be. Anticipate future equipment growth. Besides setting aside a dedicated growth path outside the server environment, leave empty rows throughout the Data Center as you assign space.

For example, say your newly-opened, completely-unoccupied Data Center contains ten server rows—one after the other in ascending order—and there are three business groups that need hosting space. Group A has enough servers to fill most of one server row, and doesn't expect any future growth. Group B has servers to occupy one row, but can't predict whether it is going to need a lot more hosting space in the future or none at all. Group C has servers to occupy one server row right away and is expected to fill a second row over the next twelve months. That is a total of three rows that need to be allocated immediately, with at least one more row definitely needed for growth.

Resist the inclination to start at one end of the Data Center and fill in from there—putting Group A in Row 1, Group B in Row 2, and Group C in Rows 3 and 4. That arrangement might be suitable when servers and networking devices are first installed, but it can lead to problems later on. For one thing, it concentrates the heating and electrical load in the Data Center into a small area, which can cause hot spots unnecessarily. Depending upon how your electrical circuits are distributed across the Data Center, it might also trigger nuisance alarms in your power distribution units. Many PDUs are sensitive to whether electrical draws are consistent from one panel of circuits to another. When one panel is providing power and another is not, the unit assumes that there is a problem and sounds an alarm.

More importantly, clustering the occupied rows together doesn't enable a group to grow into additional rows and yet still remain contiguous. Group A and B might experience more growth than first anticipated. With them boxed in by Group C's equipment, their additional servers must be located elsewhere in the Data Center. This isn't a major problem, but there are advantages to having all equipment from one organization located in one portion of a server environment.

System administrators for the group need only to work in that area, rather than walk to multiple locations. Reducing foot traffic is convenient for Data Center users and can reduce the risk of downtime.

Figure 10-1 and Figure 10-2 illustrate the two different approaches to assigning Data Center floor space.

Allocating floor space so that one part of the Data Center fills with equipment while the rest remains empty reduces future flexibility and might create an uneven draw upon the room's infrastructure.

Figure 10-1 *Server Rows Assigned in a Cluster*

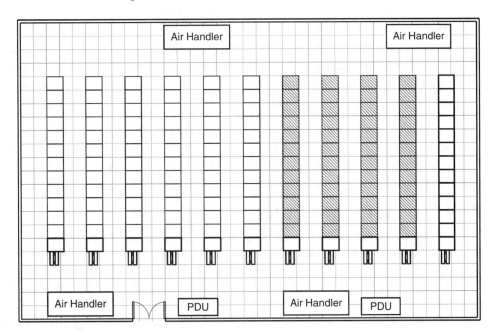

Figure 10-2 *Server Rows Assigned in a Dispersed Pattern*

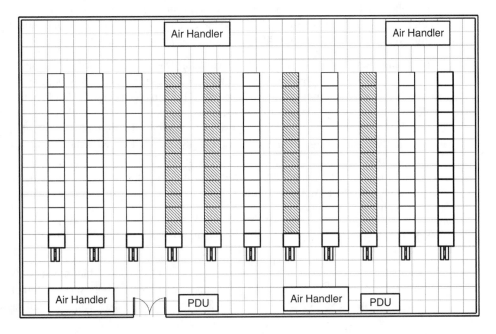

Allocating floor space so that rows alternate between empty and occupied makes it easier to accommodate future space needs by business groups as well as distributes the draw upon the Data Center's infrastructure.

Although most devices that your Data Center houses are going to patch in to the room's structured cabling, some might require direct connections to associated equipment. If any of these devices have distance limitations (for example, it must be in close physical proximity to the equipment they're cabled to) install those devices close to the center of the room rather than near a wall. If a machine needs to be within twenty floor tiles of other equipment, for instance, placing it in a row near a wall enables it to reach only twenty tiles in three directions—all out from the wall. Placing that same machine near the center of the room enables it to cover twenty tiles in all directions.

Controlling Incoming Equipment

Another way to keep firm control over how well a Data Center is organized is to diligently watchdog the machines that it hosts. Have the Data Center manager provide input into the purchasing decisions of servers, networking devices, cabinets, and other Data Center-bound equipment to make sure that these items are compatible with the room's infrastructure and physical features.

At many companies, the people who buy servers and related paraphernalia either know or care relatively little about the environment that houses them. They make purchasing decisions based upon the equipment's performance, cost, and perhaps the merits of its maintenance contract. While all of that is important, little or no consideration is given to whether an item is compatible with the Data Center, so you might end up with a square-peg machine that you must then try to fit in to a round-hole Data Center.

To avoid this, establish a review process in which all Data Center-bound items must be examined and approved before they can be purchased. Pre-approving equipment models up front in this manner can prevent future headaches. It is much easier to head off potential problems with a device while it is still on someone's shopping list than if it is sitting on your loading dock, awaiting immediate installation. This can take the form of simply ordering a different model or might require negotiating with the manufacturer for them either to mitigate a problem, such as providing a different installation kit to make a device mount into your chosen server cabinet instead of their proprietary one, or else to make outright changes to their product. Again, all of these are easier to accomplish if a piece of equipment hasn't already been purchased.

Here are several factors to consider when reviewing a device for its compatibility with your server environment:

- **Footprint**—Does the item (whether a server cabinet or floor-standing server or storage device) fit conveniently within your server rows? Many server cabinet locations are the size of two floor tiles—24 inches wide and 48 deep (61 centimeters wide and 122 deep). It is possible to accommodate larger items, but be aware that they are then intruding upon aisle space or occupying additional cabinet locations. Installing multiple oversized devices means that your server row that is designed to have twelve cabinet locations might in practice be able to accommodate only perhaps eight oversized items.

- **Power needs**—Does the device need power receptacles that are significantly different from what your Data Center typically provides? Those that require different amperage or multiple circuits can use up your server environment's electrical infrastructure very rapidly. Does the device have redundant power supplies, making it compatible with most server cabinets and less likely to suffer downtime?

Note	Over the years, I have encountered many server cabinets that have unique and sometimes outright unhelpful power configurations. Some have built-in converters that change power from one voltage/amperage to another—often unnecessarily in light of the different power configurations already in place in the Data Centers that I manage. Other cabinets have electrical components that seem overengineered—four small power strips where two would do, for example, which requires extra electrical circuits to power the cabinet. When reviewing a server cabinet suitability in your Data Center, pay close attention to how it is powered.

- **Weight load**—How much does the item weigh? The more weight that is placed in a small area, the more difficult it can be for a Data Center floor to support. Don't forget this detail when reviewing cabinets—the more that a cabinet weighs, the fewer servers it can hold before exceeding the Data Center's maximum load capacity.

- **Serviceability**—How easy is it to service or upgrade the device? Servers that are the most Data Center-compatible can be accessed and worked upon while the device remains mounted in a cabinet. Individual components can be slid out and replaced, for example. Devices that require a side or top panel to be opened don't belong in a server environment—the user is forced essentially to uninstall the device to work on it, which is time consuming and inconvenient. Even rack-mountable servers that are installed on rails and require the entire unit to be slid out for servicing aren't desirable, especially if they are heavy, because they can cause a cabinet to tip over and potentially injure someone.

- **Equipment exhaust**—Does the equipment produce an above-average amount of heat? The more heat it generates, the larger the burden it places upon a Data Center's cooling infrastructure. It is also more likely to produce hot spots and blow hot air onto nearby servers. Where does the equipment vent its exhaust? As mentioned in Chapter 8,

"Keeping It Cool," equipment with front-to-back cooling patterns are most compatible with a Data Center designed with hot and cold aisles. Avoid having a large number of devices whose air flow patterns are inconsistent with how the server environment is arranged.

- **Wheels**—Does the item have casters? If you're evaluating a server that is going to be installed in a server cabinet, you don't want wheels because the item could roll off of a cabinet shelf. If you're reviewing server cabinets and floor-standing machines, you want wheels unless you're going to bolt the items to the floor or install them upon seismic isolation platforms. Lockable casters are particularly helpful on a large device because they enable the item to sit immobile on the Data Center floor, but also be easily transported in the event of an equipment move. Make sure that the wheels that are supplied with cabinets or floor-standing servers are large and sturdy enough to enable the cabinet to roll easily over the Data Center floor—including the lip of any room entrances—and support significant server weight.

NOTE   I have participated in dozens of Data Center moves, in which dozens or even hundreds of server cabinets were transported from one server environment to another. The most common problem I see is damage to a cabinet's casters. Roll a cabinet that is loaded with hundreds of pounds of equipment over the lip of a Data Center entrance and there is a fair chance of bending something. The wheels themselves are usually fine, but the bracket that secures them to the server cabinet can bend from the torque, causing the cabinet to lean at an angle. This requires re-racking all of the devices into an undamaged cabinet, and then repairing the wheel brackets. To reduce the chance of this damage occurring during equipment moves, the custom server cabinets that I prefer are reinforced with additional steel plating around each wheel.

In addition to reviewing the physical features that a device must have before it is permitted into your company's Data Centers, establish standards for what applications and functions a server must perform. Data Center floor space is likely your company's most expensive real estate, so you want to reserve it exclusively for business-critical equipment.

Servers and networking devices that handle your company's core business transactions, host its website, and enable employees to send and receive e-mail, for example, are all excellent candidates because they are critical to the operation of your business. The exact same models of machines—if they perform less important functions or contain non-essential information—are poor ones. While those non-essential machines are certainly going to incur less downtime if they are placed in a full-fledged Data Center with a standby electrical system and other infrastructure, safeguarding them this way is overkill—like treating inexpensive place settings as if they are fine bone china and lead crystal.

NOTE   Years ago a friend of mine worked as an emergency medical technician for a private ambulance service. In addition to responding to everyday medical calls, his company provided coverage at large public events such as concerts and major sporting events. While staffing these, he would invariably be approached by someone asking for aspirin for their headache or other minor pain. To most people's surprise, the ambulance he drove didn't stock any. Why not? Because it was there to deal with serious, urgent medical issues, not minor ones.

Your Data Center is much the same. Its elaborate and expensive infrastructure is there for critical machines and applications, not minor ones. Don't waste floor space by installing non-essential equipment or storing items there.

Summary

Just as it is important to design a Data Center strategically in order to make it productive for your company, so too must you carefully manage it to make it most effective. A poorly designed and mismanaged server environment is confusing to work in, more prone to accidental downtime, might eventually require expensive infrastructure modifications, and holds fewer servers due to inefficient use of the room's space.

It is helpful to have a dedicated Data Center manager position to coordinate the different technologies involved in a server environment, enforce design and operational standards, and actively manage how floor space is allocated.

The first step in managing a Data Center is a decision on how to organize the servers it hosts—by function, by internal business group, by manufacturer, or in whatever order they happen to arrive in. Arranging by business group might distribute equipment more evenly, isolates activity within the Data Center, and enables responsibility of servers rows to be delegated to the respective business group managers. The approaches that cluster similar machines together are simple to manage at first, but might require customized infrastructure and require time and money to modify server rows when devices outgrow their initial space assignments.

When allocating Data Center floor space, stagger server row allocations to enable future server growth. Place devices with dependencies closer to the middle of the room, to maximize the radius of what other machines they can connect to.

Govern what equipment is allowed into the Data Center to ensure that items are compatible with the room's physical features and infrastructure as well as being truly critical to your business. Among the details to review are a device's footprint, electrical requirements, weight, accessibility for servicing, heat production, and transportability. Don't allocate Data Center floor space to nonessential devices.

CHAPTER 11

Labeling and Signage

This chapter discusses the role of clear and instructive Data Center labeling in promoting best use of the room's infrastructure, simplifying troubleshooting, and avoiding accidental downtime. The chapter explains different numbering schemes for a server environment and provides examples of essential Data Center signage.

Choosing a Numbering Scheme

A key element of how a Data Center is organized and labeled is what numbering scheme is assigned to the room. It is necessary to number each cabinet location in a server environment for several reasons. At the most basic level, numbering creates a common frame-of-reference for navigating and working in the space. Data Center servers and infrastructure can be assigned specific locations. Telling someone to install a device "at cabinet location 32" is more straightforward and precise than "at the sixth cabinet from the left, in the third row from the door." Labeling isn't useful only for knowing where to place servers and networking devices; it is equally important to have defined destinations for structured cabling and electrical conduits. It is extremely difficult to trace cable and electrical runs if no numbering scheme exists to designate where they run from and to. Finally, a numbering scheme lends itself to creating a database of Data Center equipment that includes location information.

While there are several possible approaches, the most common Data Center numbering scheme involves laying a virtual grid over the Data Center and establishing coordinates for each floor tile location. Think of a game of Battleship® or plotting coordinates along X and Y axes. Letters proceed in sequence on one Data Center wall, while numbers proceed in sequence along another wall that is perpendicular to the first.

Figure 11-1 shows a map of a Data Center featuring a grid numbering system.

Grid numbers are typically printed high on each Data Center wall, just below the ceiling line. This is intended to make the information visible throughout the server environment. In practice, however, these numbers can be hard to see when standing in the middle of a server row with industry-standard server cabinets. Some companies also print the grid coordinates on floor panels, which is effective as long as tiles are returned to their correct locations after being lifted to access the under-floor.

Figure 11-1 *Data Center Numbering Grid*

3F	6F	9F	12F	15F	18F	21F	24F	27F	30F	33F
3G	6G	9G	12G	15G	18G	21G	24G	27G	30G	33G
3H	6H	9H	12H	15H	18H	21H	24H	27H	30H	33H
3I	6I	9I	12I	15I	18I	21I	24I	27I	30I	33I
3J	6J	9J	12J	15J	18J	21J	24J	27J	30J	33J
3K	6K	9K	12K	15K	18K	21K	24K	27K	30K	33K
3L	6L	9L	12L	15L	18L	21L	24L	27L	30L	33L
3M	6M	9M	12M	15M	18M	21M	24M	27M	30M	33M
3N	6N	9N	12N	15N	18N	21N	24N	27N	30N	33N
3O	6O	9O	12O	15O	18O	21O	24O	27O	30O	33O
3P	6P	9P	12P	15P	18P	21P	24P	27P	30P	33P
3Q	6Q	9Q	12Q	15Q	18Q	21Q	24Q	27Q	30Q	33Q
3R	6R	9R	12R	15R	18R	21R	24R	27R	30R	33R

Grid with column numbers 1–35 and row letters A–V. Labels: PDU, Air Handler (top), Air Handler, Air Handler (bottom).

Figure 11-2 shows grid numbers printed on a Data Center wall, above a row of server cabinets.

Figure 11-2 *Data Center Grid Numbers*

An advantage of the grid system is that it is based upon physical coordinates within the Data Center and not limited solely to cabinet locations. The grid therefore can also be used to indicate the locations of major infrastructure on the Data Center floor, not just servers. Recording specific locations on the grid for air handlers, power distribution units, sprinkler heads, cylinders containing fire suppressant, or structural columns is also useful. In Figure 11-1, for example, air handlers are located at grid locations 33A, 24U, 15A, and 7U.

Another approach is the labeling of server rows themselves in sequence, like aisles in a grocery store, and then differentiation of individual cabinet locations with letters. Row 1 would contain cabinets 1A, 1B, 1C, and so on; Row 2 would contain cabinets 2A, 2B, 2C, and so on. Many people find this numbering system familiar and therefore easier to work within than the grid. Its only shortcoming compared to the grid is that it only creates location information for devices located within server rows, and can't be expanded to air handlers and other major infrastructure components.

Figure 11-3 shows the same Data Center as in Figure 11-1, with rows and cabinet locations numbered in sequence.

Figure 11-3 *Sequential Data Center Rows*

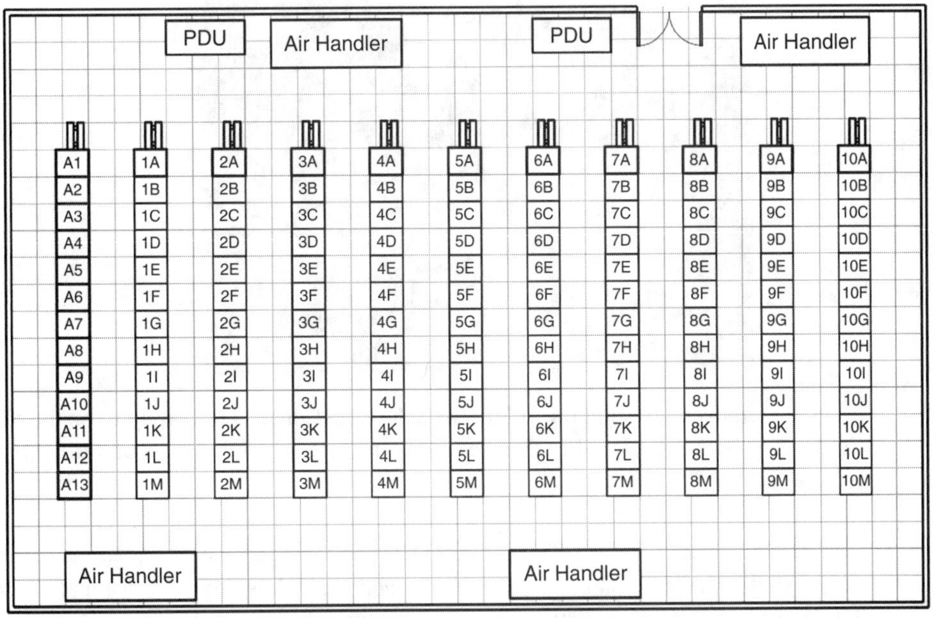

PDU	Air Handler					PDU			Air Handler	
A1	1A	2A	3A	4A	5A	6A	7A	8A	9A	10A
A2	1B	2B	3B	4B	5B	6B	7B	8B	9B	10B
A3	1C	2C	3C	4C	5C	6C	7C	8C	9C	10C
A4	1D	2D	3D	4D	5D	6D	7D	8D	9D	10D
A5	1E	2E	3E	4E	5E	6E	7E	8E	9E	10E
A6	1F	2F	3F	4F	5F	6F	7F	8F	9F	10F
A7	1G	2G	3G	4G	5G	6G	7G	8G	9G	10G
A8	1H	2H	3H	4H	5H	6H	7H	8H	9H	10H
A9	1I	2I	3I	4I	5I	6I	7I	8I	9I	10I
A10	1J	2J	3J	4J	5J	6J	7J	8J	9J	10J
A11	1K	2K	3K	4K	5K	6K	7K	8K	9K	10K
A12	1L	2L	3L	4L	5L	6L	7L	8L	9L	10L
A13	1M	2M	3M	4M	5M	6M	7M	8M	9M	10M

| Air Handler | | | | | Air Handler | | | | | |

In Figure 11-3, an additional step has been taken to differentiate the Data Center's networking row from its server rows. The networking row, located on the plan south portion of the map, uses a letter designation first. This optional step might be helpful, particularly in a large server environment that contains more than one network row.

Figure 11-4 shows how this numbering scheme appears to Data Center users, thanks to signs hung from the ceiling at the end of each server row.

Figure 11-4 *Server Row Signage*

Rows are arranged in ascending order across the Data Center. The acronyms on the adjacent signs—NSMBU, NUBU, SPLOB, and so on—refer to which business unit the server row is allocated to.

NOTE

Although it is the less common approach, I much prefer labeling rows sequentially rather than according to a grid pattern. It is a more intuitive numbering scheme, which makes it easier to navigate through the room and understand where cable runs connect to. I find this especially true in larger Data Centers. Because the grid creates coordinates for every floor tile location, it more rapidly exceeds the twenty-six letters of the alphabet and must therefore employ double letters. Which is easier for you to understand—if someone asked you to go from cabinet 3A to cabinet 20L or from grid location D10 to grid location AB25?

No matter what numbering system you use, large objects such as disk libraries inevitably overlap onto multiple coordinates. When determining the location information of a large object, don't list multiple locations. Doing so can be confusing. Instead, choose one reference point and be consistent. Establish all location coordinates based upon the center or upper left corner of the device, for example.

Recommended Labeling Practices

Once you've chosen which numbering scheme to implement within your Data Center, it is time to decide what objects to label and how.

The "what" is easy—label just about everything:

- Structured cabling
- Power receptacles and circuit panels
- Cabinets
- Raised floor tiles
- Individual servers and networking devices
- Entire server rows
- Major infrastructure components

Anything that needs to be located, serviced, replaced, or plugged in to by a Data Center user or someone who supports the room's functions should be labeled. The more relevant the information that is posted about a Data Center component, the easier it is to use the room's infrastructure correctly or to troubleshoot and remediate a problem. Even the most well thought out Data Center—if it lacks adequate labeling—can be confusing to users and therefore less effective for your company.

As for how, there are several options:

- Printing on address labels
- Using pre-printed stickers
- Ordering engraved signs
- Writing on masking tape with a marking pen

Whatever materials you use for labeling, employ large lettering with an easy-to-read font and choose a consistent format. If you decide to assign each air handler in the Data Center with a Roman Numeral, for instance, label them all that way—don't suddenly use Arabic numbers or otherwise vary from the format.

Always place labels in a prominent location—you want the information that they contain to be easily noticed by Data Center users or support staff. Put labels at eye level when possible or at least somewhere that has an unobstructed line of sight. Floor tile surfaces are excellent for providing information about the infrastructure below, for example. If an object you are marking might be viewed from multiple sides, such as the front and back of a server or the front and sides of an air handler, consider labeling each side that is visible.

Cable Runs

While all Data Center signage is important, labeling the room's structured cabling has the most day-to-day influence upon system administrators and networking engineers. This labeling is like a street sign at an intersection, telling users where the road—or in this case the structured cabling—goes.

The structured cabling should include labeling that contains what type of media is in use (i.e., 50 μm multimode or Category 6 copper) and the cabinet locations that a cable run connects from and to (i.e., from cabinet 1A to cabinet 1D). Place it everywhere that the structured cabling terminates—at the main networking row, in network substations, and at server cabinet locations. Specifically, label the fiber housings, patch panels, and multimedia boxes where Data Center users patch in to the structured cabling infrastructure.

Figure 11-5 illustrates typical labeling on a fiber housing and copper patch panel within a networking substation. The labeling indicates what type of fiber terminates there and lists the from/to locations of the structured cabling. (The substation is within a Data Center that uses sequential row numbering as shown in Figure 11-3.)

Figure 11-5 *Fiber Housing and Patch Panel Labeling*

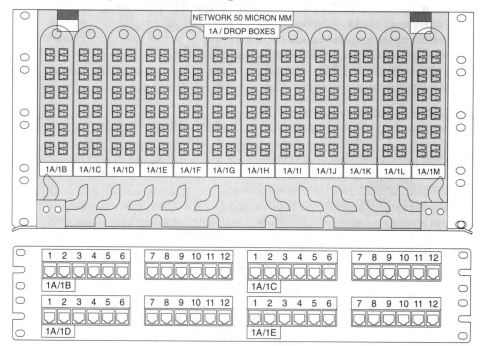

Networking substation 1A connects to other cabinet locations in the row—1B through 1M. Each panel in the fiber housing has twenty-four strands (twelve ports) of fiber running to a specific cabinet location. Similarly, twelve ports of copper are also clustered together to run to a specific cabinet.

Be aware that Figure 11-5 is only to demonstrate labeling, and therefore one copper patch panel is shown, containing connections for cabinets 1B through 1E. In practice, the substation would have three patch panels, with twelve connections each to cabinets 1B through 1M. It would also contain fiber and copper connections to the room's networking row.

NOTE   Some companies supplement the labeling of their Data Center structured cabling infrastructure by individually marking patch cords with from/to information and sometimes even the specific device and port number that they are plugged in to. (Many cable vendors sell plastic tabs for patch cords, to facilitate this practice.)

I generally believe that there's no such thing as too much labeling in a Data Center, as long as it is accurate and easy to understand. But, if a Data Center numbering scheme is clear and logical and all of the termination points within the structured cabling infrastructure are labeled, I don't believe there's a need to individually label patch cords.

When you consider the number of connections made during the installation of just a handful of servers, skipping that extraneous step can be a significant time saver—perhaps hundreds of hours over the course of a year.

Electrical Conduits

Just as Data Center cable runs should be labeled at their termination points, so too should power conduits. While data ports are labeled so that Data Center users can understand how to connect servers and networking devices to one another, power receptacles are labeled to help with troubleshooting. In the event that a power malfunction occurs or a circuit breaker trips, the facilities or Data Center support staff needs the information to trace a problem from an electrical receptacle to a circuit panel and back to the source power distribution unit. Labeling circuits also enables power to be managed so that Data Center cabinet locations are provided with electricity from different sources consistently.

Label electrical receptacles, circuit breaker panels, and power distribution units. Include circuit information, voltage and amperage, the type of electrical receptacle, and where in the Data Center the conduit terminates.

Figure 11-6 illustrates suitable labeling on a Data Center electrical receptacle. A power receptacle, shown in both NEMA 5-20R and L6-30R configurations, is fed by circuits 2 and 4 from PDU1 panel A.

Figure 11-6 *Sample Labeling of Electrical Receptacles*

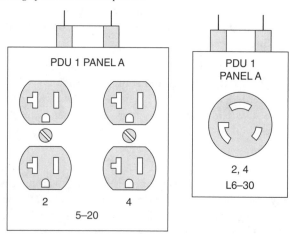

Table 11-1 shows a typical power schedule format that can be found in a single electrical panel, either as a standalone panel at the end of a Data Center row or one of several panels within a larger power distribution unit. (Although circuits are listed individually, be aware that many receptacle configurations require that a pair of circuits be used.)

Table 11-1 *Sample Power Schedule—PDU1, Panel A*

Cabinet Location	Circuit Breaker	Type of Receptacle	Cabinet Location	Circuit Breaker	Type of Receptacle
1A	1	L6-30R 208v	2A	2	L6-30R 208v
1A	3	L6-30R 208v	2A	4	L6-30R 208v
1B	5	5-20R 120v	2B	6	L6-30R 208v
1B	7	5-20R 120v	2B	8	L6-30R 208v
—	9	SPARE	—	10	SPARE
—	11	SPARE	—	12	SPARE

Depending upon how frequently alterations are made to your Data Center's electrical receptacles, it might be helpful to have additional columns on a power schedule, for information such as:

- The length of each electrical conduit
- When a circuit was last changed
- Who performed the work

Length information can be helpful for an electrician who needs to obtain conduit materials, while a date and signature for the last circuit change provides a paper trail for work completed in the server environment.

Electrical configurations in a Data Center are typically more dynamic than connectivity needs. Whenever power is changed in your server environment, whether it is running entirely new electrical conduits or simply modifying what's already in place, make sure all labeling and power schedules are updated when the work is done. It is much easier to keep this information up to date when changes are made than to have to re-inventory all of the Data Center's electrical conduits in the future.

Cabinet Locations

People who use a Data Center on a regular basis—system administrators, networking engineers, and vendor representatives—spend most of their time working at the cabinet locations where their servers have been or are in the process of being installed. Providing useful information at these spots can therefore make the Data Center easier for them to work in.

At a minimum, show what electrical circuits are powering each cabinet location and, by extension, the devices within them. Atop the corresponding raised floor panel and server cabinet, duplicate the data that's printed on the circuit panels and electrical receptacles. If power terminates above each cabinet location, circuit information should be printed on the overhead raceway near the appropriate receptacle.

Figure 11-7 shows electrical circuit information posted on the bottom rail of a server cabinet as well as on the floor tile below it. The data on the labels corresponds to what is printed on the electrical receptacles terminating below the cabinet, under the raised floor.

Figure 11-7 *Cabinet Labeling, Electrical*

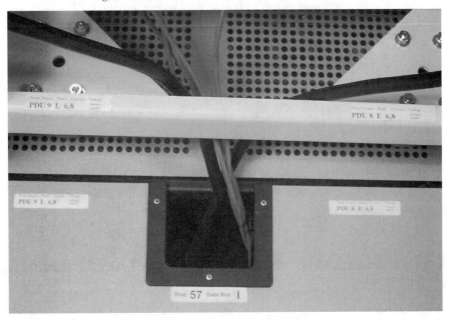

One power strip in this server cabinet is powered by PDU9 panel L, circuits 6 and 8; the other is powered by PDU8 panel E, circuits 6 and 8. The cabinet is at Row 57, cabinet I.

Although not at eye level, the labeling in Figure 11-7 is well placed. It is readily visible to anyone standing immediately behind a Data Center cabinet, which is where a person must be in order to plug in to or work on the cabinet's power.

As pointed out in the discussion of the numbering grid, it can be difficult to see over a server row to tell what specific location you are at within a Data Center. To mitigate this, put location information on each cabinet. Post it on both sides of the cabinets, because it is equally likely for a Data Center user to work on the back of a cabinet as on the front.

Figure 11-8 shows server cabinets bearing location labels. The labels are attached to the right horizontal rail of each cabinet, at eye level for someone of average height.

Figure 11-8 *Cabinet Labeling, Location*

Unless your Data Center is static, with minimal changes to the equipment that it houses, your server cabinets are likely to be relocated periodically. Be diligent about keeping their labeling up to date. Outdated location labeling can be confusing, and obsolete electrical information can lead to serious mistakes. Whenever electrical work is done in a Data Center, it is vital that individual circuits be mapped correctly to cabinet locations in the room. Just one old electrical label can mislead an electrician to shut off power to a circuit that is supporting live equipment rather than the empty server cabinet they think it is.

NOTE   Labeling is a trick I use to help keep track of which empty server cabinets in my Data Centers have been allocated for use. As soon as the cabinet is given to someone, it is adorned with location and circuit labels and then rolled to where it needs to be used. If a cabinet is unassigned, I keep it free of labels.

This practice also highlights when someone circumvents the allocation process and just takes a cabinet without permission, as their equipment will be installed in unlabeled cabinets.

Servers and Networking Devices

Assign distinct names to Data Center servers and networking devices. Clearly label them on both their front and back sides, including any related peripherals, as part of the machine's installation process. If something should malfunction on a device and trigger an audible alarm, a passing Data Center user should be able to determine immediately the name of the machine that is having a problem so they can quickly track down its owner. Reporting a problem on a particular piece of equipment is much more helpful to the troubleshooting process than simply saying "some server in the Data Center" is having a problem.

What someone specifically names a device doesn't matter. It is usually done by a system administrator, according to conventions established by the department. Some prefer very straightforward names, such as PRODSERV1, DEVBOX, EMAILSERV, and so on. Others prefer more fanciful ones, drawing names from television characters (CAPTAIN KIRK, MR. SPOCK, DR. MCCOY), everyday objects (BAT, BALL, GLOVE), or anything else that can be considered a recognizable group (VANILLA, STRAWBERRY, CHOCOLATE). Any of these patterns work fine in the Data Center, just as long as servers and other items are consistently named and thoroughly labeled.

Figures 11-9 and 11-10 show the front and back of a fully loaded cabinet, containing properly labeled servers. (Specific server names are not shown on the images, as a security precaution.)

Figure 11-9 *Server Labeling, Front*

Server Rows

One of the first challenges that new Data Center users often face is physically finding a particular server within the room. This can be especially challenging in a server environment that is very large or whose equipment isn't arranged in any particular manner. To make it easier to find specific servers as well as promote the overall organization of the room, post signs that show row numbers and which group each is assigned to. (An example of this is shown near the start of this chapter, in Figure 11-4.) If Data Center servers are arranged by type, it might instead be helpful to indicate what brand or type of equipment each row contains.

Figure 11-10 *Server Labeling, Back*

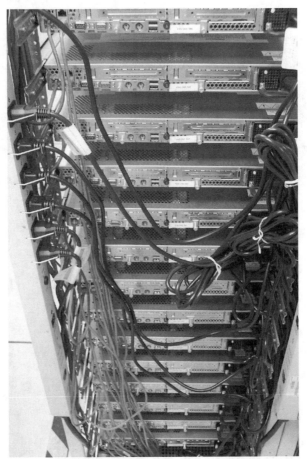

Also post an alphabetized list of equipment at the end of each Data Center row, indicating which cabinet position each device is in. Like signs in a grocery store that call out what type of foodstuffs are in each aisle, listing what servers are in a given row makes it easier for people to find what they are looking for. Provide these printed lists even if you maintain such information in an online database—it is possible that the database might be offline during a crisis.

The equipment list can be as elaborate as placards for each server or as simple as a printed piece of paper for an entire row. Whatever materials you use, make sure that they are easy to reconfigure, because the list should be updated periodically as servers are added, removed, or relocated. (Chapter 14, "Mapping, Monitoring, and Metrics," provides suggestions for regularly inventory Data Center devices.)

Figure 11-11 shows alphabetized equipment lists posted at the end of a pair of server rows.

Figure 11-11 *Server Row Equipment Lists*

Piping

Any water-bearing pipe in a Data Center presents a potential risk for leaking. Clearly mark such piping, especially any segments that are in high-traffic areas and therefore the most vulnerable to accidental damage. Such labeling is not only intended to make Data Center users more cautious around the piping, but also, in the event that water does leak in the server environment, it narrows down what piping needs to be examined as a possible source of the liquid.

Label cylinders that contain fire suppressant, as well.

Figures 11-12 and 11-13 show a Data Center air handler and its associated water pipes, which carry chilled water to and from a Data Center air handler. The pipes are labeled to indicate their contents and flow direction.

Figure 11-12 *Data Center Air Handler*

Essential Signage

All of the labeling practices mentioned to this point are aimed at providing information to Data Center users so they understand how the room that they are working in is organized— where structured cabling and electrical conduits run to and from, for instance. With this understanding, they can use the server environment's infrastructure effectively and efficiently.

Figure 11-13 *Air Handler Water Pipes*

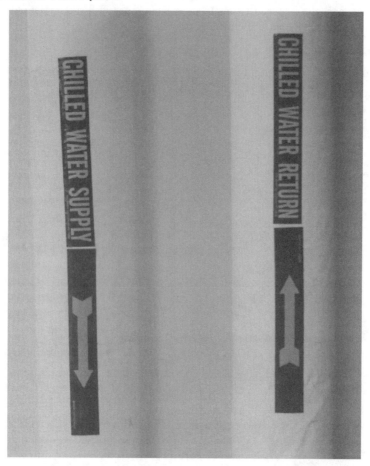

As necessary as that labeling is, it is even more important to label any Data Center infrastructure that potentially involves user safety. Typically this encompasses a room's fire suppression and electrical systems.

Fire Alarm Instructions

As outlined in Chapter 8, "Keeping It Cool," a typical Data Center can possess up to three automated elements for detecting and fighting a fire—a smoke detection system, water-based sprinklers, and gaseous fire suppression. All three systems feature alarm mechanisms to indicate when they have been activated. These alarms, all wall-mounted in multiple locations within the server environment, should also include explanatory signage that informs Data Center users of their function and what to do in the event that they activate.

Figure 11-14 shows three Data Center fire alarms—one for the smoke detection system, one for the sprinklers, and one for the gaseous fire suppression system—and their accompanying signage.

Figure 11-14 *Data Center Fire Alarms*

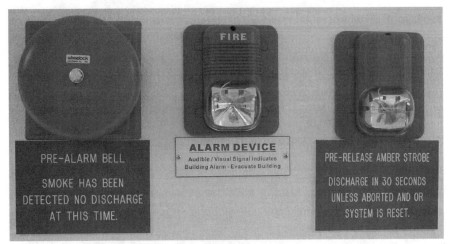

From left to right, an alarm bell indicates that smoke has been detected in the Data Center, a white strobe light shows that a building fire alarm has been activated, and an amber strobe light signifies that the countdown has begun to activate the Data Center's gaseous fire suppression system.

These placards, located next to each alarm station, are typically supplemented by large signs on the Data Center door informing users to leave the room in the event that any fire alarms engage.

Fire Suppression System Instructions

Unlike other firefighting mechanisms, a Data Center's gaseous fire suppression system features manual controls within the room that enable a person either to pause the system's automatic countdown to activation or to cause an immediate discharge. Because these controls require active participation of someone within the Data Center, they require more signage than merely explaining why a particular fire alarm has activated. Signage must be placed at the fire suppression controls that explains how someone can correctly operate them.

Figure 11-15 shows the controls and explanatory signage for a Data Center's gaseous fire suppression system.

Figure 11-15 *Fire Suppression System Controls and Signage*

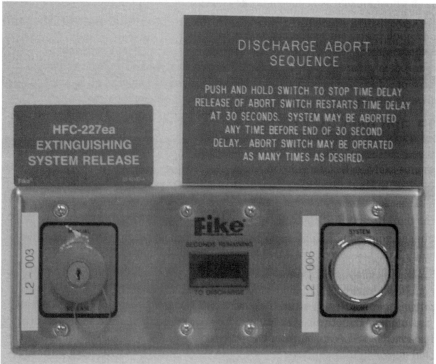

Pressing the button on the right pauses and resets a thirty-second countdown to discharge the gaseous fire suppression system; pressing the button on the left immediately discharges the suppressant. The countdown is shown on the middle display.

As important as your Data Center's overall fire suppression system is, if a small fire breaks out, it is likely that the first response of anyone in the room will be to look for a portable fire extinguisher. Make their task easier by providing signage that makes the extinguishers easier to find.

Figure 11-16 shows a wall-mounted fire extinguisher, with an overhead placard that helps call attention to it. The placard is placed just below the Data Center ceiling and protrudes outward, to increase its visibility.

Emergency Power Off Instructions

Arguably the most powerful controls in a server environment are those for the Emergency Power Off (EPO) system. Because they enable someone to shut down all Data Center servers and networking devices—literally at the touch of a button—it is vital that they be clearly and thoroughly labeled to reduce the chance of an accidental activation.

Figure 11-16 *Fire Extinguisher Signage*

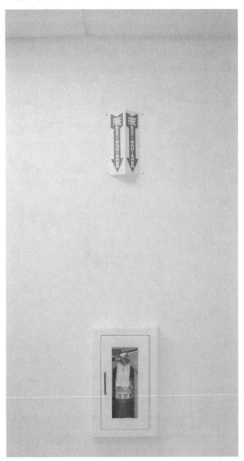

Signage must explain what the EPO controls do, how they can be activated, and what their area of effect is. EPO controls appear innocuous to those who don't know what they are for, so include an additional placard that says "Use only in an emergency" or something similar.

Figure 11-17 illustrates labeled Emergency Power Off controls, including an explanation of what the EPO system does and a map of its area of effect. Ideally these controls should also have a transparent plastic cover, for further protection against accidental activation, and a placard explaining that breaking the glass causes the button to protrude and the power to go off.

Triggering this Emergency Power Off button cuts power to all devices in the room, as shown on the accompanying map.

Figure 11-17 *Emergency Power Off Controls and Signage*

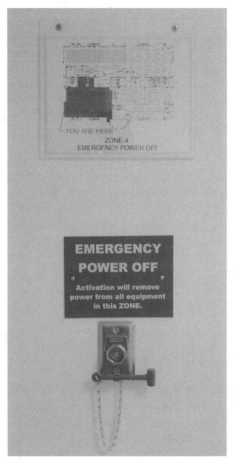

NOTE   Chapter 6, "Creating a Robust Electrical System," mentions an incident during 1999 in which a contractor pressed an Emergency Power Off push-button as he prepared to exit a Data Center, thinking it would open the door. That is not the only time I have encountered someone misunderstanding the true function of the EPO controls.

In 1997 in San Jose, California, while my manager was giving a Data Center tour and explaining the room's electrical infrastructure, a fellow employee walked behind him and, believing the EPO controls were activated by pushing a button rather than having it pop out, began unscrewing the cap that held the EPO's protective glass chip in place. My manager saw what he was doing about half-a-rotation before the man got the cap off and brought down the entire Data Center.

In 2001 a system administrator was working in a server environment in Akron, Ohio, when he heard an alarm from a power distribution unit. He could tell from the PDU display that the problem was related to a power imbalance of some sort. (In truth, the PDU had different power load levels on its individual circuit panels. Good to be aware of, but not a major issue.) When he noticed the nearby button labeled "Emergency Power Off," he thought he had the answer to his problem. He pushed the button, which certainly silenced the alarm, but also brought down all servers in the room.

Monitoring Lights

Chapter 6 recommends that you install monitoring lights that engage whenever Data Center power is being provided by an uninterruptible power source or generator instead of normal utility power. Assuming you include these monitoring lights as part of your server environment's standby electrical infrastructure, be sure to include signage that explains their purpose and whom Data Center users should contact in the event that they come on.

Figure 11-18 shows wall-mounted monitoring lights and explanatory signage.

Figure 11-18 *Monitoring Lights and Signage*

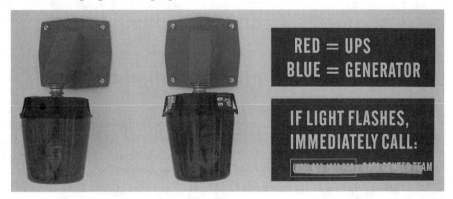

The red light (left) activates when the Data Center's electrical load is provided by UPS and the blue light (right) activates when it is provided by generator. (The phone number to call is intentionally obscured in this figure.)

Monitoring lights are typically installed at multiple spots throughout the Data Center as well as immediately outside the room's entrance. Have the accompanying signage posted at all of these locations as well.

Emergency Contacts

Even if your Data Center doesn't have monitoring lights, post lists in the room that inform room occupants whom to contact if a power outage or other infrastructure-related incident occurs. This can be just the phone number for your company's operations command center or a detailed list of people who support the server environment and how to reach them. Facilities engineers, Data Center support staff, security, system administrators, network engineers, department managers, and an abundance of on-duty paging aliases are typically included on this type of contact list.

Contact information can be arranged in several ways. One that works well is people grouped by their job role—all facilities staff, all network engineers, all system administrators, and so on—and then the names arranged in the order that they should be contacted if an issue needs to be escalated. This can be more effective than a simple alphabetized list, because it lessens the chance of someone contacting a department head before the front-line people who are intended to deal with an emergency.

Post these contact lists at all Data Center telephones.

Final Note

The purpose of all Data Center labeling and signage is to inform people how to properly use the room's infrastructure, either for their physical safety or simply so they can get their server up and running. Always make wording on signage unambiguous and easy to understand. Assume that it is going to be read by someone who is unfamiliar with the Data Center and the particular infrastructure component that the labeling pertains to. If your Data Center is in a region where multiple languages are used, consider printing signs in several dialects.

Would a visitor to your server environment know what to do in an emergency, based solely on the posted signage? How about if they had only seconds to react, perhaps to evacuate the room or pause the fire suppression system? If a person couldn't immediately figure out what to do, the Data Center probably needs better signage. That might seem like an extremely high standard, but odds are that, when an emergency occurs in the Data Center, the people in the room won't be facilities personnel who are specifically trained on the use of the electrical or fire suppression systems.

To improve the effectiveness of your Data Center signage, it is also advisable to train Data Center users on the basic functions of the room's associated infrastructure, as covered in greater depth in Chapter 13, "Safeguarding the Servers."

Summary

The first step in labeling Data Center infrastructure is a chosen numbering scheme for cabinet locations. One approach is use of a grid pattern that creates coordinates for all floor tile locations; another is server rows numbered sequentially. The first system is more common to Data Centers and can encompass more than just cabinet locations, while the second is likely more intuitive.

Prominently label infrastructure components to help Data Center users find and work with them. Label cable runs at their termination points. Include from/to information, the media type, and the number of ports. Label electrical conduits at their termination points, too. Include circuit information, the type of electrical receptacle, and where in the Data Center the conduit terminates. Maintain up-to-date power schedules at each circuit panel.

Use extensive labeling at cabinet locations, including location information and which electrical circuits the cabinet is plugged in to. Print this data on the cabinets themselves and again on either the raised floor tile below or infrastructure raceway overhead.

Label servers, networking devices, and peripheral equipment—front and back—with the distinct names assigned to them by system administrators. Put signs at the end of each Data Center row that indicate the number of the row and, depending upon how equipment is organized, either which group a row belongs to or what type of equipment it houses. Post an alphabetized server list at the end of each row.

Mark all pipes and cylinders in the Data Center that contain liquid, as they pose a risk of leaking.

Post signage near all Data Center fire alarms—smoke detection, sprinklers, and gaseous fire suppression—that explain their functions. Call out if people are required to leave the area or take other actions when a fire alarm activates.

Provide thorough instructions near the controls for the Data Center's fire suppression and emergency power-off systems. Both systems potentially require active participation on the part of bystanders. Include steps that a person must take to activate or disengage each set of controls.

If your Data Center has lights that monitor its standby electrical system, include signage that explains their function and whom to contact when they engage. Provide emergency contact lists at all Data Center telephones, for room users to call if an emergency or urgent infrastructure problem arises.

Make Data Center signage and labeling clear and understandable to all, including those unfamiliar with the room's infrastructure.

CHAPTER 12

Stocking and Standardizing

This chapter explains the value of providing standardized items within a Data Center to make the room safer to work in, more convenient for troubleshooting server problems, and easier to manage. The chapter calls out specific supplies, from server cabinets to stepladders, and details their potential benefit to a server environment.

Equipping a Data Center

The design principles in this book call for making a Data Center robust, flexible, modular, standardized, and intuitive to use. Stocking a server environment with carefully chosen consumable items and tools can significantly reinforce those qualities. Data Center consumables are the everyday materials needed by system administrators and network engineers to make their equipment function. Server cabinets, patch cords, and adapters fall into this category. Data Center tools are convenience items that, although not strictly necessary to bring a server or networking device on line, make it much easier to get work done in a server environment that has them. Pallet jacks, power tools, and tile lifters are good examples.

If your company has multiple Data Centers, be consistent with the consumables and tools that you provide in each room—right down to the make and model of the item if possible. This emphasizes standardization and creates a consistent level of convenience and functionality in each server environment. Data Center users can rely upon what materials are available for them and, if multiple server environments are located at one site, won't be tempted to shuttle supplies from one room to another. It is also easier to stock a single brand of an item rather than several different ones. While there is likely no discernable difference if your Data Centers have different brands of screwdrivers, more complex items such as server cabinets can have significantly different qualities.

NOTE   Providing the same consumables and tools in multiple Data Centers also lends itself to purchasing those items in bulk. As pointed out in Chapter 3, "Quantifying Data Center Space," as part of the discussion of Data Center sizing, buying in bulk can noticeably reduce your costs.

This chapter recommends several useful items to stock in a Data Center. Tailor these suggestions to the needs of your particular room. For example, a pallet jack is probably a necessity in a large Data Center where heavy servers and big boxes of supplies arrive frequently, but unnecessary and even impractical in a small server environment that houses little or no large equipment. A system administrator or network engineer in that same server environment, however, can get substantially more use out of a Data Center stepladder because the room's electrical and data infrastructure terminates overhead and not under a raised floor.

Patch Cords and Adapters

If you provide no other supplies in the Data Center, at least stock patch cords—pre-terminated fiber and copper cabling bearing connectors at either end. The patch cords should match whatever structured cabling exists in the server environment. That is typically 62.5/125 µm or 50/125 µm multimode fiber and Category 6 or 5E to each server cabinet location as well as a handful of singlemode fiber that leaves the Data Center from the main networking row.

While fiber patch cords are generally defined by their diameter (62.5, 50, or 8.3 micron) and type of connectors, copper patch cords are defined by their rating (Category 6 or 5E) and the orientation of the wiring pins within their RJ-45 connectors. A Data Center's copper structured cabling is always configured so that its internal twisted pairs proceed straight from one end to the other. However, those four pairs—eight wires in all—within a copper cable can actually be configured so that the wires appear in any of several combinations at the end connectors.

These various combinations are often used for patch cords. They enable a direct connection between servers and other devices whose transmitters and receivers otherwise wouldn't align correctly. (When a server connects to a network hub or switch, that device typically addresses the transmitter and receiver orientation.)

Table 12-1 illustrates the copper patch cord configurations most commonly used in Data Centers. The positioning of individual wires within a copper cable are represented by the numbers 1 through 8.

Table 12-1   *Copper Patch Cord Configurations*

Type	Connector Pins	Typical Usage
Straight Through	12345678-12345678	Ubiquitous. Used for most Data Center connections.
Rolled	12345678-87654321	Fairly common. Used primarily for console connections.
Crossover	12345678-36145278	Varies by Data Center. Connects devices without a hub or switch. Used rarely in a room with a distributed network design, more so for direct connections.

Although many servers and networking devices come with their own patch cords, there is no guarantee that they are made in the same configuration as the structured cabling that exists within the Data Center. The patch cord might be built to lesser specifications, which would then lower the performance of the device it is plugged in to. For example, if a Category 5 copper patch cord is deployed in a Data Center equipped Category 6 structured cabling. Even worse, the patch cord could have connectors that don't physically fit the jacks provided in the server environment. A server with an incompatible patch cord is as useful as a table lamp with a broken power cord—that is, not at all. Cables that are provided by the equipment manufacturer also tend to come in only one length, which is almost never the exact length that you need.

Stock an array of patch cords in the server environment. Provide cords with connectors that are compatible with both the room's structured cabling and as many incoming servers as possible. For instance, if fiber optic structured cabling in the Data Center terminates in Lucent Connector (LC) jacks, and servers that the room hosts typically contain either LC or subscription channel (SC) connections, stock LC to LC patch cords (patch cords with LC connectors on each end) and SC to LC patch cords.

Offer patch cords in multiple lengths. There should be enough variety so that a Data Center user isn't forced to use a long cable to make a short connection. Using overly long patch cords creates clutter and snagging hazards.

NOTE	I generally stock a Data Center with patch cords in lengths of 2, 3, 4, 5, 6, 8, 10, 20, and 50 feet. (That's .6, .9, 1.2, 1.5, 1.8, 2.4, 3, 6, and 15.2 meters.) Because most connections are made entirely within the patching field of a networking cabinet—at either the Data Center's main network row or a network substation at the end of a server row—the cables in greatest demand are those 2 to 6 feet (.6 to 1.8 meters) long. How many I keep on hand varies by the patch cord type and how much demand there usually is for it. I typically stock about 100 of each length of straight-through copper, 50 of each length for rolled copper and multimode fiber, and 10 of each length for crossover copper and singlemode fiber.

Slightly longer cables, 8 feet (2.4 meters), are for connections running from a device in a server cabinet to the structured cabling either below the raised floor or in a raceway suspended from the ceiling. I maintain about 50 in straight-through copper, 25 of each length in rolled copper and multimode fiber, and 10 of each length for crossover copper and singlemode fiber.

Last are the patch cords 20 and 50 feet (6 and 15.2 meters). Because the Data Centers I manage are equipped with structured cabling at each cabinet location, there is rarely a need for such long patch cords. They are strictly for emergencies or temporary use, such as keeping a server connected to a networking device while relocating from one server row to another. In fact, when a Data Center user comes asking for several long cords, it is usually a signal that they are not using the infrastructure correctly! I provide only a few of each of these lengths—in straight through copper, multimode fiber, and singlemode fiber—in the Data Center itself. I also maintain a larger stash of them elsewhere (but close by) in the event that an emergency does arise that requires them.

Providing your own patch cords also enables you to color-code them for greater clarity and organization. Knowing a data cable's characteristics without having to unplug it from a device, which you might otherwise need to do to see how a copper cable's wired pairs terminate in its connector, is invaluable.

Businesses typically color-code their Data Center patch cords in one of two ways, either by configuration—how their internal wiring is arranged—or by function—how the cable is used. For instance, one company might decide to make all of its Category 6 copper patch cords green that contain identical wiring. Any time a system administrator or network engineer sees a green patch cord, they know its type, rating, and wiring configuration. Another company might decide to implement different colors for otherwise identical cables to highlight what connections those cables are used for. Examples would be green for patch cords used to make Ethernet connections, where data is passing constantly along the cable and disconnecting the cable can cause a disruption, and yellow for console connections, which contain infrequent data traffic and can often be removed for a time without consequence.

Establish a system of color-coding patch cords for your entire business, not just those used in the Data Center. At many companies, different groups are responsible for maintaining the server environments, network closets, labs, and other areas that use patch cords. Developing a companywide standard avoids confusing circumstances, such as if the Data Center and lab groups happen to choose the same color for different patch cords. Their cables might appear identical on the outside but have different wiring inside, which can lead to considerable confusion. Adopting one system of color-coding also facilitates ordering patch cords in bulk, at a significant cost savings, and then distributing them as needed to the respective rooms and support groups.

Because patch cord connectors aren't always compatible with the data jacks found on servers, stock adapters in the Data Center as well. Adapters, which contain a connection port on either end, enable otherwise mismatched items to be linked together much like a power plug adapter enables a traveler to plug the hair dryer they brought from home into an electrical outlet in a different country. Adapters can be used to connect patch cords to servers, network devices, patching fields, or even other patch cords. So-called straight-through adapters, which have the same jack on either side, can be used to connect two short patch cords and make them serve as one longer one.

As with patch cords, provide a variety of adapters to enable connections to your Data Center's structured cabling and most commonly used servers and networking devices. Color-code adapters as you do patch cords.

NOTE   I greatly prefer color-coding patch cords and adapters according to their configuration because it reduces the chance for confusion. One color for each kind of patch cord is straightforward and mistake-proof, whereas color-coding by use of a patch cord requires the ongoing efforts of multiple employees.

Figure 12-1 shows cables, connectors, and other small Data Center items stored in a dedicated area along a Data Center wall. Cables are sorted by length and type, while other materials are grouped together by type. Storage bins with transparent fronts enable Data Center users to see the items inside, and the support staff to easily check supply levels. Each bin is labeled with what it contains.

Figure 12-1 *Dedicated Cable Bin Area*

Patch Cord Care

Over the years, I have seen some incredibly slipshod treatments of patch cords. Careless users toss patch cords on the floor, allow heavy equipment to rest upon them, and even occasionally mark cables by tying a knot in them—and yet they still expect these cords to provide a good connection!

Patch cords are the final component of your Data Center's expensive structured cabling system. To properly care for your patch cords, do the following:

- Use care when plugging in or unplugging patch cords. Excessive pressure can damage the cable.

- Keep caps on fiber patch cords and the jacks they plug in to. This keeps away dust, which can cause signal loss or even scratch a fiber cable's polished end.

- Don't drop patch cords, especially fiber patch cords. Connectors might become damaged.

- Apply the same minimum bend radius to your patch cords that you apply to your structured cabling. I recommend 2 inches (5.1 centimeters).

- Before reusing a fiber patch cord, clean it at each end and recheck it with a fiber tester. Cleaning is typically done with a lint-free wipe and a drop of 99 percent isopropyl alcohol. *Lightly* pass over the fiber tip in a figure-8, once with a moistened part of the wipe and then again with a dry part of the wipe—don't rub hard or you might scratch the fiber. After cleaning, test the patch cord to confirm that it meets the same performance standards you specify for new cords.

Server Cabinets

The next most valuable items to stock in a Data Center are server cabinets. As with patch cords, cabinets can often be provided by the manufacturer whose servers your company buys. This can seem convenient because manufacturers are often willing to install the servers into their cabinets at the factory and ship them to you—a notable time savings for your system administrators if the order involves dozens of servers or more. Spend enough on the equipment and the cost of the cabinet might even be free.

Before you accept a manufacturer's proprietary cabinets, however, make sure that they are compatible with your Data Center. Saving a couple of thousand dollars on the cost of a cabinet might not be the best business decision if the cabinet you end up with is too large for your Data Center rows, too heavy, or needs to be provided with more electrical receptacles than another cabinet would.

A preferable alternative to this is for your company to standardize on a generic cabinet design and deploy it in the Data Center as much as possible. A Data Center that houses only one model of server cabinet is much easier to manage. Data Center electrical receptacles can all be configured in the same manner, there's no mystery as to the cabinet's footprint, and the company needs to stock only one type of cabinet and related accessories. Unlike proprietary cabinets, a generic model can also be produced by multiple manufacturers, which can improve availability and possibly drive down its cost due to competitive pricing.

Server cabinet designs, just like the equipment they house, are bound to evolve over time. Using and reusing cabinets is a frugal practice, but pay attention as your cabinets age. If an older cabinet model becomes less compatible for newer servers, perhaps due to changing equipment footprints or increasing weight, consider standardizing on a newer cabinet style.

Specific features to seek or avoid in a server cabinet are outlined in Chapter 10, "Organizing Your Way to an Easier Job." How a cabinet can affect cooling in a Data Center is addressed in Chapter 8, "Keeping It Cool."

Figure 12-2 shows a row of generic server cabinets containing a variety of server models. Standardizing on one type of Data Center server cabinet simplifies room management.

Figure 12-2 *Standardized Data Center Cabinets*

How many server cabinets to keep on hand depends on the size of your server environment, how quickly new equipment might arrive for installation, and how fast an order for additional cabinets can be filled. Depending upon demand, manufacturers can take anywhere from four to ten weeks to produce new server cabinets. Shipping adds additional time, particularly if the cabinets must be delivered across a great distance and pass through customs.

Server cabinets can come pre-equipped with their own power strips or be outfitted with others. If you stock power strips as a distinct item—something that might be necessary if you have Data Centers located around the world and therefore a variety of electrical configurations to deal with—be sure to include them when stocking, ordering, calculating lead times, and so on.

Stock an ample supply of cabinet shelves in the Data Center, too. Depending upon the size, type, and number of devices that are installed within it—and whether the items can be directly rack-mounted or not—a single server cabinet might need two dozen shelves or none at all.

NOTE   At minimum, I maintain enough server cabinets and corresponding shelves and power strips on hand to occupy at least two server rows in a large Data Center. That is generally 24 cabinets, 48 power strips, and about 100 shelves per server environment. Because Data Center consumables are inevitably going to be used, I seek to buy them in great quantities whenever doing so leads to significant price breaks.

I stack spare cabinet shelves against the Data Center wall, within the buffer area of whichever power distribution unit is closest to the center of the room. This makes use of what would otherwise be dead floor space and inhibits Data Center users from placing something else there that might be susceptible to electromagnetic interference.

Tools

Provide a common group of tools in your Data Centers. This makes a server environment more usable and can save a system administrator or network engineer a significant amount of time if they need to work on a piece of equipment and don't happen to bring tools with them. This isn't just a convenience issue—when downtime occurs, every minute that doesn't have to be spent retrieving tools is hopefully how much faster devices can be brought back online.

Be aware that Data Center "tools" aren't limited to the handheld kind found in a hardware or do-it-yourself store. Anything that helps a Data Center user complete their work in the room should be considered a tool. The list that follows describes some particularly helpful Data Center tools:

- **Anti-tip brackets**—Some models of servers and networking devices are heavy enough to cause a cabinet to tip over, assuming that the cabinet isn't bolted to the ground. This can occur during the item's installation, removal, or—if the device must be slid out on rails to be serviced—regular maintenance. Equip all Data Center cabinets with their own antitip mechanisms or provide independent rails that can be attached to a cabinet when these three functions are to occur. It is obviously cheaper to stock a few sets of brackets per Data Center than to pay for them to be equipped with each cabinet, so pursue that option first.

    In Figure 12-3, a Data Center support staff member attaches antitip brackets onto a server cabinet in preparation for installing a server.

Figure 12-3 *Antitip Brackets*

Note	In addition to providing antitip brackets in your Data Center and having them integrated into server cabinets, you can further reduce the chances of a cabinet toppling by making it a standard installation practice that heavy equipment always be placed at the bottom of a cabinet. This might not be practical in a small server environment, where space is limited and you must install items wherever possible, but it can be quite effective in larger Data Centers.
	Chapter 13, "Safeguarding the Servers," outlines more recommended installation practices.

- **Cabinet screws**—Stock the Data Center with screws that are compatible with the mounting rails for your standard server cabinets. Properly threaded screws can make the difference between installing a cabinet shelf in moments and having to wrestle with it for twenty minutes or more. The tiniest misalignment can lead to stripped screws, broken tools, scraped hands, and raised blood pressure. Don't rely solely upon the screws that come with individual servers and network devices. They might not be made to the same specifications as your cabinet's mounting rails.

- **Cable ties**—These simple fasteners made of plastic, fabric, or even metal are among the most versatile of Data Center tools. Cable ties, also called zip ties, are useful for neatly gathering excess lengths of patch cords and power cables, securing bundles of structured cabling, and anchoring electrical conduits under a raised floor so that they don't drift from the specific server cabinet location they are to terminate at. In a pinch, they can even serve as temporary wire management within a cabinet. Cable ties can be ordered in a variety of lengths and, when made of the correct materials, can be rated for use in a Data Center plenum. They come in both single-use and reusable forms.

Note   I prefer single-use ties for tasks such as fastening infrastructure components and prefer reusable ties for bundling patch cords. If a Data Center user tries to "borrow" a power receptacle or box of data ports from a nearby cabinet location—something they aren't supposed to do—they must first cut a single-use cable tie so that they can reposition the item. This usually makes them hesitate and perhaps ask the Data Center support staff for assistance. If they proceed and do cut the cable tie, they generally just leave the tie where it falls, providing a clue that something has been moved without authorization. Reusable ties are excellent for bundling or securing items that might change in size, because the ties can be adjusted.

Be aware that plenum-rated cable ties can be more than ten times the cost of non-plenum ties. Using them in non-plenum areas is needlessly expensive, so stock both types and use them appropriately.

- **Equipment lift**—The manual equivalent of a forklift, an equipment lift has a shelf that can be placed under a heavy object and then, typically by the use of a hand crank, raised to eye level. Small enough to fit between server rows, this lift enables one person to elevate a heavy server or networking device and maneuver it into a server cabinet. This item is especially valuable at a small site with few employees, because it is less likely that a system administrator there can find someone to help lift and install a heavy piece of equipment.

Figure 12-4 shows an equipment lift elevating a server for installation into a cabinet.

- **Flashlights [torches]**—While server environments are generally well lit, have a few flashlights available for working under the raised floor or within the recesses of large infrastructure items such as a power distribution unit. A light source that can be placed on the ground is preferable to a typical cylindrical flashlight, because a person can use it and still have both hands free.

Figure 12-4 *Equipment Lift*

- **Handheld tools**—Stock a range of useful tools that can be used during equipment installations, servicing, or decommissions. Screwdrivers (slot and Phillips head) and wrenches are the most useful. A hammer can be helpful for tapping bent metal back into place, such as the installation tabs on a server cabinet shelf. A tape measure can also come in handy now and then.

- **Information tags**—If a member of your company's Data Center support staff comes upon a pile of server components and half-empty boxes near an empty server cabinet location, what should they do? Assume that the items are trash and toss them out? Wait to see if someone returns to claim them? Begin walking through the building to see if anyone knows who was last working in the Data Center? Eliminate mystery piles of items in the Data Center by requiring the use of information tags—preprinted, self-stick pieces of notepaper with helpful information—by anyone performing equipment installations. These tags can be custom made at most print shops or office supply stores. Tags can also be used by Data Center support staff to alert system administrators and network engineers about conditions that need to be corrected with their machines, such as missing labels or power cords plugged in to an incorrect electrical receptacle.

Figure 12-5 shows a tag for system administrators to indicate that a server is in the midst of being installed and that its components shouldn't be discarded by Data Center support staff. Work-in-progress tags include key information such as who is doing the work, how to reach them, and when it will be done.

Figure 12-5 *Work-in-Progress Tags*

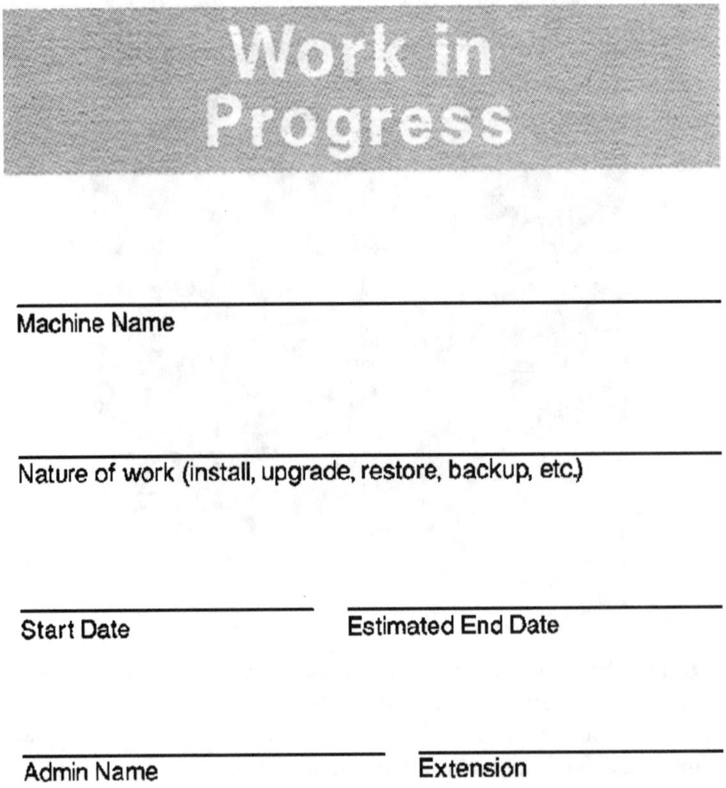

Machine Name

Nature of work (install, upgrade, restore, backup, etc.)

Start Date   Estimated End Date

Admin Name   Extension

Figure 12-6 shows a tag for Data Center support staff to flag improper machine installations or other conditions that violate Data Center policies.

Attention tags should be large enough to be seen easily and so that information can be written upon them easily.

- **Label makers**—If you want system administrators and network engineers to label their devices when they install them, provide label makers for them to do so. Label makers are also helpful for the Data Center support staff, enabling them to update immediately minor labeling in the room such as when a server cabinet is placed in a new location and needs new power circuit information.

- **Moving dolly, pallet jack, and equipment cart**—Just as an equipment lift helps Data Center users raise and install heavy servers, so do dollies, pallet jacks, and carts make it easier to move items around the room. Stock one of each in a Data Center, perhaps two if the room is particularly large.

- **Power tools**—Manual screwdrivers are acceptable for installing a few cabinet shelves and servers, but for more demanding jobs provide a power screwdriver or electric drill. Include a bit set and plenty of rechargeable batteries to prolong how often the tool can be used.

Figure 12-6 *Attention Tags*

Machine Name	Date	Location
Nature of problem		

Complainant   Extension

Note   If you do stock power screwdrivers or drills, instruct anyone who may use them to make good contact between the tool and any screws and to limit how much torque they apply. Misaligning a tool or using too much force can strip, cross thread, or otherwise damage a screw. This not only ruins the screw, but the screw may then be extremely difficult to remove from whatever hole it is in—much like breaking a key off in a lock.

- **Stepladder**—Having a stepladder in a Data Center is helpful for both system administrators and the room's support staff. They make it easier to reach servers installed high in server cabinets and hanging signs. If your server environment has infrastructure that terminates overhead, provide multiple stepladders in the room so that users always have one at hand. Obviously, choose stepladders that are sturdy. Those with rubber feet are preferable for greater stability—look for feet that are non-marking to better keep your Data Center floor clean.

- **Tile lifters**—If your Data Center has a raised floor and infrastructure that terminates in the space below, provide tile pullers so that Data Center users can easily gain access to that area. There are multiple types of devices for lifting floor panels. Most tile pullers are handheld and have twin suction-cups that can be used on blank or cut tiles. Some have an extended handle, theoretically enabling a person to lift or replace a tile without bending over. There are even lifters that consist of a small metal hook, for raising perforated tiles.

  Figures 12-7 and 12-8 each show a different floor tile lifter, one with an extended handle and the other without.

Figure 12-7   *Handheld Floor Tile Lifter*

Figure 12-8 *Long-Handled Floor Tile Lifter*

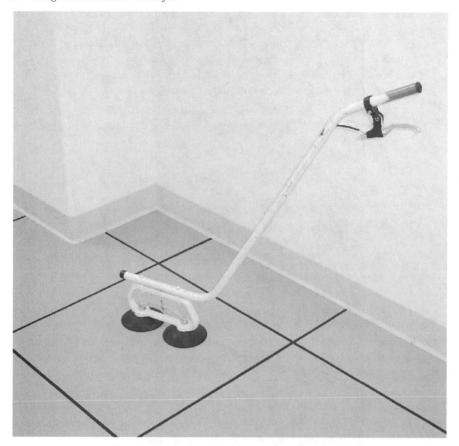

NOTE   There are two schools of thought about providing floor tile pullers and handheld tools in a Data Center. One is that these items should not be provided, because the Data Center is a fragile environment, and every time someone lifts a floor tile or touches a server there is a risk of downtime. Anyone in the room could cause an outage, and making tools available is asking for trouble. The second theory is that people who are permitted in the Data Center should be trusted to use these items when necessary.

I agree with the latter. If employees can't be trusted to act responsibly with these items, they shouldn't have been allowed in the Data Center in the first place. The presence or absence of tools won't make a difference.

Figure 12-9 shows a collection of Data Center tools, wall-mounted near the room's entrance. Provide this cluster of helpful items immediately inside each door to make them readily available for users.

Figure 12-9 *Data Center Tools*

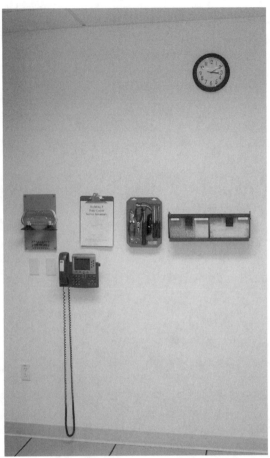

Accessories

Handheld tools go a long way toward making a Data Center more convenient for system administrators and network engineers. There are also a handful of other items that can improve the room's usability, both for Data Center users and the support staff who maintain it:

- **Cable testers**—A cable tester is useful for double-checking the quality and performance of both structured cabling and patch cords. Available for copper and fiber media, cable testers can gauge the strength of a signal as it reaches the end of a cable, measure different forms of interference, as well as map the wiring within a patch cord. It is especially important to confirm the quality of any patch cord you intend to reuse. Patch cords that have been used or discarded or both can become kinked, dirty at the connection points, or otherwise damaged. Most companies that possess a server environment actually have multiple rooms that make use of patch cords—a network room, cable distribution closets on each building floor, and possibly some form of testing labs. In each of these environments, patch cords are often dropped on the floor, either after a server or networking device is decommissioned or simply because an employee grabbed more cables than needed and didn't bother to return unused ones to where they came from. Over time this tangled yarn ball can come to contain thousands of dollars worth of patch cords. Untangling and reusing them is a good cost-saving measure as long as each patch cord is tested—and in the case of fiber, cleaned—before being put back in to service.

- **Clocks**—Having clocks in the Data Center makes it less likely for someone working in the room to lose track of time. This is helpful if a system administrator has arranged with their clients for a specific amount of downtime and must complete the upgrade of a machine on a deadline. It is also useful in the event of an unscheduled downtime or emergency, because someone in the room can immediately make note of when the incident occurred. Use battery-powered models, so they continue functioning even if power is lost to the Data Center's convenience outlets. As with server environment monitoring lights and visual alarms, place clocks high on the walls and in multiple locations so that they are easily noticed throughout the room.

- **Electrical circuit analyzer**—Say that you've installed a new server in a Data Center cabinet and for some reason the device isn't receiving power. Is the problem with the server's power supply? The cabinet's power strips? Perhaps it is the power receptacle provided to that cabinet location in the Data Center? Provide a simple three-wire electrical circuit analyzer in the Data Center. Smaller than a pack of cigarettes, this device indicates how the hot, neutral, and ground wires are configured at a given electrical outlet. It can immediately determine if a server cabinet power strip or electrical outlet is wired incorrectly. Have the Data Center support staff use the tester to check each new server cabinet power strip when it arrives in the room to confirm that its wiring is correct. A similar check should be performed by the electrician when the room's electrical infrastructure is initially installed.

- **Fireproof containers**—Try as you might to keep trash out of the Data Center by diverting incoming equipment into a build room, debris is still bound to accumulate. Instruction manuals, packaging, and installation kit leftovers all tend to drift in to a server environment when new equipment arrives. Data Center users are also known to grab handfuls of patch cords to perform an installation and fail to put back what they don't use. Decommissioned servers and their accompanying cables also become junk within the Data Center once they are turned off. Provide trash cans to discard paper products into and a larger bin to place decommissioned equipment into. Both should be fireproof.

Tip	Provide large containers in designated locations of the Data Center so that system administrators can place decommissioned servers or unneeded components there. These "donation bins" keep stray items from occupying cabinet locations while also making them available for other system administrators to use if they can.

- **Hanging bins**—Cable ties, cabinet screws, and other minor Data Center items need to be stored someplace—why not place them in wall-mounted storage bins? Install these items near each Data Center entrance to make them easily accessible and simple to keep in stock. Monitor the level of the supplies and refill the bins when necessary.

- **Spare floor panels**—Strategically placing notched, perforated, and blank tiles in a Data Center can influence air flow patterns in the room. Their location also controls where patch cords and power cables can be routed in and out of the plenum. If your server environment has a raised floor, keep a handful of extra panels on hand to facilitate such adjustments by the Data Center's support staff.

- **Tacky mats**—Place these sticky mats just inside your Data Center entrances to reduce the amount of dirt and other contaminants that people track in on the bottom of their shoes. The mats contain several layers of adhesive sheets. When the top sheet becomes dirty, you peel it away to reveal the next clean sheet below.

Equipment Spares

At many large companies, servers are purchased and supported by distinct groups. Even if multiple groups are using the same model of servers, they might or might not coordinate their efforts to make bulk purchases or obtain companywide service maintenance agreements. Because these devices are ultimately installed within the company's Data Centers, those responsible for managing these rooms might have the best global perspective as to what items are in the most widespread use.

Take advantage of this perspective by stocking spares of those servers and networking devices that are most commonly used. Stocking a few extra power supplies or data drives for the most prevalent servers can let a system administrator swap out a bad one in minutes rather than having to wait for a replacement to arrive. This dramatically reduces how long a malfunctioning system remains offline. Equipment spares can ideally be stored in the storage area that is located nearby and dedicated for Data Center-related items.

If a particular server is used in your Data Center, also consider stocking a few extra installation kits. This precaution can facilitate an installation in the event that someone forgets to order mounting rails with the common device, or if those that are ordered are damaged during shipping.

Obscure Data Center Tools

I once asked Data Center support staff members to brainstorm what items might be helpful to have in a server environment if cost, storage space, and other practical considerations weren't an issue. The only guideline was that the item had to serve some sort of relevant purpose for a server environment. As hoped, their suggestions were very imaginative. They included everything from adhesive bandages to bathroom plungers. Here's a list of the group's more creative suggestions, which you may or may not consider providing in your Data Center:

- Aspirin and Band-Aids® for minor scrapes and cuts that can occur when installing servers or moving floor tiles.

- An engraver for marking Data Center tools such as pallet jacks, tile lifters, and equipment carts, thereby reducing the odds of someone stealing them from the room.

- Knee pads that can be used for extensive work under the room's raised floor.
- A level to ensure that items mounted on the Data Center wall or installed in cabinets are straight.
- Notebooks, pens, and permanent markers for written notes that a Data Center user might need to make while in the room.
- Pedestal fans to redirect cold air in to or hot air out of a Data Center in the event of a cooling infrastructure failure.
- A pair of plungers that can serve as a substitute floor tile lifter if someone walks away with the genuine article.
- Batteries to power electric tools, clocks, label makers, and other Data Center items, rechargeable, if possible.
- Pre-moistened towelettes for wiping dust off of patch cords or cleaning a person's hands.

Summary

Having designed your Data Center to be reliable, flexible, consistent, and easy to use, stock the room with well-chosen consumable items and tools to further those characteristics. Standardize your choice of which items to provide for the same reason that you standardize Data Center infrastructure components—consistency.

At a minimum, stock your server environment with copper and fiber patch cords. Provide patch cords in multiple lengths and bearing connectors that are compatible with the ports in your server environment. Avoid patch cords that come with servers in favor of stocking your own. Color-code patch cords so that Data Center users can immediately tell a cable's characteristics, and extend this system to other cabling that your company uses in its networking closets, labs, and similar environments. Provide common adapters in the Data Center, too, to enable otherwise mismatched components or patch cords to be connected.

Use proprietary server cabinets sparingly in the Data Center. Standardize on a generic server cabinet as much as possible to avoid having to accommodate different power requirements, sizes, weights, and other characteristics. Stock enough server cabinets to anticipate numbers of incoming servers. Take into account the lead time involved with having additional cabinets manufactured and shipped, and provide an ample number of power strips and cabinet shelves as well.

Provide tools in the Data Center to make the room easier to use. Helpful items include antitip brackets, standardized cabinet screws, cable ties, an equipment lift, flashlights, handheld tools, information tags, label makers, moving dollies, pallet jacks, equipment carts, power tools, stepladders, and tile lifters.

Other items that can be useful, both for Data Center users and support staff, include cable testers, clocks, electric circuit analyzers, fireproof containers, hanging bins, and spare floor panels.

Stocking spare server components in or around the Data Center can also reduce downtime or avoid unnecessary installation delays.

Safeguarding the Servers

This chapter presents access control options for a Data Center and recommends standards of operations for people working in the room. The chapter also provides best practices for equipment installations and suggested guidelines when touring visitors through a server environment.

Physical Access Restrictions

Because your Data Center contains your company's most critical servers, applications, and data, it is important to physically secure the environment. You want to shield equipment from intentional theft or vandalism, from accidental damage by personnel not trained to work in a Data Center, and from espionage, that is, unauthorized personnel seeing or obtaining sensitive information.

The most fundamental way of physically protecting the items housed in a Data Center is control over who can enter. Door locks, access control systems, fencing, and lockable server cabinets each prohibit someone from entering a sensitive area without authorization. Video cameras can track who enters and leaves. Finally, establishing clear access policies ensures that only appropriate personnel are allowed in to the Data Center.

Door Controls

It goes without saying that Data Center doors must be equipped with a sturdy lock. At a small site with a server environment that is entered regularly by only a handful of people, it is conceivable to provide keys or a combination code to those who qualify. Keep a log of who has such access and prohibit copies of the keys from being made or the combination from being further distributed. This approach is manual, however, and relies predominantly on individual employees to ensure that the mechanisms to enter the Data Center aren't improperly shared with unauthorized people.

Most businesses choose a more automated approach for securing Data Centers and other sensitive areas, though—typically employing what is known as a card reader or badge access system. Employees, vendors, and other qualified visitors are issued an identification badge that has a photo of them and bears a magnetic stripe. The stripe contains data about the person such as an employee number. Card readers are installed at the doors to all secured areas and controlled by computer. A person presses or slides the badge across a reader device, which unlocks the door if the person has the appropriate level of clearance.

Access lists are maintained by computer, which enables a greater amount of control and flexibility than simply issuing keys to employees. Vendors and other visitors can be issued badges that expire after a limited time, for example. Access data can also be collected, who enters and leaves a Data Center when, for example. This can be useful in case a malicious event occurs in the server environment, helping ascertain who was there at the time.

Card reader systems can include even greater safeguards and identification measures. Some additionally require a person to enter a combination code, making it harder for an intruder to enter the room by using a stolen employee badge. Others involve a signature on a sensor pad. There are even biometric security features that scan the shape of a person's hand or fingerprints or focus on their voice, facial features, or iris patterns.

It is also possible to install a revolving door mechanism that allows only one person to enter at a time. This prevents tailgating, that is, following someone in to a secure area without badging in. Although card readers are generally thought of primarily as an entry control mechanism, they can be placed inside a Data Center as well, requiring personnel to unlock the door before leaving. (Emergency release controls can be included so that no one is trapped in a room in the event of a fire or other disaster.) This confirms who has left a room and also helps ferret out incoming tailgaters.

Cages

Although most Data Centers are hard-walled rooms, on occasion a company might choose to surround a specific server area with wire mesh fencing. Called a cage, such fencing is most commonly used to subdivide a large raised floor area. This might be installed to provide added physical security for select servers and networking devices. It can also be used to create distinct server areas, perhaps to house equipment belonging to different outside companies. This is fairly common in co-location scenarios, in which the servers and networking devices of various customers are physically located on their service provider's premises. A business might even use a cage to carve out separate spaces, again on one common raised floor, for Data Center and lab usage. Whatever the reason, weigh the pros and cons of a caged area before implementing it in a Data Center.

The biggest advantage of a cage is that it is an easy way to provide a restrictive barrier within a server environment. Fencing prevents unauthorized personnel from entering a given space, while still enabling the area to receive the effects of the overall Data Center's cooling, fire suppression, and other infrastructure systems. It is cheaper to build and generates less of a mess during construction than a traditional wall.

Be aware, though, that a cage still enables people to look in and know that something of value is inside. Even if the cage is covered, it attracts more curiosity than a regular room with walls. A cage also can't protect what it doesn't surround. If a cage surrounds a server row, but doesn't also encompass the power distribution units and air handlers that support that row, then the servers within that area are still vulnerable to events that affect those infrastructure items. This also applies to any electrical conduits or structural cabling that extend outside of a caged area. A break in the conduit or cabling can cause downtime to equipment within a cage, no matter where the damage occurs.

NOTE   One of first Data Centers I ever supported housed its associated materials — spare components, patch cords and other supplies, old equipment, and so on — in a storage cage. Fencing was arranged in an L against the corner of a receiving dock, forming a large square storage area. The cage had a magnetic lock, a card reader security system, and a plastic shield on the door to prevent reaching through the mesh. Along one of the hard walls, about ten steps in to the storage space, was a release button for the magnetic lock. This was required by the local building code to prevent a person from being accidentally locked in.

For some reason there were intermittent problems with the cage's card reader. Sometimes it released the magnetic lock, and other times it didn't. One such malfunction occurred when a system administrator needed to remove a server from the cage and install it immediately in the Data Center. Not wanting to wait for the card reader to finally behave again, I searched for an immediate way in to the cage. Within five minutes, I located a long pole, reached through an unshielded portion of the cage, and triggered the lock release.

I was happy to have circumvented the faulty card reader and helped the system administrator get his equipment, but was concerned about how easily someone could get in to the cage if they put their mind to it. After getting the card reader fixed, a coworker and I spent our spare time in the weeks that followed developing new ways to break in to the cage. We would then fix the vulnerability and try again. Pushing the release button with a pole? Place shielding on all fence walls, not just the door. Using a longer, angled pole to still reach the release button? Build a metal box around the button that opens by turning a knob. Defeating the magnetic lock with a makeshift pry-bar? Get stronger magnets. Bending the fencing to create a crawl space? Add support posts and make sure that the wire mesh is inflexible and secured to them.

Know the pros and cons that come with a cage before installing one. You need to decide if the vulnerabilities are acceptable to live with and, if not, know what steps to take to mitigate them.

The lesson here is that a cage provides a degree of additional protection within a server environment, but only if placed correctly. If you do cage in a portion of a Data Center, take the following precautions:

- Extend cage walls below the raised floor and above the false ceiling. Don't permit space for a person to climb above or below the fencing and enter the caged area.

- Cover cage walls with a hard, opaque surface. This prevents someone from reading information that might otherwise be visible through the fencing, or from reaching through the mesh.

- Size the cage and orient infrastructure so that as much as possible is located within the fencing. The more electrical conduits, structured cabling, and source equipment feeding them that are located outside of a cage, the easier it is for someone to cut, break, or shut down power and connectivity into the space.

One last Data Center-related use for a cage is fencing off a common area to store equipment and supplies in. This tactic is generally employed when no dedicated storage room was established for Data Center items to begin with or else when existing Data Center storage space has filled to capacity. A rarely used corner of a receiving dock or an unfinished spot of building space intended to contain cubicles are typical candidates for being transformed into a caged storage area.

Only keep Data Center items in a storage cage if no other option is available. While a cage inside a Data Center has its limitations, it at least resides within a hard-walled area and can't be seen or accessed by most people. A free-standing cage is more vulnerable to someone reaching in or cutting through its wire mesh. It is preferable to move Data Center materials into an existing hard-walled storage room and relocate whatever was in there to a caged area. The Data Center storage space is likely to contain spare server components needed to perform upgrades or repairs, equipment that is decommissioned but still valuable, and various supplies that are needed to keep the server environment functioning normally. Unless other materials that are kept in your company's storage areas are as important to keep the business running, displace them instead of the Data Center items.

Locking Cabinets

Another option for providing extra physical security for servers is the use of locking cabinets. Enclosed server cabinets, which come with doors and side panels, typically have the option of being equipped with locks as well. These locks come in several forms—key, combination, or even a full-fledged card reader system with the control options listed at the beginning of this chapter. Whatever the type, locking cabinets prevent a person from gaining direct access to whatever servers or networking devices are physically inside the cabinet.

While a locking cabinet can't stop someone from sabotaging a piece of equipment by severing structured cabling or turning off power to them from the outside, it does prevent a person from seeing or making physical contact with those devices. Therefore, the cabinet is most effective at hiding sensitive information displayed on a system and stopping someone from directly manipulating it. The card reader system might also log who opens the cabinet, which can be useful to know in the event that a problem occurs with a device.

Be aware that use of locking cabinets requires you to administrate their access controls as you do the controls for the Data Center itself. This means distributing and tracking keys or combination codes, or managing any badge access readers for the cabinets, or both.

By definition, locking cabinets are fully enclosed. If you deploy them in the Data Center in significant numbers, be aware of their effect upon the room's cooling. How to design a Data Center's cooling infrastructure and choose server cabinets so that they are compatible with one another is discussed in Chapter 8, "Keeping It Cool."

Closed-Circuit Television Coverage

Card reader logs can track who enters and leaves a Data Center, but for real-time surveillance of who enters your server environment, install closed-circuit television cameras. Cameras can be placed outside all Data Center entrances and, for greater visibility into the comings and goings of visitors, at key locations within the room. You might even consider installing cameras *under* a raised floor to view the condition of infrastructure there. Cameras are typically monitored by company security personnel and, depending upon how the system is configured, can be limited to live views or record footage for archiving and later viewing. As with the card readers, cameras monitoring the Data Center are generally part of a larger system used to protect the entire company site.

Cameras placed outside the server environment to monitor its entrances should be oriented so as to have a clear view at all times. Those installed inside the room should be placed along major aisles, for maximum coverage, and point at the room's most important servers and networking devices.

NOTE   Check with your human resources department before implementing closed-circuit television coverage in a Data Center for the first time. Some businesses have policies against tracking an employee's activities or movements during the work day. These policies can apply to both security cameras and card reader systems that record who enters or leaves an area and when. If your company has such restrictions, you might need to post warning signage (i.e., "This area under camera surveillance"), limit cameras to only a few key locations, or modify the system so that areas are viewed by a camera but no permanent record is kept.

Access Policies and Procedures

As important as a Data Center's physical controls are for protecting the room, they can be only as effective as whatever rules are put in place governing who may enter. The best lock in the world can't protect anything if everyone has keys for it.

Establish a Data Center access policy that defines who is allowed to enter the room and under what circumstances. This is usually done based on job classifications. For example, give all information technology (IT) system administrators Data Center access because they are responsible for supporting and maintaining the room's servers, while prohibiting all sales personnel because they have no compelling reason to enter. Or perhaps provide access to a limited group of network engineers and equipment vendors who are solely responsible for supporting Data Center equipment.

More sophisticated policies further distinguish between long-term and short-term access. For example, facilities personnel who maintain and repair the Data Center's major infrastructure might be permitted to enter the room any time of day or night, while an IT manager who leads client tours of the server environment might only have temporary access at the predetermined times of those visits.

Among the questions that should be addressed by your company's Data Center access policy are:

- What job functions qualify someone to enter a Data Center?

- How does an employee request Data Center access? Requests might be handled by a centralized security department or by the individual owners of secure rooms.

- Is badge access provided for vendors, contractors, or other non-employees? It is generally wise to require an escort into the Data Center for any non-employee. This restriction might be relaxed for contractors or vendors who work regularly at a company site and are badged.

- Is Data Center access all-or-nothing, or is it differentiated between short- and long-term? Where a distinction exists, short-term access is generally provided for the performance of specific tasks, such as maintenance on an air handler, while long-term access is granted to people whose jobs involve ongoing Data Center support, such as those who allocate row space, stock supplies, and inventory servers.

- How is access granted during an emergency? Any number of scenarios can occur that require someone who normally doesn't enter the Data Center to need immediate access—rescue personnel during a medical emergency or an on-call person arriving to fix a malfunctioning server or major piece of infrastructure in the middle of the night, for example. There must be an ability and process to provide immediate access in these instances, particularly at remote sites where someone might not be immediately available to provide an escort.

- How often are access privileges reviewed and by whom? Again, this is often done by corporate security or those who individually manage secure areas.

- What exceptions, if any, are permitted under the access policy? Perhaps a test server is housed in the Data Center while a lab is under construction, requiring temporary access for lab engineers. Maybe an employee doesn't have a job classification that normally qualifies for Data Center access, but he is assisting someone who does and needs to be able to enter the room.

- What are the penalties for access violations? Some companies consider tailgating or otherwise improperly entering a restricted area sufficient grounds for termination of employment.

The Sarbanes-Oxley Act of 2002

In July 2002, the U.S. Congress passed the Sarbanes-Oxley Act, establishing new standards for corporate accountability and disclosure. (The act is named after its authors, Sen. Paul Sarbanes and Rep. Michael Oxley.) The law requires chief executive officers and chief financial officers to certify that their companies' quarterly and annual financial statements are accurate and that any vulnerabilities to "internal controls" surrounding financial reporting are disclosed.

While the act doesn't spell out which company policies and procedures specifically make up internal controls, it is safe to assume that those pertaining to Data Center access are included, because a Data Center houses the servers that perform company business transactions and record its financial information. As if the safety of your company's most important servers and data wasn't enough reason to make these policies dependable, chief executive officers and chief financial officers can be held personally liable for any discrepancies.

For your access policies and procedures to be considered sound, they must truly protect the server environment. Be able to justify why each person with Data Center access absolutely must be allowed to enter. From the perspective of an external auditor, the more people who can enter a server environment the greater the likelihood of accidental downtime or intentional sabotage. If there's no compelling reason for a particular person to enter the Data Center, he or she shouldn't be allowed in.

Data Center access policies and procedures must be followed consistently. If company policy states that only IT system administrators are allowed in the Data Center, then a check of company access logs must confirm that in truth only those people have access. Any exceptions to your access rules—say, a vendor is provided badge access once a week to pick up backup tapes—shouldn't really be exceptions. Document special cases within the policy itself.

It is up to your legal department to determine the applicability of Sarbanes-Oxley to your particular business. Not all companies are subject to it because it is a U.S. law aimed at major public corporations (only those with a market capitalization of $75 million or more). Even if your company is exempt, however, it is still desirable for your Data Center access to be tightly controlled and its procedures consistently enforced.

"Do's"

Beyond standby infrastructure that keeps a Data Center running and access controls that bar unauthorized personnel, the greatest protection to a server environment can be a basic set of rules—standards of operation that guide Data Center users about how to work safely in the room and correctly use its infrastructure.

As you read the items that follow, be aware that the list is not all-encompassing. No list of Data Center rules is. First, some basic standards of behavior are left out. It is assumed that anyone visiting or working in the server environment is going to exhibit a minimum of common sense and be respectful of the infrastructure. Presumably anyone entering the room will watch where they step, treat equipment with care, and use tools for what they are intended and also resist the urge to run with scissors, start a fire, or do anything else destructive.

Second, no matter how many rules are listed, unusual circumstances are going to arise that aren't covered. Generally it is preferred that system administrators install servers within standard server cabinets, for example. However, if a vendor has a proprietary cabinet that is compatible with the Data Center and it is offering to pre-install hundreds of servers at the factory—saving an enormous amount of time for your company employees—it might be worth granting the exception.

The point is that, as valuable as the rules are, it is more important that anyone entering the Data Center simply understands the sensitivity of what is inside the room and treats those items accordingly.

NOTE   Consider establishing an orientation program to train employees and vendors on whatever standards of operations you adopt for your Data Center. Requiring people to have a certain minimum knowledge of the server environment and its rules can reduce downtime caused by user errors.

Implement Change Management

Above all else, a Data Center's job is to be reliable. Neither customers nor upper management like surprises, especially when it comes to a server environment. They want the room and equipment inside to function dependably and without incident.

While you can't eliminate surprises due to external events, say a major earthquake or commercial power grid failure, you can avoid them for planned, internal activities such as shutting down a Data Center power distribution unit for maintenance. Removing the surprise is done by implementing a change management process. Change management is a method of planning, coordinating, and communicating about activities in and around a company's vital facilities—the Data Center, Network Room, areas that house primary and standby electrical infrastructure—that are vital for the business to remain operational and serve its customers.

The idea is that, when your Data Center or other essential room is functioning normally, you want to limit anything that is potentially disruptive to it. Change management is intended to reduce unnecessary alterations to the server environment and control the necessary ones. Any actions that might change conditions within those essential rooms must be first communicated to the people who are potentially going to be influenced. This enables them to plan for what is to come and, where appropriate, ask for the activity to be rescheduled to a more advantageous time or even canceled.

Say that a power distribution unit in the Data Center needs to be taken offline for maintenance. The unit provides power to two server rows and has to be shut down for six hours for work to be completed. If those rows are powered only by that PDU, all servers and networking devices in those rows will go offline during the maintenance. If those rows are powered by multiple PDUs, any servers and networking devices with just one power supply will go offline while those systems with redundant power supplies merely have less protection—they'll go offline if the other PDU in the room that supports them happens to fail at the same time.

In either scenario, the system administrators, network engineers, and client groups who either support or do their work through the servers and network devices in those rows should be notified about the planned work. They can then plan ahead for not being able to use certain equipment during the designated maintenance period, and be aware of the additional exposure of other systems. If a server is supposed to be completing an extremely important task at the same time the maintenance is scheduled, the client group can ask to have the work delayed by a few days so as to avoid downtime or increased exposure to downtime.

Change Defined

Understanding the benefits of change management, what exactly is considered a change and to what degree should any activity in a Data Center be governed by change management? To put it another way, do you have to get permission to do *anything* in the Data Center?

Change is an alteration of any Data Center element—an infrastructure component, a server application, power availability, or connectivity status—that might affect a client or hamper the ability of a company to provide its regular services. From the Data Center infrastructure perspective, changes typically come in the form of maintenance on the room air handlers, power distribution units, uninterruptible power source, or generator. This can also include relatively minor work such as converting electrical receptacles. Some examples of non-infrastructure changes are: software upgrades, replacement of a faulty component on a server, or decommission of a networking device.

Some companies apply change management to any activity that occurs in a Data Center or could affect it. Under this strict application, a person must file a change request—the document used to provide notification of an activity—and receive approval from a governing change manager or board any time they want to enter the room. Other companies forego change requests for noninvasive activities.

What's noninvasive? The line between invasive and noninvasive is usually whether an action involves opening a server cabinet door or lifting a raised floor panel. Examples of noninvasive activities include inventorying servers, restocking supplies, updating external cabinet labeling, or giving a tour. Such activities involve no physical interaction with Data Center devices or infrastructure and are extremely unlikely to cause downtime. Ultimately, it is up to your company to decide what types of activity in the Data Center should be reviewed and approved by way of a change management process.

Typical Data Center-related activities that do require a change request include:

- Any event known to require downtime by servers or networking devices accessed by customers

- Work on major electrical infrastructure supporting the Data Center, be it a power distribution unit, uninterruptible power source, or standby generator
- Work on a Data Center air handler, chiller, or other cooling component
- Any activity involving Data Center emergency power off controls
- Work on infrastructure within the network room where Data Center connections terminate

Change Request Essentials

Under change management, plans for upcoming activity in a Data Center are spelled out in a document called a change request. Whoever wants to initiate the activity, called the requestor, must explain the work that is to be done, justify why it needs to occur, provide specific start and end times, define what systems are to be affected, state potential risk by doing the work (generally calling out whether or not there is a chance of downtime), and provide a plan to stop and return things to their prior condition in the event a problem occurs.

The requestor is typically a system administrator working on a server, a network engineer working on a network device, or a facilities engineer working on a piece of Data Center infrastructure. Even if the activity itself is done by an outside vendor or contractor, change management is an internal company process, and therefore change requests are generally made by whichever employee is responsible for the device or infrastructure that is to be worked upon.

Write change requests in plain language and include as much detail as possible. Those reading the request are not always experts in the same field as those performing the work. The system administrator whose server is expected to go offline for three hours needs a clear explanation about why electrical work absolutely has to be done on the power distribution unit, for example. A change request that merely says "maintenance is needed" isn't informative and will—or should be—rejected.

Indicate within the request all Data Center servers and networking devices that will be affected by the activity, down to the specific applications and any dependent devices. Specify both planned downtime and any potential downtime in the event that something goes wrong. Say, for instance, that structured cabling is being run to an existing network substation that has an online network device in it. If all goes correctly, there will be no downtime as a result of the work. However, list the networking device as well as all servers in the row within the change request, because they all have the potential to be affected if a cabling contractor mistakenly disconnects something.

This can seem like an excessive amount of detail, but it is better to be safe than sorry. In the event of the outage, a comprehensive change request reduces how long it takes to identify the source of a problem and understand its scope.

Following are a few sample change requests, depicting common Data Center-related activities.

Change Request for Standby Infrastructure Maintenance

The first request is to perform maintenance on a pair of standby generators. Although the work is not expected to involve any downtime, the request is sent to e-mail aliases for the company's system administrators, network engineers, IT managers, all client groups with equipment in the server environment, as well as the Data Center support staff.

CHANGE TITLE: Standby Generator Preventative Maintenance

CHANGE REQUESTOR: John Facilityguy

NOTIFICATIONS: systemadministrators@company.com, networkengineers@company.com, itmanagers@company.com, clientgroups@company.com, datacentersupportstaff@company.com.

CHANGE REQUEST ID#: 000001

START TIME: Monday, Aug-15-2005 02:00

STOP TIME: Monday, Aug-15-2005 06:00

HOSTS AFFECTED: None.

APPLICATIONS AFFECTED: None.

DESCRIPTION OF ACTIVITY: Service technicians will perform preventive maintenance on the two standby power generators that serve the Data Center in Building 1. There will be no transfer of electrical load to the generators or outage to the Data Center or building during this work. The two generators that support the Data Center will be isolated one at a time from the standby power system. While one generator is tested, the other will remain on line and support the Data Center electrical load in the event of a utility power failure.

RISK ASSESSMENT: No hosts in the Data Center will be affected by this activity. The Data Center has an N+1 standby electrical infrastructure, so it is not exposed to downtime during this maintenance procedure even if utility power fails. If a problem occurs during this procedure, the generator that is being worked upon can be brought back on line within ten minutes. The staff performing the maintenance is experienced, having completed such work more than fifty times.

BUSINESS BENEFIT: Performing this preventive maintenance work helps ensure that the standby power generators for the Data Center remain in reliable operating condition.

INSTALLATION IMPACT: Work will begin at approximately 2:00 A.M. Each generator will be completely isolated from the standby power system as it is tested. Work will be completed by 6:00 A.M. Building occupants might hear the generator start up and run during the course of the job. There will be no effect to the building. The uninterruptible power supply that supports the Data Center will continue to operate normally during the work.

BACKOUT PLAN: If bad weather or other circumstances arise that increase the likelihood of a utility outage, maintenance work will be rescheduled. If an incident occurs during the work, the offline generator will be immediately returned to normal condition.

NOTES: None.

Change Request for a Server Repair

The second change request is for work on a single server. Although the scope is more limited than the generator work, it does involve bringing the device off line. Notifications are sent to the specific clients whose work depends upon the server and to the system administrators who support it.

CHANGE TITLE: Replace faulty CPU on PRODSERV1

CHANGE REQUESTOR: Jane Systemadministrator

NOTIFICATIONS: systemadministrators@company.com, clientgroup1@company.com

CHANGE REQUEST ID#: 000002

START TIME: Tuesday, Aug-16-2005 14:00

STOP TIME: Tuesday, Aug-16-2005 16:00

HOSTS AFFECTED: PRODSERV1

APPLICATIONS AFFECTED: APP4, APP6, and APP8

DESCRIPTION OF ACTIVITY: PRODSERV1 has a faulty CPU that caused the machine to crash recently. We have arranged for the manufacturer to come out and replace the failed component. It will take about an hour to replace the CPU and boot the machine back up. Once this is done, we will confirm that the system is functioning normally.

RISK ASSESSMENT: This work requires bringing PRODSERV1 offline, but no other hosts in the Data Center will be affected.

BUSINESS BENEFIT: The new CPU will restore the server to its normal working condition and reliability.

INSTALLATION IMPACT: The server will be off line while the CPU is replaced. Downtime for this event has been scheduled with the client group, so they are prepared to not have access to this machine and its applications for two hours.

BACKOUT PLAN: If a replacement CPU is unavailable, this work will be postponed.

NOTES: None.

Change Request for Minor Electrical Infrastructure Changes

The third change request is for minor electrical work at two server cabinet locations within the Data Center. The work is to facilitate installation of incoming servers, so a notification is sent to the system administrators to provide them an expected time of completion.

CHANGE TITLE: Data Center power conversions

CHANGE REQUESTOR: John Facilityguy

NOTIFICATIONS: systemadministrators@company.com, datacentersupportstaff@company.com.

CHANGE REQUEST ID#: 000003

START TIME: Thursday, Aug-18-2005 13:00

STOP TIME: Thursday, Aug-18-2005 15:00

HOSTS AFFECTED: None.

APPLICATIONS AFFECTED: None.

DESCRIPTION OF ACTIVITY: Electrical receptacles at cabinet locations 5B and 5C in the Building 1 Data Center will be converted from a 120 volt NEMA 5-20 to a 208 volt NEMA L6-30. Sufficient internal wiring exists within the electrical conduit to support the new 30 amp configuration, so modifications will need to occur only at the cabinet locations and at the circuit panel at the end of Row 5.

RISK ASSESSMENT: Row 5 is empty of servers, so there is no risk of downtime.

BUSINESS BENEFIT: Outlets will be converted to permit the upcoming installation of DEVSERV8 and DEVSERV9.

INSTALLATION IMPACT: Work is isolated to Row 5, so there will be no effect on other equipment within the Data Center.

BACKOUT PLAN: None.

NOTES: Data Center badge access must be approved for electrician John Doe for the duration of the scheduled work. DEVSERV8 and DEVSERV9 do not need to come on line for another week, so this work can be postponed by a few days if it conflicts with other scheduled Data Center activities.

The requestor should also provide contact information, typically a phone number or e-mail address, so that the change manager or board can contact them with any questions about their request.

When to Make Changes

There are two theories regarding when significant work, that which is noteworthy enough to warrant a change request, should be performed in a Data Center, particularly in one containing servers that are accessed regularly by customers.

One approach is to conduct all work outside of traditional business hours, say after 6:00 P.M. and before 8:00 A.M. during weekdays and any time on weekends. This has the advantage of eliminating intentional downtime during peak usage hours for customers. The main drawback of this approach is that it can significantly increase the labor costs for a project. Contractors for certain trades need to be paid time-and-a-half or even double-time to work late or weekend hours. If all Data Center activities are restricted to after business hours, company employees might also face long workdays during times of great activity.

The second approach is performance of Data Center work during the regular business day. If a company has customers around the world, there aren't really any off hours during which downtime is more palatable. This approach has the benefit that, if something unexpected occurs during the work, the company's normal personnel are at the site and able to respond immediately. Employees might be harder to reach after business hours, potentially lengthening downtime that occurs.

NOTE   There's no wrong answer for when to enable changes in the Data Center. Adopt whatever approach is the most suitable for your business. Just be consistent with the policy and make sure that clients are given ample notice about upcoming work.

I prefer to schedule lesser activities, those which require downtime for only one or two devices and involve just a few employees, during the business day. Upgrading a server's memory or adding an electrical conduit to a server cabinet location fall under this category. In turn, I prefer to schedule major activities after hours and have plenty of additional personnel on site to respond immediately in the event a problem arises. These activities include replacing all of the batteries in an uninterruptible power source or relocating an entire server row of equipment.

Use Only Approved Materials

When faced with a choice between using supplies that are provided standard in a Data Center or other materials that perform the same function, system administrators and network engineers should use the provided items. Use of approved materials reinforces the standardization of the Data Center.

Items stocked in the server environment have presumably been reviewed and approved based on their suitability. For example, patch cords provided in the Data Center possess the same connectors and rating as the room's structured cabling, are color-coded by type and offered in multiple lengths, and are periodically tested to make sure they meet minimum performance standards. Patch cords provided by an outside source haven't undergone this same level of scrutiny and therefore aren't as trustworthy or compatible.

While there might be some instances in which it is acceptable to use nonstandard items, they should be the exception rather than the rule. A storage unit that is too large to fit in to a standard server cabinet must obviously be housed in another manner, for instance.

Follow Security Procedures

Your company undoubtedly has policies that address how high-security areas are to be maintained. These might include escorting visitors and making sure that all access-controlled doors remain shut at all times, that is, not propping them open and defeating the card reader system. There might also be specific asset management procedures governing the arrival or removal of company equipment to and from the site. Whatever policies your company has adopted, enforce them for the Data Center and any of its accompanying rooms where servers are kept.

"Don'ts"

As important as the rules are that Data Center users must follow are the things that they aren't supposed to do. These restrictions are intended to keep the server environment in good working condition, ensure that items are available for all system administrators and network engineers to have available when needed, and prevent the incorrect use of infrastructure.

Don't Leave Trash in the Data Center

Keeping trash out of the Data Center keeps the room looking professional, reduces contaminants, eliminates a potential fuel source in the event of a fire, and ensures that empty server cabinet locations remain ready for immediate use rather than buried under miscellaneous debris.

A clean Data Center can also reduce confusion and the loss of valuable items. Memory cards tucked in a small box are more likely to be recognized as valuable by the Data Center support staff if they are sitting on a server cabinet shelf in a trash-free server environment than if they are resting atop a pile of leftover boxes that have accumulated over several days.

Note that for the purpose of keeping a Data Center clean and organized trash is more than just empty boxes, discarded paperwork, and the drink cup that a Data Center user throws out as they enter the room. Patch cords that are functional but don't match the room's color-coding scheme, unneeded instruction manuals for servers, leftover materials from server installation kits, and any other materials that serve no purpose in the server environment are trash. Discard them accordingly.

NOTE   I see a lot of weird stuff accumulate in the server environments of different companies, especially if the spaces aren't actively managed. I have encountered coffee mugs, packing materials, ping pong paddles, sunglasses, discarded clothing, and even parts of a bicycle.

As part of keeping trash and other contaminants out of the Data Center, prohibit food and drink in the room. This policy can sometimes be unpopular, but it keeps an unnecessary source of liquid away from servers, keyboards, data ports, electrical receptacles, leak detection systems, and other vulnerable items. To put it another way, do you really want to have to explain to a company director how your fifty-cent soda damaged a $50,000 server?

More information about the importance of keeping a Data Center tidy is discussed in Chapter 15, "Maintaining a World-Class Environment."

Don't Steal Items or Infrastructure

A Data Center's infrastructure and tools are provided to make the room easier for employees to use. They therefore help accomplish the room's overall goal of increasing company productivity. To make sure that the room functions the way it was designed, Data Center users should not borrow or steal items that don't belong to them.

Using and promptly returning a tile puller or screwdriver that is stocked in the Data Center is one thing—that's what the item is provided for. Leaving the server environment with those tools still in hand, however, is something else. That deprives the next system administrator or network engineer who works in the Data Center of being able to use them.

Floor space, data ports, electrical receptacles, and tools that are provided in the room—not to mention servers and networking devices belonging to other business groups—are all in the server environment for a specific purpose. No one should take them without permission.

Don't String Cables Between Cabinets

It is generally unwise to route cabling—be it patch cords or power cables—between server cabinets. When a Data Center user does so, they circumvent the infrastructure that has been specifically installed at a given cabinet location. It can create a variety of problems.

First, stringing cables between cabinets unintentionally binds them together. If someone needs to relocate one cabinet, they are unlikely to know that devices from other cabinets are tethered to it. When they move the cabinet, they can easily yank the connecting lines free and cause unexpected downtime. If cables crisscross among multiple cabinets, this can affect dozens of servers in a row.

Second, if the cables that are strung to another cabinet are plugged in to the infrastructure at that second location, there is an additional danger of overloading the provided components. If the practice involves patch cords, the problem is simply one of occupying data ports that should be available. If power cables are involved, there is a threat of overloading either a cabinet power strip or the electrical receptacle that the strip is plugged in to. For instance, if a server in Cabinet 1B is plugged in to the power strip of adjacent Cabinet 1C, installing the normal contingent of equipment at 1C might exceed the strip's maximum electrical capacity and trip a circuit breaker.

Third, stringing cabling across cabinets leads to unanticipated vulnerabilities. In the previous example, say that Cabinet 1C is empty but its power strip has been plugged in to by a server in Cabinet 1B. Maintenance is being performed on one of the Data Center's power distribution units, and power needs to be shut down to certain electrical circuits. When the electrician checks the power schedules for the PDU and the labeling at the individual cabinets, they can't know that a device in Cabinet 1B is actually plugged in to 1C. If power is dropped to 1C, the server in 1B is either going to shut down unexpectedly or at least lose its redundant power source for the duration of the outage.

When a Data Center user does string cables between cabinets, they are usually trying to solve a problem. Maybe there are not enough data ports at the cabinet location where their server is installed. Perhaps the patch cords they have aren't long enough to reach the structured cabling under the raised floor or overhead, and it seems simpler (to them) to directly connect to an adjacent device. It might be that the person is trying to feed their servers from two different power sources, not realizing that redundant power is already provided to all cabinet locations and that plugging in to nearby power isn't necessary. Whatever the details, the causes essentially fall into two categories—either there is not enough infrastructure or the person doesn't understand the infrastructure that is there. The best way to prevent Data Center users from stringing cables between cabinets, therefore, is to make sure that an adequate amount of electrical receptacles and data ports are provided at each cabinet location and that anyone working in the room is thoroughly educated as to what is available.

Knowing all of the hazards that come with stringing cables between cabinets, is it acceptable in any circumstances? Yes, on rare occasions.

The most common exception comes when dealing with a cluster of equipment that, although occupying multiple cabinet locations, functions as one large device. Say, for example, you have a dozen servers that work in conjunction with one another to perform a function. The devices include different server models and fully occupy three consecutive cabinets in a Data Center. Some of the servers need more connectivity and some require less. As a result, the devices in two cabinet locations don't have enough data ports, but the third location has plenty to spare. The cluster acts as a single unit. If the equipment ever needs to be upgraded, decommissioned, or relocated, the entire cluster must undergo that change.

As long as the cabinets are adjacent to one another and there is no chance that a single server or cabinet might ever need to be removed from the unit as a whole, sharing data ports among the three cabinets makes perfect sense. Doing so makes full use of the structured cabling that is already provided and avoids the unnecessary cost and downtime risk of installing more. Even if the individual servers don't have a need to pool the provided infrastructure, it is okay to run patch cords between the cabinets of the cluster and make direct connections among devices. If there won't ever be a time for a cabinet to be removed from the cluster and electrical downtime to one of the server cabinet locations would halt the ability of the entire cluster anyway, there is no particular drawback to intermingling. Just make sure that the occasional installation that is connected this way is cabled neatly to avoid dangling patch cords or power cables that could pose a snagging hazard.

A similar exception might be acceptable when a Data Center must host extremely heavy equipment. If a device is small enough to fit within one cabinet location but is so heavy that the location adjacent to it must remain empty, the infrastructure for the empty location won't be used. If that device needs additional electrical conduits or connectivity, consider using what is provided in the adjacent space. In this case, it is best to physically relocate the electrical conduits and structured cabling to the occupied cabinet location and relabel the infrastructure—PDU schedules as well as electrical labeling posted on the cabinet and floor tile—to reflect the change.

Good Installation Practices

A fundamental way to protect both the Data Center itself and the servers and networking devices it hosts is equipment installed deliberately and strategically. That is, reduce exposure to accidental downtime by following good installation practices. The sections that follow describe several proven strategies.

Manage Cabinet Space

How someone arranges servers within a Data Center cabinet influences the room's capacity to house equipment, influences cabling density at certain cabinets, and might even affect user safety. If a server environment has limited floor space but ample cooling and weight-bearing ability available, servers should be installed as tightly as possible to maximize how many can fit in to cabinets. Conserving even a small amount of space between servers can accumulate and enable additional equipment to be installed. Alternately, if a server environment has difficulty with hot spots or supporting heavy weight loads, it might be best to leave server cabinets partially unoccupied. Finally, reserve space at the bottom of server cabinets for the largest devices. Putting the most weight at the bottom of a cabinet makes it more stable and less prone to tipping. This practice can also save a Data Center user's back, because it is easier to install or remove a bulky item that is closer to the ground than one that is at eye level or above.

Properly Use Rack Units

No matter how you want to install equipment into server cabinets—tightly packed or spread out, on a shelf or rack-mounted, up at the top of the cabinet or down at the bottom—you need to understand how the screw holes on a cabinet's vertical rails are configured. At first glance, these mounting holes appear to be evenly spaced. As anyone who has ever attempted to rack-mount a server can testify, however, some positions on a cabinet's mounting rails align better with a server's mounting brackets than others.

This is no accident. The screw holes on most server cabinets and Data Center devices follow a deliberate pattern, an Electronic Industries Alliance (EIA) standard that delineates rack units. A rack unit, you remember, is the measurement of installable space within a server cabinet. One rack unit equals 1.75 inches (4.45 centimeters). Screw holes on a mounting rail are spaced 1/2 (.5) and 5/8th (.625) of an inch apart—1.27 and 1.59 centimeters apart—within that rack unit span. The pattern is present on both generic and proprietary cabinets.

Figure 13-1 illustrates how screws holes are spaced on the mounting rails of a server cabinet. Screw holes are spaced in 1/2- and 5/8-inch increments. The tab of a cabinet shelf is shown below the highlighted rack unit. The rack unit is centered on the hole labeled B.

Figure 13-1 *Screw Hole Pattern on a Cabinet Mounting Rail*

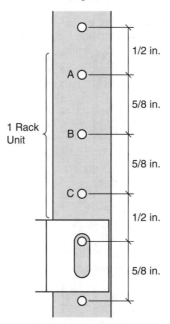

Recognizing the screw hole spacing on a cabinet's mounting rails enables you to align an incoming server correctly. Match the pattern and a device can be secured firmly and easily to a cabinet. Fail to do so and that same piece of equipment becomes harder to install.

Figure 13-2 shows two installations of the same rack-mountable server. The incorrect placement, at top, causes the screw holes to misalign and allows screws at only three of the server's nine anchor points. The correct placement, at bottom, aligns the server with the cabinet's mounting rails and permits the use of all nine anchor points. Correctly aligning a device along a server cabinet's mounting rails enables an easier and more secure installation.

NOTE	To make it easier for system administrators and network engineers to identify the rack unit pattern, horizontal lines are etched in the mounting rails of the standard Data Center server cabinets I use. The lines demarcate each rack unit, similar to the guide lines shown in Figure 13-2 but directly on the rails among the screw holes.

Although server cabinet shelves can be mounted anywhere along a mounting rail, because they need to align with only one screw hole, install them strategically as well. Whatever rests on the shelf occupies a certain amount of cabinet space. Placing the shelf slightly higher or lower can free up an entire rack unit along the mounting rail and enable an additional item to be housed in the cabinet.

Figure 13-2 *Server Alignments*

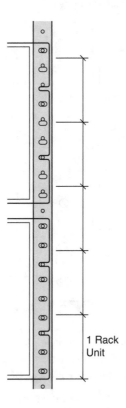

1 Rack
Unit

NOTE   Some server cabinet mounting rails employ cage nuts instead of screw holes and their
accompanying EIA rack unit pattern. A cage nut has a floating nut within a square bracket,
and can offset minor misalignments of server mounting brackets. Despite this benefit, I
dislike server cabinets that use cage nuts.

A cage nut must be clipped into a cabinet mounting rail before a server or cabinet shelf can
be attached with screws. The cage nut therefore becomes an extra consumable item to stock
in each Data Center I manage and adds a step for installing of servers and cabinet shelves—
neither of which I want.

The Balance of Power

Reduce the chances of overloading a server cabinet's two power strips by dividing the
electrical load that is placed upon them. Simply put, when you install multiple servers into
a cabinet, don't plug all of their power cables into one power strip. Alternate between the
two strips. Most Data Center users do this automatically for servers that have dual power
supplies, because they need two power sources for redundancy, but they might not be as

diligent when dealing with devices that have only one power source. Even when a server cabinet contains only servers with single power supplies, balancing power between its power strips reduces the number of devices that go off line in the event that a power strip, electrical receptacle, or power distribution unit fails. Only half of the servers can be affected when power cables alternate between power strips.

Route Cabling Neatly

Threading cables—both patch cords and power cables—so that they are well organized and carefully arranged eases troubleshooting. It also reduces the risk of someone unplugging a device by snagging a hanging cable or unplugging the wrong cable by mistake. When plugging a server in to cabinet power strips, connect them to the power strip outlets that are at the same height as the device. Plugging cords in to outlets that are significantly higher or lower leads to tangled cables.

Label Thoroughly

The importance of labeling has been stressed in several chapters of this book—for electrical infrastructure, for cabling infrastructure, and for server cabinets. Clearly label incoming servers and networking devices, too. This identification is essential when equipment is inventoried and can greatly reduce the time it takes to find a machine's owner in the event of a problem.

Data Center Tours

Depending upon the nature of your business, customers or employees might be interested in touring your server environments. Customers might want to see how data is protected or what sort of processing capability your company has at hand, while employees might want to learn more about the room for any number of reasons. Executives might want to know about the room's physical security for Sarbanes-Oxley, sales executives might want to know about the room's qualities for marketing potential, and lab managers might want to see if there are any best practices that they can learn.

Whatever the reason and whoever the guests, follow a handful of guidelines when conducting Data Center tours:

- **Keep visitors together, preferably in main aisles**—Don't allow people to wander throughout the room without supervision. A Data Center can be overwhelming to first-time visitors, and one misstep while within a server row can snag a patch cord or power cable.

- **Don't touch**—There's a reason that amusement parks tell visitors to keep their hands and feet inside the car at all times. Make sure that visitors understand they are not to touch anything no matter how innocuous an item appears. Regardless of how many warning signs are posted, emergency power off buttons and fire suppression controls are unfamiliar to the untrained eye and seem to attract curious hands.

- **Designate a demonstration area**—If you consistently highlight certain Data Center features during a tour, consider creating a dedicated area to showcase these details. For example, if you want to illustrate the redundant power provided at each cabinet location by showing the electrical receptacles under the raised floor, choose a cabinet location that is accessible from the room's main aisle and therefore easy for a large group of visitors to see. While it is fine for the cabinet in that location to contain servers, be sure that all cabling is neatly routed and not susceptible to snagging. You might want to have a tile lifter, flashlight, and warning pylons in the immediate vicinity to facilitate opening up the floor during tours.

- **Use tacky mats**—For some reason, visitors to a Data Center often treat tacky mats like a blanket of new snow—they are hesitant to walk on them and mess up the pristine surface. The mats are meant to stop dirt from being tracked in. Make sure that visitors step on rather than over them.

NOTE   With this chapter's focus on protecting Data Center items and keeping unauthorized personnel out of the room, you might assume that I'm opposed to Data Center tours. I'm not. As long as you are confident that the people who are brought in to the server environment will be respectful and not touch anything they shouldn't, bring them in.

Data Center tours are excellent for showcasing a company's best practices, particularly the reliability, flexibility, and consistency incorporated in to the room. Those are great qualities to present to customers, fellow employees, or shareholders. A Data Center highlights company values. When I tour a server environment that is carefully thought out, effective at protecting its equipment, and well maintained, I come away believing that that business will exhibit similar reliability and attention to detail in the goods and services it provides.

Whenever possible, I try to arrange for reciprocal tours. You are welcome to see my Data Center. May I see yours, too?

Summary

Protect Data Center servers and equipment from theft, vandalism, accidental damage, or sabotage by installing a card reader system. For additional security, consider features that require combination codes and prevent tailgating.

Cages are sometimes used within a Data Center to provide more physical security or subdivide the room into smaller server areas. If you install a cage, extend the fencing below the raised floor and above the false ceiling, cover the walls to obscure visibility, and contain as much supporting infrastructure within the cage as possible. Avoid keeping Data Center items in a caged storage area except as a last resort.

Locking server cabinets can also prevent someone from accessing individual devices but do not protect the electrical conduits or structured cabling that feed them.

Closed-circuit video cameras can be installed to monitor and record who enters and leaves the Data Center, providing greater information than a card reader system's logs.

Create an access policy that defines who may enter the Data Center and under what conditions. Spell out how an employee can request access, whether nonemployees must be escorted or can be badged like regular employees, and whether there are different types of access such as short- and long-term. Also explain how to gain access during an emergency, how frequently access privileges are reviewed, what access-related exceptions are permitted, and what the penalties are for violating the access policy. For public companies in the United States, pay special attention to access policies and procedures in light of the Sarbanes-Oxley Act of 2002.

Establish standards of operation so that Data Center users know how to work safely in the room and take best advantage of its infrastructure. Most important, make sure that anyone entering the room understands the critical nature of the equipment inside and treats the environment as the critical facility that it is.

Adopt a change management process to improve the planning, coordination, and communication of Data Center-related activities. Any planned actions that can affect a Data Center client or prevent the company from performing its regular functions should be controlled by way of change management. This process can be applied to any activities that touch a server environment—requiring a change request to even enter the room—or be limited to more major events such as those precipitating servers going off line.

When writing a change request, include the scope of work, a business justification, start and end times, what systems will or might be affected, and a back-out plan in the event that a problem arises. Be straightforward and provide detailed information.

Some companies restrict Data Center work to after normal business hours, hoping to reduce the impact upon clients. Others prefer to have such activities occur during the standard workday so that personnel are already on hand in the event that a problem arises.

Require system administrators and network engineers to use the standard supplies provided in the Data Center over outside materials and obey company security procedures such as not propping Data Center doors open. Prohibit them from leaving trash in the server environment or taking tools or infrastructure.

Also forbid stringing patch cords or power cables between server cabinets, because this practice ties cabinets together and makes them more susceptible to accidental downtime. Exceptions to this rule should be permitted only for devices that can be treated like one large piece of equipment, occupying multiple server cabinet locations and sharing infrastructure.

Protect servers by following good installation procedures—manage cabinet space, balance power to avoid overloading electrical infrastructure, and route cabling neatly to reduce snagging.

When providing tours of the Data Center, keep visitors together and within main aisles, prohibit touching anything in the room, establish a regular demonstration area, and promote the use of the tacky mats as people enter.

CHAPTER 14

Mapping, Monitoring, and Metrics

The chapter specifies what Data Center-related information should be documented and maintained and how such data is helpful for managing rooms, troubleshooting during emergencies, and planning future Data Center expansions. The chapter also suggests inexpensive tools that can be used to monitor a server environment and recognize problems before they affect the systems contained within.

Documenting the Data Center

Data Centers are complex environments. They are also dynamic, continually evolving as new servers arrive and older equipment is phased out. To help simplify your management of these rooms, document as much information about them as possible. The more details you collect and maintain about a Data Center, the fewer mysteries that can arise and trigger unanticipated problems or delays.

Cabinet locations, electrical and data infrastructure, server names, and installed applications are all key details worthy of keeping track of. A system administrator planning to install a server might want to know how much connectivity and what type of power is provided at specific server locations. Also important are significant Data Center-related events. Upper management might want to know about whatever incidents caused a server environment to have less than 100 percent availability. When did the Data Center go off line and for how long? What was the cause and what steps were taken so that it doesn't happen again? This information, and more, is invaluable to address Data Center-related questions.

You have several choices for how to archive this data. One option is a maintained Data Center handbook, filled with reference materials pertaining to the room. Even more effective is the information posted on a company intranet site. This makes the information accessible to all employees, no matter the time or their location. It also enables data to be updated immediately for everyone, without having to manually revise multiple handbooks.

NOTE   I joke that I write everything down about the Data Centers I manage because I'm too lazy to remember the details. In truth, I support too many rooms—from forty-five to fifty—with too many unique details to keep track of everything. Each room has its idiosyncrasies, even though they are designed to the same standard.

Some of the Data Centers came by way of acquired companies and so weren't designed with the same type or level of infrastructure as others. Some were built years apart from one another, either before or after the advent of smaller servers requiring greater server densities. Still more were designed the same, but were influenced by regional building codes and therefore have different details.

Whatever the reason, it is more reliable for me to document each Data Center's characteristics than to rely on memory. This approach also scales better, making the data available to more people.

Obviously, Data Center information is only helpful when it is accurate. Whenever alterations are made to your server environment, have those changes reflected in the documentation for the room. This is potentially a never-ending task, so choose your battles. It is reasonable to expect a Data Center map to be kept current at all times, for example, because any changes to the room's physical features require a major construction project. Staying current regarding every new server, networking device, or peripheral that is installed may be unrealistic, though. For Data Center details that change frequently, update information on a regular basis, such as monthly or quarterly. This at least provides a snapshot of the room's condition.

Floor Plan

One of the more powerful documents to have for a Data Center is a map of the room. At a minimum, an accurate map shows physical clearances, cabinet locations, the placement of major infrastructure, and the Data Center's numbering scheme. This information is helpful when allocating space for incoming servers and crucial when the time comes to expand the server environment.

More detailed floor plans can illustrate the actual paths that structured cabling and electrical conduits follow within the plenum space as well as the specific type and numbers of data ports and electrical receptacles that terminate at each cabinet location. These details are helpful in preparation for installing equipment. Having a server environment floor plan with this information enables a Data Center manager to allocate row and cabinet space in a server environment located elsewhere, because the information is available without anyone having to physically enter the room. Maps can additionally highlight weight restrictions in the Data Center, where infrastructure controls are installed, and where floor tiles are allocated.

Figure 14-1 shows a useful Data Center floor plan. The map conveys the Data Center's cabinet locations, numbering scheme, placement of major infrastructure, and the incline of its entrance ramp. Symbols mark the true locations of the room's card reader (CR), telephones (triangle), fire suppression controls (F), emergency power off controls (P), and red and blue monitoring lights (R and B) for the room's standby electrical infrastructure. Even two storage racks, where patch cords and other consumable items are kept, are represented along the south wall.

Infrastructure components and controls are represented in their actual location within the server environment. Note that identification numbers are assigned to the Data Center's power distribution units and air handlers, making it easier to distinguish among each infrastructure component during an emergency. This is particularly helpful in large Data Centers. The person who discovers a cooling problem, for example, can report a malfunction with air handler number four rather than "one of the cooling units."

Figure 14-1 *Data Center Floor Plan*

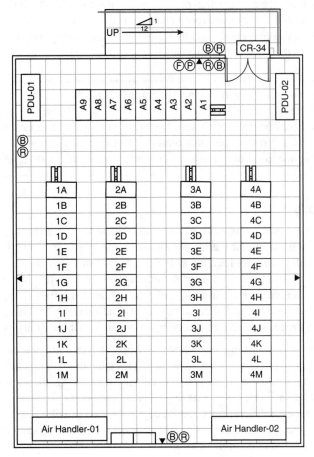

As-Builts

As part of the design package issued for the construction of your Data Center, require the respective cabling and electrical contractors to provide as-built blueprints of the room. An as-built is just what it sounds like—a document showing specific Data Center infrastructure *as it was built*. A cabling as-built shows the physical paths of all structured cabling and provides termination details: how many and what type of connectors terminate where. An electrical as-built shows the equivalent information for electrical infrastructure—conduit paths, how many and what types of receptacles, and which circuits specifically terminate where. Electrical as-builts should also include comprehensive power schedules—copies of the circuit and location information posted in each Data Center circuit breaker panel.

Even if your original design documents for a Data Center project specify what data ports and electrical circuits are to go where, obtain as-builts. Many changes, big and small, often happen during the construction of a server environment. As-built documents incorporate all of these and show how a room truly is. Ask for the information in both hardcopy and softcopy. If you possess the electronic file, you have the option of updating it as changes are made to the Data Center infrastructure.

NOTE   When you obtain as-builts, check them for accuracy by touring the Data Center and confirming that their information is correct. While as-builts are *supposed* to reflect all changes, occasionally a contractor might provide files that aren't entirely up-to-date. It is better to catch oversights immediately than to store the documents for years and then, when it is time to retrofit or expand the server environment, discover inaccuracies.

Server Inventory

Once a Data Center is operational, inventory its servers, networking devices, and other equipment on a regular basis. Include the name, make and model of machine, and corresponding cabinet location in the room. Follow the same Data Center numbering scheme that you use for cable runs and electrical schedules. Details about peripheral devices—storage devices, disk trays, monitors—are also helpful. Asset tagging technologies such as bar codes or radio frequency identification (RFID) may help automate your inventory procedures, thereby reducing how much staff time must be spent.

Periodically inventorying Data Center equipment keeps you in touch with what items are flowing in and out of the room over time. This can help you identify equipment trends, alerting you to changes that need to occur to your existing infrastructure. You might see a shift toward smaller devices that require more data ports, for example, or a new server model that needs different electrical receptacles. Recognizing these changing requirements gives you the option of retrofitting a few server rows at once rather than having to manage each installation of equipment as they arrive.

Consider recording additional physical details about your Data Center equipment as well. Knowing the height, weight, typical heat output, and electrical requirements of the servers and networking devices in your server environment makes it easier to manage the room as well as accommodate machines of the same type that arrive in the future.

Inventorying servers might even save your company money. Many businesses pay service contracts for the support and maintenance of their servers. The fees for this are typically based upon the number of machines involved. An up-to-date inventory can provide an accurate count of how many of a given server are on line and need support. This prevents you from paying for service on machines that have been decommissioned and removed from the Data Center.

NOTE   Some companies adopt rigorous asset management procedures, placing identification numbers on every piece of hardware and tracking their whereabouts, be they in a Data Center or lab space, on someone's desktop, in storage, or anywhere else. Whatever asset management policies exist at your company, make your inventory process compatible with it. It is more efficient to catalog equipment once, for both purposes, than for the task to be performed twice.

Store inventory information in an online database. Also post printed copies of the machine inventory within the server environment. Near the room's entrance, along with Data Center tools and infrastructure controls, is convenient. When the inventory data is sorted and displayed alphabetically and includes cabinet location information, it can assist room users in finding equipment. This can be particularly helpful in an emergency when connectivity—and therefore the online database—is unavailable.

After collecting location information and other server details, you might think about including that data on your Data Center floor plan. You already have both the information and a room map, so why not combine the two? In theory, it is a brilliant idea. Having a graphic representation of specific Data Center equipment, showing its footprint on the floor and perhaps even its relative location within the server cabinet that houses it is extremely helpful for planning future installations. Unfortunately, most server environments are very dynamic. The more server-specific information that is recorded on a map, the faster the document is likely to become out of date. Unless you want to devote a substantial amount of time to updating the floor plan, it is best to limit what is included on the map to those details that rarely change.

NOTE   In Data Centers that experience a lot of turnover of equipment, I prefer to inventory equipment monthly so that information remains relatively current. In server environments that experience less change, I inventory equipment quarterly.

Applications

Other valuable data to inventory are the applications running on each server within the Data Center. This information is useful for two reasons. First, if you are going to perform work on a machine that hosts a particular application, in your change request you can accurately define all servers that are going to be affected by the scheduled downtime. Second, if an application fails unexpectedly you can quickly determine the scope of the problem and what specific servers are affected.

Software applications are a unique element of Data Center servers. They typically span multiple machines, and no matter how a server environment is organized, whether by form or function, it is frequently impossible to isolate applications to a particular section of the room. Structured cabling, electrical conduits, and even networking devices can be distributed throughout a Data Center to limit the effect of a single catastrophic event, but machines might still be linked together by applications.

Be aware that application information can be more difficult to obtain and keep current than a physical inventory of servers. That's because applications are added to, upgraded on, or removed from machines more frequently than devices are physically relocated. Additionally, most of these changes take place behind the scenes. They are often performed by the system administrators or network engineers who support those particular devices and, unlike when a server is installed or removed from a Data Center, the change isn't immediately obvious.

If you do track application information, maintain it in a database that can be easily accessed in an emergency.

Processes

It is also useful to document as many Data Center-related processes as possible. Having employees follow the same procedures regardless of location ensures consistency. Thorough documentation also makes it easier to educate new Data Center users. Simply show them the written materials.

Useful processes to document include:

- **Access and change management policies**—Instructions for how to gain access to the Data Center and appropriately notify company personnel and clients about planned activities in the room.

- **Service level agreements (SLAs)**—Involving Data Center-related clients, support organizations, and vendors. An SLA is a contract between someone who is hired to perform a task or service and a customer, specifying the measurable functions and services they are to provide. Your company probably has an SLA with a regional Internet service provider, for instance, specifying expected reliability and acceptable response times for any repair work that is necessary. There might also be internal SLAs, such as a commitment from the facilities department to perform maintenance on Data Center mechanical infrastructure according to a defined schedule and to respond to outages within a certain amount of time.

- **Server installation guidelines**—Spell out for Data Center users how they can most effectively install their incoming equipment. (See Chapter 13, "Safeguarding the Servers," for several recommended practices.)

- **Equipment move procedures**—If your business is prone to relocating servers from one Data Center to another, perhaps due to acquiring another company, it is helpful to have some basic instructions on hand. Strategies for how to insulate servers during the move, when it is appropriate to rerack and consolidate equipment to save floor space, and priority lists for what types of devices need to be brought back on line first. Perhaps lists of area moving companies qualified to relocate sensitive electronic equipment.

Features and Philosophies

Last, consider documenting and publishing details about your Data Center's infrastructure as well as the design philosophies behind it. Which infrastructure systems are redundant and why? Are power and data prewired to each location or are they added when servers arrive for installation? If they're installed in advance, what's the typical amount and configuration of each? What's the maximum weight that a cabinet location can support, and how does this limit incoming servers?

Create orientation materials for employees, contractors, and visitors. The more you educate Data Center users about what the room has to offer, the less likely it is for someone to misuse the infrastructure. For example, a system administrator who understands that the Data Center is designed for redundancy and each cabinet location is equipped with electrical receptacles from two different power sources has no reason to borrow power from an adjacent cabinet. Understanding how the room is designed encourages people to use its infrastructure correctly.

Monitoring from Afar

As much as floor plans, as-builts, and equipment inventories can tell you about the condition of your server environment, they are all snapshots in time. They can't tell what's happening in the Data Center up to the moment. For that real-time information, you need tools that actively monitor the room. The greater the ability you have to "see" in to your Data Center without having to physically be there, the easier it is to manage. It is like a parent using a baby monitor, which enables them to hear or see that their child is safe while they are in another room of the house.

Data Center monitoring devices are often referred to as remote monitoring tools. Don't be fooled by the description. Even if your company has only one server environment and it is located at your site and staffed around the clock, monitoring tools can still provide valuable information and are useful to install. Even the most well-trained employee can't perceive that a server cabinet power strip is close to overloading its circuit breaker the way an amperage meter can, for example.

NOTE   I support six Data Centers in San Jose, California, on a campus that spans about 2 miles (3.2 kilometers). The site has a relatively busy city road running through it that contains half a dozen traffic signal lights. During morning or evening rush hour, it can take more than fifteen minutes to drive from one end of campus to the other. If a problem occurs in a Data Center across campus from me, it is almost always faster to log on to our internal web site from a personal computer and check the monitoring tools that are in that server environment than for me to drive. What I learn from those tools determines if I ultimately need to go to the room at all.

Web Cameras

A great way to tell what's happening in your Data Center is to deploy web cameras that leverage the room's network. Connect them to a port on your Data Center's existing networking equipment and transmit the live images across your internal network. Some cameras don't even need to be plugged in to an electrical outlet—they receive their power from the same data connection.

Install a camera so it has a clear view of the lights that monitor the Data Center's standby electrical infrastructure. (The lights and their function are outlined in Chapter 6, "Creating a Robust Electrical System.") Utility power outages are among the most common Data Center-related incidents. A quick look at the room's monitoring lights through a web camera immediately reveals whether the room is off line or running on commercial power, uninterruptible power source batteries, or generator. If the Data Center's fire alarm lights are near the monitoring lights, cover them with the camera as well. If they aren't in close proximity, install a second camera to see them.

For the small expense of one or two web cameras per Data Center, you can instantly see the condition of the room and know the status of two of its most vital infrastructure systems, all from any computer connected to your company's internal network.

Figure 14-2 is a screen capture from a web camera mounted atop a networking cabinet in a Data Center.

Figure 14-2 *A Web Camera Views Monitoring Lights Within the Data Center and One of Its Main Corridors*

Sat Oct 16 11:10:51 AM 2004

Note that these cameras are to help you keep an eye on major infrastructure. They are not security cameras. They don't record what is happening in the Data Center and aren't monitored by security personnel. For that function, use closed-circuit video cameras as outlined in Chapter 13.

Amperage Meters

An additional method of keeping an eye on your Data Center is having your server cabinet power strips equipped with amperage meters. These devices display the amount of electrical load that is put upon them. This tells a Data Center user how close they are to reaching the maximum electrical capacity of a power strip. It also helps with efforts to balance power within a server cabinet. If someone is installing a server with a single power feed, they can check which of a server cabinet's two power strips is carrying the lesser electrical load and plug in to that one.

More advanced power strips display not only this information on their faceplates but also transmit it across a network connection. The appropriate online interface can enable someone to remotely view the draw on all power strips across the Data Center, providing a detailed picture of the room's entire electrical load. Some strips additionally enable power-cycling, that is, remotely turning off and on individual sockets, which can be useful for rebooting a server without actually being at the Data Center site.

NOTE   If you opt to use power strips that can be remotely controlled, make sure that your network is very well protected. Were someone to hack in to it they could conceivably command the power strips to turn off, thereby shutting down any Data Center devices plugged in to them.

Temperature Sensors

Yet another useful thing to know about your Data Center is how hot or cold it is. Monitoring the temperature of the room can alert you to a malfunctioning air handler, air flow problems, or hot spots that are forming due to increased server density at a particular cabinet location.

You can obtain this information to some extent from the temperature sensors that are built in to your Data Center air handlers. Many servers and networking devices also enable you to check their internal temperature by entering a certain command. Both of these readings offer only a glimpse of the Data Center's true condition, however. Sensors that are part of an air handler are in the coolest parts of the Data Center—close to a source of cold air rather than near the servers that you are most concerned about. Temperature information from individual servers can also be incomplete.

To get a more comprehensive picture of your Data Center's temperature conditions, install ambient temperature sensors. These can be free-standing sensors or built in to some models of cabinet power strip. As with the amp meters, temperature sensors can plug in to your Data Center networking devices, which enables them to transmit information and be monitored through the web. Applications associated with these sensors enable you to take sensor readings in all of your Data Centers at once, archive temperature data, and send alerts by e-mail. By adjusting the alert conditions, you can be informed when room conditions are above or below certain temperatures or if a reading changes by a significant amount in a short period of time.

NOTE   Free-standing temperature sensors are installed in all of the Data Centers that I manage. They are typically mounted at the top of a server cabinet. Because these rooms predominantly use four-post, open cabinets, the sensors read the heat that rises from the server exhaust. (An alternate approach, particularly in a Data Center with enclosed cabinets, is the sensors placed on a shelf in front of a server to measure the incoming air.)

I use one sensor every other server row, unless a Data Center has hot spots that I want to monitor more closely. In that case, I can have several installed in a single server cabinet, providing an almost three-dimensional view of the heat conditions there. The online tool that controls the sensors makes an hourly sweep, sending me the data in a single e-mail. An additional alert message is sent to an on-call pager if any sensors register temperatures above 90° Fahrenheit (32.2° Celsius) or below 55° Fahrenheit (12.8° Celsius), or if conditions change by at least 10° Fahrenheit (5.6° Celsius) in an hour.

This network of sensors has proven to be an invaluable warning system, facilitating quick responses to air handler or chiller problems and preventing the overheating of small server environments on several occasions over the years.

Because the temperature sensors transmit their information over your network, you can also use them as a quick way to determine whether or not a Data Center has lost connectivity. If you trigger a sweep of the sensors in a particular server environment and they all come back with no data, likely the network is down.

Humidity Sensors

The same devices that take ambient temperature readings in a Data Center—free-standing sensors and those within server cabinet power strips—can be equipped to measure humidity as well. Humidity is generally monitored and controlled by Data Center air handlers. If a server environment is having problems with humidity—condensation or corrosion from too much moisture in the air or static from not enough—humidity sensors can help diagnose the problem.

The geographic location of your company site, including local weather conditions, has the largest influence on whether humidity is a problem in your Data Center. A server environment located in a region with generally moderate humidity conditions probably has little need for this type of monitoring equipment, while one in more extreme conditions might benefit.

NOTE   As you've read, server cabinet power strips are capable of being equipped with amperage meters, temperature sensors, and humidity sensors. Because two power strips are generally installed per cabinet location, strips can therefore provide dozens or even hundreds of points of data across a Data Center. The only drawback to these monitoring capabilities is that they are expensive. A power strip equipped with these features costs several times that of one that merely provides power.

I recommend deploying these features only where you need them. Provide amperage meters within server cabinets that are going to house a high number of servers or devices known to draw excessive amounts of power. Install a handful of free-standing temperature sensors throughout the Data Center, say one or two per server row, unless the room has hot spots or other temperature problems. Likewise, deploy humidity sensors sparingly unless moisture levels appear to be a problem in a particular server environment.

Gathering Metrics

Other information useful to have about a Data Center is metrics—measurements taken regularly to determine how the room functions over time. There are a lot of data points that can conceivably be collected about a server environment. Some are crucial, while others are simply items of trivia.

Maintaining an Incident Log

To get some perspective on the performance of your server environment and the incidents that happen in and around it, keep a log of Data Center-related events. Record the time, date, and major details of notable occurrences. Utility power failures, infrastructure malfunctions, and occasions when servers go off line are all worthy of mention. Over time, a well-maintained incident log can reveal trends that might otherwise go unnoticed: perhaps an air handler whose belts are wearing out faster than in other devices or the fact that commercial brownouts are occurring in certain parts of the world during extended periods of hot weather, because residential customers are drawing more power to cool their homes.

Also note incidents in which things go right and downtime or a catastrophic event is avoided: when utility power fails but the Data Center runs interrupted thanks to its standby generator, for example, or when a server environment's temperature sensors detect a hot spot and members of the room's support staff reposition floor tiles to correct the problem before servers are affected.

It is easy to fall in to the trap of thinking about a server environment only when something goes wrong. It is just as important to know when a Data Center is successfully protected because of its good design, the proper functioning of its standby infrastructure, or the quick actions taken by its support staff, or all three. These successes carry their own lessons, demonstrating what works and should be repeated.

An incident log that thoroughly tracks Data Center events can be extremely valuable for upper management. Such a log provides them with real-world information about the threats posed to company servers and what infrastructure and processes are (or aren't) in place to protect that equipment. Without such information, managers may assume that a company Data Center should have 100 percent availability, even if the room was never designed with the necessary depth of infrastructure to achieve it. Table 14-1 shows a sample format for tracking Data Center incidents, including some suitably noteworthy events.

Table 14-1 *Data Center Incident Log*

Date	Event	Cause	Type
Jan 14	Utility power failed to the Austin, TX, site at 10:15 P.M. local time. The Austin Data Center was supported by its standby UPS and generator for 2.5 hours. Utility power was restored around 12:45 A.M., at which time the Data Center's electrical load transferred back automatically. No servers were affected by this incident.	CP	EX
Feb 03	While testing new fiber connections in the Chicago, IL, Data Center, the cabling contractor accidentally unplugged two live patch cords plugged into PRODSERV4. The disconnects occurred around 4:40 P.M. local time. The cords were plugged back in immediately and the on-call system administrator was contacted. He pinged the server and found no apparent disruption as a result of this incident. Note: Clients were notified beforehand of the structured cabling installation through Change Request 056321.	CO	HU
Jun 05	A motor in air handler #3 in the Bangalore, India, Data Center burned out, causing room temperatures to rise. Ambient temperature sensors alarmed at 6:25 P.M. local time, alerting the on-call facilities staff. The Data Center temperature was recorded at 90.5° Fahrenheit (32.5° Celsius). Technicians arrived on site at 6:45 P.M. The air handler was on line by 9:20 P.M., and room temperatures returned to normal by 10:10 P.M. The Data Center remained operational throughout the event—no servers went off line.	AC	ME
Aug 23	Utility power failed to the Denver, CO, Server Room around 3:10 P.M. local time. The room was supported by UPS, but servers shut down around 5:10 P.M., when the outage lasted longer than the two-hour runtime of the UPS. *Multiple servers shut down from this incident.* Utility power was restored around 6:40 P.M. All Data Center servers and networking devices were back on line by 9:00 P.M.	CP	EX
Sep 14	The smoke detection system in the London Data Center registered an alarm around 5:02 A.M. local time. Facilities staff went to the site, determined there was no fire condition, and reset the alarm. Note: Three similar incidents were recorded last year. In those cases, batteries in the detection equipment had begun to run low—although had yet to trigger a "replace battery" alarm. Based on this earlier pattern, we have requested a technician to come to the site and examine the detection equipment.	MI	ME

The incident log in Table 14-1 not only documents what happens in the Data Center and when, but it also categorizes the events by type and cause. This can be helpful for identifying recurring problems. Here are several useful categories to separate Data Center-related incidents into:

- **Commercial Power (CP)**—An interruption in the power that is normally provided to the Data Center by a utility source.

- **Connectivity (CO)**—A disruption in data connections, either in the external structured cabling that feeds the company site or those within the Data Center.

- **Mechanical—HVAC (AC)**—An incident related to the Data Center's cooling system.

- **Mechanical—Power (MP)**—An incident related to the Data Center's primary or standby electrical infrastructure. (Further distinction should be provided within the description of the incident.)

- **Miscellaneous (MI)**—Events that are worth noting but don't fall in to any other categories. Perhaps a false alarm in the fire suppression system or a problem with the room's physical access controls, for example.

- **Water Leak (WL)**—An incident in which unwanted moisture enters the server environment.

All of these are obviously infrastructure-related incidents. If you choose to maintain a log of other events, such as the malfunction of an individual server, create additional categories to distinguish them.

Even more important than knowing what happened in a server environment is understanding the cause of the incident. Knowing that a row of servers went off line doesn't do you much good unless it also comes out whether the outage was caused by human error (i.e., a person incorrectly flipped off a circuit breaker) or mechanical failure (i.e., the power distribution unit malfunctioned). Such understanding enables you to put measures in place to prevent the incident from happening again, be they more training for employees or more frequent maintenance on the Data Center electrical infrastructure.

Here are some typical causes of Data Center-related incidents:

- **External (EX)**—External causes are those that originate away from your company site. Utility power failures, damage to the structured cabling that leads to a company site, or an earthquake are sample external causes.

- **Human Error (HU)**—Human error applies to incidents that occur because a person made a mistake rather than the failure of a physical component. Powering down the wrong electrical circuits, inappropriately pressing an emergency power off button, or tipping over a cabinet of servers are all examples of human error.

- **Mechanical (ME)**—A mechanical cause is the malfunction of infrastructure at the company site. A belt breaking within an air handler, UPS batteries failing to hold a charge, or a standby generator not engaging when it is supposed to are various mechanical causes.

- **Structural (ST)**—The rarest of causes are those related to a building's structural integrity. Examples of this are a roof leak or the buckling of a Data Center floor.

An event can have more than one cause. For example, say that utility power fails to a company site and then the UPS doesn't hold the Data Center's electrical load because its batteries aren't holding a sufficient charge. This event might have started due to an external incident, but the additional mechanical problem contributes to Data Center servers going off line.

NOTE   In my experience, half of all downtime-causing incidents in a Data Center are caused by human error. This perception comes from maintaining several years of incident logs as well as discussions with other Data Center managers.

I have personally experienced Data Center outages from a technician dropping a tool into a power distribution unit, an electrical contractor mislabeling a circuit breaker (leading to an outage years later when the wrong breaker was shut off to perform maintenance), and an intern severing a handful of fiber patch cords that were in use by dropping a floor tile panel on them. Other rooms I manage have had problems when a system administrator turned off an entire power distribution unit to silence an alarm, an electrical contractor neglected to turn on a circuit feeding a generator's trickle charger, and a technician installing a fire suppression system in a live Data Center tested its sensitivity with a hair dryer—not realizing this would trigger the emergency power off system and bring the entire room off line.

Whatever the specific incident, people are too often a Data Center's worst enemy. While it is maddening to have millions of dollars' worth of protective infrastructure nullified by carelessness or a stupid mistake, the bright side to this is that these incidents are largely preventable. Clear labeling, ample signage, and lots and lots of training go a long way toward preventing human error. Limit Data Center access to employees who truly need to work in the room, and make sure that they are thoroughly educated about its infrastructure.

Availability Metrics

As stated at the start of this book, availability—the degree to which a Data Center is online—is a key criterion that drives the design of the room. A Data Center's uptime is arguably the defining element of how productive it is for your company. Modularity, flexibility, standardization, and intuitiveness all contribute to the effectiveness of a server environment, but none of them are as important as its availability. Imagine owning a high performance automobile. Various features can make it the best car in the world—quickest at acceleration, best at handling, most luxurious—but none of those elements meet your transportation needs unless the vehicle can be counted on to run. Measuring your Data Center's availability therefore goes a long way toward evaluating its contribution to the success of your business.

Availability metrics can also justify the expense of additional Data Center infrastructure, either when designing a new room or when upgrading an existing one. If, for example, your server environment was designed and built with the goal of achieving 99.99 percent availability, track the number of outages that occur over a significant time period, perhaps annually, to determine what its availability has turned out to be. If the numbers are lower than your company is trying to obtain, maybe it is time to install more standby electrical equipment or incorporate more network devices to improve redundancy. If the numbers are at or above your goal, then the metrics can help justify the value of having similar quantities of infrastructure for future server environments.

You can calculate your Data Center's availability by using the following formula:

(TIME—OUTAGES) ÷ TIME = Percentage of Availability

TIME is the total number of minutes in a defined time period and OUTAGES is the cumulative number of minutes that a Data Center was offline during that period. (Any unit of time can be used, but minutes are usually appropriate to define most Data Center outages.) For instance, say a Data Center was offline for 20 minutes over the course of a 30-day month. There are 43,200 minutes in that month (30 days × 24 hours in a day × 60 minutes in an hour = 43,200 minutes). Being online for all but 20 minutes translates to 99.91 percent availability:

(43,200—20 min.) ÷ 43,200 min. = 99.95 percent availability

By keeping track of the lengths of outages throughout the year, you can calculate availability for any time period—monthly, quarterly, or annually.

If you have multiple server environments, you might want to adjust your availability metrics so that they are cumulative and incorporate the relative size of each room. This reflects that an outage involving a large Data Center has more of an affect than an outage at a small one. Say that your company has four Data Centers, two that are 5000 square feet in size, one that is 10,000 square feet, and one that is 30,000 square feet, for a total of 50,000 square feet. The unit of measurement doesn't matter; the sizes could just as well be in meters. The important part is how the Data Centers are sized in proportion to one another.

Continuing with the previous example, say that the Data Center with a 20-minute outage and 99.91 percent availability is one of the small rooms—5000 square feet. If the other three rooms all stayed on line for the entire month, what's the cumulative availability for all 50,000 square feet of Data Center space?

Adjust the formula, (TIME—OUTAGES) ÷ TIME = Percentage of Availability, to incorporate the size of each room. That is, multiply the amount of time that each room is on line (TIME—OUTAGES) by the size of that particular Data Center, and then divide the entire formula by the cumulative size of all of the rooms. The formula then becomes:

((SIZE1 * (TIME-OUTAGES1)) + (SIZE2 × (TIME-OUTAGES2)) + (SIZE3 * (TIME-OUTAGES3)) + (SIZE4 × (TIME-OUTAGES4)) ÷ (TOTAL SIZE * TIME)

SIZE1, SIZE2, SIZE3, and SIZE4 represent the respective footprints of the four Data Centers, while OUTAGES1, OUTAGES2, OUTAGES3, and OUTAGES4 are the cumulative downtimes for each respective room. TOTAL SIZE is the combined size of all of the Data Centers. Plugging in the monthly statistics for the four Data Centers, with the smallest having 20 minutes of downtime, you get the following:

((5000 sq. ft. * (43,200—20 min.)) + (5000 sq. ft. * 43,200 min.) + (10,000 * 43,200 min.) + (30,000 sq. ft. * 43,200 min.)) ÷ (50,000 sq. ft. * (43,200 min.)) = 99.995 percent availability

Note that, because the room only accounts for one-tenth of the overall Data Center space (5000 of 50,000 square feet), the downtime it suffers has a smaller effect on overall availability than if it was a company's only server environment. What, then, if it that 20-minute outage instead occurred in the largest of the four Data Centers? That is figured as follows:

((5000 sq. ft. * (43,200 min.)) + (5000 sq. ft. * 43,200 min.) + (10,000 * 43,200 min.) + (30,000 sq. ft. * (43,200 − 20 min.))) ÷ (50,000 sq. ft. * (43,200 min.) = 99.972 percent availability

Not surprisingly, because the Data Center in this example accounts for a larger amount of the overall server environment space, an outage there has a greater effect on overall availability.

To save yourself a math-induced headache every time you want to calculate Data Center availability, enter these formulas into a spreadsheet software program. With a few minor adjustments, you can quickly calculate availability numbers for Data Centers in whatever groupings you desire — large server environments versus small ones, by geographic region, or according to their level of redundant infrastructure if you happen to have Data Centers built to different specifications.

Other Useful Data

There is inevitably other miscellaneous stuff that is helpful to keep track of concerning your Data Center. This information is unlikely to help you manage or support the room on a daily basis, but can be useful for future planning and when making presentations to customers or upper management.

- **Cabinet occupancy** — How quickly are Data Center cabinet locations filling up? Tracking this helps ensure that the need to expand a server environment is identified early.

- **Consumable usage** — How many server cabinets, cabinet shelves, and patch cables are used each quarter? This information is helpful for maintaining proper inventory amounts and future budgeting.

- **Supplies and vendors** — What's the model number of the power strip in your Data Center server cabinets? Which cable contractors do you request bids from when it is time to order patch cords? Which configuration of screws are compatible with your server cabinets and which aren't? Document the items you stock in your server environment and the vendors who provide them. Include both everyday consumables (i.e., patch cords and server cabinets) and those items needed to complete a Data Center when it is first built (i.e., storage bins, signage materials, and floor tile pullers).

- **Major infrastructure changes** — If you significantly retrofit a Data Center — perhaps adding electrical infrastructure to provide greater redundancy or changing structured cabling runs from a direct-connect to distributed model — document the project and photograph key steps. "Then and now" comparisons can be very illustrative. The information can also be useful when future retrofit projects are planned.

- **Data Center trivia**—What's the biggest piece of equipment in the Data Center? The smallest? How long does it take to install a typical server? If placed end to end, how long is the server environment's structured cabling? Such trivia might not help you manage the room, but it can be powerful when explaining Data Center challenges. For example, some people are surprised to hear that a Data Center can't support a row of cabinets laden with high-density servers. Doing a bit of research shows that such a cabinet can weigh as much as a compact car. Explaining that the Data Center now has to bear the same weight as a parking garage is usually more understandable than showing a chart of how much various servers weigh.

Summary

Document as much about your Data Center as possible to simplify the overall management of the room, space allocation for incoming servers, troubleshooting, and planning for future expansion. Maintain the information both online and in printed form and keep it up to date.

A Data Center floor plan that includes infrastructure locations, a numbering scheme, cabling and electrical paths, weight restrictions, and floor tile configurations, is particularly helpful. So too are as-builts that show the paths and termination details of structural cabling and electrical conduits.

Regularly inventory Data Center servers by name, type, and location to make it easier to find these items in the room. Likewise collect information on what applications are on them.

Document Data Center-related processes, including access and change management policies, service level agreements, installation guidelines, and move procedures. Also provide details about why the server environment is designed the way it is, so that room users can understand the facility and use it more effectively.

Deploy remote monitoring tools to obtain up-to-the-moment information on all of your server environments regardless of their geographic location.

Install web cameras to view the monitoring lights for your Data Center's standby electrical and fire detection systems, equip server cabinet power strips with amperage meters to monitor the electrical load upon each of them, and deploy temperature and humidity sensors to sample air conditions in the room.

Also gather Data Center-related metrics. Maintain an ongoing incident log, with events classified by type and cause. Include not only downtime incidents but also occasions where the room's infrastructure or support staff prevent downtime.

Gather availability metrics to gauge the productivity of your Data Center. If your company has multiple server environments, it can be valuable to adjust the data to highlight rooms of different sizes or geographic location.

Other miscellaneous Data Center information that might prove useful to track is cabinet occupancy, run rates for supplies, lists of standard materials and vendors, records of significant infrastructure changes, and other Data Center trivia.

CHAPTER 15

Maintaining a World-Class Environment

This chapter discusses the importance of maintaining your Data Center in a pristine state, diligently removing unwanted materials, and having the room professionally cleaned on a regular basis. The chapter also offers instructions for contracting with a professional cleaning company and outlines common mishaps that can occur.

The Importance of Data Center Maintenance

Because your company has spent a considerable amount of money building a Data Center and populating it with servers and networking devices and that facility is where critical business transactions occur and data is stored, it goes without saying that the room must be treated with care and maintained so that it is clean and orderly. Or at least it *should* go without saying. While many companies do indeed go to significant lengths to protect and maintain their Data Centers, others are less diligent. More relaxed policies allow food and drink in the server environment, equipment to be unboxed in the Data Center, patch cords to be routed haphazardly, or items to be stored in the room.

In some cases, more lenient practices are the result of physical limitations at the Data Center site. Perhaps a proper storage room was never set aside to house Data Center equipment and supplies. Boxes might need to be brought in to the server environment and opened there simply because no other physical space is available.

In other cases, human nature is to blame. Even when a storage room is available, some Data Center users don't use the space because they consider it more convenient to leave an item in the server environment. Neatly routing patch cords through wire management, keeping boxes out of the Data Center, and returning unused supplies to their proper location can all seem like tedious and trivial tasks to system administrators when they are rushing to bring a server online. Such habits are more likely to develop if there is no single person or group responsible for managing the room and ensuring that its policies are followed.

Taking shortcuts, either in violation of Data Center standards or because no such standards exist, increases the chances for a Data Center to become dirty and disorganized, which in turn reduces the room's productivity for a company. In extreme circumstances, dirt and contaminants can interfere with the proper operation of a server. Data Center users also shouldn't have to waste time dealing with non-essential items in the room.

Send a clear message about the importance of your Data Center by keeping it well-maintained and enforcing its standards of operations at all times.

The Broken Window Theory

In 1969, Philip Zimbardo, a professor of psychology at Stanford University, performed an experiment that introduced what is now known as the Broken Window Theory. The premise is that if people perceive an item to be abandoned, even those people who are not otherwise prone to criminal behavior, they are more inclined to steal or damage that item.

Zimbardo parked a car in a rough Bronx, New York, neighborhood with its license plates removed and hood up, making the vehicle appear abandoned. Ten minutes after the automobile was left alone, its battery and radiator were stolen. The car's other valuable components were stripped within twenty-four hours; soon after that its windows were broken and upholstery was destroyed. Zimbardo parked another car in the same starting condition in an upscale Palo Alto, California, neighborhood. It sat untouched for a week, until Zimbardo smashed part of it with a sledgehammer. Within a few hours, the vehicle was flipped over and demolished.

Law enforcement authorities and government officials in many municipalities have expanded upon the Broken Window Theory, believing that, in neighborhoods where graffiti, petty crime, and decay (i.e., broken windows) aren't cleaned up, there is an increased likelihood of not just more of the same but also more serious crimes. Minor bad behavior, if left unchecked, is believed to send the message to people that no one in authority is watching and there are no consequences for that behavior.

How does the Broken Window Theory apply to your server environment? A Data Center user is more inclined to toss unused patch cords on the floor if piles of discarded cables are there already, more apt to take shortcuts when installing servers when other employees have obviously done the same, and less likely to treat a server environment with respect if the room appears poorly maintained.

Regular Upkeep

Your first line of defense in maintaining a Data Center in excellent condition is simply keeping the room picked up. Deliver equipment to and un-box it in a dedicated build room, empty Data Center trash cans regularly, and encourage room users to take pride in the server environment's condition.

Establish a time for employees to clean the Data Center as a group. Involve the Data Center's designated support staff and, if possible, include system administrators and network engineers who typically work in the room. The more people who are involved, the bigger impact they can make.

Cleaning a Data Center as a group can be quite effective. Large items that need to be moved out of a room can be easily handled, and tedious tasks—sorting and retesting patch cords, for example—can be accomplished quickly by several people rather than made the responsibility of one. There is even a degree of team-building that occurs when employees work together to visibly improve the Data Center.

NOTE   While one half of my team is distributed across multiple company sites, the other half is based at our company headquarters where there are six Data Centers. Once a week, we choose a different room and clean it together. We pick up trash, move inappropriate items from the Data Center into storage, and replace worn or outdated cabinet labels. We also flag improperly installed equipment and contact their owners to address any problems (typically poorly routed patch cords or unlabeled devices). We spend about an hour per cleaning, rotating to a different server environment each week. In this way, no room ever goes more than a month and a half without being thoroughly picked up.

Professional Cleaning

In addition to keeping the Data Center tidy on a day-to-day basis, hire a professional cleaning company to periodically clean the room. No matter how diligently your employees pick up after themselves, it is inevitable for scuff marks to appear on floor panels and particles—typically dirt, dust, lint, or metal shavings—to accumulate under floor.

Among the things that a cleaning vendor can do for your Data Center are:

- Wipe down servers
- Remove marks from raised floor surfaces
- Vacuum the room, in and out of the plenum
- Test for potentially hazardous particles
- Note the condition of the plenum and infrastructure components

NOTE   Have realistic expectations about the cleaning vendor's scope of work. Cleaners come to your Data Center to clean, not to move server cabinets, boxes, or pallets. If objects in the Data Center are in the way of the cleaning crew, blocking aisles between server rows or overlapping onto raised floor tiles, cleaning technicians aren't going to move them. Therefore, to get the most performance out of a cleaning company, you probably want to tidy the room before they arrive, so that nothing is in the way of their technicians.

Vendor Qualifications and Credentials

Choose a cleaning vendor carefully. You want a company that is experienced at working in Data Centers so that its employees know how to conduct themselves in a sensitive environment and so that appropriate cleaning materials are used.

Interview multiple vendors. Ask for professional references and check them. If you know Data Center managers at other companies, ask them who they use to clean their server environments and whether they are happy with those vendors. Word of mouth recommendations are often the most reliable.

Choose a cleaning company that is bonded and insured—the two provide financial protection in the event of theft, personal injury, or property damage. It is desirable for the cleaning company to have "errors and omissions" insurance, which covers acts that are performed or not performed. This gives your company the option of seeking reimbursement in the event that a cleaning technician causes damage or downtime because of something they do incorrectly or because they fail to carry out a task.

In addition to the cleaning company as a whole having appropriate qualifications, the specific vendor employees who are going to clean your Data Center should meet specific criteria as well. All vendor employees who are to work in your server environment must be trained in the proper use of all cleaning equipment and materials and experienced working in a Data Center. The cleaning crew's supervisor, who is to be in the server environment throughout the job, should be fluent in whatever primary language is spoken by your employees. You want to avoid any misunderstanding of your company's instructions to the supervisor, be they presented verbally or in writing.

Finally, if you want to be particularly cautious about the people who are to clean your Data Center, ask for a list of vendor personnel and enough information to perform a background check upon them.

Approved Cleaning Equipment and Materials

Due to the sensitivity of Data Center servers and infrastructure components, allow only gentle cleaning agents and limit the amount of liquid used in the room. Restrict vendors to use the following items:

- Vacuums equipped with triple-filtration high-efficiency particulate air (HEPA) or S-Class filters. Vacuums shielded to prevent the emission of electromagnetic interference are preferable.

- Cleaning chemicals that are pH neutral, static dissipative, and approved or qualified by computer hardware manufacturers. Avoid cleaning agents that contain ammonia or other corrosive materials.

- Canned air.

- Lint-free mops. Mops should have non-metal handles and sewn ends, to prevent snagging. Mop heads should have looped ends, not ends that are open or stringy or both. New mops are preferable. Prohibit dry dust mops or dust brooms.
- Lint-free, anti-static wipes and towels.
- Low-speed floor scrubbing machines. Avoid high speed buffers.
- Electrical cords that are in good condition and, if appropriate for local power configurations, have a three-pin ground.
- A stable stepladder, for cleaning items near the ceiling. Ladders should have non-marking, rubber feet so as to not scrape or mark the Data Center floor.

If the cleaning company suggests substitute materials, review the items and approve or deny their use as appropriate. You want all cleaning materials to be gentle on your Data Center. Avoid strong chemicals, fabrics that produce static or lint, or equipment that might damage Data Center infrastructure components or emit electromagnetic interference.

NOTE   What are HEPA and S-Class filters? A HEPA filter is a tightly woven paper made up of tiny glass fibers. It is rated to remove 99.97 percent of all particles as small as .3 µm from a stream of air. That means that, for every 10,000 particles passing through a HEPA filter, a mere three get through. HEPA filters were first created in the 1940s by the United States Atomic Energy Commission as top-secret technology to remove radioactive dust from plant exhausts. An S-Class filter is the European equivalent of a HEPA filter.

Pre-Cleaning Steps

After you have chosen a vendor, have it come to your company site and provide its representatives a tour of the Data Center that is to be cleaned. The tour should be attended by a management representative of the cleaning company, the work crew supervisor who will be present during the actual cleaning, the manager of your Data Center, and whoever from your Data Center support staff will be present during the cleaning.

Provide a map of the Data Center, designating which electrical outlets are for the contractor's equipment and use during the cleaning. Point out any relevant physical details or procedural issues about the Data Center and provide a copy of the standards of operations for the room. This meeting is also an opportunity to cover miscellaneous items, such as whether the cleaning crew is allowed to have a radio playing while it works.

While it is advisable to have a company employee in the Data Center to supervise the cleaning, if that is not practical, provide escalation instructions and contact information to the work crew supervisor. They must be able to reach someone from your company immediately in the event that a problem arises.

Standards of Operations

When your Data Center is professionally cleaned, the people doing the work come into contact with practically all servers, networking devices, structured cabling, and electrical conduits in the room. Because the work requires such direct contact with these sensitive items, it is vital that the vendor's staff understands and adheres to the room's standards of operations. At a minimum, the cleaning crew should obey the following:

- Don't bring food or drink in the Data Center
- Don't prop open Data Center doors
- Don't admit unauthorized or unbadged personnel in the Data Center

To avoid possible misunderstanding, go over all Data Center rules with representatives of the cleaning company during the initial interview with them. Also, review your company policies on the day of the cleaning with the crew members who come to your site. Do this even if you employ a cleaning company on a regular basis, and it should be familiar with your Data Center procedures. The vendor might have a turnover of employees, and you want to ensure that anyone who is new understands the server environment.

In addition to following your Data Center's standards of operations, require the cleaning crew to observe the following:

- **Wear identifiable clothing**—Most Data Center visitors are individually escorted by company employees. That might be impractical for a cleaning crew with several people, so have all crew members wear some form of company attire so they can be easily identified. Shirts bearing the cleaning company logo are common. Additional identification, such as company-issued picture badges, is helpful.

- **Stay within designated areas**—Members of the cleaning crew should remain within areas of the company building that they need to be in to perform their work. It is reasonable for workers to have access to a restroom or janitor's closet—preferably such rooms that are relatively close to the Data Center—but people must not wander through the building. Ideally your employees won't be leaving sensitive materials out on their desks, but it is better to be safe than sorry. If your company has security procedures for employees, contractors, or visitors to follow—perhaps signing a log sheet when entering or leaving the building—make sure that the cleaning crew obeys them.

- **Mark off open floor tiles with pylons**—Server cabinets are usually so tall that someone walking through the Data Center can't see what is happening between server rows until they reach a row's end and look in. If they are walking quickly, they might step in to an open floor tile before realizing that there is a hazard. Prevent this from happening by placing brightly colored cones or pylons around open floor tiles.

- **Plug cleaning equipment into only identified power sources**—Provide the cleaners with a Data Center floor plan that has convenience outlets highlighted.

- **Make minimal contact with Data Center equipment**—It is common to have a cleaning crew remove dust from servers and networking devices by wiping them down. When doing this, workers must be extremely careful not to dislodge any patch cords or power cables. If a cable, connection, or piece of equipment ever seems precarious, workers should leave the item undisturbed and inform your company representative about it.

NOTE	On occasion, my team has had a cleaning vendor make an excellent impression during an initial interview—looking well-dressed in company attire, exhibiting a professional demeanor, and offering good credentials—only to later have the people who show up on the day of work appear poorly dressed, inexperienced at cleaning a server environment, and certainly unfamiliar with the ground rules of working in one of our Data Centers.

If this happens to you, ask the supervisor of the cleaning crew to send those people home. If you feel like the skills of the cleaning crew were misrepresented in the interview, send the entire group away. You don't want untrained people working in your Data Center, especially if those people are going to be lifting floor tiles and potentially coming into direct contact with servers, structured cabling, and electrical receptacles. The risk of an accident happening is too great. |

Cleaning Procedures

Many companies choose to perform environmental tests within their Data Center immediately before and after the room is cleaned. This helps quantify the benefit a company is receiving from having its server environment professionally cleaned. If you desire this, have the vendor begin its work by performing the following tests:

- **Particle count**—A portable airborne particle counter is used to measure particle concentrations at different locations in the Data Center. The counter itself typically employs a laser and is similar to the mechanism in a Data Center's smoke detection system.

- **Ferrous metal test**—This procedure is performed to detect fine metal shavings or flakes that, although difficult to see with the naked eye, can be carried through the Data Center by its cooling and air circulation system and get in to sensitive hardware. Typically for this test a medium-powered magnet is wrapped in white paper and then rubbed on the subfloor deck in an area the size of a floor tile.

- **Temperature and humidity test**—If your Data Center lacks temperature or humidity sensors, be aware that many cleaning vendors also have portable equipment that can take these measurements as well. Unlike the prior tests, temperature and humidity results aren't likely to change after a server environment is cleaned. The data is merely a snapshot of your Data Center's environmental condition, which can be informative if you aren't otherwise monitoring these qualities.

Once the true cleaning of your Data Center begins, the cleaners should start at the highest point in the Data Center they will clean and then proceed downward. Starting from a high point prevents a cleaning technician from dislodging dirt or other contaminants and having the material fall down onto items that have already been cleaned. Similarly, cleaners should begin near Data Center air handlers and work outward from them. This removes particulate matter along an air handler's outgoing air flow path, rather than going against the air stream. Imagine sweeping dirt while a breeze is at your back versus sweeping dirt into a headwind.

Specific cleaning procedures for different layers of the Data Center are covered in the sections that follow.

Above-Ceiling

If your Data Center has a false ceiling and the area is used for air distribution, have the space cleaned. Any dirt or contaminants in this plenum are obviously going to circulate through the entire server environment. Instruct the vendor to clean the area as follows:

- Lift and displace ceiling panels to gain access to the space. Be careful not to damage the tiles or structural supports.

- Use a HEPA or S-Class vacuum to clean the top of the ceiling panels—the side that faces the plenum—as well as structured cabling or electrical conduits.

- Replace all ceiling panels.

  This area of the Data Center is typically seen less than any other—who bothers to look above the ceiling tiles unless additional infrastructure has to be run? Specifically direct the vendor to make note of any unusual conditions. These might include:

  — **Loose ceiling tile brackets**—Unsecured brackets obviously need to be resecured to the ceiling. A heavy item such as a light fixture might be the cause.

  — **Damaged ceiling tiles or infrastructure**—Stained ceiling tiles are a sign of a water leak. Physical damage might indicate the presence of rodents.

  — **Exposed fiber strands**—If cabling terminates in faceplates that are directly mounted to the ceiling rather than in a raceway below the ceiling, an insufficient bend radius might strain the cabling and cause the protective jacket around the fiber to pull away.

NOTE   Don't rely solely upon a cleaning vendor's inspection of your Data Center's rarely seen spaces to be aware of their condition. While it is logical to ask the cleaning crew to look around, because they are poking around in those spaces anyway, it is ultimately your responsibility to monitor and maintain these areas. Consider the vendor merely an additional set of eyes.

If your Data Center doesn't use the space above its false ceiling for air distribution, it is less important that the area be cleaned on a regular basis. Dust and debris that accumulate in a nonplenum ceiling are unlikely to circulate through the server environment.

Below-Ceiling

While the bottom surface of blank ceiling tiles don't typically need to be cleaned, vented panels and any raceways or cable trays that are suspended from the ceiling do. Direct the cleaning vendor to do the following:

- Use a HEPA or S-Class vacuum to clean the horizontal surfaces of vented ceiling tiles, raceways, and cable bundles. Use canned air to dislodge dust in areas that cannot be reached by the vacuum.

- Wipe down the vertical surfaces of raceways with lint-free cloths treated with antistatic chemical.

Light fixtures come in different configurations, whether flush with the false ceiling or suspended. As appropriate, have the cleaning vendor remove dust from the overhead lights in your Data Center.

Servers and Networking Devices

Advise the cleaning vendor to exercise particular care when working around Data Center servers and networking devices. Technicians should avoid disturbing patch cords or power cables, touching keyboards, moving hardware, or spraying chemicals directly onto equipment. Instruct the vendor to clean equipment and cabinets as follows:

- Use a HEPA or S-Class vacuum to clean the horizontal surfaces of all equipment. Use canned air to dislodge dust in areas that cannot be reached by the vacuum.

- Wipe down the external surfaces of all server cabinets, servers, networking devices, and other equipment with lint-free cloths treated with antistatic chemical.

If your Data Center employs enclosed cabinets, specify whether you want technicians to clean only the exterior of the cabinets or if you want them to open cabinet doors and clean equipment surfaces within.

Other Above-Floor Items

Although the main goal of having your Data Center professionally cleaned is the removal of contaminants from servers, infrastructure components, and the plenum, consider having nonessential items in the room cleaned as well. If your company's regular janitorial crew doesn't clean in your Data Center—and it probably doesn't because its people aren't experienced working in a server environment—dust can accumulate in corners over time.

Have the cleaning vendor clean the Data Center's door frames, unused cabinet shelves, storage racks, observation windows, and so on. This prevents dust particles from ultimately being drawn in to the Data Center's air circulation system and puts the finishing touches on making the entire room clean.

Floor Surface

The condition of your Data Center floor—dirty or clean, worn or new-looking—makes a significant impression upon visitors to the room. Unfortunately, the floor's surface is subjected to a significant amount of wear and tear over time, due to both people traffic and equipment. Have the floor cleaned regularly to freshen its appearance. Direct the cleaning vendor to clean all accessible portions of the floor in the following manner:

- Use a HEPA vacuum or S-Class to clean the top of all floor tiles—blank, notched, and perforated.

- Treat smudges, stains, and black marks with an approved cleaning solution and scrub them with a medium grade scrub pad.

- Use a low-speed floor scrubber. Don't apply a finish or wax to floor tiles.

- Mop the floor with a damp—*not wet*—mop, using clean, warm water. Use a two-bucket system, one for mopping and one for rinsing. Frequently change the water in both buckets.

NOTE   If you attach printed labels to your Data Center floor, perhaps to provide cabinet location or electrical information, the labels are going to become faded and dirty over time as people and equipment pass over them. Rather than ask the cleaning vendor to maneuver around the labels with the floor scrubber, allow the labels to be scraped off. You can then apply a fresh set of labels on the newly cleaned floor.

Also ask the cleaning vendor to identify any damaged floor tiles that it discovers.

Subfloor

The last section of your Data Center to be cleaned, assuming that the room is equipped with a raised floor, is the plenum below. Instruct the cleaning crew to clean the area as follows:

- Lift and remove panels to access the under-floor area. Remove tiles in a checkerboard pattern to avoid exposing floor pedestals to damage. No more than ten percent of the Data Center's total floor tiles should be removed at one time.

- Use a HEPA or S-Class vacuum to remove dust and particles within the subfloor. Avoid moving any structured cabling or electrical conduits. Use canned air to dislodge dust in areas that cannot be reached by the vacuum.

- Wipe down the raised floor system's pedestals and stringers with water-moistened towels.

- Manually remove any large debris and place it in the trash.

When removing floor panels, the vendor should follow the recommended handling practices outlined in Chapter 5, "Overhead or Under-Floor Installation?"

As with the area above the false ceiling, your server environment's subfloor likely receives limited attention most of the time. Data Center users might lift a floor tile or two to plug in to infrastructure, but there is no reason for those employees to truly inspect the room's subfloor.

Ask the cleaning vendor to make note of any of the following conditions:

- **Damaged floor pedestals or stringers**—Damage to any components of the raised floor grid can compromise the grid's ability to bear weight. Replace damaged components immediately.

- **Floor cracks**—Shallow cracks in the Data Center floor are probably only an indication of minor settling of the building, but might be the first symptom of a more serious structural issue. Consult with your facilities personnel and a structural engineer to be sure.

- **Worn sealant**—A Data Center's subfloor is sealed to keep it from releasing concrete dust. As with other particles, such dust will otherwise be carried everywhere by the room's air handlers and enter sensitive servers. Many cleaning vendors offer a sealant service and are therefore very sharp at spotting deteriorated sealant on a subfloor.

- **Moisture**—Free-standing water under a Data Center floor can be the result of condensation or a leak. Either condition is undesirable and should be reported.

- **Room integrity**—Breaches to the Data Center "cocoon"—holes in the wall or improperly sealed conduits for cabling, for example—reduce the effectiveness of the room's gaseous fire suppression system. The suppressant can't smother a fire completely if outside air leaks in or the suppressant itself leaks out. A server environment's temperature and humidity controls also have to work harder if the room is not sealed.

- **Excessive litter**—Some debris under a raised floor is inevitable but an excessive amount is cause for concern. Cable tie scraps, cabinet screws, and dropped tools are understandable, while items such as cardboard scraps, candy wrappers, or cigarette butts signify that people have brought items into the Data Center that violate the room's standards of operations.

Post-Cleaning Steps

As soon as the Data Center has been cleaned, have the vendor perform a second particle count and test for ferrous metals. Testing should be done in the same locations as before so that the findings are comparable.

Obtain a written report from the cleaning vendor on the status of the Data Center. The report should include a thorough description of all work that was performed, data from before-and-after tests, and a summary of any unusual Data Center conditions encountered during the cleaning. It is unlikely that members of the Data Center support staff regularly inspect the area below a server environment's raised floor, so having the cleaning company document what they find can be informative. Moisture, litter, or cracks are all details worthy of being reported.

Zinc Whiskers

If your Data Center has a raised floor, carefully examine the underside of your floor tiles for zinc filaments before having the room professionally cleaned. Called whiskers for their tendency to grow from metallic surfaces, these tiny strands are believed to form due to molecular stress. Zinc is used in floor panels to keep the steel on their bottom side from rusting, and the filaments emerge as the zinc tries to separate itself from the steel.

Zinc whiskers are extremely small and therefore difficult to see with the naked eye. The filaments are typically 2 µm in diameter and a few hundred µm long. Over time, they can grow to just under half an inch (about one centimeter). The phenomenon is also known to occur with tin and cadmium.

Figures 15-1 and 15-2 show zinc whiskers under the magnification of a scanning electron microscope.

Figure 15-1 *Zinc Whiskers Growing from a Floor Tile*

Image provided by courtesy of NASA Goddard
Space Flight Center

Figure 15-2 *A Closeup of Two Zinc Filaments*

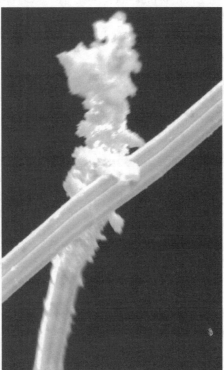

Image provided by courtesy of NASA Goddard
Space Flight Center

Although the whiskers are harmless while growing on your floor tiles, they become dangerous if dislodged. The Data Center's cooling and air circulation system distributes the filaments through the room, where the tiny strands can get into sensitive hardware. Zinc conducts electricity and can trigger an electrical short. Ironically, then, when you have your server environment cleaned to remove contaminants—and hundreds of floor tiles are lifted as part of the process—you might actually harm your servers if certain precautions are not taken.

Zinc whiskers were first discovered in telecommunications rooms in 1948 by Bell Laboratories. The filaments haven't been a significant problem until relatively recently. Today's servers are smaller and installed in greater concentrations than in the past and therefore believed to be more vulnerable to the filaments. Today's Data Centers are also older, giving the whiskers time to grow on floor tiles. Filaments have even been found growing in electronic hardware, on server mounting rails, and within server cabinets.

How do you know if your Data Center has zinc whiskers? The primary symptom is the server environment experiencing a high rate of equipment failure throughout the room and those failures involving equipment from different manufacturers. To look for zinc whiskers, dim the surrounding light, carefully lift a floor panel, and shine a bright light at the underside of the tile. Look for a sparkle or reflection off of the filaments. The whiskers are easier to see at an angle.

Figure 5-3 shows zinc filaments on the bottom of a raised floor tile.

Figure 15-3 *Zinc Whiskers on the Bottom of a Floor Tile*

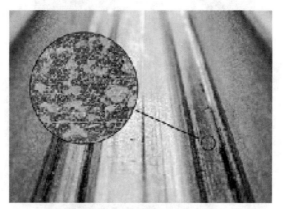

Image provided by courtesy of
Prabjit (PJ) Singh of IBM

To treat zinc whiskers, cleaning companies recommend outright removing all floor panels that have the whiskers. Temporarily reduce air flow to the problem tiles to reduce circulating any filaments that break free, carefully bag and remove the panels, clean the plenum with HEPA or S-Class vacuums, and then install new tiles. Some manufacturers are working to develop coatings to inhibit the formation of zinc filaments, but to date no materials have proven to do so reliably.

Frequency

How often you should have your Data Center floors professionally cleaned depends upon how much the room is exposed to contaminants, both from foot traffic and the surrounding environment. How many people work in the Data Center? Are they allowed to bring in food or drink? Are cardboard boxes or wood pallets ever brought in to the Data Center? Is the company site exposed to smoke or pollutants, which then might enter the Data Center as part of the outside air that is circulated in? Is building construction occurring at the site? The more of these factors that apply to a Data Center, the dirtier the room is likely to get and therefore the more frequently it should be professionally cleaned.

Companies with the most rigorous requirements have their server environments cleaned on a quarterly basis. Others might go years between cleanings. Let the condition of your Data Center guide how often it is cleaned. If floor labels begin to look worn and visitors to the room are leaving as much dirt on the room's tacky mats when they leave as when they enter, it is probably time for a cleaning.

NOTE	The major Data Centers I manage are professionally cleaned below the raised floor once a year and above it every three months. A cleaning is also performed after any significant construction is performed within a server environment. For example, if a pair of server rows containing direct-connect cabling has its structured cabling removed and replaced to a distributed model, it is a requirement of the project that the areas above and below the floor be cleaned.

Common Problems

If something goes wrong during a Data Center cleaning, it is inevitably attributable to human error. There just aren't many mechanical devices involved in cleaning a server environment, and those that are guided by a person and therefore can cause damage only when that person makes a mistake. Here are some common pitfalls to avoid:

- **Tripping a circuit breaker**—Plugging a vacuum cleaner into a server cabinet power strip already feeding server equipment can overload the strip and trip a circuit breaker. Don't allow anything to be plugged in to a server cabinet other than servers, networking devices, and peripheral equipment. Require cleaning equipment to be plugged in to the Data Center's designated convenience outlets

- **Disconnecting a patch cord or power cable**—Any time a person is working near server cabinets or under a raised floor, there's a risk of dislodging a cable. A cleaning crew is no more prone to do this than anyone else, but because it comes into contact with hundreds or thousands of servers and infrastructure components while doing its job, there's certainly an increased opportunity for a problem to occur. Safeguard against this by educating the cleaning crew about working carefully in the server environment and also by training Data Center users to secure patch cords and power cords and fully use the room's wire management.

- **Misusing Data Center controls**—Emergency power off and fire suppression system controls must remain accessible to people in the Data Center, and so there is a chance of someone inappropriately activating them. If you feel that your Data Center's standard signage for its fire suppression and emergency power off controls aren't enough to warn someone away, consider posting temporary signs during cleaning events. A simple sheet of paper with DON'T TOUCH and USE ONLY IN EMERGENCY printed in large block letters might be attention-getting enough to help. That's obviously only a short-term fix to a larger problem—upgrade your permanent labeling at the first opportunity.

- **Getting servers or infrastructure wet**—Allowing water in the Data Center always brings with it the risk of a spill. Minimize this during the cleaning process by using low quantities of water for mopping and keeping mop buckets atop blank tiles—*not perforated or notched*—at all times. This limits the ability of a small amount of spilled water to reach infrastructure components under the raised floor.

Summary

Your Data Center is a critical environment containing millions of dollars worth of infrastructure and computer hardware, and should be properly maintained. Allowing the server environment to become dirty and disorganized reduces its productivity.

Have the users and support staff of your Data Center regularly pick up the room as a group.

Hire a professional cleaning company for removing dirt and dust and performing various environmental tests. Choose an experienced company that is insured and bonded. The vendor's employees must be familiar with working in and cleaning a Data Center.

All equipment and materials used to clean your Data Center are to be gentle—nonacidic, nonstatic generating, and nonlinting as appropriate.

Go over your Data Center's standards of operations with the vendor before cleaning begins. In addition to these rules, require cleaning technicians who come to your site to wear company clothing, stay within designated areas, mark any openings in the raised floor with pylons, plug cleaning equipment into identified power sources, and make minimal contact with Data Center servers and networking devices.

At the start of the cleaning, you might want the vendor to take particle counts, test for ferrous metals, or record temperature and humidity levels, all at various locations in the Data Center. Begin the actual cleaning at the high point in the room and work down. Check for the presence of zinc filaments on the underside of raised floor tiles before having the floor cleaned.

Have any plenum above the false ceiling, any ceiling-mounted infrastructure, server cabinets and the equipment they house, the raised floor surface, and the subfloor cleaned. Instruct the cleaning vendor to look for and report any evidence of damage, from water-stained ceiling tiles to cracks on the subfloor.

Repeat any testing that was done prior to the cleaning, so that comparisons can be made.

How often you clean the Data Center depends upon how much the room is exposed to dirt and other foreign particles.

Mistakes to watch out for and avoid during the cleaning of your server environment include plugging cleaning equipment into a server cabinet power strip and tripping a circuit breaker, bringing a server offline by dislodging its patch cords or power cables, wrongly activating the room's emergency power off system, or spilling water on equipment or infrastructure.

GLOSSARY

A

adapter. A device that enables otherwise incompatible patch cords, data ports, servers, or networking devices to connect to one another. The term is also used to identify the mating point of fiber optic connectors through a bulkhead.

as-built. A construction document illustrating how a building was constructed. Typically drawn for a Data Center to show the location of electrical circuits and structured cabling.

attenuation. A reduction in signal strength during transmission. Attenuation is measured in decibels and normally occurs over long distances. Also known as loss.

availability. The degree to which Data Center infrastructure is operational and ready for use. This is represented as a percentage of time, such as 99.999 percent.

B

bend radius. The radius of curvature that a cable can bend without suffering damage and reduced performance.

British thermal units (BTUs). The amount of heat needed to raise the temperature of 1 pound of water by 1° Fahrenheit (.56° Celsius) at its maximum density. This occurs at 39.1° Fahrenheit (3.94° Celsius). Heat output of servers are rated in BTUs, as are the capabilities of most cooling equipment.

build room. A dedicated area for system administrators and network engineers to unpack, set up, and preconfigure equipment that is ultimately bound for the Data Center. Also known as a fitup room, staging area, or burn-in room.

busbar. An electrical conductor that makes a common connection between multiple circuits.

C

canned air. Compressed air in a spray can that is discharged through a long nozzle. Useful for removing dirt or dust from servers and small Data Center infrastructure components.

change management. A methodology of planning, coordinating, and communicating about activities in a Data Center. The goal of change management is to notify stakeholders of and track and control infrastructure alterations to a company's critical facilities in order to minimize downtime.

characteristic impedance. The opposition that a cable or component gives to the flow of an alternating electrical current.

cladding. The glass layer that surrounds the core of a fiber optic cable. Cladding has a lower index of refraction than the core, enabling light to travel great lengths even along a curved fiber cable.

cold aisle. A Data Center aisle, located between two inward-facing server rows, that contains perforated floor tiles for the purpose of directing cold air to the intake of servers.

colocation. Data Center space available for a customer's servers and networking devices. Colocation space typically consists of a large raised floor environment that is physically divided into sections, each of which contains equipment owned by a different customer.

concentrated load. Weight applied on a small area of a floor tile, such as where the pegs or casters of a fully loaded server cabinet touch the floor. Also known as point load.

convenience outlets. Electrical outlets provided in a Data Center, usually around the walls, to power noncritical items.

core. The central glass of a fiber optic cable, through which light is transmitted.

crosstalk. When the signal carried along one set of cable (metal) wires interferes with the signal on a nearby set. This is known as either near end cross talk (NEXT) or far end cross talk (FEXT) depending upon whether it is measured at the end closest or farthest away from the transmitter. Measured in decibels.

D - E - F - G

delay skew. The difference in time it takes a signal to travel down different pairs of wires within a single cable. Specifically, the difference between the fastest and slowest pairs. Measured in time, usually nanoseconds.

electromagnetic interference (EMI). When an electromagnetic field interrupts or degrades the normal operation of a piece of electronic equipment or signal. Also known as radio frequency interference (RFI).

equal level far end cross talk (ELFEXT). The measurement of crosstalk at the opposite end of a cable where a signal originates, minus the attenuation of a signal due to cable length.

far end cross talk (FEXT). The measurement of crosstalk at the opposite end of a cable from where a signal originates. *See* also crosstalk.

gauge. Wire conductor sizes. The lower the number, the thicker the wire's diameter and greater connectivity it provides. Different gauge standards are used in different regions of the world. American Wire Gauge (AWG), sometimes called Brown and Sharpe Wire Gauge, is the standardized set of wire conductor sizes in the United States. British Imperial Standard (SWG) is used in Great Britain and Canada.

growth path. A dedicated area for the future expansion of a Data Center. This space usually consists of employee cubicles, storage rooms, or conference rooms, which are easy to demolish, relocate, and replace.

H

HEPA. High-Efficiency Particulate Air. A filter capable of removing 99.97 percent of particles as small as .3 μm from a stream of air. The standard for vacuum cleaner filters used to clean a Data Center. A European S-Class filter has the same capability.

hot aisle. A Data Center aisle, located between two outward-facing server rows, that typically contains a ducted return in the ceiling above for the purpose of drawing hot exhaust away from servers.

house air. Slang for a building's standard air conditioning system used in the general office or standard work areas. Most Data Centers require a dedicated or separate cooling system, but a very small server room might be adequately cooled by house air.

HVAC. An abbreviation for heating, ventilation, and air conditioning. Used generically to refer to all environmental controls in a building or Data Center.

I - J

impact load. The force put on a raised floor by a dropped object. This is defined by the weight of the item and distance it falls.

interoperability. The ability of a system to use the parts or data from another system. A necessary capability of a building management system used to coordinate and monitor Data Center infrastructure.

jack. A female connector. Applied to copper, fiber, or voice cabling components.

jacket. The outer coating of a data cable. Also called a sheath.

L - M

latency. In networking, the time it takes for a packet of data to go from one point to another. Synonymous with delay.

load bank. A device that creates an electrical load. Used to test standby infrastructure to ensure that it can support a Data Center's electrical needs when the room is operating at full capacity.

low smoke/zero halogen cables. Cables rated to produce little smoke or toxic fumes during combustion. Used predominantly in Europe rather than plenum-rated cables.

micron. One millionth of a meter. Used to express the diameter of a fiber cable's core and the size of tiny contaminants in the air. The symbol for micron is μm.

multiplexing. Sending multiple streams of information as part of a single, complex signal.

N

N. Abbreviation for need. Need refers to the level of infrastructure required to support all servers and networking devices in the Data Center, assuming that the space is filled to maximum capacity and all devices are functioning. The term can apply to all types of Data Center infrastructure, but is most commonly used when discussing standby power, cooling, and the room's network. Redundant infrastructure levels are indicated as N+1, N+2, N+3, and so on, or N, 2N, 3N, and so on.

nanometer. One billionth of a meter. A measurement of the wavelength of light. Abbreviated as nm.

nanoseconds. One billionth of a second. Used to measure signal delay times associated with structured cabling. Abbreviated as ns.

near end cross talk (NEXT). The measurement of crosstalk at the end of a cable where a signal originates. *See* also crosstalk.

networking room. A centralized area where all structured data cabling for a site, including from the Data Center, terminates. Also known as a data room, communications (comms) room, or campus distributor.

noise. Unwanted interference that disturbs a signal's normal function.

non-plenum cables. Cables used in general-purpose cabling installations. Acceptable for use in Data Center areas that are not used for air distribution. Non-plenum cables produce smoke and toxic gases during combustion. Also sometimes called riser-rated cables.

O - P

Operations command center. A workspace in which employees remotely monitor Data Center servers and coordinate efforts to fix malfunctions that occur. Also known as a call center, control room, or network operations center (NOC).

patch cord. A copper or fiber cable that contains a connector on both ends. Used to provide connections among servers, networking devices, and structured cabling infrastructure.

plenum. A separate space in a structure used for air distribution. In Data Centers, this term typically refers to the spaces below the raised floor or above a false ceiling or both.

plenum cables. Cables rated for use in Data Center areas used for air distribution, such as below a raised floor or above a false ceiling.

power sum. Adding all combinations of possible interference from adjacent cable pairs.

power sum equal level far end cross talk (PS-ELFEXT). The cumulative interference of adjacent cable pairs, as measured at the opposite end of a cable where a signal originates, minus attenuation due to cable length.

power sum near end cross talk (PS-NEXT). The cumulative interference of adjacent cable pairs, as measured at the end of a cable where a signal originates.

R

rack unit. A unit of measurement for the height of internal, installable space within a server cabinet or rack. 1 rack unit = 1.75 inches (4.45 centimeters). Abbreviated as U, as in "1U server" or "42U server cabinet."

radio frequency interference (RFI). *See* electromagnetic interference (EMI).

relative humidity. A percentage of how much water is in the air compared to how much water the air could hold at whatever temperature it happens to be when you measure it.

return loss. The ratio of an outgoing signal's power to that of a return signal caused by an impedance mismatch. The return signal is created when the outgoing signal encounters a jack or other piece of connecting hardware. Measured in decibels.

reverse fiber positioning. Installing a single flip in the relative position of the two strands in structured cabling. This ensures that the transmitters and receivers on Data Center devices remain correctly aligned in relation to one another.

rolling load. Weight rolled over an area from passing equipment. This load is defined not only by the weight of the object but also the size and hardness of the wheels that make contact with the floor and how many passes are made.

run time. The amount of time that a standby infrastructure device, such as a battery system or generator, can support an electrical load. This figure should be calculated based upon a Data Center being at maximum capacity.

S

service level agreement (SLA). A contract between a person or group expected to perform a task or service and a customer, specifying the measurable functions and services that are to be provided.

shielded twisted pair (STP). A cable containing multiple pairs of twisted copper conductors, which are gathered in a single sheath. Individual wires are surrounded by plastic insulation, and each pair is wrapped by a metal braid or foil to shield against electromagnetic interference.

short cycling. In Data Center cooling, when cold air exits an air handler and returns immediately to its intake without mixing with hotter air in the room. Since a handler's temperature sensors are in the return airflow, the unit believes that the room is cooler than it is and shuts off prematurely.

standby power. The system responsible for supporting the Data Center's electrical load when normal utility power fails. Devices in this system traditionally include a bank of large batteries or a generator or both.

storage area network (SAN). A dedicated network that enables servers to connect to networked storage resources.

T

tailgating. Closely following a person into a secure area and thereby circumventing its physical security system.

ton. In cooling, the amount of heat involved in melting one ton of ice in a day. Data Center air handler capacity is typically rated in tons. One cooling ton equals 12,000 BTUs.

total internal reflection. An optical phenomenon in which light attempting to pass from one medium to another at a given angle is reflected back toward the center rather than continuing through the boundary.
Total internal reflection is what enables light to continue traveling down a long, curving fiber optic cable.

U

Ufer grounding. A technique, often used for server environments, that uses the properties of concrete to improve conductivity for grounding.

ultimate load. The minimum weight that exceeds a floor tile's ability to support a load. Essentially the breaking point of a floor panel, past which an object crashes through to the subfloor.

uniform load. Weight distributed evenly over an area, such as large equipment that sits flush on the Data Center floor with no support pegs or wheels. This load can also be an accumulation of point loads. Also known as static load.

unshielded twisted pair (UTP). A cable containing multiple pairs of twisted copper conductors, which are gathered in a single sheath. Each individual wire is surrounded by plastic insulation.

W - Z

whip. Colloquial name for a flexible conduit containing electrical wires.

zinc whiskers. Tiny conductive filaments that form on the underside of raised floor tiles due to molecular stress. Hazardous to servers when dislodged and distributed throughout a Data Center by the room's air circulation system.

INDEX

A

above-ceiling cleaning, 342
access restrictions, 293
    cages, 294–296
    cameras, 297
    door controls, 293–294
    locking cabinets, 296
    policies, 297–299
    rules, 299–306
accessibility of Data Centers, 46
accessories, stocking, 288–290
acquisition of servers, 230–231
adapters, stocking, 274–278
affect load, 124
air handlers
    chilled liquid cooling, 196–198
    floor grids, 86
    positioning, 204
    raised floors, 120
    spacing, 91
    temperature sensors, relocating, 224
air pressure, 202
air sampling, 209
airborne particle counts, 341
airflow
    floor tiles, 125
    raised floors, 121
aisles, 93–94, 204
alarms
    fire signage, 264–265
    fire suppression, 210
amenities (Data center site selection), 49
amperage meters, 325
analyzing power needs, 47–49. *See also* evaluating
antitip brackets, 280
applications, mapping, 317, 321
architectural firm (design considerations), 27
Argonite, 207
Arrhenius Rate Law, 195
Arrhenius, Svante, 195
as-built blueprints, 319
asset tagging, 320

associated Data center support rooms, 73–79
attention tags, 284
attenuation, copper cabling, 167
AutoCAD, 84
automated house air, 198
automatic sprinkler heads, 117
automating inventory procedures, 320
availability, 17, 18
    metrics, 330
    services, confirming, 53–54
avoiding
    dirty power, 142
    single points of power failure, 136

B

backup rooms, 78
backward infrastructure installation, 105
bandwidth, cabling, 166
bar codes, 320
batteries, standby power, 148
behavior (promoting good habits), 14
below-ceiling cleaning, 343
best practices
    installation, 310–312
    labeling, 253–263
blueprints, as-built, 319
brackets, antitip, 280
Broken Window Theory, 336
budget decisions, 22–23
buffer zones, 93
Build Rooms, 14, 75–76
building code for Data Centers, 34
buildings
    mapping floor grids, 84–88
    planners, 27
    obstacles, 102–103
building-to-building connectivity, 179–180
business groups, organizing by, 240
bypass options, 136

C

D

G

H

I - J

Q

T

DISCUSS
NETWORKING PRODUCTS AND TECHNOLOGIES WITH CISCO EXPERTS AND NETWORKING PROFESSIONALS WORLDWIDE

VISIT NETWORKING PROFESSIONALS
A CISCO ONLINE COMMUNITY
WWW.CISCO.COM/GO/DISCUSS

CISCO SYSTEMS

THIS IS THE POWER OF THE NETWORK. now.

Cisco Press

NETWORKING TECHNOLOGY GUIDES
MASTER THE NETWORK

Turn to Networking Technology Guides whenever you need **in-depth knowledge of complex networking technologies**. Written by leading networking authorities, these guides offer theoretical and practical knowledge for **real-world networking applications and solutions**.

Look for Networking Technology Guides at your favorite bookseller

Cisco CallManager Best Practices: A Cisco AVVID Solution
ISBN: 1-58705-139-7

Cisco IP Telephony: Planning, Design, Implementation, Operation, and Optimization
ISBN: 1-58705-157-5

Cisco PIX Firewall and ASA Handbook
ISBN: 1-58705-158-3

Cisco Wireless LAN Security
ISBN: 1-58705-154-0

End-to-End QoS Network Design: Quality of Service in LANs, WANs, and VPNs
ISBN: 1-58705-176-1

Network Security Architectures
ISBN: 1-58705-115-X

Optimal Routing Design
ISBN: 1-58705-187-7

Top-Down Network Design, Second Edition
ISBN: 1-58705-152-4

Visit **www.ciscopress.com/series** for details about Networking Technology Guides and a complete list of titles.

Learning is serious business.
Invest wisely.

CISCO SYSTEMS

Cisco Press

CISCO SYSTEMS

Cisco Press

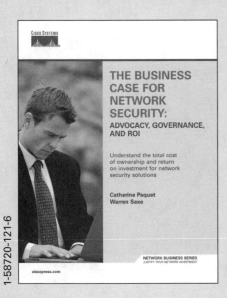

Cisco Press

Learning is serious business.

Invest wisely.

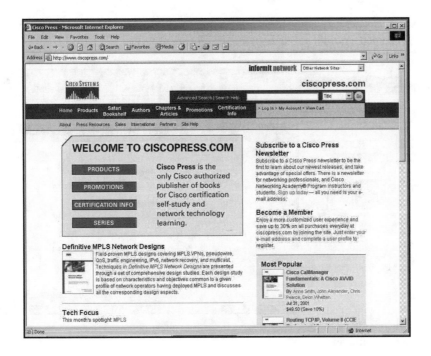
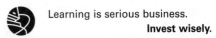

SEARCH THOUSANDS OF BOOKS FROM LEADING PUBLISHERS

Safari® Bookshelf is a searchable electronic reference library for IT professionals that features thousands of titles from technical publishers, including Cisco Press.

With Safari Bookshelf you can

- **Search** the full text of thousands of technical books, including more than 130 Cisco Press titles from authors such as Wendell Odom, Jeff Doyle, Bill Parkhurst, Sam Halabi, and Dave Hucaby.

- **Read** the books on My Bookshelf from cover to cover, or just flip to the information you need.

- **Browse** books by category to research any technical topic.

- **Download** chapters for printing and viewing offline.

With a customized library, you'll have access to your books when and where you need them—and all you need is a user name and password.

TRY SAFARI BOOKSHELF FREE FOR 14 DAYS!

You can sign up to get a 10-slot Bookshelf free for the first 14 days.
Visit **http://safari.ciscopress.com** to register.